FREEDOM TO DIE

Moral and Legal Aspects of Euthanasia

Revised Edition

by

O. Ruth Russell

 **HUMAN SCIENCES PRESS**
72 Fifth Avenue   3 Henrietta Street
NEW YORK, NY 10011 ● LONDON, WC2E 8LU

To all who suffer needlessly
while awaiting laws
that would permit painless death.

Library of Congress Catalog Number 77–3383

ISBN: 0-87705-311-1

Copyright © 1975 by Human Sciences Press, a division of Behavioral Publications, Inc., 72 Fifth Avenue, New York, New York 10011

Revised Edition 1977

Printed in the United States of America
89 9876543

Library of Congress Cataloging in Publication Data

Russell, Olive Ruth.
  Freedom to die.

  Bibliography: p.
  1. Euthanasia. I. Title. [DNLM: 1. Euthanasia. W50 R965f]
R726.R8   174'.24   74-8946

CONTENTS

Foreword

Euthanasia is defined in Webster's Dictionary as "granting painless death to a hopelessly ill patient with a non-curable disease." What a blessed thing to grant! Many persons throughout the ages have prayed for such a death. Many others pray that they will not outlive their usefulness and become a burden to their next of kin, forcing them to spend large sums of money only to postpone the inevitable.

Man is a reasoning, but not a reasonable creature. He is more considerate of his pets than of his fellow man. A free society strives to allow people personal freedom, provided it does not interfere with the lives of other people or infringe upon their rights. A loving family will strive to grant any reasonable wish to a beloved one suffering from a terminal illness except that last great wish—to be released from life when all significance of life has gone. Often the family wishes to comply, but society objects. What right does society have to insist that a person live as long as possible? The problem becomes progressively more serious as medical science is able to keep a body "alive" almost indefinitely with a respirator, pacemaker, renal dialysis and artificial feedings—all this at great expense to the family or to society. Now that man can be kept alive by these measures, it becomes extremely important, and indeed only just, for those who do not wish to be kept alive to have the legal right to die. Viewed objectively, what right has society to forbid a man to die painlessly and with dignity?

The strongest argument against euthanasia is the fear that it will be abused. Perhaps no law has ever been written that cannot be or has not been abused. Nevertheless, every society has its laws and tries to live with them; in truth, people cannot live together without laws. Furthermore, what society really wishes, it can achieve. Surely a country that can send men to the moon and bring them back safely is capable of writing a good euthanasia law if it so desires.

This book, which discusses the many aspects of euthanasia and the necessary safeguards of good legislation, should help to make euthanasia one of man's basic rights and grant him the freedom to die as he chooses.

Helen B. Taussig, M.D.
Professor Emeritus of Pediatrics
The Johns Hopkins Hospital
Baltimore, Maryland

Preface

Unexamined traditions and emotions, reinforced by opposition from organized religion and the medical profession, have long prevented the legalization of euthanasia for anyone, no matter how hopeless his condition or how earnestly he might plead for death. It is now time to ask why society should deny a person the right to choose death with dignity when the only alternative is prolonged, futile suffering or a meaningless existence or unconsciousness.

As a result of the ever increasing ability of the medical profession to prolong life, a growing number of people live to become the victims of degenerative diseases and senility. Thus, in the absence of any new legislation, the chances are every day increasing that you, the reader, will some day plead, to no avail, to have your physician end your life. Present law does not permit him to do so no matter how great your distress and that of your loved ones.

This book is written in the hope that it will stimulate discussion and appropriate action in dealing with this pressing problem. It outlines the development of thought and action on euthanasia and discusses arguments pro and con. It also proposes legislation that would make it permissible, in accordance with legal safeguards, for a patient, or his guardian, if the patient is not of testamentary capacity, to request euthanasia and have a physician's assistance in bringing it about.

Almost unquestionably the time will come when euthanasia in certain circumstances will be accepted practice, and we will wonder how society could have continued so long its cruel customs in dealing with hopeless human suffering. To an incurably ill patient, who wants only to die as soon as possible, the subject is not one to be either brushed aside or endlessly debated. It is one of great urgency. Fortunately there is now greater concern than ever on the part of clergymen, physicians, nurses, lawyers, and the public—especially the elderly. Under present law doctors are more and more faced with the dilemma of having to choose between allowing prolonged suffering, or mercifully granting a request for death in violation of criminal law. This dilemma ought not to be. A reasonable and humane society should not encourage covert action by doctors in order for them to grant a terminally ill person's plea for merciful release; it should instead enact laws that would safeguard both the individual's right to live and his right to die.

The author wishes to express her gratitude to the many who have assisted her by helpful discussion and those who have related personal experiences that graphically demonstrate the urgent need for laws that would permit a patient to have hopeless suffering terminated. The assistance and suggestions of Marjorie Nordlinger and Don Burgess have been especially appreciated, and the encouragement and help of Dr. Ruth Roettinger, a political scientist, who has assisted with the research on court cases and legal aspects of the problem, have been invaluable. My special thanks also to Ruth Hoberman for her meticulous care in editing the manuscript.

PREFACE TO THE SECOND EDITION

Since this book first went to press, the public has become
increasingly aware of and concerned with the problems pertaining to death and dying. One positive change is that discussions exploring this once hushed-up topic are now being encouraged. Evidence of this is in the questions and arguments
being orchestrated in a rising volume of publications, seminars,
courses, conferences, television and radio programs, court decisions, and legislative proposals. Cases of individuals who have
acted to end hopeless suffering also support this new outlook.

In this second edition, a Supplement has been added to
bring the record up to date.

We have yet to settle the arguments that surround death
and dying. Among the most provocative questions raised are:
What is death? Is it a process or an event? Is it indicated by
cessation of activity of the heart or the brain? Does death occur
when the person is no longer able to communicate as a human
being? Should man or God alone make decisions about when
life shall end? Complicating these issues is the fact that medical
technology has become so advanced that what is ordinary and
what is extraordinary treatment of the dying has become ques-
tionable. There is much disagreement about whether everything possible to prolong life must inevitably be started, and
whether any process may be stopped once it has been started.
Perhaps the greatest controversy is that over the question of
whether death may ever be hastened under certain circumstances.

Many doctors and nurses, philosophers and lawyers, both
individually and in their professional organizations, are leading
in efforts to develop new guidelines and solutions to these

problems. To further their cause they are expressing their views more openly and with much more clarity than in the past. The opposition of the Catholic hierarchy, the timidity of the Protestant churches, and the resistance of organized medicine continue to impede open and clear discussion of legislation regarding any deliberate termination of life. In spite of this situation, there are some Catholic and Protestant theologians who are giving courageous leadership by breaking with the dogmas of the past.

As freedom of choice regarding planned parenthood, abortion, and birth control has been won, we should feel encouraged. The struggle for legislation that will permit freedom of choice pertaining to suicide and euthanasia keeps gaining momentum and seems on the verge of success.

Among the highly significant developments in 1976 alone are the first international conference on euthanasia held in Japan, the first legislation in the United States dealing with the "right to die" enacted in California, and the introduction of "right to die" bills in at least 16 other state legislatures. There have also been significant legislative efforts in Great Britain and Europe. A high-water mark in judicial recognition of human rights is the decision of Chief Justice Hughes of New Jersey in the Karen Quinlan case. Justice Hughes stated that "Ultimately there comes a point at which the individual's rights overcome the State interest." The Justice's use of the constitutional concept of "the right of privacy" opens the way for legal recognition of the right of the individual to choose whether he shall live or die. Also, euthanasia societies in at least six countries are stepping up their campaigns to find a solution to the problems of hopeless suffering.

These remarkable developments will certainly speed the day when it will be legally permissible for an individual to exercise a choice regarding his own fate. An individual's responsibilities to society and his dependents must first be discharged by him. But once this is done, should he not then have freedom to die when "the ending of life is the best that life offers?" This is the heart of the matter dealt with in these pages.

I wish to express my sincere appreciation to Dr. Ruth Roettinger for her major role in preparing this Supplement.

Chevy Chase, Maryland
October 1976

O. Ruth Russell

Part I

CHANGING ATTITUDES TOWARD DEATH AND DYING

Chapter 1

OUR NEW POWER OVER
BIRTH AND DEATH

Framework for Discussion

In this century, and especially in the past decade, we
have witnessed amazing changes in man's power over both
birth and death. Radical changes have taken place in beliefs
and practices pertaining to the beginning of life. Family
planning and birth control, instead of being condemned,
are now accepted as a duty and responsibility, and the
battle to legalize abortion has been won in many places. It
is hard to believe that it was less than 60 years ago that
Margaret Sanger served a month in jail for conducting her
crusade for the freedom of every woman to determine the
number of children she will have. In spite of strong opposition, especially from the medical profession and organized
religion, she persisted in her efforts until today birth control is accepted practice throughout much of the world.

Now new kinds of control of birth are generating concern. Due to the potential power resulting from biomedical
research in such areas as genetic engineering, test tube
babies, cloning, and artificial insemination, man appears to
be on the threshold of being able to determine his own

characteristics—the so-called fabricated man. In 1969 a human egg was successfully fertilized in the laboratory by a human sperm for the first time, and in 1970 British scientists were able to grow human embryos in the laboratory up to the age of one week. At the 1970 meeting of the American Association for the Advancement of Science, the president, Dr. Bentley Glass, internationally known biologist and geneticist of Johns Hopkins University, told of the startling progress being made by a group of researchers at Cambridge University. He predicted the birth in the future of "deep freeze babies," conceived from eggs and sperms preserved in a frozen state.

In the United States there are now several frozen sperm banks and it is estimated that from five to ten thousand children are now conceived each year from frozen sperm.

But when in 1966 Dr. Hermann J. Muller, Nobel Prize winner and professor of genetics at the Univeristy of Wisconsin, speaking at a Ciba Foundation seminar in London, proposed a national program to promote human betterment by "genetic choice," he created something of an uproar. He advocated artificial insemination conducted on a voluntary basis in which only the sperm of men selected for their physical, mental, and moral superiority would be used.

Clearly the march of science is shaking the very foundations of our society and will continue to do so even further in the future. There is potential for both great good and great harm and abuse in man's capability to control the kinds of persons that will be born, and these questions are matters of great concern for all thoughtful people. Many theologians, among them the Reverend Dr. Paul Ramsey of Princeton University and Canon Michael Hamilton of the Washington Cathedral, as well as numerous scientists, have been warning of the urgent necessity for man to accept responsibility for the wise use of the new knowledge and skills acquired from laboratories throughout the world.

In testimony before the United States House Science Subcommittee in 1971, Nobel Prize winner James D. Watson, professor of Molecular Biology at Harvard, described the imminence of test tube babies and the need to recognize that such new developments raise the most profound questions of law and ethics and a challenge to guard against unwise use. He, like the Secretary General of the United Nations, called for an international commission to be set up to study the tremendous medicomoral questions arising from man's rapidly increasing power over birth and death. Senator Walter F. Mondale has been trying since 1967 to have a National Advisory Commission established in the United States to study the ethical, social, and legal implications of changes brought about by biomedical advances.

Many view man's new power over birth as a great opportunity for the improvement of man and his society and for the avoidance of hereditary diseases and congenitally defective children; but they see it also as a potential threat. Some fear that if we use our power by creating men and women of a predetermined type, a totalitarian society such as Aldous Huxley's *Brave New World* or George Orwell's *1984* will result. To avoid such a danger, vigilance and wise planning are essential; the longer we fail to accept responsibility to govern the use of new knowledge the greater will be the risk of abuse.

The spotlight is now being focused also on the other end of life—on man's new power over death. Due to the amazing successes of medical science and technology, physicians are now able to keep the body functioning long past its natural span, long after the mind and spirit have ceased to exist, sometimes almost indefinitely by artificial means. They can produce what some have called a living death, or, as David Hendin has said, "Dying is rendered obscene by technology."

This power has reached such a stage and keeps increasing so rapidly, that many people are now asking, what are we doing with this new power to prolong life—power undreamed of only a few years ago—and what are our moral responsibilities in regard to it? Many of the epidemics and diseases that only a few years ago killed people off in great numbers have been replaced by long chronic illnesses and degenerative diseases, and the proportion of the aged ill and defective children who survive is constantly increasing. As the end of life approaches, many patients have their lives prolonged against their wishes and against all good sense. By means of respirators, oxygen tanks, heart-lung and kidney-dialysis machines, intravenous feeding, drainage tubes, and other modern devices and medications, many are forced to live on when they want nothing so much as to die. Today there is a groundswell of indignation and revolt against many such efforts in hospitals throughout the land.

We are faced with a crucial question: Will we use our knowledge and new power intelligently, or will we let it be a force leading us blindly while we adhere to dogmas and beliefs that have no relevance for this age of biological revolution, population explosion, and spectacular medical skills? We must ask not merely what man can do but what he ought to do. It is absurd to argue that "man must not usurp God's power" and "God alone must determine when life shall begin and when it shall end;" man is already exerting very great power over both birth and death. And in any case it seems doubtful God's will would require of doctors that they persist in prolonging life as long as possible regardless of the patient's suffering and wishes or beyond the point when life has meaning to him. It is doubtful that God would disapprove of shortening life when it is done out of compassion and in accordance with the safeguards law and the medical profession could provide. It is more likely, on the contrary, that man has a moral obligation to permit avoidance of useless suffering.

A new freedom is being demanded today: the freedom to choose death. More and more people are now realizing that the right to die with dignity, so long denied to countless people, is a basic human right that should be available to those hopelessly ill patients who request it.

Law does not now recognize this right, nor does it distinguish between a merciful act of hastening the death of a dying or hopelessly ill or incapacitated person and an act of murder; neither does it clarify when it is permissible for doctors to discontinue treatment or not initiate efforts to prolong the life of terminal patients who want to die. In order for such persons to be assured that they will be permitted and assisted in carrying out their wish to avoid futile suffering or a meaningless, degrading existence, it is necessary to develop new medical guidelines and enact legislation that will recognize the right to choose death with dignity under the protection of carefully devised safeguards.

What is Euthanasia?

The word euthanasia is derived from the Greek word "thanatos" meaning death and the prefix "eu" meaning easy or good. Certainly no one could disapprove of an easy or good death. But over the years dictionaries have added a new element to the basic concept.

According to Webster's *Third International Dictionary* (1965), euthanasia is: "(1) easy death or means of inducing one, (2) the act or practice of painlessly putting to death persons suffering from incurable conditions or disease." Dorland's Medical Dictionary (1965) gives as its first definition, "An easy or painless death," and as its second, "Mercy death: the putting to death of a person suffering from an incurable disease." The 1970 edition of the American Heritage Dictionary defines it as (1) "the action of inducing the painless death of a person for reasons assumed to be merciful," (2) "an easy or painless death."

These definitions add to the original one the concept of merciful action willfully taken to induce good death. Most people would call this active or positive euthanasia, and some would restrict the term euthanasia to such positive action—sometimes referred to as mercy killing or mercy death. But death may result also from the omission of action which would prolong life; this is usually called passive or negative euthanasia. Some who condemn any deliberate hastening of death approve of withholding or stopping measures that uselessly prolong the agony of dying; they say they merely want to permit natural death to occur and they object to calling this euthanasia. Hence there is some confusion in the use of these terms.

This confusion has not been cleared up because in many quarters the subject has been as taboo as sex was in the days of Queen Victoria. Condemned by church authorities and legally indistinguishable from murder, the very concept of euthanasia has tended to shock and distress people. Also, the word was used improperly in connection with the Nazi crimes of World War II, and this has made many people disapprove of any suggestion of euthanasia because they associate it with that perverted use of the word.

Confusion arises also from what is usually referred to as the principle of double effect, which has been much emphasized by the Roman Catholic Church. It involves the question, if a physician acts deliberately to relieve pain with the knowledge that by so doing he is shortening the life of his patient, is that fundamentally and morally different from willfully hastening the death of his patient? In each case the effect is the same: the patient's life is shortened. In the former, while the intent is to relieve pain, the effect is to hasten death; in the latter, the inevitability and desirability of death are openly admitted and agreed upon and deliberate action taken to induce it.

It is the official position of some religions that there is an overriding moral difference between these two kinds of action, and that while the former is permissible even if it hastens death, provided the intent is only to relieve pain, the latter is strongly condemned. While the moral difference may be none too clear to some the law does make such a distinction.

CLASSIFICATION OF EUTHANASIA

"Medical" euthanasia is a general term sometimes used to describe euthanasia administered by or authorized by a doctor for the benefit of the individual—to end hopeless suffering or a meaningless existence. It is the only kind discussed in this book. No consideration is given to eugenic euthanasia, which has as its objective the genetic improvement of society; nor is there any discussion of compulsory or state imposed euthanasia of any kind except to strongly condemn it.

It is fairly customary to classify euthanasia into two major pairs of categories: (a) *Active* versus *Passive,* or some prefer the terms *Positive* versus *Negative;* and (b) *Voluntary* versus *Involuntary.*

Active or positive euthanasia means a positive merciful act taken deliberately to end futile suffering or a meaningless existence. It is an act of commission; death is induced either by direct action to terminate life or by indirect action such as in giving drugs in amounts that will clearly hasten death.

Some would limit the use of the term to direct, intentional action to end life, which under present law is murder. If the intent in giving drugs is to hasten death as well as to relieve pain, that too is now a criminal act, though proof of such intent might be difficult to establish. Even if a physician merely provides the means for a patient to end his own life, he is acting illegally in most states in that he is aiding a person to commit suicide.

Passive or negative euthanasia means discontinuing or desisting from the use of "extraordinary" life-sustaining measures or "heroic" efforts to prolong life in hopeless cases when such prolongation seems an unwarranted extension of either suffering or unconsciousness. This includes acts of omission such as failure to resuscitate a terminally ill or hopelessly incapacitated patient or a severely defective newborn infant. It is refraining from action that would probably delay death and instead permitting natural death to occur.

Recent court decisions have varied regarding the legal status of such inaction or negative action. Some doctors maintain that no new legislation is needed to permit the termination of useless treatment, but others disagree, and many legal experts have warned that failure to take all steps possible to prolong life could result in a charge of criminal negligence or manslaughter. Therefore a large number of doctors refuse to take the risk of "pulling the plug" of the oxygen tank or discontinuing or failing to use other life-supportive treatment. It is true that a competent adult has the right to refuse treatment, but if he is in a hospital and refuses the treatment prescribed, he can be discharged from the hospital, which in many cases would cause distress and great hardship. If his competence is questioned, treatment may be ordered regardless of his wishes or those of the next of kin.

The difference between active and passive euthanasia is often less real than is generally assumed though some persons strongly condemn the former and approve the latter. It should be recognized that to refrain from or discontinue life-sustaining measures requires a conscious decision and a deliberate act of a negative kind. To argue that it should be acceptable in some cases to terminate treatment but that any intentional hastening of death should be prohibited and condemned seems difficult to justify on moral or compassionate grounds, though under present law the latter is murder while the legal status of the former is less clear.

Voluntary versus involuntary euthanasia is an incomplete and objectionable classification. *Voluntary* means at the will of the person, and *involuntary* usually implies contrary to the person's will, i.e., compulsory. There should be a third category which might be called *nonvoluntary.* It would pertain to cases of persons incapable of making their wishes known, such as those in an irreversible coma or severely defective infants. For such individuals, euthanasia at the request of the next of kin or legal guardian who has the responsibility of making decisions on the patient's behalf must be differentiated from compulsory or involuntary euthanasia; it would be without the patient's request but not contrary to his wishes insofar as they could be known or anticipated.

We would all agree that compulsory, or state imposed euthanasia is wrong; it is unthinkable in a free society. But it is time to give serious consideration to what might be classified as (a) *euthanasia at the request of the patient* and (b) *euthanasia at the request of the patient's legal guardian* in cases in which the patient is not of testamentary capacity. It is this writer's belief, however, that euthanasia should be permitted and administered only in accordance with the safeguards that would be specified in a good euthanasia law.

Because medical science and technology have now made it possible to prolong the life of the body almost indefinitely in many cases, the act of dying is often prolonged to horrifying lengths. It therefore seems urgent to enact appropriate legislation to protect the rights of both physicians and patients. Without it, many persons will be denied relief from suffering and the right to death with dignity and might even be denied the right to live as long as they wish. An adequate euthanasia law would doubtless provide also that a person while in good health could make an advance declaration of his wish for euthanasia in the event that he became incapacitated in the future. Such a provision was proposed in the 1969 British Voluntary Euthanasia Bill and in different forms in bills in Montana, Florida, Washington, and Oregon in the early Seventies.

Whether considering voluntary or nonvoluntary euthanasia, the role of the physician may be either positive or negative. Dr. Joseph Fletcher, in discussing classification, has used the terms "dysthanasia" and "anti-dysthanasia" as well as "direct euthanasia" when describing the doctor's role. The word dysthanasia is derived from the Greek prefix "dys" meaning bad, and "thanatos" meaning death; hence it means bad death, i.e., the opposite of euthanasia. It may be used to designate useless prolongation of life which only increases suffering. Fletcher used the term anti-dysthanasia to designate desisting from or discontinuing such prolongation, but this is now more frequently called passive or negative euthanasia. More recently he has used the term "elective death" to describe death brought about at the request of the patient; this seems to be a good term and would apply both to euthanasia at the request of the patient or at the request of his legal guardian.

Table 1 may be useful in thinking of the doctor's role.

Some believe that the patient's physician should not be the person to administer euthanasia. Certainly no physician, nurse, or any other person should ever be required to take any action contrary to his conscience, religious beliefs, or judgment. Some have suggested that an anesthesiologist or other specialist who might be known as a thanatologist be available for this purpose, or that a paramedical member of hospital staffs be specially trained.

Table 1

CLASSIFICATION OF EUTHANASIA

DYSTHANASIA (bad death)	EUTHANASIA (easy or good death)		
	Passive or Negative Euthanasia (Anti-dysthanasia)	Active or Positive Euthanasia	
		Indirect	Direct
Prolongation of suffering; use of extraordinary means or "heroic" efforts to prolong life uselessly.	Desisting from or discontinuing useless prolongation. An act of omission which permits natural death to occur.	Indirectly causing death by use of drugs to relieve pain but which clearly hasten death.	Deliberately inducing death in order to terminate hopeless suffering or a meaningless existence.

THE NEW CONCERN WITH DEATH AND DYING

Research and Discussion

The great increase in the amount of discussion and research on the subject of death and dying during the past decade is truly remarkable. This long neglected subject has become the focus of much attention by leaders in various professions, medical and theological schools, foundations for research and education, and government. There is also a new awareness on the part of the medical profession that the care and treatment of patients often involve not only medical skills but decisions requiring ethical and social judgments. This recognition led in 1961 to the establishment by the American Medical Association of a Department of Medicine and Religion to arrange for dialogue between the two disciplines in dealing with problems of life and death.

Many interdisciplinary conferences and seminars have been conducted recently on problems confronting the medical profession in dealing with hopelessly ill patients, especially in making decisions which in effect determine who shall live and who shall die and when. There is a new recognition of the need for consultation and concensus in making value judgments involving basic human rights and vital decisions.

At the First International Conference on Social Science and Medicine held in Aberdeen, Scotland in 1968, the problems presented by impending death and the need to replace evasion and secrecy with open and sympathetic discussion were emphasized. And at the 1971 White House Conference on Aging, one of the recommendations to be given high priority was, "Religious bodies and government should affirm the right to, and reverence for, life and recognize the individual's right to die with dignity."

This recommendation led Governor Tom McCall of Oregon to call for a series of public discussions to bring the subject of "death with dignity" "out of the forest of superstition and into the light of discussion." He urged that the problem be discussed in rational rather than emotional terms. In 1972 a resolution was introduced into the House of Representatives of the state of Hawaii calling for hearings "in the area of euthanasia, exploring all its facets including the social, judicial, and public health and welfare implications of such a practice." A similar resolution was introduced in Illinois in 1973.

In addition, the United States Senate Special Committee on Aging, under the chairmanship of Senator Frank Church, held three days of public hearings in August 1972 on "Death With Dignity: An Inquiry Into Related Public Issues," in order to consider questions raised by the White House Conference.

Bills to legalize either passive or active voluntary euthanasia have been introduced in at least ten state legislatures since 1969, and in England efforts continue to get a voluntary euthanasia bill enacted. Also in England, in 1972, people from all parts of the country attended a conference called by the Department of Health and Social Security to discuss the problems of dying and to consider the desirability of making euthanasia legal under certain circumstances.

During the past decade, the number of books and articles on the subject of death and dying has increased many times over what it was during the preceding ten years. Books such as those by Kübler-Ross, Eissler, Feifel, Hinton, Weisman, and Hendin have done much to focus attention on and bring new understanding of the problems of dying. Articles in medical and law journals, magazines, and newspapers have brought prominence to the question of euthanasia, and there have also been many discussion programs on television and radio. A front-page article in the *Wall Street Journal* by Ellen Graham in 1972 was headed, "A Good Death: Increasing Support for Euthanasia Spurs Heated Medical Debate. Doctors Ponder Their Duty as Dying Patients Plead to Have Treatment Ended. When is Life Really Over?" *The National Observer* published a similar article by Lawrence Mosher. "When There is No Hope . . . Why Prolong Life?" And on July 3, 1973, an editorial entitled "The Right to Die" appeared in the *New York Times.*

Several foundations are now conducting and sponsoring research on death and dying. The Foundation of Thanatology was established in 1968 in New York City for the promotion of scientific and humanistic research on the psychological aspects of dying, the needs of the dying, reactions to death, and recovery of the bereaved. Its board of directors represents a wide variety of disciplines.

Another interdisciplinary organization, the Institute of Society, Ethics and the Life Sciences, was founded in New York in 1970. Its purpose is to carry on research, organize conferences and seminars, and in general "to stimulate professions to make ethical problems an important focus of their attention." Its scope is much broader than the subject of death and dying, but it has launched a three-year research program to inquire into the adequacy of present definitions of death, current medical practices in the care of the dying patient, professional and legislative codes pertaining to death, and present philosophical and theological understandings of the meaning of death. It has conducted nationwide seminars that include discussion of euthanasia. One such conference was held jointly with the American Association of University Women in 1972.

The Russell Sage Foundation in 1970 published a collection of essays by noted persons in the fields of medical and behavioral sciences entitled *The Dying Patient* edited by Orville Brim, president of the Foundation. A recurrent theme running throughout the book is the need to develop new attitudes toward death and dying and new guidelines

with legal safeguards for dealing with the problems arising
out of man's increased ability to prolong life. The book
explores the medical, social, economic and ethical issues
raised by man's new control over death and dying and asks:
How far will man accept the new responsibility thrust upon
him?

In this Russell Sage book the Dean of the School of
Medicine of Stanford University, Dr. Robert J. Glaser,
wrote, "For those of us in medicine, the preservation of life
remains a noble goal; but in seeking this objective we must
more and more concern ourselves with the quality of life we
preserve." He called attention, too, to the tremendous economic and emotional costs of prolonging life in the presence of irreversible disease.

Similarly, Dr. Osler L. Peterson, a professor of preven-
tive medicine at Harvard Medical School, pointed out that
the dramatic new treatments possible today have forced
both the medical profession and society generally to con-
front problems involving value judgments and policy decisions. He pointed out the urgent need for guidelines with
legal safeguards: "It clearly is not healthy to tolerate increasing disparity between what is legal and what is done."

Professors Sol Levine and Norman A. Scotch, both of
Johns Hopkins University, in discussing "Dying as an
Emerging Social Issue," dared to ask what proportion of
health resources should be used for keeping dying patients
alive. "Painful and repugnant as it may be, those who de-
ploy resources in the health field must decide how much
they wish to allocate for the prolongation of life as opposed
to other types of investments in health. . . . The problem
may still be in its infancy . . . it may mushroom and demand
increasing attention of policy makers."

They continued:

Most of all perhaps we should not overlook the fundamental
human dimensions of the problem—the anguish, the suffer-

ing, and the frustration of dying patients and their kin. Though their numbers are legion they are dispersed throughout the land. They are not an organized or visible public. Their agony is experienced quietly and privately. Society . . . has developed efficient ways to shield itself from the daily tragedies of the dying so that it can go on with tasks, unperturbed and uninterrupted. Hence, society is not confronted with the collected anguish or the outcry of the dying and their loved ones.

Universities and medical schools are at long last giving attention to this subject. Some universities have recently established programs of research and training on death and dying, and many medical schools, schools of nursing, and divinity schools are considering or have already established courses of training for the care of dying patients. To the average citizen it is incomprehensible that such training has been missing all these years, but death has indeed been a taboo subject.

The University of Minnesota in 1969 established the Center for Thanatology Studies, which has conducted valuable conferences. Wayne State University has established the Center for Psychological Studies of Dying, Death, and Lethal Behavior. Harvard has established an Interfaculty Program in Medical Ethics—a venture of the Faculties of Medicine, Public Health, Divinity, and Arts and Sciences—whose aim is to examine the ideas, events and traditions which influence the ethical behavior of physicians, medical institutions, and Western society toward illness, and to attempt to reappraise the role society should play in developing new standards of conduct. There is also a new Kennedy Institute for the Study of Human Reproduction and Bioethics at Georgetown University; in 1971 it conducted an international conference in Washington, D.C., where the tragic problems of seriously defective infants were discussed.

The Texas Medical Center in Houston, with its Institute of Religion and Human Development has become a liaison between doctors and clergy in the matter of medical decisions involving ethical judgments and religious values. Also among the universities now making interdisciplinary studies of life and death or care of the dying are the University of Chicago, Stanford University, University of Oregon, Case Western Reserve University, Columbia, Tulane, and Tufts. And in 1973 the School of Education of the University of Massachusetts organized a Death Education Research Group that is preparing a curriculum for use in secondary schools on the subject of death.

Defining the Moment of Death

Since early in the Sixties the medical profession has become more and more concerned with the need for a new definition of death. This need had long been recognized, but it was the success in transplanting human organs, especially hearts, that precipitated the urgent need to know, for purposes of transplantation, when a person could legally be pronounced dead. Also, many physicians, clergymen, and laymen have openly protested the useless prolongation of the lives of terminal patients, especially those who were already in the irreversible coma or comatose state which has been termed "psychological death." During the past few years these matters have been discussed at many national and international conferences.

At the 1964 meeting of the American Medical Association, Dr. Hannibal Hamlin of Harvard Medical School urged physicians to adopt a flat EEG (electroencephalograph) as a criterion of the time of death, for it is an indication of the cessation of all brain activity. He said, "When the brain is dead, the person is dead." This criterion differs from the traditional, legally accepted definition that a person is not dead until heart and pulmonary functioning have ceased.

At the International Meeting of Forensic Medicine in Copenhagen in 1966, Dr. Keith Simpson, Professor of Forensic Medicine at Guy's Hospital Medical School, London, said, "We should distinguish between being alive and a live state that can be maintained artificially. . . . We can say that death has occurred if the brain is no longer in a living state, even if it can be maintained as living tissue by artificial means."

Also in 1966 the French Academy of Medicine recommended that doctors should be empowered to certify death of a patient in whom cerebral function had failed, even though a state of artificial survival was being maintained by mechanical means. This is a greater deviation from the traditional definition of death than is the flat EEG; the cerebral cortex may cease to function long before there is a flat EEG; absence of function of the cerebral cortex indicates that though parts of the brain may still operate, it is no longer possible for the individual to function as a human person capable of communicating with others. It is well known that in cases in which the brain is deprived of oxygen for from five to eight minutes, the cells of the cerebral cortex are destroyed thus ending all possibility of life as a conscious, aware person.

The World Medical Association in its Declaration of Sydney in 1968 approved a flat EEG criterion only as a supplement of clinical judgment. It stated: "No single technical criterion is entirely satisfactory in the present state of medicine, nor can any one technological procedure be substituted for the overall judgment of the physician."

The much publicized 1968 report of the Ad Hoc Committee of Harvard Medical School, whose chairman was Dr. Henry K. Beecher, recommended acceptance of a flat EEG as the chief criterion for the determination of death provided it remained flat for at least 24 hours, and provided that the decision to pronounce the patient dead was made by physicians who were not involved in any effort to transplant organs or tissues from the deceased individual. Dr. Beecher has pointed out that desperate efforts to save the seriously injured often enable the heart to continue beating but the brain remains irreversibly damaged. "The burden is great on patients who suffer permanent loss of intellect, on their families, on the hospitals, and on those in need of hospital beds already occupied by these comatose patients," he wrote. He also pointed out that society could ill afford to discard the tissues and organs of hopelessly unconscious patients, when these are so greatly needed to help those who could recover.

A 1972 court case in Richmond, Virginia, regarding the transplantation of the heart of a fatally injured man, Bruce Tucker, appears to be the first time the question of brain death in connection with organ transplantation has come before a court. The seven man jury decision that the physicians were not guilty of killing Tucker was widely interpreted as an acceptance of brain death as evidence of the death of an individual. But the medical record in the case and the rulings and instructions of Judge A. C. Compton indicate that the legal acceptance of brain death was not clearly established.

On May 24, 1974, the *New York Times* reported the outcome of an intriguing legal contest in California over the definition of death that illustrates clearly the need for formal legislation. When Samuel M. Allen Jr. was shot by Andrew D. Lyons, he was pronounced "neurologically dead" by the hospital to which he was taken. With the consent of his family, doctors then removed his heart and transplanted it. At the manslaughter trial of Mr. Lyons, his lawyer contended that because doctors removed the heart when it was still beating with the assistance of life-supportive systems, Allen was not actually dead until the heart was actually removed. Adherence to the traditional concept of heart activity as the criterion for death would mean that it was the removal of the heart, and not the gunshot wound, that was the cause of death, and hence Lyons could not be guilty of manslaughter. The Oakland court, however, did find Lyons guilty, although the case is expected to be appealed. The *Times* pointed out that there is currently no legal definition of death in California, although the legislature is considering a bill naming brain function as the crucial factor.

Acceptance of brain death as definitive appears to be a major factor in the success of transplant surgery. Experts claim that if a transplant operation is to succeed, the organ or tissue should be removed at least 30 minutes before total biological death occurs. And Dr. Robert S. Schwab, in an address to the American Academy of Neurology in 1969, said that to have to wait even 24 hours after the first recording of a flat EEG would largely negate the value of organs for transplantation.

It should be noted that if a flat EEG should become an acceptable criterion of death, this would fall far short of solving most of the problems of useless prolongation of life. One well-known case demonstrates that brain death can occur long before a flat EEG is registered. A brain-damaged young man in Minnesota was in a coma for more than 13 years, cared for day and night by a special team of nurses. The family's finances were decimated, and the strain had other very serious effects on the family. The care of the patient was finally taken over by the State at a cost of about 60,000 dollars annually. In commenting on this case at the Euthanasia Educational Council, Dr. Schwab related similar cases, one of whom had been in a coma for ten years and several for about four years. He deplored the cruelty of such cases and the waste of medical and nursing services, labeling our present approach totally primitive.

At least three states in the United States have enacted laws providing new criteria for deciding when a physician

may give up in his efforts to prolong life and declare the
patient dead (Kansas in 1970, Maryland in 1972, and Virginia in 1973). These statutes permit a physician to declare
death if there is no spontaneous brain function and further
attempts at resuscitation or supportive maintenance seem
unlikely to restore either spontaneous brain function or
spontaneous respiratory or cardiac functioning. These statutes have been both widely praised and criticized. A similar
new definition of death was approved by the House of
Delegates of the Connecticut State Medical Society in
1970, reading, "In patients whose cardiorespiratory system
is being supported by artificial means, death may be determined on the basis of complete and irreversible loss of
function of the entire brain."

It is to be hoped that in order to avoid variations in
definitions from state to state, some nationally recognized
body such as the National Conference of Commissioners
on Uniform State Laws, in conjunction with the medical
profession, will prepare a model definition and guidelines,
as they did in the Uniform Anatomical Gift Act of 1968.
Significant work toward clarification of and agreement on
this problem is being done by the Task Force on Death and
Dying of the Institute of Society, Ethics and the Life
Sciences, directed by Robert M. Veatch. Under the spon-
sorship of the Institute, Alexander M. Capron and Leon R.
Kass have proposed a new definition of death (see appendix). The move for legislative action may well be slowed by
the December 1973 stand of the AMA that there is no need
for a definition of death by statute in precise, scientific
terms. But their view that such a statute would be inflexible
and repressive may well change, as increasing ambiguity
makes the pronouncement of death more and more com-
plicated.

But there is an urgent need for society to go beyond
even the questions of biological or brain death, to a recognition of psychological death—that is, death of the individ-

ual as a conscious person. Dr. W. Spann of the Institute of Legal Medicine in Helsinki is quoted by Richard Restak as saying, "It is not a question of the scientific boundary between life and death, but what is involved is a value judgment as to what is considered *human* life in its real sense. This kind of judgment is not a matter for . . . the doctor on his own authority."

It should be noted that much of this new concentration on death and dying is not necessarily directed to the subject of euthanasia, and among those who stress the importance of death with dignity, there are many for whom even the word euthanasia is anathema. These people say they merely want doctors to refrain from useless prolongation and help the patient die a "natural death" as comfortably as possible, with dignity; they condemn any action that intentionally hastens death. But to think that death will be easy and dignified if only doctors refrain from prolonging life by heroic efforts is a delusion. The fact is that many people will go on suffering in great distress and indignity unless active steps are taken to induce death.

With all this new concern with death and dying and research into the experiences of the dying, and with the increasing medical skill to prolong life, it was inevitable that there would be a fresh surge of interest in and a demand for freedom to choose euthanasia.

Chapter 2

CHANGING ATTITUDES
AND THE NEED
FOR NEW SOLUTIONS

Some Indications of the Problem

The magnitude and scope of the problem of personal choice regarding whether one lives or dies cannot be recorded statistically. Nor can one know how many people would request euthanasia if law made it permissible. Many polls, however, have indicated that a large number would choose it in certain circumstances if they could, and most adults know someone who has longed for and asked for death. It is common knowledge that most people hope that "when their time comes" they will go quickly, and polls have indicated that an overwhelming majority of elderly people have a much greater fear of prolonged dying than of death.

In two combined National Opinion Polls in Britain, in 1964 and 1965, a total of 2,000 general practitioners taken at random from the Medical Register were asked: "Have you ever been asked by a dying patient to give him or her final relief from suffering which was felt to be intolerable?" Nearly half (48.6 per cent) of those who replied said yes. Dr. Eliot Slater, distinguished British psychiatrist, has

35

asked, "Is there really any valid reason why a doctor should have to refuse to grant such a request?"

There are countless numbers of hopelessly ill or incapacitated people in hospitals, nursing homes, homes for the aged, and institutions for the insane and mentally defective for whom life is nothing but a tragic burden. For those who have never visited such institutions, it is difficult to realize the human tragedy that exists there. No matter how much money is spent trying to improve their care and living conditions, many are doomed to utter despair year after year. Others equally incapable of any satisfaction in living wait in their homes longing for death, often at the cost of the health and happiness of the person who must care for them. Can a humane and rational society condone this futile suffering?

Following an article by this writer published in the *New York Times* in 1972 entitled "The Right to Choose Death," many elderly persons wrote thanking her for the article; only one was critical. The following are excerpts from a few of the letters received; they indicate the demand for freedom to choose euthanasia.

Mrs. G., an 86-year-old woman from Colorado, told of having visited nursing homes where corridor after corridor contained the dying, many of whom had lost all power of reason. She said, "Voluntary euthanasia would be like freeing a living spirit from a burdensome body. . . . When the right has been established by law, such an act would be accepted and honored. An effort to that end must engage all my future days." She pleaded for legislation that would enable her "to go out with decency and self-respect." She wants her doctor to be permitted to give her "a pill" which she can take when she is ready to go.

Mrs. M., an 89-year-old in New Hampshire, wrote that she was deaf, blind, arthritic, and fast approaching senility. She referred also to "poor old souls who don't even know their own children," and urged that the medical profession do something about "the cruelty of their [Hippocratic] oath" so doctors may help such persons "go to eternal rest."

Mrs. McC. of Florida told about her mother, who died at 87 after five years of senility during which she did not know any of her children. She had been an intelligent woman, and loved her independence and freedom, so her children decided that she would never go to a hospital or nursing home, but would continue to live in her own house with nursing care. But when she fell and broke her hip, she had to be taken to the hospital where she developed pneumonia. Her children were shocked at how they found her:

> She had many tubes and drains in her, was being fed intravenously, was in an oxygen tent and had her hands bandaged into large balls so that she could not pull out the tubes. She was in a coma most of the time but at one time when we were with her, she mumbled "awful, awful." She had two heart attacks, but the hospital 'heart rescue squad' revived her. We spoke to the doctor in charge and said we wanted her to be left alone and to die in peace; however, they continued with their so-called "heroic efforts." This went on for two and a half weeks before she died, and I think we will always remember it with horror and sadness.

The president of a liberal arts college who is also an ordained minister said that he was in full agreement with the view that one should have the right to choose death. He told of his father and mother, both of whom had been in their nineties and hospitalized for a long time. Each had reached a point where life had little meaning for them. "Each was just waiting for death to come; in fact, they were both desirous that it would come quickly." Yet the physician "felt it was his obligation to keep them living as long as possible." The president said, "I hope that if the time comes when I reach that point, I will have that right."

Mrs. S. of New York City wrote: "I am now pushing 72, and along with many of my contemporaries worry about our future, lying for months in hospitals at great expense, with tubes to and from every orifice. How nice it would be to be able to say, 'this is enough,' and have the doctor respond accordingly."

Dr. F. of New York City, a 76-year-old physician, wrote: "I know many doctors who have made pacts with each other that if they are ever in one of those terrible illnesses where a patient can be kept alive . . . by means of injections, etc., that they will pull out all the needles and let the sick one die in peace."

Professor B. said he had been "fortunate far beyond my deserts," but that of late his mental and physical health were such that "I feel I *must* at long last find a way—a graceful way—out."

THE RIGHT TO REFUSE TREATMENT

Recent Court Cases

Mrs. Carmen Martinez of Florida, age 72, was afflicted with a fatal form of hemolytic anemia, a blood disease which destroys the red blood cells. She was admitted to the hospital where she was kept alive for almost two months by virtually continuous blood tranfusions that had to be forced into her withered veins by surgical incisions. Then she was told by her doctor that she would need to have her spleen removed as well as continue the transfusions in order to avert death. She was told that the operation would not cause her extreme pain, but she preferred death. She begged her family and her doctor, "Please don't torture me any more."

Her doctor, Dr. Rolando Lopez, was caught in a double-bind. If, on the one hand, he granted her request, he might be charged with negligence or with aiding and abetting a suicide. On the other hand, if he operated, he could be charged with treating a patient against her will. Dr. Lopez took the problem to court, where Judge David Popper ruled, "A person has the right not to suffer pain. A person has the right to live or die in dignity." The surgery was not performed, and the transfusions were stopped. She died peacefully less than 24 hours later. This ruling was in effect a condoning or approval of passive or negative euthanasia at the request of the patient.

Mrs. Gertrude Raasch of Milwaukee also won a legal battle to refuse surgery. She had spent 17 years in and out of hospitals and nursing homes, and had undergone two major operations for gangrene of the leg. Doctors then insisted that amputation of the leg was necessary for survival. Mrs. Raasch refused to consent to the operation and said she would rather die. She appealed to the court and Judge Michael T. Sullivan went to her hospital room to hear her testimony. She explained her feelings to the judge, who ruled that she had the right to refuse the operation even though it meant death from gangrene. He said, "It is not the prerogative of this court to make decisions for adult, competent citizens, even decisions relating to life or death."

The case of Clarence A. Bettman, a 79-year-old investment banker in New York, ended less happily. To sustain his life, a new pacemaker was required. Although this would involve relatively minor surgery, his wife claimed that he was unaware of his condition and incapable of making a decision; she refused to authorize the operation. The doctors took the matter to court. State Supreme Court Justice Gerald P. Culkin named the hospital director as Mr. Bettman's legal guardian and authorized the hospital to "perform whatever medical and surgical procedures were necessary to protect and sustain the health or life" of Mr. Bettman.

When Mrs. Bettman heard the decision she asked "What has he got to live for? Nothing. He knows nothing, has no memory whatsoever. He is turning into a vegetable. Isn't death better?" She said her refusal was "the greater compassion."

The case of Delores Heston of New Jersey is another case of a court decision regarding one's right to refuse treatment. A 22-year-old member of Jehovah's Witnesses, she was badly injured in an auto accident and needed surgery for a ruptured spleen. She also needed a blood transfusion, but she and her family adamantly opposed a transfusion on religious grounds. Miss Heston had no desire to die, but her religious faith forbade the treatment prescribed, and she believed a clear conscience to be more important than life.

Physicians and nurses said Miss Heston was not competent to make a decision so when it appeared that she would die without prompt treatment, the hospital made application at 1:30 A.M. to a Superior Court judge to appoint a guardian for her with authority to consent to blood transfusions "for the preservation of the life of Delores Heston." The judge issued an order appointing a guardian, and at 4:00 A.M. surgery was performed and blood administered.

Miss Heston recovered and asked the court to vacate (annul) the order. The controversy was moot since Miss Heston was well, but the Supreme Court of New Jersey accepted the issue because it felt that "the public interest warrants a resolution of the cause." Previous court decisions had held that children might be given blood transfusions and other medical treatment without their consent or that of their parents, under state laws designed to protect neglected children, but there have been very few precedents involving adults.

Chief Justice Joseph Weintraub, speaking for a unanimous court, asserted: "It seems correct to say there is no constitutional right to choose to die." The judge held that since New Jersey might intervene to prevent suicide (a provision repealed later that year), whatever interests justified such intervention also supported the overriding of an individual's refusal of lifesaving attention—"if the State may interrupt one mode of self-destruction, it may with equal authority interfer with the other."

One comment on the case was that a court, a physician, or a hospital is perilously near legally forbidden territory when it imposes an unwanted medical procedure on a competent adult who has religious reasons for not wanting it. Judge Alfred Burka, a District of Columbia judge, refused to enter this forbidden territory in the April, 1974 case of Patricia Bentley. Citing the restrictions of the Bill of Rights and the 14th amendment on governmental invasion of personal liberty and religious belief, Judge Burka ruled that the right of privacy "extends to an election to die." Miss Bentley refused on religious grounds to agree to receive a blood tranfusion if judged necessary to save her life during a cesarian operation. Finding Miss Bentley "an intelligent, rational and informed patient," the judge found "no compelling state interest" to restrict her right to refuse the transfusion, and after eight hours of medical and legal testimony, he ruled, "The court finds with great sorrow that the mother does have a right to die."

Some Publicized Cases not Taken to Court

Flip was a tall, handsome boy of 22 who was first thought to have a deformed kidney, but when operated on in a Brooklyn hospital was found to have cancer. He was then transferred to a hospital specializing in cancer research and care, where he had a second operation. After five hours of surgery, doctors told the family that the cancer was already too widespread to treat; there was no hope, and there was no cure.

Flip lived for 11 months after that, and according to his sister-in-law Deborah Josephs, he was "never once out of pain, never once feeling good, and in the end, telling us that he was more afraid of living than of dying." Cobalt treatments and other therapy continued and there were more operations. Mrs. Josephs said that decisions were made without consulting the family and they were told that since Flip was not a minor they had no authority to make decisions for him. She said they were made to feel that their questioning of a doctor was "a blatant infraction of their rules." She also reported that "Never in all that time, were we asked if we could afford continued hospital expenses."

Many have told similar stories of hospitals persisting in very expensive, futile, and painful treatment for hopelessly ill patients who were required to leave the hospital if they refused further treatments or surgery.

The stand taken by Mrs. Joyce Franks was reported by Charles S. Johnson in *The Sunday Missoulian*. After the death of her 86-year-old father, she appeared before the Bill of Rights Committee of the Montana Constitutional Convention and pleaded with the committee to provide in the new state constitution a guarantee of the right to die. She described the lingering death of her father and his great suffering. After he had broken a hip and was told that an operation would be necessary, he asked for "something to put him to sleep right then." As his condition deteriorated, he made the request again, to no avail. Mrs. Franks said that her father had been a farmer and a compassionate man, and that he could not stand to see animals suffer when they were severely mutilated or dying. He asked for himself the same mercy that he showed to helpless animals. His daughter resolved to try to make such merciful action available to other human beings—action that had been denied her father.

Mrs. Franks's proposal was that "every citizen be allowed to choose the manner in which he dies." This proposal was not adopted and there is no way of knowing what influence Mrs. Franks may have had, but one wonders what judicial interpretation may some day be made of the provision in the new Montana Constitution under "inalienable rights" of "seeking health and happiness in all lawful ways. In enjoying these rights, all persons recognize corresponding responsibilities." Mrs. Franks is still working for legislation to permit euthanasia.

Dr. Arthur E. Morgan, former President of Antioch College and the first chairman of the Tennessee Valley Authority, has related the experience of his wife, who was in a nursing home. Mrs. Morgan had fallen and suffered a severe cerebral hemorrhage. She recovered sufficiently to recognize and express affection for her husband, to whom she had been married 60 years, and she showed some interest in affairs. But, Dr. Morgan said, for the last few months, since she is

> blind and unable to hear well enough to understand and unable to speak so that she can be understood, I have few ways of communicating with her. I think she is now just enduring existence. . . . The other day when I was there at meal time, I found her trying to refuse food, but with the nurses prying her mouth open with a spoon to force her to eat. When I took the matter up with the directress of the nursing home, she said it was a rule to keep everyone alive as long as possible. I protested forced feedings and told her that Mrs. Morgan should be allowed to die if she wished. She said, "Should we not allow God to decide that?"

In an article written 34 years before this incident called "On Drinking the Hemlock," Mrs. Morgan told of several members of her family who had lived to an average age of 80 and been incapacitated for long periods before death; she described the plight of many other elderly people and said:

> We do wish we might help to bring about a change in public opinion so that it would be recognized as honorable and proper for a person who has done a good life's work and is honestly weary from the burden, to so signify. We feel that

after mature consideration, such a one should be allowed to
drink the hemlock in some dignified and simple way.

EVIDENCE OF CHANGING ATTITUDES

Among the Clergy

During the 1930's and 1940's organized efforts were
made in England and the United States to legalize voluntary euthanasia, and although no legislation was enacted,
much interest in the subject was evoked—both for and
against it.

In 1957 Pope Pius XII made some very significant pronouncements in regard to the care of dying patients in
which he made an historic departure from traditional doctrine about the redemptive value of suffering. Though he
still condemned any deliberate hastening of death and anything called euthanasia, he gave moral approval to desisting from or terminating the use of extraordinary measures
to prolong the life of the dying patient in certain circumstances, and said it was permissible for a physician to administer drugs in terminal cases in quantities sufficient to
relieve pain even when it was known that by so doing the
patient's life would be shortened. Though he warned that
it would be unlawful to take action with the intent to hasten
death, this allocution is nonetheless important to the euthanasia movement; it has opened the door to a more humane and reasonable approach to the problem of human
suffering, an approach less bound by early religious dogma.

Many distinguished Protestant leaders have in recent
years asserted that euthanasia is not only morally acceptable in certain circumstances, but highly desirable; they
have given leadership in efforts to enact legislation that
would make it permissible in accordance with legally established safeguards. Several Protestant denominations are
now reexamining their former stand on the issue and have

committees at work with a view to making new statements regarding their positions.

The Reverend Dr. Joseph Fletcher, one of America's most highly esteemed ethicists, wrote in *Harper's* in 1960 that it is the right and responsibility of human beings to use intelligent control over physical nature rather than to submit beastlike to its blind workings. "Death control like birth control is a matter of human dignity. Without it persons would become puppets." He has said that the practice of "keeping vegetables going" and dragging them back to "life" only to prolong the agony or continue a meaningless existence is to be deplored, and that to bow to blind, brute nature is outrageous to the limit.

Dr. Fletcher has been in the forefront in emphasizing the need to put the human personality rather than the biological organism at the center of our thinking. It is the person that is sacred and possessed of rights, and as a responsible creature he should have freedom of choice in regard to whether or not he shall exist in a painful or helpless state when it is clear that he can no longer have any satisfaction in living.

The Very Reverend William R. Matthews former Dean of St. Paul's in London, also stressed the idea that it is the person rather than the body that is sacred, saying, "It seems to be an incontrovertible proposition that when we are confronted with suffering which is wholly destructive in its consequences and, so far as we can see, could have no beneficial result, there is a *prima facie* duty to bring it to an end." And the Reverend Cornelius Trowbridge, former Chaplain of St. Luke's Hospital in New York, has said, "From my point of view as a theologian, I want to say that the body is of importance only as long as it can serve as a vehicle for the mind and spirit. When it has reached the point of no return, the quicker it goes the better."

Dr. Leslie Weatherhead of the City Temple, in London, in response to the argument that death should be left to God, wrote in *The Christian Agnostic*, "We do not leave birth to God. We space births, we prevent births. We arrange births. Man should learn to become the lord of death as well as the master of birth." This world-renowned theologian has also written, "I sincerely believe that those who come after us will wonder why on earth we kept a human being alive against his will when all the dignity, beauty and meaning of life had vanished; when any gain to anyone was clearly impossible, and when we should have been punished by the State if we kept an animal alive in similar physical conditions."

Among Physicians

Although organized medicine has generally opposed or avoided open discussion of euthanasia, some of the most respected members of the medical profession have taken the lead in this humanitarian movement. Physicians are increasingly protesting useless prolongation and in June, 1973, following two mercy-killing indictments—one against Dr. Vincent A. Montemarano of New York, accused of ending the life of a dying cancer patient, and the other against Lester Zygmaniak of New Jersey, who shot his paralyzed brother—Dr. Malcolm C. Todd, president-elect of the American Medical Association, told the press that mercy killings "have their place" in certain "uncorrectable" fatal illnesses, but that decisions in such cases should not be left to the attending physician alone. According to the *New York Times,* June 28, 1973, Dr. Todd suggested that a commission of doctors, lawyers, clergy and the public be formed to study the matter.

Recently the question of keeping hopelessly defective infants alive has been receiving special attention. In a case at the Johns Hopkins University Hospital, the parents of a grossly defective mongoloid infant refused to give permission for the operation necessary to correct an intestinal defect. Some doctors proposed that an appeal be made to the courts for permission to perform the surgery, but their legal counsel said they would probably lose the case since the child was not normal mentally. The doctors then decided that they should not use "extraordinary" measures—in this case, intravenous feeding—to keep the child alive, so to the dismay of many, it was left to starve to death. Not until 15 days later did it finally die. No one could possibly be happy about this kind of death, although it could be described as "natural" death, with no effort made either to prolong or shorten the infant's life. The parents, however, were convinced that it would be less cruel to let the child die "naturally" than to force it to endure a tragic existence, and the doctors refused to take any action to induce death. This now famous case has led the hospital to set up a review board to advise its medical staff, presumably as to both broad policy and individual cases. This would seem to be a step in the right direction, but only a first step.

The distinguished American surgeon Dr. H. Leslie Wenger of New York has stated that there are times when it is morally right to speed life's end. "Prolonged and hopeless physical anguish degrades and dehumanizes. When medical science can no longer cure or relieve the pain of terminal illness, a man has the right to die in peace and dignity with no further suffering." Dr. Wenger was so convinced of the rightness of this view that he became a charter member of the Board of the Euthanasia Society of America more than 30 years ago and gave strong leadership to efforts to enact a voluntary euthanasia bill in New York.

The well-known British surgeon Dr. John Rowan Wilson has deplored the vast amount of irrational sentimentality surrounding death. He, like Fletcher, denounces the practice of "waiting for the last agonies imposed by blind and cruel nature. . . . If death alone can bring relief, it is wrong to withhold it." He said that for a doctor to withhold treatment in hopeless cases is not to act unethically but rather to accept the responsibility of his profession. He stressed that to make this legally permissible requires a change in the current laws.

Dr. Arthur A. Levisohn, Professor of Medical Jurisprudence at the Chicago Medical School, in a 1961 article on voluntary euthanasia made a strong plea for doctors and others to replace traditional ways of thinking with new values and attitudes appropriate to our rapidly changing world. He said that we must not allow religious bias to hinder the course of progress, but rather permit proper legislation to remedy the evils which advanced medical knowledge has inadvertently created. "The history of civilization reveals how laws have resulted from society's need and effort to meet situations which arose out of scientific advancement."

More recently Dr. Arthur F. Schiff, a general practitioner in Florida, writing in *Medical Economics,* challenged doctors to examine their beliefs and personal convictions and decide where they stand in this matter. He said that for those who are unalterably opposed to the principles of euthanasia under any circumstances, there is only one position they can take. But for those who believe that euthanasia is reasonable and needed in certain circumstances, there are two courses open: one is to act clandestinely, the other is to work for new laws. He urged the latter course and said, "What appears remote today may be commonplace tomorrow. . . . the sands of time are shifting; the signs are changing. . . . Whether you accept or reject, agree or disagree, like or dislike, I believe that in the decade now beginning man will revise his present ethical code in the matter of keeping people alive at all cost. He will extend to all the right to die as well as the right to live."

THE NEED FOR NEW SOLUTIONS

From the beginning of time man has been innovative and creative in finding ways to understand and solve problems pertaining to himself and his environment; he must now find a solution to this problem of needless human suffering. In civilized countries ancient superstitions and taboos have been repudiated in almost all areas of life except death and dying. The rise of modern science has led to radical changes in man's view of himself and his universe. He now knows that he is able in large measure to determine his present condition and the future of the human race; he has forsaken his older view of man as a helpless victim of natural forces. Many traditional religious doctrines, superstitions, and rule-of-thumb guides for behavior no longer meet the needs of today. Death must be redefined, our conceptions of life re-examined, and our role in controlling our own destiny re-evaluated. Emphasis has shifted away from the quantity of life to its quality; no longer can we attribute any inherent value to longevity— it has been the cause of too much suffering.

The time has come to stop viewing death as necessarily an enemy, and to recognize instead that sometimes it is a welcome friend. It is time to ask who wants to go on living indefinitely in an oxygen tent, with intravenous feeding, colostomies, or other devices that prolong life artificially, when there is no hope of recovery? Many do not want to go on using precious blood for transfusions when they know their case is hopeless and that that blood could save the life of another person who would probably otherwise die—perhaps a younger person whose desire to live is great.

And if the prognosis is that there is no reasonable possibility of recovery, and the difficult decision has been made to terminate treatment and distress continues, who would not hope that he could be eased out of life painlessly without further delay at a time of his own choosing? Perhaps some of the terminally ill honestly want to endure their suffering or helpless condition until death takes over; certainly they should not be denied that choice. But one might predict that their numbers would dwindle rapidly if the twin forces of religion and law were to assure them that it is permissible to choose death in certain circumstances.

In any case, just because there may be some who would not want positive euthanasia for themselves no matter how hopeless their condition, that is no reason to deny to others the right to choose euthanasia when life no longer is of value. Surely this is a matter of conscience for each individual to decide for himself, as long as the decision does not do harm to anyone else or deprive society of useful services.

Part II

HISTORICAL REVIEW
OF THOUGHT AND ACTION
ON EUTHANASIA

Chapter 3

THOUGHT ON EUTHANASIA
PRIOR TO 1930

FROM ANCIENT TIMES TO THE TURN OF THE CENTURY

The concept of euthanasia goes back to ancient times, and interest in the subject has waxed and waned over the years. Many Greek philosophers advocated euthanasia. Socrates and Plato justified the elimination of maimed children and contended that no elaborate attempt should be made to keep alive invalids for whom there was no hope of recovery. In Aristotle's ideal state defective children were not to be allowed to survive, and Epictetus endorsed the right of every person to an easy death. Historian Morris H. Safron of Rutgers Medical School has stated that the preponderance of Greek and Roman thought makes man the master of his own body, with the right to decide his own fate.

According to some historians, there existed on the island of Cos—the birth place of Hippocrates—an ancient custom whereby very old people who had outlived their usefulness to society might gather annually as if for a banquet, and leave this world by drinking together a lethal potion; and in one of the oldest Greek colonies (modern Marseilles) it was the custom to make available in a public depository a death potion for those who could justify before the Senate their desire for death.

In the first century A.D., when there was great indifference to human suffering, the Roman philosopher Seneca said:

> If I can choose between a death of torture and one that is simple and easy, why should I not select the latter?—Why should I endure the agonies of disease—when I can emancipate myself from all my torture?—I will not depart by death from disease as long as it may be healed and leaves my mind unimpaired—but if I know that I will suffer forever, I will depart, not through fear of pain itself, but because it prevents all for which I live.

Marcus Aurelius even defended the right of the individual to emancipate himself from the danger of "intellectual decrepitude."

In the fifth century, however, Saint Augustine, the great leader of the early Christian Church and author of the *City of God,* writing at a time when many Christians were committing suicide, proclaimed that "suicide is detestable and damnable wickedness." This view has been cited by many who condemn euthanasia—which is sometimes termed "assisted suicide." It has persisted throughout the history of the Catholic and other churches, though even Saint Augustine justified some exceptions, among them the suicides of saints and martyrs, saying that they had been specially commanded by God. Saint Augustine's chief arguments against suicide were that (1) it is a violation of the Sixth Commandment, "Thou shalt not kill," (2) suicide deprives a man of the opportunity of repentance and penitence, and (3) one should endure what suffering life brings; to avoid it by suicide, is an act of cowardice. St. Augustine's point of view, however, may have been based partly on practical considerations, since a high birth and survival rate among Christians at this time was crucial to the spread of Christianity.

These views set the stage for many cruel rulings by both religious and secular authorities, and were reflected in church law and criminal law. For instance, those who committed suicide were denied the rites of Christian burial, and secular laws were passed in many countries requiring the forfeiture of the property of such persons, even though nowhere in the Bible is suicide specifically condemned. Many of these customs and laws have persisted to the present day, although there is no longer a legal prohibition of suicide in the United States and in many other countries.

The strong opposition to taking one's own life expressed by Saint Augustine in the fifth century was further reinforced in the thirteenth century by that great theologian and scholastic philosopher of the Roman Catholic Church, Saint Thomas Aquinas. It was contended by Saint Thomas that to commit suicide is to usurp God's power over creation and death. He proclaimed that since we are God's property, it is for Him to determine when we die. He also stressed the idea that self-destruction is contrary to man's natural inclinations and natural law, and furthermore that man has no right to deprive society of his presence and activity by suicide.

After reading the views of these great church leaders who not only adamantly opposed suicide and any action that would shorten the suffering of a dying man, but even extolled suffering, it is refreshing to those who believe in the right to an easy death to read the views of the noted sixteenth century British statesman and scholar Sir Thomas More, who was canonized by the Roman Catholic Church in 1935, four centuries after his death.

Sir Thomas presented his idea of a model society in *Utopia,* published in 1551. In his description of the treatment of the sick, he displayed compassion, comprehension and conviction. He wrote:

> The sick they see to with great affection, and let nothing at all pass concerning either physic or good diet whereby they

may be restored again to their health. Them that be sick of incurable diseases they comfort with sitting by them, with talking with them, and to be short, with all manner of helps that may be. But if the disease be not only incurable, but also full of continual pain and anguish; then the priests and the magistrates exhort the man, seeing he is not able to do any duty of life, and by outliving his own death is noisome and irksome to others and grievous to himself, that he will determine with himself no longer to cherish that pestilent and painful disease. And seeing his life is to him but a torment, that he will not be unwilling to die, but rather take a good hope to him, and either despatch himself out of that painful life, as out of a prison, or a rack of torment, or else suffer himself willingly to be rid of it by others. And in so doing they tell him he shall do wisely, seeing by his death he shall lose no commodity, but end his pain. . . . But they cause none such to die against his will, nor they use no less diligence and attendance about him, believing this to be an honourable death.

Thus Sir Thomas More outlined what may be regarded as a forerunner of present-day proposals to provide for the administration of euthanasia with legal safeguards. Of course his views met with strong opposition, but in the seventeenth and eighteenth centuries, John Donne, Dean of St. Paul's, David Hume, the Scottish philosopher, and others joined Sir Thomas in challenging the doctrine that to take one's own life was necessarily wicked.

Hume, in his 1777 "Essay on Suicide," said that a man who retires from life does no harm to society; he only ceases to do good. He said that if a person cannot promote the interests of society but rather is a burden to society, his resignation from life is not only innocent but laudable. And in 1790, France, due chiefly to the influence of Montesquieu, Voltaire, and Diderot, enacted a statute legalizing suicide.

In 1798 Dr. John Ferriar published his *Medical Histories and Reflections,* which included a fascinating chapter entitled "On the Treatment of Dying." Dr. Ferriar, who was then physician to the Manchester Infirmary, Dispensary, Lunatic Hospital and Asylum, did not advocate any hastening of death, but the statement "Disturb him not—let him pass peaceably," was given a full page in his book, and he made a strong plea for physicians and attendants to make the dying patient as comfortable as possible.

During the latter part of the nineteenth century a few books and essays appeared with the word euthanasia in the title or a chapter heading. The first of these was an essay in 1872 by S. D. Williams entitled "Euthanasia," published in England. This appears to be the first time the word euthanasia was used in the modern sense of inducing death, though William Mountford came close to it in his *Euthanasy: Or Happy Talk Towards the End of Life,* published in 1848 and in its fourth edition in 1852.

Williams' essay was followed the next year by one entitled, "The Cure for Incurables," by the Honorable Lionel A. Tollemache. Tollemache, a British philosopher, defended the thesis of Williams and systematically refuted the arguments advanced against it by its critics. These scholarly and practical essays made a highly significant contribution to thinking about euthanasia. In 1884 the article by Tollemache was incorporated in his book *Stones of Stumbling.* This book included excellent chapters on related topics such as "The Fear of Death" and "Fearless Deaths." He attributed much of the fear of death to the preaching of Christians about hell and the torments of life after death, and the idea that suffering is punishment for sin.

Tollemache not only discussed the pros and cons of euthanasia but gave strong support to the idea that the laws should be changed to permit it. He quoted and supported Williams' view that "in cases of incurable and painful illness the doctors should be allowed, with the patient's consent, and after taking all necessary safeguards, to administer so strong an anaesthetic as to render all future anaesthetics superfluous; in short, there should be a sort of legalized suicide by proxy."

Tollemache added, "Any of us may one day have to bear—many of us certainly have to witness—either cancer, creeping paralysis . . . or a mortally wounded soldier who wishes to die. . . . So even from the most selfish point of view we all have an interest that this question should be speedily discussed." He said we must consider also the friends who, besides the immediate suffering of nursing the sick man, often permanently impair their constitutions and nervous systems.

In his rebuttal of the argument that there would be abuses if euthanasia were made legally permissible, Tollemache questioned the right of the state to forbid the sick man to choose his own way of "severing himself from his friends," and he said "if we rejected all reforms which might lead to contingent and remote evils, no reform whatever would be passed and we should be in a state of . . . stagnation." He envisaged adequate safeguards to prevent the abuse of power in the proposed legislation.

An 1887 book by Dr. William Munk, a Fellow of the Royal College of Surgeons, was entitled *Euthanasia: or Medical Treatment in Aid of an Easy Death.* Another was *Euthanasia: the Aesthetics of Suicide,* by Baron Harden-Hickey in 1894.

In Munk's book, as in Ferriar's a century earlier, the word euthanasia was used in its original meaning, an easy or good death; the author made a plea that the dying patient be made as comfortable as possible, using opium when necessary to relieve pain. He quoted the famous Lord Verulam who two centuries earlier had said that it was "as much the duty of a physician to smooth the bed of death, and render the departure from this life easy and gentle, as it is to cure diseases and restore health." Both Munk and Ferriar made a strong plea for the medical profession to make the subject of euthanasia part of their medical training and their studies and writing—a plea that has gone largely unheeded until very recently.

It seems clear that in spite of the doctrines of the Christian religions (and especially the Roman Catholic) regarding the value of suffering and the belief that God alone should determine how much suffering each person should have, forces were at work advocating a more humane approach to the problems of dying.

The views of these nineteenth century scholars and physicians seem so sound it is hard to believe that now, nearly 100 years later, euthanasia for the hopelessly ill or incapacitated is still not legally permissible.

1900–1930

During the first three decades of the twentieth century, although several articles were written denouncing euthanasia, little was written in support of it except for one very significant article in 1901 by a prominent British physician, Dr. Charles E. Goddard, entitled, "Suggestions in Favor of Terminating Absolutely Hopeless Cases of Injury and Disease."

Dr. Goddard, who later became Medical Officer of Health for Harrow, England, advocated euthanasia not only for people dying from incurable and painful disease who demanded relief from their suffering, but also for certain cases of hopeless idiots, imbeciles, and monstrosities; these latter he described as "Those who, having no will power nor intelligence of their own, and being a burden to themselves and especially to their friends and society, [and] of course, absolutely incapable of improvement." He said their cases should be considered and their fate determined by a "Committee of Experts," who, being convinced of the eligibility for such relief, would arrange the proper method for the termination of their miserable existence.

Dr. Goddard said there was need for a new attitude on the part of the public regarding this "somewhat gruesome subject." He thought the first step should be by the medical profession. He said,

> I am satisfied of this, that when once it was recognized that it was lawful to accept the means of relief at all, it would be gratefully accepted by thousands of suffering creatures in the years to come as a God-given escape. It would be regarded as a providential help in a time of terrible need. I am sure more than half the opposition will arise from cruel prejudice. Some of us are old enough to remember in our practice people who were prejudiced against the use of anaesthetics on the supposition that pain was never intended by the Almighty to be avoided in this way.

Thirty years later another physician, Dr. C. Killick Millard, picked up the torch and gained so much support that a Euthanasia Society was founded in England in 1935 for the purpose of obtaining legislation to legalize voluntary euthanasia under certain circumstances.

In the meantime in the United States, the advocacy of euthanasia by Dr. Charles Eliot Norton of Harvard, a distinguished scholar and humanitarian, brought forth denunciation in a January 6, 1906 editorial in the *New York Times* which said that Norton had been moved by an "unfortunate impulse," and called euthanasia a "curious delusion." In spite of this climate of opinion, a bill for the legalization of euthanasia for certain incurable sufferers was introduced in the legislature of the state of Ohio, January 23, 1906. This appears to have been the first such bill introduced into the legislature of any English-speaking country. The bill, described in the *New York Times*, January 24, as "Concerning administration of drugs, etc., to mortally injured and diseased persons," was introduced by a Mr. Hunt at the request of Miss Anna Hall, who drafted the bill following the death of her mother. Miss Hall said she deeply regretted that she had not been permitted to end her mother's suffering with chloroform.

The Ohio bill would have provided that when an adult of sound mind had been fatally hurt or was so ill that recovery was impossible, or if he was suffering from extreme physical pain without hope of recovery, his physician, if not a relative and if not interested in any way in his estate, might ask him in the presence of three witnesses if he wished to die. If he indicated that he did, then three other physicians were to be summoned in consultation and if they agreed that the case was hopeless, they were to make arrangements to put the person out of pain and suffering with as little discomfort as possible.

A motion to reject the bill was defeated by a vote of 19 yeas to 79 nays, so the bill was given a first reading and referred to the Committee on Medical Jurisprudence, but it was finally defeated by a vote of 23 to 79. Much publicity and much hostility ensued.

The editor of *Independent* (February 1, 1906) expressed surprise and dismay that a woman would draw up such a "cruel" bill and he deplored the reported support the bill had received from Dr. Norton. An article in *Outlook* (February 3), "Shall We Legalize Homicide," enumerated a long list of objections—including such hackneyed fears as: the way would be opened for guardians and relatives to rid themselves of their burdens, for quacks to conceal their failures, for heirs to resort to corrupt practices, for confidence in the medical profession to be eroded, and "it would add to the terrors of the sick bed by stimulating fears . . . the patient would look forward to the visit of the physician with dread."

An editorial in the *New York Times* on January 25, 1906, called the Ohio proposal "something considerably worse than ignorant folly—something that verges close upon, if not into, the criminal." Ironically, the following day the *Times* reported the assertion of Dr. Walter Kempster of

Milwaukee that he had given a fatal dose of morphine to a woman who had been fatally burned. He said, "There are others to whom a law providing death might be applied with benefit. If such a measure is contemplated it should include in its provisions such members of the community as are suffering from incurable diseases, lunatics, and idiots." Another *New York Times* editorial, on February 3, 1906, spoke of "morbid sensitiveness to suffering" and compared the practice of euthanasia to "practices of savages in all parts of the world."

In England, as in the United States, opposition was expressed by various doctors and others. Dr. S. Russell Wells, in a paper presented at the annual meeting of the Medico-Legal Society, London, in 1906, said he was astounded to discover how many doctors supported the views expressed in the Ohio bill. He, too, enumerated the dire consequences that would follow the passage of such a bill. However, in spite of his strong opposition to any such legislation, he conceded:

> When one visits the numerous lunatic asylums, each of which contains many cases of the hopelessly insane; when we enter and see those in the last stages of general paralysis of the insane, where, as far as our knowledge goes, there is absolutely no hope of recovery; when we see such cases kept alive by artificial feeding, only to drag out more weeks or months of the most hopelessly disgusting and animal existence; and when we enter a criminal asylum and see people confined and kept alive whose instincts are worse and whose actions are more ungovernable than those of savage beasts, I must admit that it is only natural to say, 'Qui bono?' Why should these people be kept alive? Were it not better to give them an overdose of morphia, and painlessly end their miserable existences?

Bertrand Russell (later Earl Russell) claimed that Dr. Wells had not argued against the principle of putting the incurable to death, but had merely demonstrated the need for safeguards.

In 1912, Sara Harwis of New York, suffering almost constant pain and distress from an incurable disease, created a sensation when she announced that she was sending a petition to the Legislature of the State of New York asking for such a relaxation of the homicide laws as would permit her physician to put her painlessly to death. Her petition was not granted, but it was widely publicized and the press reported much hostility to it.

In 1917, at the sixth annual convention of the American Association of Progressive Medicine in Chicago, Dr. William A. Guild of Des Moines advocated legalized euthanasia for the aged, infirm, and those suffering from incurable maladies. A resolution calling for a commission to submit to every state legislature a proposal for legalization of euthanasia was adopted by a vote of 87 to 24. But apparently the desired action was not taken since Dr. Guild presented the same proposal in 1931 to the Illinois Homeopathic Medical Association, and again no action seems to have been taken.

In July 1917 Dr. Harry J. Haiselden of Chicago allowed a baby girl born with a microcephalic head to die when he could have saved her life. Forty doctors had looked at the child and agreed with Dr. Haiselden's decision. In a November trial which acquitted him, Dr. Haiselden was supported by 15 doctors. He said he had followed the same course in a similar case in 1915.

It seems clear that at this time the climate of medical opinion regarding the legalization of euthanasia was not favorable, but the debates stimulated by Dr. Goddard and the Ohio bill seemed to indicate that perhaps the winds of change might be stirring, as indeed, they were.

Chapter 4

THE 1930's

Decade of Organized Action

During the Thirties there was a remarkable upsurge of action in support of euthanasia and its legalization. Many scholarly articles and a few books by theologians and physicians dealing with the subject were published. Books by two of Britain's most distinguished clergymen—the Reverend Dr. William R. Inge and Canon Peter Green—in 1930 and 1931 did much to challenge traditional thinking and religious beliefs and dogma, and persuade people of the need for new thinking, new attitudes, and new practices in regard to matters pertaining to life and death. An address and article on euthanasia by Dr. C. Killick Millard in 1931 sparked organized action and the support of many medical doctors. Discussion and support of euthanasia grew so widespread in 1931, that it is often referred to as the beginning of the euthanasia movement, although not until 1935 was a euthanasia society founded in England, and three years later in the United States. In both countries attempts were soon made to enact bills to legalize voluntary euthanasia. Throughout the period there was, of course, active opposition as well.

ENGLAND TAKES THE LEAD

The Role of Dr. C. Killick Millard

In spite of the traditional belief that doctors are bound by the Hippocratic Oath to save life at any cost, it was a highly respected British physician, Dr. C. Killick Millard, who gave strong leadership in the organization of the movement to deal more humanely with problems of futile human suffering. And, as already noted, it was also a physician, Dr. Charles Goddard, who 30 years earlier challenged his colleagues to recognize that their obligation to prevent useless suffering should sometimes outweigh their obligation to prolong life.

In 1931, in his presidential address to the Society of Medical Officers of Health in London, Dr. Millard chose as his subject, "A Plea for the Legalization of Euthanasia," and in an article later in *Fortnightly Review* he presented his proposals for a bill which with slight modification was introduced into the House of Lords five years later. (See p. 68.) Dr. Millard's article represents another milestone in the literature on euthanasia. He spoke and wrote of the fear people have of a slow, lingering dying and of the mental anguish of loved ones and the fears caused by the increase in cases of cancer which "tends to kill by inches." He advocated euthanasia only for the dying who requested it; while he shared Dr. Goddard's concern for cases of hopeless idiots and monstrosities, he thought advocacy of euthanasia for them presented a different and more difficult problem and was too much in advance of public opinion at that time.

Opposition to euthanasia he attributed chiefly to the historic teaching of the Church, and he singled out the condemnation of suicide by Saint Augustine as one of the chief reasons for the opposition, since it led to the belief that a person who ended his life was committing the most grievous of sins and was doomed to eternal perdition. Dr. Millard added, "With all respect and humility, I suggest that Saint Augustine, great man though he was, need not be regarded as infallible." Truth is progressive, he said, and should not be bound down by the dead hand of the past. Though life is sacred, "it is not something to be selfishly clung to after it has permanently ceased to be useful, and especially if we have become a burden to others."

To the ethical and religious argument that life is sacred and God alone has the right to decree an end to it, Dr. Millard said the argument is meaningless as long as war and capital punishment are permitted. He also pointed out that the Biblical injunctions are prohibitions of acts calculated to injure others and there is a fundamental difference between murder, and suicide or euthanasia: "In murder we are committing a most grievous wrong against another, in that we are robbing him of his life; whereas in suicide we are taking only that which humanely speaking, is our own, and we are not necessarily doing any wrong to others; indeed, in some cases we may be benefiting them. . . . The morality of euthanasia and suicide should surely be judged by the motives underlying them. It may be an act of highest altruism."

To arguments of possible abuses, Dr. Millard enumerated the safeguards of his proposed bill and stated that they were sufficient to prevent abuse. As for the practical aspects of administration, he proposed that regulations be made by the Ministry of Health which could be revised from time to time as necessary, without any need for amendment to the act itself.

In his *Fortnightly Review* article Dr. Millard reported on the many letters he had received from people strongly supporting his position, among them the Reverend Dr. A. S. Hurn, who said, "I am convinced that the case he makes out is unanswerable. Our moral judgments cannot ultimately rest on custom or prejudice, but on the ever advancing enlightenment of the conscience of mankind."

The Founding of the Euthanasia Society

Dr. Millard's proposals received much publicity in the press and medical journals, both favorable and unfavorable. They were strongly supported by many of Britain's most distinguished intellectuals and physicians. His efforts led to the formation of the Voluntary Euthanasia Legalization Society, on December 10, 1935, under the presidency of Lord Moynihan of Leeds, former president of the Royal College of Surgeons, and generally regarded as the most progressive surgeon of his time. Dr. Millard was honorary secretary. The objective was "to create a public opinion favorable to the view that an adult person, suffering from a fatal illness for which no cure is known, should be entitled by law to the mercy of a painless death if and when that is his expressed wish; and to promote this legislation." The *British Medical Journal* fully reported the founding and objectives of the Society.

Among the distinguished supporters of the Society and the proposed bill were such notables as Julian Huxley, Sir James Jeans, H. G. Wells, G. Bernard Shaw, Eleanor Rathbone, A. A. Milne, Vera Brittain, and Sir Harold Nicolson; there were many prominent physicians, and such well-known clergymen as Dr. William R. Inge, former Dean of St. Paul's Cathedral, and his successor Dr. W. R. Matthews; Canon Peter Green, Canon H. R. L. (Dick) Shepherd, and Canon Harold Anson of City Temple; Dr. F. W. Norwood, President of the National Free Church Council, and Dr. Rhondda Williams, Chairman of the Congregational Union.

At the first meeting of the Society, Lord Moynihan reported that a strong consultative Medical Council had been formed which, with the assistance of legal experts, had drafted a Parliamentary Bill, based on Dr. Millard's bill. The meeting and the proposed bill received much publicity.

The 1936 British Bill to Legalize Euthanasia

The bill, known as the Voluntary Euthanasia (Legalization) Bill, was introduced in the House of Lords on November 4, 1936 by Lord Ponsonby, and given a first reading. It was the first such bill ever presented in the British Parliament, and appears to be the first to be introduced into a legislative body in any English-speaking country since the Ohio Bill in 1906.

The bill's major safeguards and provisions included:

(1) An application must be made by the dying person who desires to receive euthanasia stating that he has been informed by two medical practitioners that he is suffering from a fatal and incurable disease (as defined in the act), and that the process of death is likely to be protracted and painful; that he desires to take advantage of the provisions of the act; that his affairs are in order; that his near relatives (as defined in the act) have been informed; and that he knows of no valid reason why he should not be granted the necessary license or permit. This application must be duly attested by a magistrate or commissioner of oaths.

(2) The application must be accompanied by two medical certificates—one from the ordinary attendant, and one from an independent medical practitioner of a specified status who must not be related to the applicant, nor be financially interested in his death.

(3) The application, with the certificates, must then be sent to an official medical officer appointed for the purpose, who shall then examine the papers and see that they are all in order and interview the applicant and the near relatives.

(4) The application and certificates will then come before a court of summary jurisdiction sitting *'in camera.'*

The proposed bill concluded: "Assuming that the time

has come when the applicant, having discussed the matter with those near and dear to him, and with his spiritual adviser, decides to act upon his permit, he will send word to the practitioner concerned and arrange date and other details. The procedure for administering euthanasia would be governed by regulations to be made by the Minister of Health."

It was Dr. Millard's view that the responsibility for the actual *"coup de grace"* might rest with either a physician or the patient—a lethal dose might be placed within his reach to be taken by his own act.

In the debate in the House of Lords, the two speeches that were most eagerly awaited were those of Lord Dawson and Lord Horder. Lord Dawson, who has been described as one of England's wisest and most esteemed physicians, made it clear that he believed that there were times when the physician should terminate the suffering of a dying patient.* He said that life should be looked at more from the point of view of quality than of quantity, and he rejected the idea that the only duty of the doctor was to save life. "There has gradually crept into medical opinion, as it has crept into lay opinion, the feeling that one should make the act of dying more gentle, and more peaceful, even if it does involve curtailment of the length of life." He said there were diseases that reached stages when the profession knew that a cure was not possible, and though in the nineteenth century it was the accepted traditional view that it was the duty of the medical man to continue the struggle for life right up to the end, medical opinion had changed and "we now think it the doctor's duty to relieve pain."

However, Lord Dawson then noted that the medical profession was a conservative one, and to the great disappointment of many, he concluded that the matter should be left to "The gentle and slow growth of opinion among both

*For reference, see Parliamentary Debates in bibliography; also see Voluntary Euthanasia Society, 1962 listing.

the laity and the medical profession." He disliked the provision in the bill which would require that the sick chamber be visited by officials, and altogether he thought it better to leave the matter at that time to the discretion of the doctors.

Lord Horder, King George VI's physician, seemed to agree with Lord Dawson. He expressed the view that the medical profession should not be asked to give leadership in matters of the legalization of euthanasia, since putting an end to life was outside the doctor's responsibility. The Archbishop of Canterbury said there were some cases in which euthanasia seemed justifiable on compassionate grounds, but he seemed relieved when it was suggested that the matter be left in the hands of the doctors.

The Earl of Listowel strongly disagreed with the view that the matter should be left to the discretion of the individual doctor. That would put a far heavier responsibility upon him than the responsibility that the bill would put upon him. He also thought it unfair to expect a doctor to risk being charged with a criminal act in order to satisfy his moral conscience: that was the gravest responsibility that could be imposed upon him.

The Lords rejected the motion on second reading by a vote of 35 to 14, thus defeating the bill. The Society recognized that the safeguards proposed had been too elaborate and had contributed to the defeat. Its efforts were renewed after World War II, and in 1950 the House of Lords debated a motion in favour of the principle underlying voluntary euthanasia, but it was withdrawn without a vote. Not until 1969 was another bill voted on in the British Parliament.

Another debate on the bill of special interest was conducted by the Hunterian Society of London and reported in the *British Medical Journal* on November 21, 1936. Leaders in medicine, law and religion debated arguments for and against euthanasia and the bill. Dr. Millard said that the problem was not essentially medical, theological, or legal, but sociological. He expressed the view that "the substitution of a quick and painless death in certain cases for a death which was slow and agonizing would be regarded hereafter as one of the great reforms of the age." One doctor said that euthanasia was contrary to all the tenets of the medical profession; another shocked many of his listeners when he stated that he had administered euthanasia ever since he had been in practice, and would go on doing it whether it was legalized or not. Canon Harold Anson stated that it was sometimes asserted that euthanasia was constantly being practiced by the medical profession for patients who requested it, though many doctors strongly denied this. He said that if it was being done, then "Surely the position was more fraught with criminal possibilities than if euthanasia were carried out openly and by legal process." A member of the legal profession said it was intolerable that any professional man should be placed in the dilemma of either refusing to do what humanity dictated or committing a breach of law.

Sir Walter Langdon-Brown noted that public opinion moved slowly, but it moved, and he citied the fact that when he was a boy, cremation was regarded with horror, but now it was common practice. He mentioned persons serving prison terms for having advocated birth control, but noted that now the Ministry of Health issued circulars on the subject.

ORGANIZED EFFORTS IN THE UNITED STATES

The Nebraska Bill

In February, 1937, a bill to legalize the practice of euthanasia was introduced in the Nebraska State Legislature by Senator John H. Comstock. It was sponsored by Dr.

Inez C. Philbrick, a seventy-year-old physician, formerly a member of the faculty of the University of Nebraska. This appears to be the first such bill to be introduced in the United States since the Ohio bill in 1906. Dr. Philbrick, who had been an advocate of birth control and other controversial issues, defended the measure saying that euthanasia is not contrary to the Oath of Hippocrates: "This fourth century B.C. oath, in some particulars, is more honored in the breach than in the observance, and it may need an amendment to meet the need of the twentieth century, A.D."

The legislative committee of the Nebraska State Medical Association opposed the measure and many clergymen spoke against it. The bill, which was similar to the British bill, was referred to a committee and indefinitely postponed, the *New York Times* reported in February of 1937.

American Euthanasia Society Organized

The Euthanasia Society of America was organized in New York on January 16, 1938. Its original title was "The National Society for the Legalization of Euthanasia." Its purpose was to conduct a national campaign of education so that bills might be introduced in state legislatures and in Congress. It subscribed to the belief that with adequate safeguards, the choice of immediate death rather than prolonged agony should be available to the dying.

Its founder and first president was the Reverend Dr. Charles Francis Potter, a prolific writer of books on religion and other topics, and founder in 1929 of the First Humanist Society of New York. The *New York Times* said, "The name of Charles Francis Potter needs no introduction. It is a name that is today at once a symbol and a slogan. Of the liberal in religion, he is the apostle." He had left the Baptist Church to become a Unitarian minister and later a New Humanist.

The secretary was the energetic Mrs. F. Robertson Jones, honorary president of the American Birth Control League. The Board of Directors consisted of prominent leaders in various professions, and among the Advisory Council were such well-known figures as Sherwood Anderson, author; Dr. Foster Kennedy, Professor of Neurology, Cornell Medical College; Dr. William McDougall, Professor of Psychology, Duke University; and Dr. Horatio H. Newman, Dean of the College of Science, University of Chicago; also such distinguished Englishmen as Havelock Ellis, Julian Huxley, the Earl of Listowel, and H. G. Wells. Those added to the council at a later date included Dr. Harry Emerson Fosdick, Freda Kirchway, W. Somerset Maugham, Margaret Sanger, and Robert E. Sherwood.

Dr. Potter, in a public debate reported in the *New York Times* on January 17, 1938, said that the problem of euthanasia is one which sooner or later confronts every practicing physician. "My experience as a clergyman for many years has forced me to recognize the necessity for laws permitting euthanasia in certain cases under proper restrictions." Regarding the most common argument of opponents that it is against the commandment "Thou shalt not kill," Dr. Potter said:

> It seems that if the killing is done wholesale and in anger and bitter hate, the Ten Commandements can be set aside; but when you come to an individual case, and the killing is done in mercy, to release a sufferer from intolerable agony, then the Ten Commandments are suddenly in force again. . . . Perhaps the time has come to forget Moses and listen to the words of Jesus, "Blessed are the merciful." . . . There really is no logical argument against euthanasia. All opposition is based on emotional and religious prejudices or on misunderstanding of the proposed procedure.

He spoke of the safeguards that would prevent foul play by unscrupulous and impatient heirs who might want to hasten the death of a wealthy person.

Euthanasia for defective newborn babies and the chronically insane was also advocated by Dr. Potter, but on the advice of some members of the Euthanasia Society, and influenced by a questionnaire that indicated greater support for voluntary euthanasia, he did not include them when helping to draft the proposed bill.

The Proposed New York Bill to Legalize Euthanasia

A bill to legalize euthanasia in the State of New York was proposed publicly by the treasurer of the Euthanasia Society, Charles E. Nixdorff, a lawyer, on January 26, 1939. It was similar to the British bill (see p. 68) and pertained only to voluntary euthanasia. In spite of efforts on behalf of the bill, it was never introduced into the legislature, and during the war years efforts were temporarily discontinued. But much public controversy ensued and it was further sparked by a debate before the Society of Medical Jurisprudence at a meeting held in the New York Academy of Medicine.

Dr. Oscar Riddle, a biologist at the Carnegie Institute, said that euthanasia for the incurably ill, under proper and indispensable safeguards, would contribute to the welfare of mankind in shortening suffering and in lightening the burden of emotional strain and financial expense that lies so heavily on the families of the dying. He spoke also of the relief it would be to many to know that if they should become incurable sufferers, there would be a way out because there would be recognition in law of one's right to choose death.

Dr. Foster Kennedy, professor of neurology at Cornell Medical College and director of the department of neurology of Belluevue Hospital, surprised some of his listeners, according to the *New York Times* (February 14, 1939), when, instead of advocating only voluntary euthanasia, he urged the legalization of euthanasia upon application of the guardians of infants born defective who were doomed to remain defective. He said that sometimes the decision to grant euthanasia should be ratified twice at four month intervals. It is "absurd and misplaced sentimental blindness that seeks to preserve the life of a person who is not a person. . . . If the law sought to restrict euthanasia to those who could speak out for it, and thus overlooked these creatures who cannot speak, then I say as Dickens did, 'the law is an ass.' It's time the law changed its mind." Regarding terminal patients, Dr. Kennedy objected so strongly to some of the terms of the proposed bill, he said that he was willing "to take a chance of penal servitude to help my man out." His views were more fully expressed in *Collier's*, May 20, 1939, and April 22, 1950. (See page 113).

EVENTS AND VIEWPOINTS IN THE THIRTIES

Further interest in euthanasia was stimulated by the writings of Dr. Harry Roberts, a highly regarded British physician, and of the American physician, Dr. George W. Jacoby; and also, following the death of Charlotte Perkins Gilman, by an article by Dr. Abraham L. Wolbarst.

Dr. Roberts, in an article in *Living Age* called "May Doctors Kill?" made the plea, "Do unto others as you would that they should do to you," saying, "The most horrible thing in the world, for us living and sentient beings, is inexorable suffering, and we must be barbarous, or stupid, or both at once not to use the sure and easy means now at our disposal to bring it to an end." He quoted Bacon as having said, "I esteem it the office of a physician not only to restore health but to mitigate pain and dolors; and not only when such mitigation may conduce to recovery but when it may serve to make a fair and easy passage." He related cases in which patients had begged him for relief from their hopeless suffering and said, "biographical history is full of such instances."

Though an ardent advocate of euthanasia, Dr. Roberts was very critical of the bill proposed by Dr. Millard for two reasons: its safeguards were too cumbersome, and its scope was too limited. Important as it was to permit euthanasia for terminal patients who requested it, he felt it was even more important to permit it for hopelessly incapacitated or defective individuals, such as imbeciles and idiots, who were not capable of making a request. He made a strong plea on behalf of these helpless individuals. And rather than accept the cumbersome safeguards in the proposed bill, Dr. Roberts said that he personally would not hesitate to end the life of an individual suffering from a painful and incurable disorder such as cancer of the larynx. "When our sympathy outweighs our fear of the law, let us act on it," he wrote.

Dr. Roberts' 1936 book *Euthanasia and Other Aspects of Life and Death* appears to be the first book on the subject in English since the classic by Tollemache in 1884. A review in the *British Medical Journal* said of it, "His book is pervaded from cover to cover with common sense, sympathy, understanding."

In the United States, the 1936 book *Physician, Pastor and Patient* by Dr. George W. Jacoby, former president of the American Neurological Association, had a chapter on "The Euthanasia Problem" in which he asked, "Has the incurable person a right to relief from suffering?" He answered in the affirmative.

Dr. Jacoby deplored the influence of superstition and religion on medicine and its effect in preventing legislation that would permit such things as euthanasia for those who would be "better off dead," and abortion for those who should not be born. He pointed out that in 1163 the Edict of Tours forbade the shedding of blood, making surgery impossible; similarly the dissection of the body after death fell under the ban of the Church, believing as it did, in the material resurrection of the body. However, in the sixteenth century the Church succumbed to pressure and issued an edict that as dissection of cadavers served a useful purpose, its practice was thenceforth countenanced. However, many religious leaders still censured such humane measures as the use of chloroform in childbirth until late in the nineteenth century.

The suicide in 1935 of Charlotte Perkins Gilman, great-granddaughter of Lyman Beecher, sparked much controversy and publicity. Mrs. Gilman, lecturer and author, named by Carrie Chapman Catt as one of the 12 greatest women in the world, said she preferred chloroform to cancer and left a note in which she called "justifiable suicide" the simplest of human rights. She also left an article for publication in which she stated:

> Our mental attics are full of old ideas and emotions, which we preserve sentimentally but never examine. The advance of the world's thought is promoted by those whose vigorous minds seize upon inert doctrines and passive convictions and shake them into life or into tatters. This theory that suicide is a sin is being so shaken today.

In defending the right to avoid prolonged agony and refuting the idea that whatever happened was God's will, she said, "Astonishing calumnies have been believed of God."

Mrs. Gilman's plea for a more enlightened attitude toward euthanasia brought forth an editorial in *Survey* magazine which noted that her decision had a parallel in the suicide three years earlier of George Eastman, manufacturer of cameras and patron of music and education in his city of Rochester, who left a note for his friends saying that since living was over, why wait? And the editor of *Forum* responded by publishing a debate entitled "The Right to Die," by two physicians, Dr. Abraham L. Wolbarst and Dr. James J. Walsh.

Dr. Wolbarst, a distinguished New York physician, under the title "Legalize Euthanasia," made a reasoned plea for euthanasia not only for those suffering from terminal illness and for imbeciles and others severely mentally defective or deformed, but also for those who had been insane for many years. Euthanasia for the insane, he said, would present many problems, but he suggested that legislation establish a limit of perhaps ten years, during which it could be determined if there was any chance of recovery. "When that limit has been passed," he wrote, "and recovery becomes out of the question, there is no further purpose in maintaining a burdensome life any longer. . . . [it would be] better for all concerned if these incurables, determined in the crucible of time, could be aided in passing from their earthly miseries." Dr. Wolbarst urged that consideration be given also to the relatives and friends whose suffering is often even greater when it spans long years of hopelessness.

It was Dr. Wolbarst's view, however, that euthanasia should be administered only in accordance with law, and accordingly, he became one of the leaders in the fight for its legalization.

Dr. James J. Walsh took the opposite position in the *Forum* debate. Under the title, "Life is Sacred," he said, "Suffering is one of the great mysteries of life and we do not know the meaning of it. . . . Man who has suffered is more human." He added that patients "recognize that they deserve some punishment for . . . slips from grace in past moments of weakness, and become persuaded that their pain may represent punishment." The condemnation of euthanasia was continued in the *Forum* by Zona Gale, who claimed that any taking of life was an antisocial act and a primitive impulse: "The idea of suicide with its twin brother, euthanasia, belongs to the fundamentally antisocial mind."

In 1939, four years after his *Forum* article, Dr. Wolbarst published in *Medical Record* what appears to be the

first article in an American medical journal to clearly advocate euthanasia and its legalization. Dr. Wolbarst said that
every passing day made increasingly evident the rapid
growth of public sentiment in favor of euthanasia. He
noted that life is a precious thing and that the craving for
it is instinctive, but it is not how long we live but how we
live that is important. He traced the history of man's struggle for liberty and happiness and spoke of the tremendous
advances in medicine and surgery that began with the introduction of anesthesia. We now control pain whenever
possible, he pointed out, and no longer regard suffering as
a divine visitation of Providence. "Euthanasia aims to advance this humanitarian progress by easing the final passage when further suffering is useless and without
purpose." He thought that to refuse terminal sufferers the
release of death should be regarded as a denial of the
physician's solemn obligation to relieve pain and suffering.
He suggested that doctors and others ask themselves what
they would choose for themselves, if they were faced with
a slow, agonizing death.

One objection often raised by physicians is that a
stigma would be attached to a doctor who administered
euthanasia, whether or not the law condoned it. Dr. Wolbarst challenged this view and described the analogous
situation with reference to abortion. While all abortion was
illegal, those who performed it were committing a criminal
offense and were regarded as medical outlaws. But when
abortions were made legally permissible in certain circumstances, they were no longer viewed with disapproval, and
doctors soon had no hesitation in performing them in accordance with law. Dr. Wolbarst thought the same might
some day be said of euthanasia.

Earlier an editorial in *Medical Record* on March 4, 1936
had asked, "Have we the Right to Choose Death?" and
stated, "More and more frequently is this question being
asked by today's children, members of a social order already sophisticated and trained in rational thought pro-

cesses as compared with mental levels of population not more than fifty years ago." The view was expressed that the time would come when man would be master of his fate and each would be permitted to choose for himself.

A nonmedical writer, Anthony M. Turano, writing in *American Mercury,* denounced the "terrifying dogma" of the Church and described as barbarous the social policies and "gruesome ethics" that prevent merciful release from suffering. He said, "The Reformation brought about some abatement of the horrors of the Hereafter, but the soul-toughening value of misery on earth continued to be asserted."

"Five Times I Have Taken a Life" was the title of an anonymous article that appeared in the *London Daily Mail* just prior to the founding of the Euthanasia Society in England. In it a "kindly" elderly country doctor related that he had taken five lives: a newborn child clearly doomed to imbecility, a child born without a skullcap, a farmer suffering from an incurable and agonizing disease, and two patients in agony "beyond the torment of the damned." His conscience never troubled him, the doctor said, and he asserted that not only would he willingly face any tribunal in the world, but would do the same again in similar circumstances.

The story received worldwide attention and led to similar admissions by other doctors, mostly anonymously, with the result that discussion of the problems involved and of the need for legislation increased.

Among the doctors in this period to oppose the legalization of euthanasia was Dr. Morris Fishbein, editor of *JAMA,* Journal of the American Medical Association, and former president of the AMA.

According to *Time* (November 18, 1935), Dr. Fishbein's view of mercy killing was, "The average doctor frequently faces the problem, and when it is a matter between him and his patient he may generally decide it in his own way without interference." This seemed to typify the response of a great many doctors to proposed euthanasia legislation.

Time, in November, 1935, in its coverage of opposition to euthanasia legislation among the medical profession related the story of Ann Becker, a bedridden nurse in Buffalo, New York, who had appealed to the Erie County Medical Association to appoint a doctor to take her life "after 749 horrible days since an auto crash." She made her plea "in the name of mercy" but the medical society merely replied that the law forbade its taking any action, and Dr. Fishbein made what seemed a cold and irrelevant comment: "Any dying person is irrational and not responsible for what he says. If he recovers, his attitude is entirely different. I deplore the publicity that this case has received."

In a paper before the New York Psychiatric Society as well as in later articles, Dr. A. A. Brill, a well-known psychoanalyst, denounced euthanasia on the ground that man's sadistic, savage impulses would be unleashed if euthanasia were to be legalized even in the most restricted manner. "Merciful killing of incurables, no matter how humanely applied, would demoralize society," he said.

Dr. Felix Deutsch, writing in the *Psychoanalytic Quarterly,* gave interesting examples of deathbed scenes and then generalized that "Euthanasia occurs when all aggressive reactions subside, when the fear of death has been dispelled, and when there is no further sense of guilt." Even granted that many patients are likely to die more happily if their conscience is clear and they have no fear of death, there remain nonetheless countless people who have neither feelings of guilt nor fear of death, who suffer for weeks, months, or even years after they are ready and want to die. Thus, Dr. Deutsch's conclusions, based on a rather outmoded application of Freudian principles, are directly con‑ tradicted by clinical practice.

Strong opposition to the legalization of euthanasia was reported in several Catholic magazines. *Commonweal* condemned as unchristian the view that the suffering of apparently incurable people is the greatest possible evil. Instead, it should be seen as "the greatest possible source of heroism, purification and redemption." And the Catholic College Press Association, which said it spoke for 18,000 students in 17 colleges and universities, expressed unalterable opposition to all attempts to legalize euthanasia.

Literary Digest quoted many people with differing viewpoints, and *Reader's Digest,* in November 1938, "Shall We Legalize Mercy Killing?" presented articles by two anonymous writers, Mr. Pro and Mr. Con.

Mr. Con discussed the problem of medical prognosis and said "incurable" is a tricky word. He noted that some diseases regarded as incurable a few years ago are now curable and said, "No doctor can ever be sure that, in giving way to the soft-heartedness of the mercy killer, he is not robbing his patient of some chance of normal life." He said that some people would want to save money by ridding society of such nuisances as the incurable, feebleminded and insane so that their taxes might be a little lower. Mr. Con failed to state that when certain stages of some terminal illnesses have been reached there is irreparable damage that prevents all possibility of further normal life. He also made no reference to the safeguards provided in the proposed bill that would prevent action motivated by self-interest, and ignored the fact that compassion—not economic gain—was the motivation for the legislation.

Mr. Pro said that man has progressed only by using facts intelligently. He thought that to permit legal euthanasia would be to use death intelligently, while at present we use death only with stupid brutality. Of the present practice of letting dying patients suffer uselessly he said, "It sounds like a situation purposely created by a sadistic maniac. ... When confronted with the poignant facts in an actual case, public sentiment is miles ahead of the law. . . . Present regulations are as barbarous as if they wantonly prohibited the use of anesthetics because heaven intended man to suffer pain. Some people felt that way about anesthetics a hundred years ago. A hundred years from now our descendents will find our attitude toward euthanasia equally shocking."

In an article in *19th Century* supporting euthanasia, Robert Harding told of how his dying wife had begged that her life be ended, only to have her request refused by the doctor, who said, "I am not even allowed to consider that." Mr. Harding wrote, "Then I vowed that, if ever it should be in my power, I would lay before others the bitter lesson learned in the school of sorrow."

MERCY DEATHS IN THE THIRTIES

Throughout the 1930's the press reported many cases of mercy deaths. These deaths were often the response of relatives to pleas from their loved ones for release from suffering. Sometimes they involved the decision by a parent to end the suffering of a hopelessly deformed or severely defective son or daughter. Among the cases receiving most attention were the following:

In 1934, Mrs. May Brownhill of Leeds, England, terminated the life of her 31-year-old imbecile son Denis by giving him an overdose of aspirin and placing a gas tube in his mouth. Mrs. Brownhill was described as a "quiet, friendly little woman of 62 years." For 31 years she had taken care of her son, but when she required a serious operation and feared he would be left alone if the operation should prove fatal, she gave him the lethal dose from which he died. The jury convicted her of murder with a strong recommendation for mercy, but the judge ignored the recommendation and sentenced her to death. Later the Home

Office intervened, and she was pardoned by the King and set free in response to national sentiment.

In 1938, Harry C. Johnson of New York State asphyxiated his cancer-stricken wife; psychiatrists adjudged him "temporarily insane" at the time of the killing, and the grand jury refused to indict him.

In 1939 the case of Louis Greenfield, who used chloroform to end the life of his 17-year-old imbecile son, attracted attention in the press. He was tried and acquitted of the charge of first-degree manslaughter. *Time* reported the case under the heading, "Better Off Dead: Greenfield Case." And the same issue of *Time* reported that the Euthanasia Society had stated: "(1) 'mercy killings' now occur in the United States at the rate of one a week; (2) 'mercy killers' are almost never convicted; and (3) the stiffest penalty imposed in recent years was three months in prison."

One of the most famous cases was that of Louis Repouille, whose trial in 1939 for slaying his 13-year-old imbecile son dragged on for eight years. (See p. 99.)

PUBLIC OPINION POLLS

Fortune Magazine, in July of 1937, reported a survey it had made of public opinion regarding mercy killing. The questions were:

> Some people believe that doctors should be permitted to perform mercy killings upon infants born permanently deformed or mentally handicapped. Under what circumstances would you approve this?
>
> The same thing is suggested for persons incurably and painfully ill. Under what circumstances would you approve this?

The conclusion was that "a small majority would approve euthanasia for defective infants, but not for incurable adults."

In the case of defective infants, the total number approving of euthanasia, administered with the permission of the parents and/or medical board, was 45 per cent; 40.5 per cent said "under no circumstances"; and 15 per cent had no opinion.

For incurably ill adults, 37 per cent of those polled expressed approval of euthanasia provided the permission of the patient and/or his family and physician or medical board were obtained, while 47.5 per cent said "under no circumstances"; and 15 per cent expressed no opinion. No specific mention was made in the questions of laws that would permit euthanasia with safeguards.

In 1937 and again in 1939, the American Institute of Public Opinion conducted a poll asking, "Do you favor mercy deaths under government supervision for hopeless invalids?"

The public was almost equally divided, showing 46 per cent in favor, and 54 per cent opposed each year. Men were more inclined to favor the idea than women, and younger persons were more favorable than their elders. The votes of these groups were as follows:

	Per cent	
	For	*Against*
Men	49	51
Women	42	58
Persons under 30	52	48
Persons 30 to 49	44	56
Persons 50 and over	41	59

As part of the 1937 poll, doctors were polled separately; 53 per cent of them were in favor and 47 per cent were opposed, according to the *New York Times*.

A similar poll of the public was conducted by the British Institute of Public Opinion. It showed that 69 per cent of those responding, or more than two out of three, endorsed the principle of euthanasia according to the *New York Times*, April 23, 1939.

Clearly then, the period of the Thirties was a time of increasing support for euthanasia and its legalization. In both England and the United States, efforts to obtain such legislation were not successful, but, they continued, nonetheless.

Chapter 5

THE 1940's

A Temporary Halt
and Renewed Action

Preoccupation with World War II caused a marked reduction in action and publications pertaining to euthanasia. The war took up too much of everyone's energy to leave room for such humanistic efforts as the euthanasia movement; indeed, public sentiment was so revolted by the mass murders of the Nazis that the movement suffered a setback at the hands of those who grouped mercy killings with genocide and shrank from any talk of legalized euthanasia. In the latter half of the Forties, however, the euthanasia societies renewed their efforts.

AT THE START OF THE DECADE

War or no war, the talk about euthanasia went on, and, in fact, in 1940, one of the first articles on the subject to be published in a law journal appeared. It was a paper in support of euthanasia legislation read by Judge W. G. Earengey at a meeting of the Medico-Legal Society in England.

Judge Earengey discussed the nature of man's rights. From earliest times, he said, the interests of the community have necessarily restricted the claim of the individual to full freedom of thought and action. But, he deplored the fact that recently in totalitarian states, especially Germany and Russia, the cause of the state had been espoused to such an extent that freedom of the individual might be said to be nonexistent. While it is almost universally agreed that the state is entitled to prohibit the commission of crime and inflict punishment when law is violated, he observed, there are natural rights that belong to the individual, and "in that sphere he is free to act as he pleases, subject to his observing similar right to others. To this extent he has the right to live his own life. Does he have the right to end that life, if he is so minded?"

Judge Earengey answered his own question:

> The criterion for us today . . . is not what the philosophers and churchmen thought in bygone ages, but what is now in the best interests of the State and the individuals who compose it. And, bearing in mind that organized religious opinion (so far as it extends) is not uniform, one may be permitted to turn to less spiritual considerations in order to ascertain what guidance can be found.

Judge Earengey made a strong plea for voluntary euthanasia and the right to end life when it had become only a burden to oneself and others, though he disapproved of suicide or euthanasia for those who still had the ability to be of service. He insisted that legislation was necessary; to those who claimed that the matter should be left to the conscience of the physician, his answer was, "the realm of law is not to be excluded by the desires of a particular profession, however eminent." He thought it unfair to doctors to ask them to run the risk of prosecution, and unfair to patients who want euthanasia to have to be dependent on whether or not their physician is willing to risk violating law.

Also in 1940, *Quarterly Review* published two articles on euthanasia. One was by the distinguished British theologian, R. F. Rattray, who agreed with Judge Earengey that the granting of this mercy should not be left to the judgment of any one doctor. He also contended that painless death was a right for those who qualified in accordance with the safeguards of the law. In opposition to these views was an article by Sir Arthur Hurst, a distinguished physician, which expressed the traditional view that these matters should be left to the judgement of the physician. Hurst opposed the British Bill and claimed that every humane doctor kept the pain of a dying patient under control even though this might shorten life. Interestingly enough, he said, "Cases do certainly occur in which euthanasia appears to be most desirable, but unfortunately these do not come within the scope of the Euthanasia Act, which requires the expressed wish of the patient that his life be terminated." As examples of such cases he mentioned newborn infants with severe deformities and cases in which patients are unable to communicate their wishes, but made no plea for legislation to allow them to die.

A Poll of New York Physicians

The Euthanasia Society of America reported in 1941 that a questionnaire had been sent to the medical doctors of New York asking: (1) Are you in favor of legalizing voluntary euthanasia for incurable adult sufferers? and (2) Are you in favor of legalizing euthanasia for congenital monstrocities, idiots and imbeciles? Replies were received from approximately 4,000 doctors, i.e., about 16 per cent. Approximately 80 per cent of the respondents answered that they were in favor of the legalization of euthanasia for incurable adult sufferers who asked for it, and about 27 per cent were in favor for severely defective children. Unfortunately the question did not differentiate between newborn versus older defectives.

This poll played a part in the decision of the Euthanasia Society to continue to limit its program to voluntary euthanasia, even though some polls of general public opinion had shown that about as many persons favored euthanasia for grossly defective infants as for incurable adults.

THE IMPACT OF THE NAZI WAR CRIMES

The war crimes of the Nazis have a two-fold significance for the euthanasia movement. They serve as a lasting testament to the tremendous potential for evil possessed by medicine when it is exploited by the state; and they remind us that when the meting out of death becomes an extralegal function, unlegislated and uncontrolled, it is likely to be abused, and result in a denial of human rights and tragedy.

There are those who cite the Nazi crimes as an argument against the legalization of euthanasia, but surely this argument is based on fallacious reasoning. There can be no comparison between the merciless and secret cruelty of the Nazis, and humane legislation aimed at protecting the rights of the individual.

The motives and methods of euthanasia legislation advocates and those of the cold-blooded, secretive and deceptive program of the Nazis are on opposite ends of the moral spectrum. It is time to recognize that rather than opposing legislation on the ground that euthanasia bears too close a resemblance to Nazi genocide, it is more sensible to support it, for secrecy of action outside the law is what must be shunned above all else. The lesson of World War II, then, is that we must exercise vigilance, controlling medicine through legislation, while at the same time closely watching the state to see that it stays within the bounds of its own laws. Carefully thought-out euthanasia legislation is in perfect agreement with this aim.

Killing for the Convenience of the State

Lest time has dimmed the memory of the shocking crimes, we cite the following statistics supplied by two well-known writers. In an article entitled "Germany Executes her 'Unfit'," Michael Straight reported in the *New Republic:*

> In September, October, and November, 1940, 85,000 blind, incurably ill or aged Germans were put to death by the Gestapo. They were put to death as casually as the SPCA chloroforms old and helpless dogs. They were not killed for mercy. They were killed because they could no longer manufacture guns in return for the food which they consumed; because the German hospitals were needed for wounded soldiers; because their death was the ultimate logic of the national socialist doctrine of racial superiority and the survival of the physically fit.

And William L. Shirer reported in his *Berlin Diary,* and later in an article in *Reader's Digest:*

> Since last fall the Gestapo, with the approval of the German government, has been systematically putting to death the Reich's mentally deficient . . . number is not known, but a trustworthy German has estimated 100,000. That may be high but the figure certainly runs into the thousands.

Mr. Shirer reported that families were never called to their loved ones before death came. Many received a warning not to demand explanations or "spread false rumors." Crimes were also committed—for the most part by or under the direction of physicians—in the name of scientific medical experimentation. The Nuremberg records show that at least 200 doctors participated in the mass exterminations and experimentations, and perhaps another 300 were aware of what was going on.

Medical experiments, as reported by Rusk, Ivy, and others, included such atrocities as operating on prisoners who needed no operation and without their consent in order to develop surgical skills; painful mass sterilizations of Jewish women; X-ray treatments that caused severe burns; amputation of healthy limbs in order to test reactions to infections, and other unbelievably cruel experiments such as exposing political prisoners to subzero temperatures to see how much cold they could stand before death took over.

The question naturally arises, how could such atrocities be performed by so many members of a profession as noble as medicine and in a country famous for its superior medical skill? Many attempts have been made to answer that question. According to Gregor Ziemer the answer given by George Ables of the Nazi Health Office was simply "We're not thinking of individuals but of the race. The race is bigger than the individual." He said that to keep alive people who could not contribute to the state was to squander the nation's money. At the Nuremberg trials, the defense claimed that most of the experimental crimes involved a search for the answer to a worthy medical question; it rationalized that the end justified the means.

The true explanation, however, lies deeper than this rationalization. Secrecy of action, an atmosphere of dictatorial repression, and total disregard for humanitarian principles and individual rights, along with a ruthless drive for power made these acts possible.

"From Small Beginnings"—The Wedge Argument

One of the American medical consultants at Nuremberg, Dr. Leo Alexander, a psychiatrist at Tufts College Medical school, and Director of the Neurobiologic Unit at Boston State hospital, has been widely quoted by the opponents of euthanasia. In an article entitled "Medical Science Under Dictatorship," he said, "Whatever proportions these crimes finally assumed, it became evident to all who investigated them that they started from small beginnings.

... They started with the acceptance of an attitude, basic to the euthanasia movement, that there is such a thing as a life not worthy to be lived, and then spread to all 'useless eaters' and politically and socially unwanted persons." Dr. Alexander raised the question as to whether there were not danger signs that some American physicians have also been "infected with a Hegelian, cold-blooded, utilitarian philosophy."

In a country where secrecy cloaks the actions of doctors, and citizens permit dictatorship and disregard for law, such warnings of disaster are justified. However, in using the "wedge argument" to oppose the movement to legalize euthanasia, Dr. Alexander fails to stress the fundamental difference in motive and method between the Nazi program, in which secret agents selected hundreds of thousands of "unwanted persons" and ordered them exterminated with no regard for the wishes or rights of the persons selected or their families, and the compassion and openness of those who advocate the right to choose euthanasia in accordance with legal safeguards that would protect their right to live as well as their right to die. The danger lies not in the belief that life sometimes becomes not worth living, but in the idea that secret agents of the state—doctors or others—should be permitted or ordered to terminate the lives of those they decide were unwanted or "useless eaters."

Reactions of the World Medical Association

At the 1950 meeting of the World Medical Association (WMA), the accredited representatives of the German medical profession, in seeking readmission to that body, presented a declaration in which they confessed their guilt and asserted that certain German doctors, both individually and collectively, had participated in "numerous acts of cruelty and oppression, and in the organization and perpetration of brutal experiments on human beings without their consent." They acknowledged that their acts and experiments had "resulted in the deaths of millions of human beings," and pledged, "We will exact from our members a standard of conduct that recognizes the sanctity, moral liberty and personal dignity of every human being." The General Assembly of the WMA then admitted German doctors to membership by a vote of 33 to 3, in spite of strong protest by the representatives from Israel, Great Britain, and Czechoslovakia.

At the same meeting of the WMA, after heated discussion, the General Assembly voted to approve a resolution recommending to all national associations that they "condemn the practice of euthanasia under any circumstances." The resolution was strongly opposed by the delegates from Great Britain and India; they favored mercy deaths in certain circumstances. Delegates from the United States were among those that supported the resolution condemning euthanasia.

It is understandable that in an atmosphere charged with emotion and revulsion against the crimes committed by the German doctors, the members of the Assembly were in no frame of mind to consider the topic of euthanasia with dispassion or logic. Moreover, it was not surprising that delegates from Catholic countries would denounce it, but the opposition of the United States seemed inexplicable. One possible reason is that Dr. Morris Fishbein, a former president of the American Medical Association, well known for his conservative views, was an influential U.S. representative, and played a vital role in determining the antieuthanasia stance of the United States.

THE EUTHANASIA BILL PROPOSED FOR NEW YORK

Starting in 1946, groups of clergymen, doctors, and others became active in support of a euthanasia bill for New

York State. This activity in turn stimulated further opposition, especially from Roman Catholic groups and some medical societies.

A statement signed by 54 New York City Protestant ministers expressing approval of voluntary euthanasia for victims of painful, incurable disease was widely publicized in 1946. These clergymen announced that in their view voluntary euthanasia, under the circumstances outlined in the proposed bill, should not be regarded as contrary to the principles of Christianity. The list of signers, as reported in the *New York Times,* September 28, 1946, was an impressive one, and included such well-known people as Dr. Harry Emerson Fosdick and Dr. Henry Sloane Coffin.

This statement brought forth strong opposition from Monsignor R. E. McCormick, the presiding judge of the ecclesiastical tribunal in New York's Catholic Archdiocese, who denounced not only euthanasia, but the clergymen who had signed the statement, as well. He said that the proposed bill was "Anti-God, un-American, and a menace." However, when challenged to a public debate by Dr. Potter, he declined.

The Euthanasia Society announced in 1946 that a committee of 1,776 physicians for legalization of voluntary euthanasia had been formed, and that its chairman was the noted gynecologist, Dr. Robert Latou Dickenson, who during his distinguished career had been president of the American Gynecological Association, director of the American College of Surgeons, chairman of the obstetrical section of the AMA, and vice-president of the Planned Parenthood Federation. Dr. Dickenson, with the aid of such other distinguished physicians as Dr. Abraham Wolbarst, drafted a new bill similar to the earlier one.

This bill, which was presented to the legislature in 1947, provided that any person of sound mind over 21 years of age who was suffering from a painful and fatal disease attested by the attending physician to be incurable, might by a written and witnessed petition to a court of record request euthanasia. The court would then appoint three persons, of whom at least two should be physicians, to investigate all aspects of the case and report back to the court; whereupon if the committee gave a favorable report and the patient still wanted euthanasia, the court would grant the petition and euthanasia would be administered by the physician or person chosen by the patient or the committee. The bill was permissive, not mandatory. Neither patient nor physician was compelled to act. The bill provided that the request for euthanasia must originate with the patient, who would be free to change his mind at any time.

Opposition to the bill was expressed in a resolution passed at a joint convention of the American Physicians Association and the New York State Naturopathic Association; a plea was made for the legislature "to resist firmly the efforts of those doctors who would legalize mercy killing" (*New York Times,* November 27, 1948). The resolution warning of the evils of legislation completely ignored the safeguards that were written into the bill, which would assure protection of the individual's right to live.

The year 1949 brought forth more organized support from churchmen. A petition signed by 379 Protestant and Jewish clergymen was sent to all the members of the New York legislature on January 4, proclaiming that a person suffering continual pain from an incurable illness has the right to die; it urged that legislation be enacted to permit voluntary euthanasia under specified circumstances and conditions, according to the *New York Times,* January 6, 1949. (See Appendix).

This petition raised a fresh storm of controversy. Senator Walter J. Mahoney of Buffalo termed it "shocking," and Monsignor John S. Middleton, preaching at a solemn mass in St. Patricks's Cathedral, at which Cardinal Spellman presided, said "The 379 Protestant and Jewish clergymen . . . were disobedient to the law of God. . . . Those who seek to legalize voluntary euthanasia are motivated by a 'pagan mentality.' . . . It is an 'inhuman humanism' that calls murder 'mercy.' " Monsignor Middleton extolled what he called the "mystical beauty of pain," and the editor of *Commonweal* offered the prayer, "St. Joseph, patron of the dying, pray for us—and for the 379 clergymen who signed the petition submitted to the New York State legislature."

At the end of 1949, the proposed bill had still not been introduced into the New York legislature.

PUBLICATIONS

Publications appearing toward the end of the decade included several articles supporting euthanasia and a book by the Reverend Joseph V. Sullivan condemning it and presenting the Catholic position.

In Canada, some court cases and an article by Sidney Katz entitled "Are They Better Off Dead?" stimulated controversy. Katz, a highly respected Canadian journalist, described several cases in which relatives had been charged with murder for ending the life of a hopelessly ill person or a grossly defective infant, as in the Ramsberg case.

In one such case parents were brought to trial for terminating the life of their two and one-half-year-old son who was dying from cancer in pain and blindness; many doctors had asserted that nothing could be done to save the child's life. At the trial the parents confessed their action and told of the pathetic, hopeless condition of the child. In concluding his address to the jury, the judge said, "They loved their child and could not bear to have him suffer. If you acquit them, it may begin a new era in which decent people will not be classed with murderers and cutthroats because they have been merciful." After ten minutes of deliberation the jury returned a verdict: not guilty. Katz noted in his article that such leniency on the part of the courts was common to many of the euthanasia cases that had recently come to the attention of the Canadian public.

Several doctors interviewed by Mr. Katz admitted to him confidentially that they had administered euthanasia in one or more utterly hopeless cases. But they said that to make such an admission and come out openly for euthanasia would be the same as announcing retirement from medical practice. Many said, however, that they knew from long experience that the greatest mercy they could bestow in some cases was to end the unfortunate victim's life quickly and peacefully. One doctor said "When you look down at the pain-twisted face of a patient, week after week, and know that he is beyond your help, it seems barbarous and stupid not to [end his suffering]." Katz concluded, "Failing an enlightened ruling from the public, the physician at the bedside . . . must continue to make his own decision."

An article in *Survey Graphic* by Selwyn James, a teacher at the New School for Social Research in New York and formerly a reporter for the *Manchester Guardian,* quoted many prominent doctors in both England and the United States who had either openly advocated or clearly indicated the need for euthanasia legislation. He reported that a well-known British doctor said, "I know many doctors of the most transparent honesty who have admitted to me that they have given way to a patient crying for mercy." And a prominent Chicago psychiatrist said:

> Most physicians of wide experience have, at one time or another, been brave enough to risk a trial and possible conviction by conferring the bliss of death upon a hopeless sufferer. The stark fact is that euthanasia, in one form or another, is practiced by many sincere and able American physicians in cases where doomed patients, facing months of intolerable agony, plead for it. However, no doctor worthy of his degree will deny that illegal euthanasia is socially undesirable.

A book by the Reverend Joseph V. Sullivan entitled *Catholic Teaching on the Morality of Euthanasia,* published in 1949, expressed much concern over the rapid growth of the euthanasia movement. In explaining the Catholic doctrine of suffering Sullivan said, "It is rather the mark of a good and holy God that he permits so many of his children to undergo suffering here on earth. Suffering is almost the greatest gift of God's love . . . by suffering we become Godlike. This is the Catholic philosophy of suffering. Anyone who lives by it could never request or support a request for euthanasia under any circumstances."

However, in discussing care of the dying, he said that if patients were in severe physical agony, the use of sedatives was permissible even to the point of coma, if the patient is spiritually prepared to die, but that it was not lawful to render a person unconscious by drugs just because he is in fear of approaching death, "since this is a part of the sacrifice that God demands for the sins and the faults of life; and even when these have been atoned for, there is great spiritual value in accepting death with love and devotion to God."

MERCY DEATHS IN THE FORTIES

Throughout the Forties, as in the previous decade, the press reported many cases in which a member of a family had finally ended the life of a loved one who was a hopeless sufferer. The two most famous and most prolonged court cases in the United States pertaining to euthanasia administered by a relative were the Louis Repouille and the J. F. Noxon cases. These cases have been described in many law journals as well as in the press.

Louis Repouille, a 31-year-old elevator operator in New York City, on October 12, 1939 put to death by chloroform his 13-year-old imbecile son Raymond. He initially pleaded not guilty to murder, but entered the plea of first-degree manslaughter, and was released on 5,000 dollars bail. While Repouille insisted that his deed was an "act of mercy" because the boy was blind, mute, and paralyzed as well as being a bedridden imbecile with the mentality of a two-year-old, the defense attorney tried to show that the deed was the result of Repouille's "mental aberration at the time" and did not present the deed as mercy killing. Repouille admitted that he had read of the similar act by Louis Greenfield who had chloroformed his imbecile son nine months previously, and said he believed the acquittal of Greenfield had been justified.

At the trial on December 5, 1941, although he had previously said that his mind "went perfectly blank" at the boy's death, Repouille said, "The idea of putting my son to death came to me thousands of time," and told how the boy had cried night and day for years. He also stated that he had obtained the chloroform two years earlier from a hospital where he had been an employee for ten years.

The jury deliberated less than an hour and brought in a verdict of guilty of manslaughter in the second degree. The maximum penalty in such a case was 15 years in prison, but the judge freed Repouille on a suspended sentence of five to ten years and ordered him to report regularly for probationary supervision.

Judge Goldstein said many factors had entered into his decision—appeals for leniency had been made by the jurors and other citizens and Repouille's lack of a criminal record—but Repouille was disappointed at the sentence and said that the jury should never have convicted him. He appealed and also petitioned for naturalization. The case dragged on until 1947, when the United States Circuit Appeals Court ruled that the "L. L. Repouille's 1939 slaying of imbecile son shows lack of 'good moral character'," and the petition for naturalization was dismissed.

Of this Repouille case Judge Learned Hand said:

> It is reasonably clear that the jury which tried Repouille did not feel any moral repulsion to his crime. Although it was inescapable murder in the first degree, not only did they bring in a verdict that was flatly in the face of the facts and utterly absurd . . . but they coupled even that with a recommendation which showed that in substance they wished to exculpate the offender.

John F. Noxon, Jr., a 52-year-old former Pittsfield Massachusetts, attorney, was convicted and sentenced to death for the "murder" by electrocution in September, 1943, of his six-month-old mentally deficient son. In August, 1946, the death sentence was commuted to life imprisonment by Governor Maurice Tobin of Massachusetts. There was further appeal and on December 24, 1948, Governor Bradford recommended to the executive council that Noxon be paroled from the life sentence. A majority of the council indicated that they would approve a reduction of Noxon's sentence, so he was released from prison under parole for the rest of his life.

Professor Yale Kamisar of the University of Minnesota Law School has commented that seldom has the punishment for administering euthanasia been as severe as in the Noxon case. Legal history shows that in the United Stated most "mercy killers" have been acquitted, been given a suspended sentence, or been sent to a mental hospital, or the charges have been dropped.

The case of G. R. Long, a 46-year-old paper-mill worker in England who killed his seven-year-old daughter by gas because she was deformed and an imbecile, received sympathetic attention in the United States. *Time* described it under title "Good bye." Mr. Long testified at the trial in 1946 "I loved my daughter very much, more so than if she had been normal—bringing about her death is the hardest thing I have ever done." He pleaded guilty and was sentenced to death—a sentence required by British law "unless the Crown's mercy intervened." The next day he was given a reprieve. Later the sentence was commuted to life imprisonment, and doubtless that was changed later.

In 1947 Mrs. Ella Haug of Pennsylvania admitted killing her invalid mother. She told the jury how her mother had pleaded for "eternal sleep" after having been bedridden for two and one-half years. Mrs. Haug gave her an overdose of sleeping tablets and then, in a moment of grief and hysteria, took 12 herself. "We started to say the Lord's Prayer together," she related to the court. "Mother's voice grew weak. We came to the part, 'Deliver us from evil,' and then her voice died away. . . ." When the "not guilty" verdict came, the courtroom exploded into spontaneous applause. Friends, neighbors, even jurors rushed forward to congratulate her.

A case that received much attention in 1949 was that of Carol Paight, of Connecticut, a college student, who killed her cancer-ridden father. She was acquitted on the ground of temporary insanity.

The Forties ended with the indictment of a physician, Dr. Hermann Sander of New Hampshire, who attracted national and international attention. The trial took place the following year, and will be discussed in the next chapter.

PUBLIC OPINION

A poll on euthanasia, conducted by Dr. Gallup in the United States, was reported June 30, 1947. The question was: "When a person has a disease that cannot be cured, do you think doctors should be allowed by law to end the patient's life by some painless means if the patient and his family request it?" The answers were as follows: Yes—37 per cent; No—54 per cent; no opinion—9 percent. People in their 20's were divided about 50–50; people over 50 opposed euthanasia by a ratio of two to one. The wording of the question is disappointing in that it did not include any assurances that there would be adequate safeguards.

The 37 per cent of "yes" answers is the same as that in the *Fortune* poll ten years earlier and 9 per cent less than in the 1937 and 1939 Gallup polls. How much the difference in the percentages is due to the difference in the questions and how much to other factors cannot be known. No doubt one factor was the revulsion to the Nazi crimes and perhaps another was the increased publicity given to the opposition to the legalization of euthanasia.

Chapter 6

THE 1950's

Reaction and Support

The early years of the Fifties were marked by much adverse reaction but also by support for euthanasia. Opposition increased chiefly as a result of the efforts that had been made to legalize voluntary euthanasia, and the continuing reports of and revulsion to the Nazi crimes. Also, the trial of Dr. Sander sparked fresh controversy.

In the middle of the decade books by three distinguished people strongly supported euthanasia, and in 1957 the highly significant allocutions of Pope Pius XII provided an impetus to new and more liberal thinking on the subject. Also, medical and law journals for the first time published many articles, pro and con, as did some Protestant church papers, and toward the end of the decade some excellent articles appeared in popular magazines in support of euthanasia.

THE CASE OF DR. SANDER

A trial that attracted the attention of much of the world originated in the action on December 4, 1949 of Dr. Hermann Sander, a 41-year-old general practitioner of New Hampshire, when he injected forty cc's of air into the vein of a cancer patient, Mrs. Abbie Burotto, age 59, who was on the verge of death.

About a week later Dr. Sander dictated into the hospital record, "Patient was given ten cc's of air intravenously, repeated four times. Expired ten minutes after this was started." About two weeks after that, Josephine Connor, the record librarian of Hillsboro County General Hospital where Mrs. Burotto died, reported this to her superiors. Dr. Sander was then arrested. After one night in the Hillsboro County jail, he was released on 25,000 dollars bail, since he agreed, in spite of the disapproval of his lawyer, to discontinue medical practice until the case was resolved. This is believed to have been the first time in New Hampshire court history that a person facing trial on a first-degree murder charge was allowed to be at liberty, but the Attorney General said he had no objection because of Dr. Sander's "high moral character and standing in the community."

On the day following the arrest, Dr. Sander said that he had done no "legal or moral wrong" and that he would be vindicated. Later he said, "I did it in a moment of weakness but what I did was morally right. I have no regrets. I have broken the law but I committed no sin."

Immediately after Dr. Sander's arrest there was an outpouring of support for him. An article in the *New York Times* on January 2 was headed, "Neighbors Uphold Doctor on 'Mercy': 90% of them Sign Petition to Aid Dr. Sander as two Pastors also Give Him Their Support." The article stated that within six hours, a group of volunteers, including the pastor of the Congregational Church of Candia, where Dr. Sander lived, had obtained the signatures of 605 of Candia's 650 registered voters to a statement expressing confidence and faith in Dr. Sander. Some were not at home, but no one who was approached refused to sign. The petition stated "We have known him as a man of Christian virtue devoted to the highest interests of human welfare at all times . . . and unselfish devotion to his tasks." Also, in nearby Goffston, where the patient died, another petition was signed by more than 200 persons urging the grand jury to drop the case. The Reverend Mark B. Strickland of Manchester's First Congregational Church, where Dr. Sander occasionally worshipped, said in a broadcast statement, "If this man is guilty, then I am guilty, for I have prayed for those who have suffered hopelessly—prayed that they be eased into the experience of death." About the same time a group of 22 Unitarian ministers announced their support of euthanasia and of Dr. Sander.

At the Hillsboro County grand jury hearing on January 3rd, the judge warned:

> the law must be enforced as it stands . . . it is not up to you to say what the law should be. . . . No one under the laws of this or any other jurisdiction in the United States, as far as I know, has the right to take arbitrarily the life of another whether the motive for taking is said to be humane or otherwise. . . . We live in a society governed by law.

The grand jury indicted Dr. Sander on a charge of first-degree murder after deliberating about an hour and a half, stating he had "willfully and of malice aforethought . . . made the injections well knowing that they were sufficient to cause death." State officials announced that they would prosecute to the letter of the law.

On hearing the Attorney General describe Dr. Sander as "a killer who must answer for his deed before the law of man and of God," Harvard anthropologist Earnest Hooten, according to *Time*, January 16, 1950, said, if "Thou shalt not kill" is a law of God that convicts Hermann Sander, "let us have done with such a savage and inhuman deity and substitute a God of Mercy and loving kindness."

Following the indictment, support for Dr. Sander continued to be strong although of course there was opposition as well. Hundreds of Dr. Sander's fellow townspeople, patients and colleagues offered to testify for him, and 2,700 persons contributed 18,000 dollars to a fund set up on his behalf.

At the trial, which started on February 20, 1950, Dr. Sander pleaded not guilty to the indictment and denied that his act had caused the patient's death. The defense was successful, and Sander was acquitted on March 10. One of the witnesses, Dr. Albert Snay, a physician who had examined Mrs. Burotto the morning of her death, testified that he could find no pulse, and that she might already have been dead when Dr. Sander gave her the injection. A nurse also testified that she had thought that the patient was dead, even before Dr. Snay saw her.

Medical organizations were less kind to Dr. Sander than the jury. Both the Massachusetts State Board of Medicine and the New Hampshire State Registration Board revoked his license to practice medicine although there was a provision that he might apply for reinstatement in two months. The Hillsboro County Medical Society dropped him from membership, but he was eventually reinstated and his medical practice increased. However, the *New York Times* reported that the two nurses at the Hospital who testified for Dr. Sander were demoted, and one of them quit.

Reactions

At its annual meeting on January 24, the Euthanasia Society voted to support Dr. Sander, holding that his action was not morally wrong. And speaking in Boston, Dr. Potter said:

> Overwhelmingly the people of New Hampshire who know him and the facts of the case say that Dr. Sander was morally right but legally wrong. We maintain that what is morally right should be made legally right, or else all respect for law will be gone.

> Dr. Sander, purposely I believe, did not cover up, as
> most doctors do. Martyr or not, he has focused attention on
> the fact that the time has come to demand that our laws be
> brought into line with public opinion.

Dr. Potter refuted the idea that euthanasia was forbidden in the Bible, and he challenged the assumption that it is prohibited by the Hippocratic Oath.

In England the Secretary of Euthanasia Society, Dr. C. Killick Millard, was reported by the Society's *Newsletter* to have said, "As far as I know, there has never been a case of prosecution of a doctor for mercy killing in Britain . . . the prosecution of Dr. Sander will help bring home the need for legal euthanasia." Also in England, during the pretrial period, reaffirmation of support for euthanasia took various forms. The *Empire News* of London, on January 9, 1950, reported that an anonymous British doctor had said that he had administered mercy deaths to three patients, and Dr. Leslie Weatherhead, renowned Minister of City Temple, restated in a sermon his support of euthanasia for those suffering from incurable illness.

There was also vocal opposition to Dr. Sander from various prominent individuals.

Dr. Billy Graham, the well-known Baptist evangelist, addressing an audience of 6,000 in Boston, was reported by the *New York Times,* January 9, 1950, as saying that Dr. Sander should be punished "as an example. . . . Anyone who voluntarily, knowingly or premeditatively takes the life of another, even one minute prior to death, is a killer. I don't say that Dr. Sander deserves death, but if we let this pass, who is to say who is to die and who is to live."

And Archbishop Richard J. Cushing of Boston, quoted by *Time* (January 16, 1950), said, "Human life is sacred because it came from God. . . . The state itself does not have the right to take the life of a sick person." He added that the legalization of euthanasia would "imperil the life of every human being who is stricken with a serious disease."

THE FIGHT AGAINST EUTHANASIA

The American Council of Christian Churches (a fundamentalist organization not to be confused with the National Council of Churches) voted its disapproval of euthanasia in 1950; the Newark Methodist Conference Committee condemned it; and in 1951 the United Presbyterian Church General Council expressed its opposition, saying: "Euthanasia is in direct conflict with the interpretation of the Sixth commandment, and legislation would open the door to more dangerous and vicious practices." In 1952 the members of the General Convention of the Protestant Episcopal Church passed a resolution which stated that they placed themselves "in opposition to the legalization of the practice of euthanasia, under any circumstances whatsoever."

Condemnation by the Catholic Church was expressed in February of 1950 by the editor of *Linacre Quarterly,* the official Catholic medical magazine, and by the Reverend Gerald Kelly writing in the official journal of the Catholic Hospital Association of the United States and Canada; and many other Catholic periodicals also opposed it.

Some medical groups were also active in expressing their opposition. In 1950 the heads of the American Academy of General Practice succeeded in keeping the issue of euthanasia from reaching the floor of its annual conference; the New York State Medical Society stated its opposition; the Massachusetts Medical Society denied that mercy killing was common among doctors. As previously reported, the General Assembly of the World Medical Association passed a resolution in 1950 condemning euthanasia at the same meeting in which it accepted the confessions of guilt by German doctors and readmitted them to membership.

Support and efforts for the legalization of euthanasia, however, continued in both the United States and England.

ACTIVITIES OF THE EUTHANASIA SOCIETIES IN ENGLAND AND THE UNITED STATES

Petition to the United Nations

The Euthanasia Society in England announced January 3, 1950, that it had sent to the Euthanasia Society of America for formal presentation to the United Nations a petition signed by 356 prominent Britons asking for an "Amendment of the Declaration of Human Rights to include the Right of Incurable Sufferers to Voluntary Euthanasia." In the United States 2,157 names were added, making a total 2,513.

Of the Americans who signed, about one-third were physicians, a third were clergymen, and a third consisted of prominent people in the fields of science, law, education, and the arts. Among the British signers were six members of Parliament, as well as representatives of the various professions and churches. (For the text of the petition, see Appendix.)

The petition was presented to Mrs. Eleanor Roosevelt, Chairman of the Commission on Human Rights, in 1952. Mrs. Roosevelt was sympathetic to the idea, but she advised that since the Commission was then concentrating on the Genocide Convention, it would be an inopportune time to present the petition on euthanasia. However, more recently, some members of the British Society have proposed that efforts be renewed to amend the Declaration of Human Rights to specify the right of incurable sufferers to euthanasia.

Other Activities of the Euthanasia Societies

The Euthanasia Society in England continued its efforts to get a euthanasia bill enacted. In 1950 its activities resulted in debate in the House of Lords on a motion in favor of the principle underlying voluntary euthanasia. The motion was withdrawn without a vote, however, due to strong opposition. Not until 1962 was a new bill drafted and publicly proposed, and not until 1969 was one voted on.

Following the trial of Dr. Sander, the New York office of the American Society reported a deluge of requests for literature and speakers. And during the first five months of 1950, speakers were supplied for 51 meetings and literature provided for countless sermons, addresses, debates, public forums and libraries all over the country. Inquiries and requests came also from various other countries where leaders in law and medicine were interested in forming their own euthanasia societies.

Membership in the organization kept increasing. Among the many well-known people to be added to the Board were the Reverend Dr. Nathan A. Perilman, president of the Association of Reform Rabbis of New York City; the Reverend Dr. John Paul Jones, former chairman of the Civil Liberties Union of New York; and Dr. Alan F. Guttamacher, obstetrician and gynecologist, and President of Planned Parenthood Federation of America. Margaret Sanger, founder of the latter organization, urged more national advertising and suggested that each member speak up in local press in order to get laws enacted as soon as possible.

At the annual meetings of the Society, addresses were given by prominent figures in the fields of law, medicine, and religion. All of the following citations are from talks given at these meetings, which are reported in the Euthanasia Society Bulletin for that year. Dean Wesley A. Sturges of Yale Law School urged extensive education of the public to a firm belief in the philosophy of euthanasia. Professor Glanville Williams, a noted British jurist, based his appeal for legislation on the ground that the most essential of all commandments is to love. He believed a physician was morally justified in ending the life of one suffering from a painful and incurable disease if he acted truly and honestly to spare the patient and not merely for the convenience of the living.

Dr. Claude E. Forkner, Professor of Clinical Medicine at Cornell Medical College, in his address to the society in 1954, said, "It is not death that people fear . . . it is ceaseless pain, endless suffering, excessive use of the family financial resources, lifelong incompetence, hopeless dependency." Euthanasia, he said, embodies one of the strongest commandments of the Bible, which says "Do unto others as thou wouldst have them do unto you." Dr. Heinrich F. Wolfe, an 84-year-old consultant at Mount Sinai Hospital, described many cases in which life had been prolonged cruelly and futilely. He deplored the zeal of many doctors to demonstrate their scientific skills at the expense of their dying patients.

Dr. Harry Emerson Fosdick, then minister of Riverside Church, New York, addressing the Society in 1956, countered the old argument that only God has the right to determine the ending of life by pointing out that man has been responsible for increasing the average lifespan from approximately 30 years in early colonial days to 70 today. By doing so, he has extended the hopeless suffering of those whom nature, left to herself, would release. Dr. Fosdick insisted that "man must shoulder the responsibility thus thrust upon him, and must devise some way of mercifully liberating the hopelessly ill from needless agony."

Dr. Julius Kaunitz, a New York physician and charter member of the Board of the Euthanasia Society, speaking to the Women's Business and Professional Club in 1957, said that people should not be forced to attempt suicide in order to escape their suffering. He spoke of the aged and incurable in hospitals everywhere—often only half-conscious from the effects of a narcotic; some muttering, others complaining of pain, some too feeble to raise a cup of water to their lips. Most of these people want to die; many ask the doctor to please put an end to their misery. If death alone can bring relief, said Dr. Kaunitz, it is wrong to withhold it. But he added, "Taking a person's life is too serious a matter to be left to the judgment of any one man." He strongly advocated that voluntary euthanasia be legalized, with carefully thought-out safeguards written into the law.

PUBLICATIONS IN THE FIFTIES

Discussion in Church and Popular Magazines

One of the first articles on euthanasia in a Protestant church periodical was published in *Christian Century* in 1950. Under the title "Is Euthanasia Christian?" E. N. Jackson discussed the moral and religious aspects of the problem. He cited the infinite regard of Jesus for every distressed human soul. "Our final judgment must be based . . . on regard for the rights and privileges of the human soul involved." It can be assumed that on the basis of the Christian concept of the soul, we would not feel that the soul itself is injured by what a physician might do to the bodily structure. He felt confident that laws with adequate safeguards could be devised to prevent unwise or unscrupulous action.

The following year *Theology Today* published an article by Dr. Joseph Fletcher advocating euthanasia, and one by the Reverend Dr. John Sutherland Bonnell opposing it. But not until the Sixties was there much further discussion of the subject in Protestant publications.

In 1950, Dr. Foster Kennedy's article of 1939 advocating euthanasia for hopelessly defective infants was reprinted in *Collier's*. "Nature's mistakes," he insisted, i.e., infants born with a brain damaged beyond repair and lacking the power to grow, should not be forced to endure a life of suffering. He related cases of hopeless idiots that had made family life impossible—cases such that there could be no error in diagnosis and no hope for a near normal life. A few months later the Catholic publication *Jurist* revealed that the great number of protest letters received by *Collier's* in response to the Kennedy article were the result of a united campaign by Catholic groups.

Strong condemnation of euthanasia was expressed in many Catholic publications such as *Catholic World* and *America*. The editor of *Commonweal* seemed to take a somewhat less rigid position when he said "When the matter of mercy killing is finally argued, it will of necessity be a religious issue. People of all faiths and no faith will argue about legal, medical, and practical aspects of euthanasia . . . but primarily and fundamentally, they will be arguing because they believe it is right or wrong in the sight of God."

Many letters expressing various viewpoints on euthanasia were published in the London *Spectator* in April of 1950. One writer told of his visit to an old women's home in which there were about 50 "poor old souls" sitting around a large room who could neither read nor write, and who spent most of their time praying that "the dear Lord would take them home." He thought they should have the right to die. Another made a plea on behalf of those who have nothing left to live for and feel they are a burden to others.

Many magazines and newspapers such as *Time, The Nation, New Republic,* and the *New York Times* kept the subject of euthanasia under discussion during the early Fifties, but there was a lull in the controversy in the mid-Fifties that lasted until the end of the decade, when several articles in support of euthanasia drew fresh attention to the subject.

Professor N. J. Berrill, of McGill University in Montreal, in an article entitled "Abnormal Babies Should Not

Be Encouraged to Live," described cases of "babies doomed to a dismal existence no matter how well cared for they might be," who should never have been permitted to live. In a later article Dr. Berrill also deplored the practice of keeping worn-out bodies alive for an extra few days or months. He said that this is sometimes done by physicians as a test of their personal skill or of their new hospital equipment, and they are often encouraged to do so by families who are loath to relinquish their hold on their loved one. But there is no end to this business once we ignore the person and concentrate on the body: "All this is a nightmare world and what may be useful in an emergency to save the life of a young person is sheer horror when inflicted upon the aged who are about to die." Every person, he thought, should have the right to die in peace.

The British writer John Beavan, in an article in 1959 entitled "The Patient's Right to Live and Die," presented the case for euthanasia and reported interviews with many physicians. His conclusion was that the greatest single factor acting against legalized euthanasia was the willingness of so many doctors to act compassionately and morally despite the possible legal consequences. In their willingness to risk prosecution and administer euthanasia when necessary, they saw no need for legal changes.

Discussion in Law and Medical Journals

LAW JOURNALS.   Law journals in the Fifties began for the first time to publish articles on euthanasia, many of which reflected the reactionary atmosphere during the early part of the decade. One such article, by the Catholic theologian Dr. Thomas Owen Martin, appeared in *Jurist*, a journal of the School of Canon Law of the Catholic University of America. Dr. Martin used the Nazi crimes and the wedge argument to oppose the legalization of euthanasia, and in criticizing the proposed New York bill, he ignored its safeguards.

Many of Dr. Martin's arguments and statements were very misleading. He said, for instance, "As a matter of fact, where euthanasia has been established by law in Western civilization, it has been extended to all who were considered socially unfit." This sentence implies that euthanasia had been established by law in some countries, which seems not to be the case. In Germany, the one country where horrendous crimes were committed, there was no law that made euthanasia legal. Hitler's orders were given with the greatest of secrecy and in violation of German law, and with utter disregard for the rights and wishes of the individuals concerned and their families. In the few countries where laws have been changed to make a distinction between murder and a merciful act motivated by compassion, there appears to have been no evidence of abuse.

Opposition came also from a well-known non-Catholic law professor. In 1958, Yale Kamisar, an Associate Professor of Law at the University of Minnesota Law School and later Professor of Law at the University of Michigan Law School, in a lengthy and much quoted article in the *Minnesota Law Review,* sharply criticized legalized euthanasia, and specifically, many of the views of Glanville Williams, as expressed in his book *The Sanctity of Life and the Criminal Law.* Kamisar took the position that the many who desire euthanasia should be denied the right to choose it because a few who might still "have some relatively normal and reasonably useful life left in them" might irrationally choose euthanasia, or be the victim of a mistaken diagnosis. He chose not to discuss the safeguards legislation would provide to prevent any reasonable possibility of error or abuse.

Professor Kamisar admitted that emotional strains in cases of terminal illness are often great for the patient, his family, and the doctor. He admitted that the case for voluntary euthanasia is strong, and said he would hate to have to argue that "the hand of death should be stayed in certain incurable and intolerable cases if there was a rational desire to die," but he warned that under present laws, a doctor might be charged with criminal homicide for failing to prolong life. While granting that freedom to choose euthanasia might well be regarded as a special area of civil liberties, he maintained that in practice, laws to legalize euthanasia would create more problems they they would solve.

Although the title of his article was "Some Non-Religious Views Against Proposed 'Mercy Killing' Legislation," Kamisar quoted chiefly traditional Catholic views. Using the mass killings in Nazi Germany and the wedge principle as grounds to reject any proposal to legalize euthanasia, the primary appeal of his argument was to fear rather than logic. Somewhat ironically he chided the advocates of voluntary euthanasia for limiting their proposed legislation to cover only those able to request that their lives be ended; he asked what of the congenital idiot, the permanently insane and the senile and other hopeless sufferers who have made no previous request and who could not speak for themselves.

A positive approach to the problem was presented in one Catholic journal, *Notre Dame Lawyer,* by John C. Hirschfeld, who suggested that the law should make a distinction between a merciful act and murder. Hirschfeld described many instances in which a relative was tried for ending the life of a loved one. Among the cases he described was the Werner case (Illinois, 1958) in which a 69-year-old man suffocated his wife, a hopelessly crippled, bedridden arthritic patient. In arraignment proceedings, the state waived the murder charge and permitted the defendant to enter a plea of guilty of manslaughter. The court found him guilty on his admission but later, after hearing the testimony of the defendant's children and pastor concerning his unfailing care and devotion to his wife, and a letter from the doctor attesting to her excruciating pain and mental despair, the judge allowed the defendant to withdraw his plea and entertained a plea of not guilty, whereupon he was acquitted.

Hirschfeld said, "The instant case is another in a steadily expanding galaxy of examples of apparent disrespect for the written law in euthanasia cases." He said that a brief examination of cases such as the Greenfield and the Repouille cases disclosed the impact of this charge: all exemplified verdicts returned in open disregard of the facts. Although he did not approve of legislation to legalize euthanasia, he thought there might be a "special niche in the law" that would distinguish between a merciful act and murder and inflict a lesser punishment for the former. Ethical approval should be withheld, he said, but when the act was clearly motivated by compassion, the crime should be classified as less reprehensible than other forms of premeditated homicide. This proposal is similar to legislation enacted in some countries.

The *University of Pennsylvania Law Review* carried an article in 1954 by Dr. Helen Silving of the University of Vienna, a Research Associate in Law, Harvard Law School, on the subject "Euthanasia: A Study in Comparative Criminal Law." This frequently cited study describes and compares the laws pertaining to euthanasia and suicide in various countries. (See page 252).

The *New York University Law Review* in 1956 reported a symposium on "Morals, Medicine and Law," in response to Fletcher's *Morals and Medicine* (see page 123). The moderator, Thomas A. Cowan, noted that the evolutionary process has now brought mankind to the point where he has the power, or the illusion of power, to say yes or no to life. Cowan asked, "Are we prepared to take control of our life process?"

Horace M. Kallen, Professor Emeritus of Social Philosphy at the New School for Social Research, was one participant in the symposium. His topic was "An Ethic of Freedom," and he asserted:

> Safeguarding a person's right to die when and as he chooses, so long as the exercise of this right works no violence on the rights of others, seems to me a proper function for the laws of a free society of free and educated men. The fantasy that existence as such, regardless of its how and wherefore, is better than nonexistence is a quirk of metaphysical verbalization and not an inference from the actual experience of actual people.

Professor Kallen expressed the view that one of the prime attributes of one's humanity is concern for reduction of suffering; he thought that most of those who oppose euthanasia do so because they have never themselves experienced the agonies of incurable distress. He regarded it as immoral not to end futile suffering.

The two lawyers on the panel, Professor Harry Kalven, Jr. of the University of Chicago Law School and Morris Ploscowe, a former New York City magistrate, deplored the inadequacy of the law and the inconsistency of courts in dealing with these problems. Ploscowe, however, thought that until there was more universal agreement on euthanasia, "The law must limp along in these areas with an illogic which is peculiarly its own." He thought it better for the time being to accept the lack of coherence and logic than to attempt to change the law and have to face the bitter conflict that would ensue.

MEDICAL JOURNALS.   The *Cumulative Index Medicus* lists more than 20 articles that appeared during the Fifties dealing with euthanasia, and many more articles are classified under death, whereas formerly these subjects were rarely discussed in medical journals. Many of the articles and editorials were in Catholic journals, and most expressed opposition to euthanasia. However, it was significant that at last medical journals were opening up these subjects for discussion. The need for a new look at current practices was emphasized by many articles, and toward the end of the decade many doctors were openly protesting futile prolongation of the lives of hopeless terminal patients. In an article in *Medical Economics* in 1950, Dr. H. A. Davidson pointed out that economic ruin often befalls the family in which there is prolonged illness. The patient, he said, was often unwilling to see his savings wiped out and his loved ones pauperized in a futile effort to preserve his painful existence. According to Davidson, doctors recognized this as a justification for euthanasia, but seldom talked about it in public. And in the *Nebraska State Medical Journal,* Dr. Edwin Davis deplored the misery caused by medical success in keeping the aged alive. He spoke of the great increase in surgery performed on the aged and the fact that many of them had little reason to be grateful for it.

The editor of the *New England Journal of Medicine* expressed distress at "the ghoulishness and cruelty of much of the dying today," especially in large hospitals, and said solutions to the problem must be found. An article by N. Mitchison in London's *Medical World* in 1956 appears to be the first in a medical journal to call attention to "the right to die."

In a "Symposium on Euthanasia" in 1953, arranged by a Joint Committee of the Maryland Medical and Bar Associations and reported in the *Maryland State Medical Journal,* Dr. George Boas, Professor of History of Philosophy at Johns Hopkins University, traced the history of the concept of "The Sanctity of Life." He ridiculed the double standard that has been applied in the Christian era in regard to the sanctity of life. In Old Testament times and the Middle Ages this sanctity was frequently disregarded at the convenience of those in power. The Inquisition, for example, sanctioned the killing of countless heretics, and in modern times the Church has supported one war after another. While the theory is that life is sacred, the practice demonstrates that its sacredness has often been ignored. As an illustration of inconsistencies in current practices, Dr. Boas cited the case of a 60-year-old woman who took care of her imbecile brother for 30 years before she finally gave him the preparation which put him out of his misery. The irony was that "life is sacred and she must not take it, but, nevertheless, the state takes her life" for performing a merciful act.

One member of the symposium's panel warned that we must not expect a "moral slide rule" which will automatically solve our problems, and a psychiatrist warned doctors of the need to beware of certain interfering factors within themselves such as feelings of guilt because they could not save their patient. "The prospective death of one of his patients will act as a threat to the omnipotence of the physician."

The most influential medical journal article of the decade was undoubtedly that by Dr. Edward H. Rynearson, of the Mayo Clinic. Writing in *CA*, the *Bulletin of Cancer Progress* two years after the 1957 allocution of Pope Pius XII, he called for a new approach in the treatment of dying cancer patients by doctors when "every conceivable avenue of treatment has been explored with total failure, and his patient, moreover, is suffering excruciating pain and is pleading for release." He said that once the physician and his associates are in unanimous agreement as to prognosis, this is the time for open discussion with the patient, his family, and his spiritual adviser in order to decide what course of action should be taken.

Dr. Rynearson strongly protested the practice of keeping hopelessly ill patients alive indefinitely by the use of modern devices, though he did not discuss the possible legal problems that might arise from terminating treatment under current laws. He limited his discussion to cases in which all the patient's physicians, attendants and family were in agreement that no further effort should be made to prolong life. By so doing he minimized the possibility of a charge of negligence. He did not discuss positive steps to hasten death, and in an address to the American Medical Association in 1962, declared that he had never advocated such measures.

The cover of this issue of *CA* presented a woodcut entitled "Death the Friend." An old man is sitting peacefully by an open window facing the sunset, his book laid aside, his expression one of quiet resignation and peace. Opposite him is Death, dignified and quiet, with a grieved expression as he bends to the task of pulling the bell rope signalling the flight of another soul. The caption is: "To him, as to the properly managed terminal cancer patient, Death is no horrible specter."

The Rynearson article evoked release of a lot of pent-up emotion by many members of the medical profession regarding useless prolongation of life; it ushered in a new era of protest against modern practices in this regard and stimulated open discussion of a subject that had formerly been regarded by most doctors as unmentionable.

The January–February 1960 issue of *CA* was devoted entirely to this subject and reported a poll it had taken of doctors, clergymen and others to learn their reaction to the Rynearson article. Of the physicians who responded, only five expressed disagreement, while 34 expressed approval —a ratio of seven to one in favor of passive euthanasia. Many wrote long letters strongly supporting Dr. Rynearson's views; a typical response was, "I could not approve more thoroughly or sincerely." The strongest opposition came from the former director of the American Cancer Society, Dr. Charles S. Cameron, who said that over the years he had strongly advocated the philosophy of fighting for the life of the cancer patient as long as possible.

One of the articles in this issue of *CA* was by Dr. David A. Karnofsky of the Memorial Center for Cancer and Allied

Diseases in New York. He wrote a scathing denunciation of
Rynearson's point of view and a rather frighteningly illogical defense of the traditional practice of keeping patients
alive as long as possible. His reasons were not only that a
cure might be found, but that the patients were needed for
research as well, and provided an opportunity for young
doctors to get experience. No mention was made of the
wishes of the patient, or of his right to refuse to be used as
a guinea pig. Ironically, though Dr. Karnofsky used the
tragic acts of the Nazis as a reason to condemn any euthanasia and to warn against it, he tried to justify his position on the basis of two factors that had led to the cruelest
of the Nazi crimes—desire to do research and the wish to
provide practice opportunities for young doctors.

Three Books in Support of Euthanasia

Around the mid-Fifties three influential books—by a
theologian, a psychiatrist, and a jurist—were published in
which each author unequivocally defended the view that
euthanasia would be morally justified if administered in
accordance with the provisions and safeguards of the law.

In 1954 Dr. Joseph Fletcher, then professor of pastoral
theology and Christian ethics at the Episcopal Theological
School in Cambridge, Massachusetts, and author of many
books and articles on ethics, published *Morals and Medicine.*
He noted that while there was a great amount of Catholic
literature and organizational activity opposing euthanasia
and extensive instructions regarding medical practice, no
Protestant or Jewish bodies had made attempts to instruct
doctors. No fraternity of non-Catholic physicians existed
and there were no Protestant medical journals, although
there was the *Hebrew Medical Journal* and several Catholic
ones, most importantly *Linacre Quarterly.*

Dr. Fletcher traced the long difficult struggle to free
medicine from religion and superstition, pointing out that
as late as 1895 cremation had been considered a revival of

paganism. Anesthesia as well had been feared and condemned for many years, and surgeons who proposed or used it had been vilified. "It was a long journey," he wrote, "from the savage belief that the disease afflicting men had a divine origin and served as punishment, hex, or magic . . . to the blunt opinion of Martin Luther that 'No malady comes from God.' "

Dr. Fletcher noted that many of the problems faced by physicians today were never dreamed of in the time of Hippocrates—they are moral issues that should be decided on the basis of conditions today and in collaboration with the patient and his family. "The dimensions of our moral responsibility expand of necessity, with the advances made in medical science and medical technology. . . . The ethics of medical care have to change, to grow, and to engage constantly in self-correction."

Fletcher has been in the forefront of those emphasizing that the person cared for is vastly more than just a patient whose life should always be prolonged—the physician should recognize the *person* and his rights. During the past 20 years he has been the most persistent and influential voice in the United States advocating euthanasia legislation.

Fletcher deplored the double standard common in Christian societies; in regard to war and euthanasia, he wrote:

> We are, by some strange habit of mind and heart, willing to impose death but not permit it; we will justify humanly contrived death when it violates the human integrity of its victims, but we condemn it when it is an intelligent voluntary decision.

To illustrate the irony of this inconsistency, Dr. Fletcher said, "A commission of American Protestants recently concluded that the mass extermination of civilians by atom bomb blasts can be 'just,' although many members of the commission would hesitate to agree that fatal suffering could be ended righteously for one of the victims burned and charred externally and internally, not even as a response to the victim's plea."

The well-known psychiatrist Dr. K. R. Eissler, in *The Psychiatrist and the Dying Patient,* discussed theories and beliefs about death. He said that while some hold to the view that death often can be regarded as "the best friend of mankind," others still believe the myth of the fall of man and the idea that death follows sin. He said, "This identification of death with sin destroys man's deepest link with nature," and is responsible for much of the fear of death. "However strongly I am convinced that euthanasia is not an offense against ethics as they practically prevail in contemporary society and that it is not incompatible with Christian ethics when the content of the whole Bible is considered, I believe nevertheless that the tendency of modern ethics may go contrary to the acceptance of euthanasia."

Dr. Glanville Williams, in *The Sanctity of Life and the Criminal Law,* examined attitudes toward the control of human life from conception to death in the light of law, science, medicine and social history. He said, "A man is entitled to demand the release of death from hopeless and helpless pain, and a physician who gives this release is entitled to moral and legal absolution for his act." He described the Catholic defense of suffering as a sort of religious masochism, and said that the "wedge argument" against euthanasia could be used against any desired action because "there is no human conduct from which evil cannot be imagined to follow if it is persisted in when some of the circumstances are changed."

Perhaps the most important part of Williams' discussion pertains to his analysis of the "Principle of Double Effect" and the "Doctrine of Necessity" as applied to the administering of drugs to dying patients. In discussing the former, which is espoused by Roman Catholics who condemn euthanasia but defend the use of drugs in quantities sufficient to relieve pain, Williams said, "It is altogether too artificial to say that a doctor who gives an overdose of a narcotic having in his mind the aim of ending his patient's existence is guilty of sin, while a doctor who gives the same overdose in the same circumstances in order to relieve pain is not guilty of sin, provided that he keeps his mind steadily off the consequence which his professional training teaches him is inevitable, namely the death of his patient." Williams thought that such teaching can only encourage a hypocritical attitude toward moral problems.

He continued, "What is true of morals is true of law. There is no legal difference between desiring or intending a consequence as following from your conduct, and persisting in your conduct with a knowledge that the consequence will inevitably follow from it, though not desiring that consequence. When a result is foreseen as certain, it is the same as if it were desired or intended."

Williams thought it far more reasonable to justify the act, in the circumstances supposed, as the result of a necessity. The doctrine of necessity in the common law refers to a choice between competing values, where the ordinary rule has to be departed from in order to avert some greater evil. Thus, due to the constantly increasing doses of drugs needed to relieve pain, the doctor must sooner or later choose between administering what is likely to be a fatal dose and leaving the patient without relief. Therefore, the question is whether it is lawful in such circumstances to administer the fatal dose:

> The excuse of necessity would likely be accepted by a judge, and to this extent it may be held that euthanasia is permitted under existing law. It is, however, most doubtful whether a judge would go any further, and permit a physician to anticipate matters by administering a fatal dose—say, doubling the previous dose of morphine—in order to save the patient from dragging out a numbed, miserable, and hopeless existence.

Williams warned doctors of the danger of administering the "humane overdose" even though prosecuting authorities are reluctant to take action against a doctor of repute for an act done in good faith to relieve suffering. He cited the case of Dr. Sander who, though acquitted by the jury, had to forfeit his medical practice for a time. Regarding omission of acts to prolong life (passive euthanasia), Williams said this is probably lawful, but a physician is normally under a duty to use reasonable care to preserve life.

Although Professor Williams had argued well for support of the 1936 British bill to legalize voluntary euthanasia and had supported later efforts to obtain such a bill, he became discouraged with the prospects for such legislation and in this 1957 book, on the theory that half a loaf is better than none, he made a legislative suggestion that is a very disappointing compromise. He suggested that legislation be enacted to relieve the doctor of any liability in accelerating the death of a seriously ill patient if he acted in good faith, with the consent of the patient, to relieve pain in an illness believed to be of an incurable and fatal character. Under this proposal, it would be for the prosecution to prove that the physician acted upon some motive other than the humanitarian one allowed him by law.

This proposal would leave the issue to the discretion of the doctor and so lessen the fear of prosecution that now hangs over him. It would not, however, recognize the patient's right to choose euthanasia, nor would it provide adequate safeguards to protect the patient's rights. It would be a doctor-oriented rather than a patient-oriented law and would fall far short of fulfilling the need Williams expressed when he said, "A man is entitled to demand the release of death from hopeless, helpless pain." His continued belief in this right, however, was shown in 1969 when he supported and assisted in drafting a new British Voluntary Euthanasia bill which would recognize this right of the patient to choose euthanasia and provide him with adequate safeguards.

THE STAND OF THE POPE

In an allocution to the seventh International Congress of Catholic Doctors in the Hague in 1956, Pope Pius XII stated, "Medical jurisprudence is subordinate to medical ethics which expresses the moral order willed by God. Medical jurisprudence cannot therefore in any circumstances permit doctor or patient to carry out euthanasia directly, nor may a doctor ever perform it either upon himself or upon anyone else."

However, in an address to a Symposium of the Italian Society of Anesthesiology in 1957, the Pope answered three questions that had been submitted to him by the president of a committee appointed by the ninth National Congress of that Society, which had met in Rome a few months earlier. The three questions dealt with "the religious and moral implications of pain prevention in the light of natural law and especially of Christian doctrine as contained in the Gospel and taught by the Church." The answers given by Pope Pius represent a most welcome change from earlier, more rigid doctrine; they represent the thin edge of the wedge so feared and opposed by the Church in the past. Many see them as the forerunners of other doctrinal changes that will result in further reduction of futile human suffering.

The questions were:

1. Is there a general moral obligation to refuse analgesia and to accept physical pain in a spirit of faith?

2. Is it in accord with the spirit of the Gospel to bring about by means of narcotics the loss of consciousness and the use of a man's higher faculties?

3. Is it lawful for the dying or the sick who are in danger of death to make use of narcotics when there are medical reasons for their use? Can narcotics be used even if the lessening of pain will probably be accompanied by a shortening of life?

Before answering these specific questions, Pope Pius discoursed on the spiritual value of suffering, and on the justification of seeking relief from it if one so desired, for, he said, "in the long run, pain prevents the achievement of higher goals and interests." The individual should adopt the solution best adapted to his own case, provided "it is a means to progress in the inner life, to more perfect mortification, to more faithful accomplishment of one's duties, and to a greater readiness to follow the promptings of grace. In order to be sure . . . a man will have recourse to an experienced spiritual director."

To the first question, which pertains to the suppression of pain, the Pontiff replied, "The patient desiring to avoid or relieve pain can in good conscience use those means discovered by science which, in themselves, are not immoral."

In response to the second question, about the suppression of consciousness, he said there was no moral objection to the use of narcotics, provided they do not prevent the patient from fulfilling his duties. "Within the limits laid down, and provided one observes the required conditions, narcosis involving a lessening or a suppression of consciousness is permitted." The Pope spoke of the need for making final arrangements with family and friends, and said the conscientious doctor will help the patient carry out his obligations.

In answering question three, the Pope warned that "every form of direct euthanasia, that is, the administration of a narcotic in order to produce or hasten death, is unlawful." However, in summing up his answer to the crucial question "Can narcotics be used even if the lessening of pain will probably be accompanied by a shortening of life?" the Pontiff said: "The answer must be 'Yes'—provided that no other means exist, and if, in the given circumstances that action does not prevent the carrying out of other moral and religious duties." Christian heroism does not require the refusal of narcotics, he said; "Everything depends on the particular circumstances. The most perfect and most heroic decision can be present as fully in acceptance as in refusal."

To some readers these instructions may seem explicit and satisfactory, but to many others the Pope seems to confer on the physician a power of decision that should not be left in the hands of any single person. He did not mention the need for legal safeguards or even consultation with another physician; the wishes and rights of the individual seem only a secondary consideration. Moreover, some of the statements are ambiguous, if not contradictory. It almost seems that the Pope was objecting more to the word "euthanasia" than to the administration of it. If it is morally permissible for the doctor to render the person unconscious, thereby effectively ending the life of the "person," would it not be reasonable and wise to conclude also that it is senseless to keep the biological organism functioning after the person and the soul no longer exist? And would it not be more forthright and humane to administer the lethal dose of narcotic deliberately and directly rather than doing it in slow agonizing stages merely to conform to the doctrine that life may be shortened in certain circumstances but only on the condition that the doctor's intention is to ease pain and not to hasten the end of life, no matter how earnestly the dying patient desires a speedy and permanent release?

A few months later, when addressing another international audience of physicians, Pope Pius gave instructions to Catholic doctors on the use of extraordinary means to prolong life. His pronouncements must have come as a surprise and perhaps a shock to those who argue that doctors are bound by the Hippocratic Oath to strive at all costs to keep a patient alive as long as possible. Though he spoke approvingly of efforts in some cases to bring a seemingly dead person back to life after the heart had stopped beating and said that these modern resuscitation techniques contain in themselves nothing that is immoral, he made it clear that when life was ebbing irrevocably, physicians might abandon further efforts to stave off death—in fact, relatives might ask them to desist "in order to permit the patient already virtually dead, to pass on in peace." He said the physician is not obligated to use extraordinary devices unless that is the only way to fulfill some other moral duty. According to his view it is the duty of the physician to take all reasonable measures to preserve life, but this duty necessitates only that treatment which is standard for the person, area, epoch, and civilization in question.

Regarding the role of the patient's family, Pope Pius said that relatives are generally under no moral obligation to ensure more than conventional medical treatment; if some of the advanced techniques in seemingly hopeless cases represent for the family a great hardship, they may ask the doctor to end his efforts to prolong life. The exact time of death, he said, was a task for the physician, not the Church, to determine; Catholic doctrine defines death as the moment of complete separation of body and soul, but in practice, these terms lack precision, so the Church leaves to science the verdict on when death has taken place.

These papal instructions are indeed a welcome change from the traditional doctrines. Though they neither dealt with the legal aspects of the problem, nor suggested legal safeguards, they clearly sanctioned passive or negative euthanasia under certain circumstances. Also, by giving approval to the use of drugs in quantities sufficient to relieve pain even when such doses shortened the patient's life, the Pontiff was coming close to expressing approval of active or positive euthanasia, in spite of his denunciation of it.

The following year, the highly regarded Jesuit theologian the Reverend Gerald Kelly published an updated version of 60 directives that provide a "Code of Medical Ethics for Catholic Hospitals." The directives state that it is the duty of authorities in Catholic hospitals to see that the sick are cared for in accordance with Catholic principles, and that the directives concern all patients, regardless of religion, and must be observed by all physicians, nurses, and others who work in Catholic hospitals.

On the subject of euthanasia Father Kelly quoted Directive 21 as holding that all forms of "mercy killing," with or without the consent of the patient, are absolutely wrong and forbidden. He said that euthanasia is against the "law of God," and "the entire philosophy behind the euthanasia movement is anti-Christian."

The Protestant and Jewish religions do not provide any such official directives to doctors or hospital officials.

FURTHER EFFORTS FOR LEGISLATION IN THE UNITED STATES

New York

In 1952 a third attempt was made to get the New York State Legislature to consider the euthanasia bill that had been proposed in 1947 (see page 95). A petition signed by 2,000 voters and measuring nine by three feet was taken to Albany by officers of the Euthanasia Society and presented to the president of the Senate, the Honorable Arthur H. Wicks, in the hope of getting a bill introduced in the Legislature, but Mr. Wicks was unwilling to take action.

The Euthanasia Society decided that further effort at that time would be fruitless, and it appears that the New

York bill, in spite of its extensive support from physicians, clergymen and others, was never introduced into the Legislature.

New Jersey

Letters were sent by the Euthanasia Society to 2,200 New Jersey physicians asking them to sign a petition to their State Legislature requesting legalization of voluntary euthanasia for the incurably ill. 174 doctors responded affirmatively, and the petition was presented to the Legislature in 1957; when the list of signers was made public, a few protested and withdrew their names, reducing the total number to 166. (See Appendix.)

Some religious and medical groups objected to the proposal, and the State Medical Society issued a statement expressing its opposition. No legislative action was taken.

Connecticut

A new chapter of the Euthanasia Society was organized in Connecticut in 1950. The executive committee considered changing the name to include the word "voluntary"; it later chose the name "The Society for the Humane Treatment of Incurable Sufferers." Dr. Mildred H. Clarke a physician reported in the *Euthanasia Society Bulletin,* Summer 1950, on a proposed bill for the state of Connecticut. It was similar to the 1947 New York bill but with three important differences: (1) it defined euthanasia as "the termination of human life by painless means for the purpose of avoiding unnecessary suffering," whereas the New York bill limited the purpose to "ending severe physical suffering;" (2) it specified that a petitioner must be "of sufficient age and maturity to understand the nature and purpose of the petition, not necessarily over 21," whereas in the New York bill he had to be over 21 and "of sound mind;" and (3) it provided for the signing of a request for euthanasia in advance of any illness just as one makes a will in advance of death, whereas the New York bill made no such provision.

The society sent a questionnaire to 2,000 physicians asking each if he would be willing to (1) keep a patient free from pain regardless of consequences if there were no known cure and the patient requested it; (2) refrain from prolonging the life of a sufferer at his request; and (3) do either if protected by law. Though many doctors were unhappy about the questionnaire, and the Connecticut Medical Society's House of Delegates adopted a resolution opposing euthanasia, the Euthanasia Society sent the following petition to the Senate and the House of Representatives of Connecticut:

> Whereas, in reply to a recent questionnaire, some five hundred physicians of Connecticut stated that, without protective legislation, they would not dare administer drugs sufficient to keep incurable sufferers insensitive to pain, and
>
> Whereas, friends and relatives are distressed and impoverished by the futile prolongation of the patient's life by blood transfusions, intravenous feedings, etc. in terminal cases, and sometimes even take the law into their own hands to end the intolerable pain of a loved one;
>
> We, the undersigned, petition the Senate and House of Representatives to enact into law the Bill hereto annexed entitled, "For the Protection of Physicians and Patients."

Finally, in 1959, a bill with some further changes was introduced in the Connecticut General Assembly but was defeated. Though some early drafts avoided the word euthanasia, this bill (No. 2527) was called "An Act to Legalize Euthanasia." The statement of purpose was: "To legalize euthanasia to allow those afflicted with severe physical suffering to have their lives terminated by painless means under the sanction of law." Its provisions were the same as the New York proposed bill, except that it provided for the signing of a request in advance, a provision also made by the 1969 British bill (For the text of the bill, see Appendix.)

MERCY DEATHS IN THE FIFTIES

In 1950 the *New York Times* reported, "Every year in the United States about 25 cases of euthanasia—'mercy killings'—are prosecuted in the courts. Many others take place but are never reported. . . . In the great majority of cases, the person responsible has been acquitted or his sentence suspended." Nearly always the judge and jury are so moved with compassion that they refuse to convict the person, no matter how evident the defendant's guilt. Typical of the defendants in these cases were a woman who killed her husband who was dying of cancer, a man who ended his invalid wife's life, a man who killed his son who was suffering from cerebral palsy, and a woman who was charged with the murder of her epileptic son.

One of the most widely publicized cases of 1950 was that of Eugene Braunsdorf, the Detroit Symphony musician who for 29 years had done everything in his power to make his spastic daughter Virginia happy and comfortable. At the age of 21, she was four feet tall, could talk only in gobbling sounds that her father alone could understand, and was unable to hold her head upright. At last Mr. Braunsdorf, who was attempting to hold four jobs due to financial difficulties, succumbed to the strain and fell ill. Virginia was put in a private sanitarium. When her father had recovered sufficiently, he visited her regularly, but was so worried about her future, that he took her out one day and shot her. He then tried to kill himself, but he survived and was charged with murder. The jury's verdict was "not guilty by reason of temporary insanity at the time of killing." Spectators in the courtroom cheered, and some of the jurors wept.

In one of the few cases that resulted in a conviction for voluntary manslaughter, Harold Mohr of Pennsylvania was sentenced in 1950 to three to six years in prison and fined 500 dollars for slaying his blind, cancer-ridden brother who had made urgent and repeated requests for death. This severe sentence was apparently given because relatives testified that the defendant had been drinking before the shooting.

"British Physician Stirs Wide Discussion in Cancer Case"

In 1959, Dr. Maurice L. Millard, whose father had founded the Euthanasia Society in Britain in 1935, created widespread controversy when he addressed a Rotary Club in what he thought was a private meeting. The talk, however, was reported in the *New York Times,* March 6, 1959, and in *Newsweek,* May 18, 1959. Millard advocated legislation to legalize euthanasia and then told his audience of a fragile 80-year-old woman incurably ill with cancer who had asked her doctor to give her a fatal dose that would end her futile suffering. The patient, a devout Christian, put her worldly affairs in order, discussed her condition and her wishes with her relatives and her doctor, and then called them together for a brief service at her bedside. At her request the doctor read a prayer and then "gave her something to make her sleep." She soon went into a coma and died in peace. Dr. Millard then said he was the doctor.

Reactions to the story were many and varied. Dr. Millard received many letters and messages praising him for his courage and compassion, though a few condemned him and equated euthanasia with murder. Many members of the medical profession hedged in their statements when asked about it. Some said that the only difference between Dr. Millard's act and that of the average doctor was that the average doctor does not talk about such things. One doctor said, "I would guess that the average doctor does this thing perhaps half a dozen times a year."

Altogether, the press reported relatively little outright condemnation of Dr. Millard's action by either the medical profession or the churches. This seems in marked contrast to the tremendous opposition evoked by Dr. Sander's actions in 1950. Granted, the cases were different in that Dr. Sander was tried on a murder charge while Dr. Millard's action was not known until long after the event, but it seems fair to assume that public opinion had changed, and a generally more permissive attitude had developed.

PUBLIC OPINION POLLS

In 1950 a nationwide Gallup Poll was conducted in the United States using the same question as the 1947 poll. The number of "yes" answers remained about the same— 36 per cent, as opposed to 37 per cent in 1947. Undoubtedly the organized efforts by the opponents of euthanasia were effective in counteracting the efforts to legalize it. Nevertheless, when the question was reworded to "would you approve of ending a patient's life if a board of doctors appointed by the court agreed the patient could not be cured," 7 per cent of those who had answered "no" or "no opinion" now answered "yes." Thus there was a total of 43 per cent who were "in favor of mercy killing in certain circumstances."

Ten years later a much more favorable public opinion was indicated by a poll in Canada. In December of 1959 the Canadian Institute of Public Opinion released a report of a Gallup Poll of Canadians under the heading, "Belief that 'Mercy Killing' for Some Is Right Spreads." The report continued, "Ten years ago, the Gallup Poll reported that 62 per cent of Canadian people could not think of any circumstances in which a doctor would be justified in taking the life of a patient. People feel differently today for certain cases." The results were reported separately for Protestants and Roman Catholics. In spite of the fact that the questions did not include a statement regarding safe-guards, 55 per cent of the Protestants and 29 per cent of the Catholics indicated that they thought that if a person were dying and in great pain and asked for a fatal drug, his doctor should give it to him. If the patient were not suffering, only 21 per cent of the Protestants said yes, and only 15 per cent of the Catholics. When asked "And what about the mercy killing of hopelessly deformed or mentally deficient very young children, if the parents consent?" 44 per cent of the Protestants said yes, 42 per cent said no, and 14 per cent gave no opinion; 23 per cent of the Catholics said yes, 70 per cent said no, and 7 per cent gave no opinion.

Thus the poll indicated that well over half (55 per cent) of the Protestants favored euthanasia for those dying and in great pain, and close to a third of the Catholics favored it; for severely defective very young children, 2 per cent more Protestants favored it than opposed it, while about one in every three Catholics who expressed an opinion favored it.

Chapter 7

1960 THROUGH EARLY 1974

The Sixties ushered in a new era in attitudes toward death and dying. There developed a fairly widespread recognition of the need for open discussion of this subject and an increased demand for changes in practices in caring for the dying and hopelessly incapacitated.

Several Protestant churches organized national committees to study the problem of euthanasia, and church periodicals that had previously had very little to say on the subject began publishing articles in support of it. Physicians and clergymen organized seminars in many places to discuss the problems surrounding the dying, and emphasis was placed on the need for a team approach in making vital decisions.

Law journals discussed euthanasia, emphasizing the need for improvement in laws pertaining to it. Perhaps the most significant development was the increase in the number of physicians who spoke out openly not only against useless prolongation, but also in support of hastening death in certain circumstances. Many medical journals carried articles in support of passive euthanasia and several in support of active euthanasia as well. Much less opposition to euthanasia was expressed in the 1960's than in the 1950's.

The Sixties was also a period of spectacular break-throughs in surgery, including the first transplantations of the human heart. The demand for transplantable organs such as hearts and kidneys skyrocketed, and the need for a new and more precise definition of death became evident. Technological breakthroughs were presenting doctors with more and more questions for which there were no easy answers.

At the same time social concerns were raising questions in everyone's mind: overpopulation and pollution, the plight of the elderly, the rapidly rising costs of medical and hospital care, the shortage of personnel to care for the sick, and the cost to the taxpayer as well as the patient and his family of prolonging useless treatment of dying or moribund patients—all took on a new urgency in the Sixties. Medical schools were urged to face up to these problems and teach the human side of medicine. Several foundations were established to do research and arrange public discussion of the ethical, moral and social problems pertaining to man's new power over life and death, and to develop more humane ways of managing death when life has become an unconscionable burden to all concerned.

Views of Physicians

Following the favorable response to Dr. Rynearson's advocacy of passive euthanasia in 1959, many doctors spoke out in favor of euthanasia.

Dr. Long

In 1960 an article by Dr. Perrin Long, editor of *Medical Times,* entitled "On the Quality and Quantity of Life," was instrumental in attracting much support for euthanasia. The next year Dr. Arthur A. Levisohn, in the *Journal of*

Forensic Medicine, reviewed the movement to legalize voluntary euthanasia and made clear his own support for such
legalization.

Dr. Long expressed concern over the obsession with
the quantity rather than the quality of life and urged a more
humanitarian approach to the problem of human suffering.
He said that many doctors had become troubled over the
practice of prolonging life uselessly, but in their efforts to
avoid disturbing and difficult decisions, they clung to the
doctrine that life must be prolonged as long as possible
regardless of its quality.

Long described pathetic hospital scenes and asked,
"Who among us, after such sights, can be proud of what we
have wrought? Are we really behaving as thoughtful and
ethical humanitarians?" He deplored the many hours and
thousands of dollars spent in "heroic" efforts to save patients only to have them emerge again into a painful, hopeless existence. Among the scenes on a hospital ward that he
cited was a 35-year-old Mongolian idiot "playing in a pool
of his own urine and feces, saved from an early death from
infection by the miracle drugs," a senile gibbering old
woman who had been abandoned and totally rejected by
her family, and "Grandma," who had reached the age of
"second childhood," and sat staring vacantly into space.

Dr. Long discussed the difficulty of distinguishing between "extraordinary" and "ordinary means," and said
that the wording of the papal encyclical of 1957 raised
several questions. What is "reasonable" expense? what is
excessive or inconvenient? And regarding that part of the
Hippocratic Oath that reads: "never will I give a deadly
drug, not even if I am asked for one," he said, "Now obviously, we modern physicians do not interpret this literally
. . . Thousands of refillable prescriptions are written for the
digitalis alkaloids (which are the deadliest of drugs) daily."

Long asked:

> Has not the medical profession missed the point in certain of its endeavors? Are we not piling up one Pyrrhic victory after another, while gradually losing the war? Are we not causing . . . untold anguish to the patient and his friends, insupportable financial burdens for the family and community, the diversion of resources from those who could use them more effectively, and a great increase in the cost of hospitalization for the average patient, just because we are more interested in increasing the "quantity" of life no matter at what painful cost to the individual or his community?

Long thought that the issue was one of the toughest the medical profession would have to face within the next decades, since it deals with religious and ethical ideas and has social and political aspects. Nevertheless, he said, "this issue must be faced by our profession . . . We cannot escape the problem. . . . Who among us has the right to exercise the power to deprive one of death . . . of withholding for weeks or for months that one comfort . . . of dying?" Thus without using the words, Dr. Long appears to have advocated not only passive euthanasia, but the right to choose death and to have the assistance of a physician in bringing it about.

Dr. Levisohn

Dr. Arthur A. Levisohn, a professor of medical jurisprudence, at the Chicago Medical School, asked "Is it ever morally right to take the life of an innocent human being and should the law be modified so as to make killing not murder in certain circumstances?" His answer was an unequivocal yes. He said that "mercy killing" as a concept undoubtedly presents a challenge to traditional religious points of view, but it is a challenge that must be faced rather than evaded.

Levisohn called for civilized efforts to preserve human dignity and asserted that due to the advances in medical science and technology more people than ever before are faced with a tortured, hideous death. He thought that if we allow this to continue without a legal remedy, it will be a disgrace to our civilization. Traditional ways of thinking must be replaced by new values and attitudes as social conditions change. He pointed out that medical progress in increasing the lifespan and consequently increasing the number of elderly persons suffering from degenerative diseases, including cancer, has presented society with an urgent need for new legislation that would enable a physician to know where he stands when confronted with a dying patient's request for euthanasia, and enable him to confer openly with his medical colleagues, the patient, and members of the family.

According to Dr. Levisohn, there is an inadequate public awareness of the problem since it has not yet beset every family, but the problem is increasing and none is exempt from the possibility of having a painful and lingering death. He cited many cases illustrating the horror of such deaths, and said such instances could be multiplied endlessly.

Levisohn's discussion was limited to euthanasia at the request of an adult. He did not discuss cases of defective infants or the senile or comatose, though he indicated concern for them and seemed to favor legislation pertaining to them also. In discussing the legal aspects of the problem, he said that since any hastening of death by even a few minutes is murder under present law, and since medical and legal opinion is divided regarding the legality of a physician's failure to prolong life as long as possible, it is necessary to enact laws pertaining to both active and passive euthanasia. He deplored the way judges and juries circumvent the law when cases of "mercy killing" arise. He pointed out the many fallacies in the religious arguments against euthanasia and said, "They would have come to some other very startling different conclusions had their reasoning preceded their conclusions instead of succeeding them in order to bolster a conclusion already established." Regarding the statements of Pope Pius XII in 1957, he said that while euthanasia was condemned in name, "the most essential contention of the euthanasists is conceded."

Dr. Levisohn cited a poll he had taken of 250 Chicago internists and surgeons, and also one he had made of 250 active members of large civic organizations. Of the 156 physicians who replied, 61 per cent expressed the belief that many physicians actually practice euthanasia, either positive or negative but 72 per cent said they were not in favor of legalization. Thus only a little more than a quarter of the physicians favored making legal what they believed was actually practiced and was morally right. Many other polls have produced similar findings.

In contrast, Dr. Levisohn's poll of nondoctors showed that 76 per cent of the 134 who replied said they favored the legalization of euthanasia. Only 20 per cent of the Catholics favored it, but 100 per cent of those with no religious affiliation were in favor. These findings seem to support his view that the basic objections to the practice of voluntary euthanasia relate to religious ideology. Similar findings have been reported in various other polls. Levisohn argued that criminal law should not be based on beliefs that pertain only to certain religious teachings.

Dr. Williamson

Dr. William P. Williamson, a professor of surgery at the University of Kansas Medical School, made an important contribution to the discussion of euthanasia and decisions pertaining to the dying by his emphasis on the necessity for a team approach. In an address entitled "Life or Death—Whose Decision?" given at the First National Congress on Medical Ethics and Professionalism in 1966, he said that the very fact that such a congress had been arranged was reassuring evidence that the medical profession is deeply concerned that its science not surpass its art and that doctors be merciful humanitarians—not cold, aloof scientists.

Williamson maintained that there should be consultation between the patient (when able to express his wishes), the family, and the physicians concerned. The decision should rest primarily with the patient when that is possible. As long as there is a chance of a cure or of prolonging a reasonable life, it is of course the physician's duty to treat the patient with every medical means at his disposal. But there are times, Dr. Williamson said, when the doctor should ask such questions as "Should he lengthen a man's life a few months at the cost of leaving the man's wife and children penniless?"

In a later article, in *Medical Economics* Dr. Williamson said, "To resort to lifesaving measures when a patient is certain to die seems a travesty." Of patients who have been "saved from death" by modern devices, he said, "Often they have merely been condemned to a more painful and prolonged dying—in which patient, family and doctor suffer in futility together. . . . Increasingly the real issue is not life or death, but what kind of death."

Is turning off the respirator murder? Is there any moral or ethical difference in not starting the respirator as compared to stopping it once it is started? His answer was that while there is no logical difference between refusal to put a patient on a respirator and a decision to take him off it, there certainly is an emotional difference.

Although Dr. Williamson did not advocate positive euthanasia, and unlike Doctors Long and Levisohn, said he opposed its legalization, he asked "Should we not be able to do something for a loved one that we can do for a dog?" He also said that in some cases, a stage is reached when the patient should merely be made as comfortable as possible and "at this stage almost any measure is justified." While not supporting euthanasia himself, the questions Dr. Williamson raises certainly seem to indicate strong evidence in its favor.

Dr. Ayd

In 1962 Dr. Frank J. Ayd, Jr., a well-known Catholic psychiatrist writing in *JAMA,* opposed any deliberate hastening of death, but said that physicians must recognize man's right to live and die peacefully and must respect the patient's right to refuse treatment. He strongly advocated passive euthanasia if the patient is clearly dying, though he objected to calling that euthanasia. He said there are many instances when the outcome is recognized as inevitable and imminent and "If the physician concludes that what is being done is a useless gesture which he is permitting solely to avoid suit or criticism, then he is morally obligated to desist at once."

Dr. Ayd told of the resentment of loved ones being shoved out of the hospital room, displaced by gadgets and personnel striving to delay the inevitable, depriving them of the opportunity to share the waning moments of life with the dying patient. He did not discuss the legal problems that could arise from a decision not to prolong life, but did say the doctor should protect himself by consulting with colleagues and informing relatives of the whys and wherefores of his conduct. However, he did not propose that there be a witnessed statement by the patient of his wishes or those of his surrogate. He did not discuss the possibility of some relative or nurse or other medical personnel bringing a charge against him of negligence or manslaughter; nor did he discuss the fact that medical opinion is divided regarding both the professional and legal obligation under the present law and present medical standards. Thus while he asserted the patient's right to die, he would do nothing to ensure that that right be legally recognized.

In 1970 Dr. Ayd said,

Also there should be no need or demand for positive euthanasia if physicians unhesitatingly administer whatever
amount of painrelieving drugs a dying patient needs. The
medical profession has the power to erase any demand for
legalized euthanasia. All doctors have to do is apply their
skills prudently as they are morally and legally [sic] empowered to do.

What Dr. Ayd has advocated seems a dangerous course
for both doctors and patients, and for society. He has so
distorted the moral issues that one could almost claim he
is advocating the surreptitious administration of positive
euthanasia.

The danger and inadequacy of a position such as Dr.
Ayd's is recognized by many people. Dr. Walter Sackett,
who is, like Dr. Ayd, a Catholic physician, is also a member
of the Florida State Legislature, and is working for the
enactment of a bill which would permit doctors to terminate treatment provided legal safeguards were observed.

Dr. Williams

An influential voice among medical doctors in support
of euthanasia legislation during the past few years is that of
Dr. Robert H. Williams, a professor of medicine at the
University of Washington Medical School, who in his 1969
presidential address to the Association of Professors of
Medicine forcefully deplored the failure of law to differentiate between murder and a merciful act of euthanasia (reported in *Archives of Internal Medicine*). He noted the irony
of society refusing to permit the termination of the life of
a suffering, dying patient for whom life has no further value
while at the same time condoning wars, in which millions
of young are killed.

Dr. Williams thought that more attention should be
given to the wishes of a person who desires an end to life.
He thought euthanasia preferable to suicide and said the
mere fact that the patient could know that euthanasia might
be permitted if and when the situation became intolerable

would in itself help alleviate many anxieties. Some patients, he said, have carefully weighed the pros and cons and have decided that what they would contribute by continuing life is not justified by the agonizing mental or physical distress involved.

Dr. Williams spoke of the vast amount of suffering endured by many patients, their families, and friends, and called special attention to those who have been mutilated from very extensive burns and explosives, and those with great stress from spinal cord transection and quadruplegia, or severe sclerosis. Still others face the hellish torment of severe psychiatric disorders. "Why should we reject their strong desire to be relieved of their agony?" he asked. He expressed special concern too for the great number of aged lonely patients and congenitally defective children whose lives are extended unduly by drugs and other measures. He urged the establishment of a realistic policy to deal with these problems so that the long, hard work of instituting change could begin. "Whereas many of our goals will be temporarily thwarted, I hope we will have the courage, determination, and dedication to attain them," he said (see report of his questionnaire to doctors, p. 153).

Other Doctors

In 1970 Dr. Arthur F. Schiff, a general practitioner in Florida, writing in *Medical Economics,* appealed to doctors and society to face these problems realistically and honestly and work for legislation that would make it possible to deal with them openly and compassionately, and in accordance with safeguards law would provide for both doctors and patients.

But Dr. Henry A. Davidson, Past President of the New Jersey Psychiatric Association, seems unwilling or unable to accept Dr. Schiff's challenge. In an article, "Should Doctors Play God?" he said, "As a scientist I conclude that logic is all on the side of euthanasia but as a physician I will not take the power to put someone to death." Nevertheless he pointed out that keeping some unconscious patients alive can cost 50,000 dollars or more a year.

That some doctors are still vigorously opposed to the legalization of any kind of euthanasia was evident in testimony by Dr. Laurence V. Foye, Jr., of the Veterans Administration given before the U.S. Senate Special Committee on Aging in 1972. Dr. Foye, who was formerly associated with the National Cancer Institute, expressed the view that it is the solemn duty of doctors to prolong life as long as possible in every case.

He defended his position on the grounds that mistakes in prognosis are sometimes made, and no one can ever be absolutely certain of the outcome in a specific case. He mentioned instances in which doctors had predicted a rapidly fatal outcome and had been wrong and cancer cases in which the patient had lived longer than had been predicted and sometimes had been able to return to work. But Dr. Foye failed to differentiate between the young or middle-aged who want to live, and the aged or incapacitated, already irreparably damaged by their illness, who want to die. He objected to the idea that some people were being kept alive "uselessly" and said, "Neither I nor anyone else knows how to decide when being alive becomes useless." Many would challenge such statements that deal only in absolutes and divert attention from the real problems and from the need to be willing to make judgments based on all the facts available in each specific case.

Attitudes in England and Commonwealth Countries

In England various medical journals kept up a lively discussion of euthanasia in editorials, letters to the editor and articles. The editor of *The Lancet* in 1962 suggested that the tragic consequences of prolonging life in hopeless cases should be brought to the attention of the public. In cases such as severe head injuries, when the patient is in a coma for months or years, the impossibility of recovery is usually evident from the start. To keep such people alive requires the services of a skilled team of doctors and nurses. He calculated that, assuming the average length of a patient's stay in the hospital is two weeks, a bed occupied by an unconscious patient for a year could have been used by 26 other patients, whose admission had been correspondingly delayed; prolonging the life of one may have resulted in loss of life to 26. To sustain a parody of life might end in serving nobody and nothing except pride in one's technical competence. Ironically, and inconsistently, the editor instead of endorsing euthanasia allowed the grip of tradition to cause him to oppose it and the British Voluntary Euthanasia Bill; he merely advocated an increase in hospital beds and personnel.

However, the same issue of *The Lancet* published letters expressing support for euthanasia and the British Bill. One such letter was from the distinguished physician Dr. Leonard Colebrook, who was at that time chairman of the Euthanasia Society in Britain. He expressed the view that the time had come for a serious reappraisal of the advantages as well as the difficulties and possible dangers that might result from the legalization of voluntary euthanasia. He pointed out that the Suicide Act of 1961 had profoundly altered the situation by making suicide no longer a legal offense. But, he said, patients often cannot act on that choice; the means for ending their lives are not available to them, and many would be unable to use them if they were. Moreover under the law then, as now, a doctor could not give a patient the relief he asked for without committing a criminal act and jeopardizing his career.

Later *The Lancet* published a letter by T. H. Gillison who declared, "Some day, Sir, I believe people will claim the right, if and when life for them becomes intolerable, to demand an easier death; much like motherhood has claimed and won an easier childbirth."

Such prominent British physicians as Dr. John Rowan Wilson and Dr. Eliot Slater strongly supported the 1969 Voluntary Euthanasia Bill. Dr. Wilson praised the provision allowing a person to make an attested declaration in advance authorizing doctors to carry out euthanasia, or to withhold resuscitation, in certain circumstances. These circumstances, Wilson suggested, should include incurable progressive illness or the irreparable loss of normal mental faculties. If such a patient wants to die, why should he be kept dragging on in misery to satisfy somebody else's conscience? Why should he not be entitled to enlist the help of his doctor in relieving him of a life which is a misery to himself and a burden to others?

Dr. Wilson has written of the practical problems of keeping some old people, such as those with senile dementia, alive as long as possible. "To say that society should spend its money on this kind of care is one thing, but with an increasing population of the aged, how on earth are we going to find the people to [care for them]?" He deplored the sentimentality and dogma that have hindered a rational approach to the problem, and urged that society accept the fact that it is the value of life to the individual that is important in deciding whether or not life should be prolonged or death hastened.

Writing in *Contemporary Review* in August of 1971, Dr. Slater also urged doctors and society to take a rational approach to the problem. Expressing special concern for the aged, he spoke of the hardships that come with accumulating disability and increasingly intense loneliness. Doctors who work in geriatric wards, he said, know that about one in five of their patients would prefer death to continued survival.

Dr. Slater said the preservation-of-life principle can be taken to lengths which are patently absurd, and the present state of affairs pertaining to it in law and in practice are also absurd. While pain can often be controlled if the patient is in a place where injections can be repeated at short intervals, this is rarely possible at home; moreover there are many other distresses that cannot be controlled, such as nausea, difficulty in breathing and the feeling of being wretchedly feeble, ill, and lonely. "It is quite common for circumstances to arise in which the doctor has to choose between the preservation of life and the relief of suffering since the suffering can only end with the end of life." He thought no one could claim that it was of any service to the patient, his family or society to keep some patients alive.

Medical journals in other English-speaking countries also carried articles protesting useless prolongation of life. The editor of the *Canadian Medical Association Journal* in 1965 asked if a man in an irreversible coma is entitled to all the protection the law provides a living person. An article in the *Medical Journal of Australia* in 1966 deplored the last ditch stand some doctors take in a desperate defiance of death. The author described scenes in intensive care wards of old or totally paralyzed patients enduring months of dreadful consciousness in surroundings of great horror —listening to the rhythmic click of the respirator, waiting for the periodic jab of the antibiotic needle, or the daily ride in the tumbril to the deep X-ray department. The anonymous writer, described as a distinguished surgeon, said that surgery which inflicts an unutterable burden on the patient and relatives in exchange for slender and irrational hope is difficult to justify. He said it becomes a hard decision to stop all this, but the courage must be found to do so; the abasement of an individual to a vegetable status, for instance, is not an achievement to awaken pride.

A *New Zealand Medical Journal* article, written in 1967 by Dr. C. G. Riley, Director of Medicine of Christchurch Hospital, urged doctors to develop better communication with the dying patient and his family regarding when life-prolonging treatment should be withheld.

POLLS OF PHYSICIANS

A poll conducted by the medical journal *New Medica Materia* in 1962 indicated that more than 30 per cent of American doctors felt that euthanasia was justified in some cases; almost 40 per cent indicated approval of it for severely defective infants; and 41 per cent indicated that they believed the states should enact legislation to permit euthanasia with legal safeguards.

Dr. Robert H. Williams of Seattle reported in *Archives of Internal Medicine* his study of the views of doctors teaching in medical schools. He sent a questionnaire to each member of the Association of Professors of Medicine and of the Association of American Physicians—a total of 344 questionnaires to which all but 11 doctors responded. The chief findings were that 80 per cent said they practiced negative euthanasia to some extent, and about 18 per cent indicated that they favored positive euthanasia for patients who requested it, provided there were an appropriate change in law with adequate safeguards. Dr. Williams thought the number of physicians favoring positive euthanasia would increase if it were sanctioned by public opinion and law.

In his book *To Live and to Die,* Williams said he thought negative euthanasia is practiced either too late, too little, or not at all in more than 99 per cent of the cases where it should be. He said the answer to the question "When should one live or die?" depends upon the balance of the advantages and disadvantages of living or dying to the individual, his friends, and society. He defined negative euthanasia as planned omission of therapies that probably would prolong life, and positive euthanasia as the institution of therapy that it is hoped will promote death sooner than otherwise.

An excellent study of the views of doctors was conducted in 1970 by Dr. Norman K. Brown and other associates of Dr. Williams. They noted the rapidity with which issues involved in the preservation of human life are changing, and decided to make a beginning toward quantification of the evolution of thinking on euthanasia by first studying the attitudes of physicians.

Questionnaires were sent to 460 doctors in two Seattle hospitals, one a university hospital and the other a private community hospital. The doctors were assured that replies would be kept confidential. Ninety-two per cent responded; the report was based on 418 replies. The chief findings were:

About one-third of the physicians (31 per cent) favored change in social attitudes and current standards of medical practice which would permit negative euthanasia following consent of and a signed statement by the patient or family, and positive euthanasia for certain carefully selected patients.

Thirty-eight per cent said they had had requests by patients for negative euthanasia, and 54 per cent said they had had such requests from the family. The requests for negative euthanasia were higher at the community hospital than at the university hospital.

If a signed statement requesting it were presented, 59 per cent said they would practice negative euthanasia. About 20 per cent said they would practice it without such a statement; another 20 per cent said they would not practice it even if such a signed statement were available.

Twenty-seven per cent signified that they would practice positive euthanasia in selected cases if the evolution of social attitudes permitted; 12 per cent said they had had requests from patients for positive euthanasia and 9 per cent said they had had such requests from the family.

The authors of this Seattle study spoke of the fears of physicians of malpractice suits, the pressures of tradition, the Sixth Commandment, and the Hippocratic Oath as factors influencing attitudes. Nevertheless, it is evident from this survey that for selected patients with terminal conditions, more than half the physicians would not preserve life and more than one-fourth would hasten death in certain circumstances if law permitted.

When the questions used by Williams were given to medical students at the Washington School of Medicine, Dr. E. Harold Laws and colleagues found that 46 per cent said they believed they would practice positive euthanasia in appropriate circumstances if it were legalized.

A National Opinion Poll was taken of 2,000 general practitioners in England, selected at random from the Medical Register—1,000 in 1964 and 1,000 in 1965. The chief combined findings were: almost half (48.6 per cent) said they had been asked by a dying patient to give final relief from suffering; more than half (53.9 per cent) said such a request created a conflict for the physician as the law stands; more than a third (35.8 per cent) said they would be willing to administer voluntary (positive) euthanasia if it became legally permissible to do so; three-fourths (75.5 per cent) thought some doctors already administer treatment that causes some shortening of life. They were equally divided when asked if they thought adequate legal safeguards could be devised. The number who expressed no opinion to the various questions ranged from 5 to 17 per cent.

In view of the opposition of that very conservative body the British Medical Association, it is encouraging to the advocates of euthanasia to find in this excellently conducted national poll that so many doctors really favor euthanasia and admit that new laws are needed.

From these various polls it would appear that perhaps as many as three quarters of all doctors practice negative euthanasia, though to do so under present law presents a conflict for many; others continue to refuse to do so until the legal question is clarified. About a third indicated willingness to practice positive euthanasia if the law permitted it. Teaching doctors in medical schools seemed less willing to endorse euthanasia than those physicians more regularly engaged in caring for the sick and dying. Perhaps David Dempsey was right when he said that few doctors subscribe to the principle of mercy killing, but there are equally few who do not practice it.

Surely it is time to devise wise laws to end this unsatisfactory way of dealing with the problem. Might we not agree with Dr. Henderson Smith who said in the *British Medical Journal*, "The philosophical acceptance of death as a merciful episode, rather than as an ultimate catastrophe, is an element of wisdom which medical practice appears to have lost as a result of the enormous powers modern science has provided."

The Stand of Medical Associations

In spite of their traditionally conservative attitudes and resistance to social change, some medical associations are now giving consideration to the subject of euthanasia. Some have expressed support for passive euthanasia, although it appears that none has expressed support publicly for active euthanasia.

At the meeting of the World Medical Association in Sydney in 1968, a declaration was adopted stating that doctors did not see it as their role to be the deliberate agents of euthanasia, in the sense of deliberately hastening death. It was evident, however, that new questions, new thinking, and new attitudes were developing.

Abortion and euthanasia were among the topics discussed at a Conference on Ethics in Medicine and Technology held in Houston, Texas in 1969, according to Kenneth Vaux's report in his book *Who Shall Live?* An appeal was made to keep up discussion of these emotional topics in the hope of reaching agreement among people of all religious convictions.

The British Medical Association has been unbending in its opposition to euthanasia and in 1969 passed a resolution condemning it. Many British doctors, however, deplored the BMA resolution, which was based on a report by its Central Ethical Council. They pointed out that many of the members of the Council were elderly men bound by tradition, and many were specialists unaware of the misery of dying patients. Critics of the Council's report accused the BMA representatives of making many misleading statements and half truths—for instance, the idea that pain can be kept under control and that most deaths are peaceful.

As the famous physician Sir William Osler said, while the end stage may be "peaceful," it is often preceded by utter frustration that makes each day and night a "death in life." Moreover, the BMA report completely ignored the patient's right to self-determination. These and other criticisms of the BMA report are set forth in a 1971 booklet prepared by the Voluntary Euthanasia Society entitled *Doctors and Euthanasia.*

In 1970 the General Council of the Canadian Medical Association took a significant step toward a more flexible stand on prolonging life when it approved a change in the code of ethics which stated, "An ethical physician will allow death to occur with dignity and comfort, when death of the body appears inevitable." It stated also that he need not prolong life by unusual or heroic means when clinical death of the mind has occurred.*

In January of 1973, the American Hospital Association made public its new "Bill of Rights" for patients which stated, "The patient has the right to receive from his physician information necessary to give informed consent prior to the start of any procedure and/or treatment," and "The patient has the right to refuse treatment to the extent permitted by law and to be informed of the medical consequences of his action."

Also in January, the governing board of the Medical Society of the state of New York announced that its 23-man

*For 1974 action by the CMA, see page 162.

council had adopted the following statement that had been prepared by its Committee on Ethics:

> The use of euthanasia is not in the province of the physician. The right to die with dignity, or the cessation of the employment of extraordinary means to prolong the life of the body when there is irrefutable evidence that biological death is inevitable, is the decision of the patient and/or the immediate family, with the approval of the family physician.

It appears that the New York Medical Society is the first to make such a statement. Its vice-president stated that the Society considered its statement more explicit than and superior to that of the Hospital Association because it requires the approval of the family physician in concert with the patient and/or the immediate family. He said a person suffering from a curable depression could by the AHA bill withhold consent to a procedure that could save his life.

It should be recognized that the Medical Society's statement pertains only to passive euthanasia. Nevertheless many see it as a highly significant breakthrough in medical thinking. The first sentence in the statement—"The use of euthanasia is not in the province of the physician"—is a wise one, and a significant move in the direction of legislation. Decisions to administer euthanasia should not be left to physicians alone, certainly not to any one physician acting without consultation. Perhaps the next step will be a courageous endorsement by physicians of the principle of positive euthanasia in certain circumstances rather than evasion or opposition, just as after years of opposing birth control and abortion, the medical profession changed its stand on these controversial subjects.

A committee of the House of Delegates of the California Medical Association, known as the Committee on Evolving Trends in Society Affecting Life, stated in a 1972 report that, "Society as a whole will decide sometime in the future whether negative euthanasia will become accepted practice. . . . It is self-evident that the burden of the vital decision should not rest on the individual physician." This was published in *California Medicine* and attracted considerable attention.

And in its 1973–74 annual report, which was approved by the Delegates in March, 1974, the Committee stated, "During the past year the Committee has devoted its major efforts to a study of the problems and issues associated with the subject of euthanasia." According to its preliminary findings, the report added, the following formulations of policy are essential:

> The first requirement is that the medical profession adopt criteria which can serve as a basis for physicians to determine when death has occured. The second requirement is that the medical profession encourage the creation of representative community Advisory Committees to hospital medical staffs, in order to assist physicians in those special instances involving decisions regarding the termination of artificial life-supporting mechanisms.

On the subject of the "Living Will" (see page 181 for further discussion of the Living Will), the report concluded, "The Committee reiterates legal counsel's conclusion that the Living Will is not legally binding upon the physician and that reliance upon such a document may invite allegations of malpractice."

While the American Medical Association has taken no official stand on euthanasia, the subject was discussed at the AMA's Fourth National Congress on Medical Ethics held in Washington, D.C., in April, 1973. Also in April, the House of Delegates of the Connecticut State Medical Society approved a resolution suggesting that a healthy person be entitled to sign a statement asking not to be kept alive by "artificial means or heroic measures" in the event that he contracted a terminal "physical or mental and spiritual disability" and was unable to make decisions about his own future. It was pointed out that such a statement would not bind a doctor or a family but would be a guide in dealing with a terminally ill person.

This resolution was submitted by the Connecticut delegation to the AMA Convention in June, 1973, and was referred to the AMA Judicial Council for study. Also at that June convention, Dr. Malcolm Todd told a news conference that the Association is "going to hear more and more about mercy killing," and called for an AMA commission consisting of doctors, lawyers, clergy, and the public to study the issue.

In December of 1973, the AMA House of Delegates adopted the following statement:

> The intentional termination of the life of one human being by another—mercy killing—is contrary to that for which the medical profession stands and is contrary to the policy of the American Medical Association. The cessation of the employ- ment of extraordinary means to prolong the life of the body when there is irrefutable evidence that biological death is imminent is the decision of the patient and/or his immediate family. The advice and judgment of the physician should be freely available to the patient and/or his immediate family.

CONFRONTATION AND CONTROVERSY

The Neasden Hospital Controversy

In September, 1967, many newspapers gave promi- nent coverage to an incident at Neasden Hospital in north- west London in which the Superintendent, Dr. William McMath, posted on the bulletin board a notice instructing his staff that certain patients were not to be resuscitated. The notice, which went unnoticed for 16 months, read in part as follows:

> The following patients are not to be resuscitated: very el-
> derly, over 65; malignant disease. Chronic chest disease.
> Chronic renal disease . . . Top of yellow treatment card to be
> marked NTBR (i.e., not to be resuscitated)

When this was reported in the press, a public furor ensued. Even strong advocates of euthanasia expressed their disapproval. Many persons were distressed and angry at the idea of a doctor making such a decision alone, without the consent of the patient or family.

In spite of the protest, the Regional Hospital Board upheld the action of Dr. McMath, but criticized the wording of his instruction and his allowing it to be publicly displayed. Such guidance, it said, should be communicated in confidence to the staff.

This incident did much to focus attention on the problems and dangers which arise when such decision-making power is left in the hands of hospital or doctor with no protection of the right of the patient or his relatives to make the decision. However, many doctors confirm privately that in many hospitals it has become common practice to indicate on the patient's record that heroic efforts are not to be used to resuscitate or prolong life.

Dr. Vickery's Address

Dr. Kenneth O. A. Vickery made world headlines in 1969 by an address to the Congress on the Hazards of Retirement, held by the Royal Society of Health in England. He stated that one of the cruelest hazards of retirement was the prolongation of dying or what he called "medicated survival." He pleaded that old people beset with the pain, misery, and indignity of degenerative disease should be spared the prolongation of their suffering which is often increased by the use of wonder drugs and modern machine resuscitation. He called for a reconsideration of the assumed obligation upon doctors and nurses to keep a dying person alive in such circumstances.

Many press reports carried scare headlines. One in the *London Daily Mail* read: "Let the Old People Die at 80." Newsmen kept the issue alive by quoting reactions of famous people. Reaction was particularly strong to the idea that an arbitrary cut-off point could be agreed upon, after which treatment would be terminated. Dr. Vickery's reply was that he had never suggested any specific age.

Dr. Vickery said letters poured in from the four ends of earth—from aged sufferers, relatives, doctors, and nurses who knew first-hand the agony experienced by so many old people. They were incensed that the media had missed the point and pleaded, "When the autumn of life is far spent and we have run our course, there should be no undue effort to prolong it." Dr. Vickery cited President Eisenhower as "a painful example of the prolongation of a living death" by mechanized and medicated means and said, "If this is to be the case for the rest of society, we are in for a hell of a time." He thought such heroic measures in terminal cases should be withheld after open discussion with the patient, relatives and other medical people.

CANADIAN MEDICAL ASSOCIATION ACTS

The General Council of the Canadian Medical Association, at its annual meeting in 1974, passed by a vote of 75 to 66 a resolution which stated that there are times when it may be ethical for a physician to write "no resuscitation" on the chart of a terminal patient. According to the *Globe and Mail* (Toronto, June 25, 1974), a former CMA president, Dr. Duncan Kippon of Winnipeg, said that there are situations where it is inhumane to undertake cardiac resuscitation. Dr. F. N. Brown of Ottawa contended, however, that a doctor should never write no resuscitation on the medical record, because he might be accused of malpractice. But Dr. T. W. Ibbott of Vancouver said that doctors are failing in their responsibility to their patients and to nurses by refusing to put their orders in writing and instead letting it be known by word of mouth that the patient is not to be resuscitated. It would seem obvious that new guidelines are needed that would have the sanction and protection of law.

The Council expressed concern also about human experimentation and genetic engineering and announced its decision to set up a committee with the Canadian Bar Association and the Medical Research Council of Canada to establish guidelines to help people who will have to make decisions in these areas. The committee will be enlarged later. One dares to hope that this committee will concern itself also with the subject of euthanasia.

HOSPITAL CHAPLAINS, NURSES, AND SOCIAL WORKERS SPEAK OUT

Many hospital chaplains and nurses have been speaking out in the past few years, describing the suffering they have witnessed. They are asking society, doctors and hospitals to face honestly the problems of the dying and aged and to find more humane ways of helping them leave life more easily, more gently.

Writing in *Hospital Topics* in 1965, Chaplain Edgar E. Filbey described tragic cases of defective infants and other hopeless cases that seemed to provide convincing evidence of the need for new legislation that would permit, after proper consultations, euthanasia for such individuals.

Chaplain Fred W. Reid of North Carolina Memorial Hospital, writing in JAMA in 1967, emphasized the need for a team approach in dealing with these life and death problems, and urged that the church and society press for

changes in laws in order to make legally right what is believed to be morally right.

Chaplain R. B. Reeves of the Presbyterian Hospital in
New York City has said,

> We must find some way of working out an honorable exit to
> life when personhood is gone . . . [we must] find an honor-
> able equivalent to Spartan exposure on the rocks at one end
> of life and the Eskimo hole in the ice at the other end of life.
> . . . We have perverted the Judeo-Christian tradition into a
> belief that biological existence *per se* is of supreme value, and
> on the basis of that interpretation have been sidetracked into
> an ethical dilemma of ghastly proportions.

Reverend Reeves stated that the positions of the religions
—Jewish, Roman Catholic, and Protestant—are now far
more in agreement and permissive regarding the issue than
is generally supposed.

Chaplain Cornelius Trowbridge, formerly of St. Lukes
Hospital in New York, has for many years been an ardent
advocate of the right to die and the legalization of euthanasia. He has said, "The body should be the temple of
the soul and not its prison." In a letter to the president of
the Euthanasia Educational Council published in its 1971
publication *Dilemmas of Euthanasia* he stated:

> As a clergyman I made frequent visits to nursing homes,
> some . . . pretty ghastly places. Whenever I left one, I would
> thank God that no one close to me had ever been exposed
> to that atmosphere. Recently, however, after two months in
> the hospital, I chose to go to one . . . an exceptionally good
> one. The building was new and well kept, the staff on the
> whole were cheerful and efficient. . . . But it was the patients,
> the poor pathetic men and women in their wheel chairs who
> created an atmosphere that was utterly depressing. All but
> two of them were old, mainly in their eighties, some in their
> nineties. A few of them were mentally alert. The majority
> were senile or worse. They were fed, given their pills, taken
> to the bathroom, and then wheeled into the corridor where

they sat slumped over in their chairs, until it was time to be fed again and finally put to bed and another day was over. ... This was a place where they had been put to die. The irony of the situation is that these places are the expression of our humanitarianism.

But, said Dr. Trowbridge, surely there can be no kindness or compassion in prolonging the life of someone in acute misery. He cited the case of the woman across the hall from him, who kept up a continual wailing cry until she was sedated. And another patient, whom he said he could never forget, would cry out at intervals, "Oh, God, won't somebody help me?" Dr. Trowbridge concluded, "This experience has strengthened my conviction that euthanasia, properly protected, provides the only solution to this tragic problem."

Nurses have also been protesting the way we let people die, and some have openly deplored the deceptive practices some doctors employ in response to a patient's wish for death. A considerable number of nurses have spoken at recent annual conferences of the Euthanasia Educational Council, especially in 1971 and 1972. Among them was Barbara Allen Davis, a geriatric nursing specialist, who pointed out that it is nurses rather than doctors who are usually with the patient as death approaches, and she thought they should play a greater role in discussions of euthanasia. She pointed out that passive euthanasia alone is not a satisfactory solution. For instance, she said that if oxygen therapy is helping a dying patient have less distress in breathing, she would be unwilling merely to terminate the therapy.

Eileen Strauss, a supervisor of nurses at Bellevue Hospital, protested the way doctors give written or verbal orders not to resuscitate some patients, but then disobey their own orders if they are on the ward, by giving life-saving measures. She implied that it was unfair for the doctor to suggest that she omit measures that would prolong life when he himself was unwilling to do so. More and more nurses are now making similar protests.

Jennifer MacPherson, a nurse in the pediatric intensive care unit at Bellevue Hospital, protested the heroic efforts so often made to prolong the lives of grossly retarded children with irreversible brain damage. She said parents may ask that efforts to save a child continue but she thought they should consider what they will do twenty-five years later if they can no longer care for their totally dependent child.

Nurse Sharon Curtin, in her book *Nobody Ever Died of Old Age,* relates in a poignant way her experiences as a nurse in a state mental hospital, an "Old Folks Home," and as a visiting nurse. She tells of the dread old people have of "the period of helplessness and hopelessness when any further independence will be over." Of those forced to go to a mental hospital when they can no longer care for themselves, Ms. Curtin writes of the "institutional shock," the stigma of being locked up in a state hospital, the realization that they cannot leave and the only way out is by death. She challenges society and old people themselves while they are able to "rise up in anger" and revolt against the role of the elderly in our society. Those capable of being of service should be permitted to serve a useful role instead of being forced to retire at a fixed age, and for those too ill, debilitated, bedridden or senile, we should recognize that death is a part of life and make provision for it to occur with dignity. Ms. Curtin says that even in expensive nursing homes many elderly are treated like infants, deprived of privacy, sedated if they fail to submit fully to authority, and given busy work that is an insult to their intelligence.

When a questionnaire was sent to 5,000 members of the Geriatric Division of Nurses, 1,000 responded and the conclusion was drawn that most nurses who care for elderly and dying patients think they should be allowed to die without heroic efforts. And when a straw vote was taken at a convention of the Colorado Nurses Association in 1970 the nurses voted 173 to 109, (61 per cent) in favor of mercy killing, i.e., terminating the lives of incurably ill patients who want to die. A study in 1971 by Norman K. Brown and others of the University of Washington indicated that 85 per cent of the nurses questioned would practice negative euthanasia if there were signed consent and proper authority.

That the protests of nurses are justified seems to be confirmed in a 1965 study by B. G. Glaser and A. L. Strauss. These sociologists made a study of terminal patients in six hospitals in San Francisco. The findings are shocking in that they indicate the great amount of evasion and clandestine activity and unwillingness to face problems squarely.

Many doctors perform what is sometimes referred to as "the invisible act," and here the nurses often get involved in covert activity that they are rebelling against. The doctor may decide to ease the person out of life by ordering or suggesting that the resident doctor or nurse manipulate the patient's narcotics, giving either an overdose or a premature dose, or "accidentally" disconnecting life-saving equipment. In some cases it is known that the patient and his family would approve of such action, so the risk of trouble for the doctor may be small. Nevertheless, many nurses and doctors are now openly protesting any clandestine way of dealing with the problem.

Social workers also have recently been calling attention to the great amount of needless suffering endured by patients of all ages. Karen Lander of the pediatric department of Memorial Hospital for Cancer and Allied Diseases in Manhattan has expressed disapproval of the fact that very, very sick children and young people for whom there is no hope of recovery are often treated with chemotherapy, radiation and repeated surgery which make them only more uncomfortable. And Marjorie Beckman of Lenox Hill Hospital in New York has spoken not only of the dehumanizing effect of some intensive care treatment, but

also of the demoralizing effect of nursing homes and
chronic care facilities in which almost every vestige of privacy is denied.

STUDIES OF ATTITUDES TOWARD DEATH AND EXPERIENCES
OF THE DYING

Suffering and Death

Only rarely before the 1960's were there any empirical
studies of the attitudes and experiences of those facing
death or old age, or of the attitudes of others toward death
and dying. In ancient and even modern times such subjects
were generally discussed only in theological terms, which
concentrated on the rewards and joys of heaven and the
horrors and torments of eternal punishment in hell. Freud,
Jung, and other psychoanalysts theorized about death, but
not until the Sixties did there emerge much interest in
conducting systematic research in this area of human experience. A significant exception was the work of Sir William
Osler, who in 1906 made a study of 500 dying patients. He
found that slightly more than 20 per cent clearly experienced pain or bodily distress; the extent of the anxiety and
mental distress was less clear.

Various studies in the Sixties supported Osler's
findings. They also confirmed what is well known to those
who have witnessed the agony of loved ones for weeks or
months before death, namely that dying is sometimes a
very ugly business. Studies have shown also that most people fear prolonged dying much more than they fear death.
Nevertheless many doctors divert attention by using such
clichés as, "We are now able to control pain in terminal
cancer," and "most people die peacefully in their sleep."

The truth is that various studies have shown that about
one patient in five experiences physical suffering in the final

stages of dying, and many have mental distress. An unknown number of people endure intense suffering for long
periods before death occurs or before receiving doses of
narcotics sufficient to induce unconsciousness. Even the
highly respected British physician, Dr. Cicely Saunders,
Medical Director of St. Christopher's Hospice in England,
a strong opponent of any legalization of euthanasia, admits
that in order to control pain, drugs are often given in quantities that cause loss of consciousness and have the effect of
hastening the patient's death.

Various drugs have been used in efforts to relieve the
anxiety of dying patients. Jerry Avorn, writing in *Harper's*,
tells of experiments at the Maryland Psychiatric Research
Center in which LSD and other psychedelic drugs are used
to ease the transition from life. The director of these experiments, according to the report, encourages dying cancer
patients to take LSD in the hope that the experience will
somehow reconcile them with death.

While this practice may have merit under present laws,
the use of LSD is still in an experimental stage, and to many
its use is an affront to human personality and may become
as discredited as the lobotomies and electroshock treatments that were common a few years ago. It is a tragic
commentary on our society that instead of permitting terminally ill patients to choose death, we force them to live
on in a drugged condition that makes them a travesty of
their former selves.

Attitudes of the Terminally Ill

In 1958 Dr. Wendell M. Swenson, a psychologist at the
Mayo clinic, was one of the first to demonstrate that attitudes toward death could be measured objectively. He presented a checklist of questions to more than 200 individuals
over the age of 60, many of whom were in homes for the
aged. He concluded that fear of death was relatively nonex-

istent in the conscious thought of the aged. Only a small number (10 per cent) admitted having any fear of death. Almost half (45 per cent) said they looked forward to it. Responses included, "It will be wonderful," and "All troubles will be over." Unfortunately, Swenson did not ask specifically about their fear of prolonged dying.

A 1961 study by Dr. Daniel Cappon of the University of Toronto revealed that of 254 persons ranging from healthy to dying, 95 per cent of the nonpatients and 90 per cent of the dying patients clearly expressed their wish to avoid a lingering death whether from disease or old age. They wanted to die suddenly even if it meant some shortening of life. When asked about euthanasia, it was found that 73 per cent of both groups favored it, though some were ambivalent. Dr. Cappon said the study showed clearly that the popular view that people want to hang on to life at all costs is false. He found that the majority wanted some control over the time and manner of their exit from life. When doctors and medical students were asked the same questions, 100 per cent said they wanted to die suddenly.

Using the same questions the *Toronto Daily Telegram* made a survey of more than 300 residents of the city of Toronto in which the findings were similar, according to a report by Ron Lawrence. It then combined the findings of the two surveys and concluded that almost 80 per cent would prefer to die suddenly, if possible, and approximately 70 per cent of this group favored positive euthanasia.

A poll conducted by the National Opinion Research Center of the University of Chicago revealed that of 1,482 adults interviewed, 80 per cent said death is sometimes a blessing. Where death is feared, it is usually because it will cut short achievement of desired goals or present problems for survivors. This finding agrees with the views of Aldrich, Eissler and others who have said that it is the interruption of interpersonal relationships that is of greater concern than the threat of death.

In 1961 the British physican Dr. A. N. Exton-Smith conducted a study of 220 elderly terminal patients in a geriatric unit, 60 per cent of whom were bedridden at the time of admission and 82 per cent of whom died within three months. It was found that more than 20 per cent experienced moderate to severe physical suffering; 41 per cent were mentally confused during at least part of their illness and for many there was such complete personality disintegration that they were oblivious to their plight. For patients suffering from malignant disease pain was controlled, but for many others pain and distress were severe over long periods. As death approached more patients showed depression and distress from unrelieved suffering; 40 per cent died in a coma, 15 per cent died suddenly; of these, some died from exhaustion, and some in their sleep.

In a study conducted by the well-known British professor of psychiatry Dr. John M. Hinton, reported in *Quarterly Journal of Medicine,* it was found that of 121 patients in a teaching hospital who were expected to die within six months, at least half, especially among the elderly, came to acknowledge openly and to accept the nearing of death. He found that he was able to give "adequate relief" to 82 per cent of the patients in pain, but that 37 per cent experienced nausea and 18 per cent breathlessness that could not be controlled. He found that the struggle for breath caused much distress of mind as well as body. For many there was overwhelming exhaustion. Mental distress was sufficiently common for a significant number to consider suicide. For many there was a progressive impairment of consciousness; very few were conscious just before they died, in many cases because of drugs. This, Hinton said, was fortunate, because it spared the patient a potentially distressing remnant of life. He said that post mortem examinations of the elderly often have shown the presence of a number of chronic conditions, indicating good reason for suffering.

This pilot study was followed by several others, and Hinton's conclusion was that the agony of many chronically ill or dying is very great and that the problem is becoming ever more serious. He said that for many there was the terror of progressive helplessness, he spoke of the loneliness of the dying in hospitals, especially in intensive care units or wards for the terminally ill, separated from loved ones just at the time when they are most needed. Dr. Hinton discussed the complexity of the problems of decision making, and he described many of the arguments often raised against any euthanasia, but in his book *Dying* he said, "Certainly there are some powerful arguments in favor of allowing voluntary euthanasia as an end to suffering."

Dr. Avery D. Weisman of Harvard Medical School, in his book *On Dying and Denying,* also reported that many of the dying patient's fears are based on an inner feeling of helplessness; the fatal disease has the patient "squeezed into a relentless grasp." However, he said that each person's personality and psychosocial conditions impose traits upon terminality that are unique to the individual. And Dr. Robert H. Williams of the University of Washington Medical School is one of the many who have emphasized the marked feeling of loneliness and despair experienced by many of the dying and aged. For them there is the realization that instead of being able to contribute to life, their agonies and incapacitation make them a great burden to their families and society.

Hinton, Glaser and Strauss, and others have told how old people in nursing homes and hospitals who are about to die are often secluded during their last days in a room alone so that other patients will not be upset. Sometimes the dying patient is moved away from his friends because of uncontrollable groans or sobbing or unpleasant odors; some are put in a room with a comatose patient. Those who are put in intensive care units are often isolated from their families. All of these can be frightening experiences.

David Sudnow compared the experiences of patients dying in a public hospital where there were indigent patients with those in a private patient hospital. He said that in the private hospital the fact that death was imminent increased the sense of medical responsibility. In the public hospital, on the other hand, such a prediction often resulted in virtual abandonment of the patient; doctors were less likely to give up in the cases of private patients, and the relatives were given more consideration. However, the purpose here is not to emphasize class differences, though it is well known that they exist, but to call attention to the gradual rejection from the social group and the loneliness of those who are conscious as death draws near.

Another often cited experience of the dying—especially the elderly—is the desire to die at home. Yet in the United States more than two-thirds of all deaths occur in hospitals or other institutions—a commonly stated figure is 80 per cent. One reason for this high proportion is that for many there is no possibility of being cared for at home, and perhaps more significant is the fact that more than half the doctors do not make house calls. Also, professional nursing care at home, especially in rural communities, has become prohibitive for most people unless they are wealthy.

The Research of Elisabeth Kübler-Ross

A courageous study that has received much publicity is one by Elisabeth Kübler-Ross, a Swiss psychiatrist who in 1965 became a member of the faculty of the University of Chicago and the staff of the University's Billings Hospital. In her book *On Death and Dying,* she describes the origins and outcome of her study of the dying.

Dr. Kübler-Ross started her experiment after some theological students said they wanted to study the ultimate human crisis of facing death. Dr. Ross responded that when she wanted to know what it was like to be schizophrenic, she spent much time with schizophrenics; why not do the same with the dying? She realized this was a matter too long neglected and therefore decided to find dying patients who would be willing to talk. Immediately she ran into opposition by doctors and other hospital workers who feared she would disturb patients. However, she found many patients welcomed the opportunity to talk with her.

Dying patients went to a seminar room with a one-way glass screen where the patient would talk with Dr. Ross and the Chaplain, Carl Nighswonger, with the knowledge that there were medical and theological students, nurses, and social workers listening and observing from the other side of the screen. In a four-year period the seminar heard from 150 patients, many of whom were young or middle-aged. During that time there were only four patients who refused to participate. The loneliness of hospital life and the particular isolation of pain were broken by the chance to speak to sympathetic listeners; patients were motivated also by the thought that such seminars might eventually help others in their struggle with death.

From the evidence gained from these and other interviews with dying patients who freely expressed their thoughts and feelings, Dr. Ross concluded that there are usually, but not always, five successive emotional stages in life's last journey.

The first is *denial,* which often occurs following the person's initial awareness of the fatal nature of his illness. The patient seems unwilling or even unable to accept the real nature of his predicament. The second stage is *anger.* The patient, enraged by his illness and increasing pain, may become angry at his doctor or his family and be very demanding and difficult. Following this is the *bargaining* stage. A difficult patient may suddenly turn cooperative in the hope of staving off the inevitable by striking a bargain for an extension of life or a short period without pain. After the bargaining stage, the patient generally sinks into a profound *depression.* He realizes what is happening to him and sees that denial and bargaining are of no real use. He is apt to grieve for himself and for the impending separation from loved ones. After this period of depression he usually arrives at the fifth and final stage of *acceptance.* Even though he may still have some faint glimmer of hope, he is ready to let go. For the young and those in the prime of life, many studies show that it is likely to be more difficult for them than for the aged to reach this stage of acceptance.

Dr. Ross and her associate followed each patient through the several stages and attempted to assist them and help their families to understand and learn how to be of greatest comfort. Dr. Ross says it was not death they feared but dying and separation from what they held dear. In *On Death and Dying,* and in other publications, Dr. Ross leaves the impression that after a patient has all his affairs in order and has accepted death, he will die quickly and peacefully. But this is by no means always true. For many patients, especially very elderly ones, the heart persists in beating long after they have begun to wish for death. In the survey of 2,000 British doctors reported earlier, nearly half indicated that they had been asked by patients for a lethal drug to end their misery.

THE THALIDOMIDE BABIES AND THE TRIAL OF MADAME VAN DE PUT

The tragic story of the thalidomide babies became front-page news throughout most of the Western world in 1962 when Madame Suzanne van de Put of Belgium was tried for killing her seriously deformed eight-day-old daughter Corinne. The case precipitated new debate on an age-old question—the morality of keeping congenitally defective and seriously abnormal infants alive.

Ralph Nader has reported that between 1960 and 1963 several thousand babies (some authorities say as many as 10,000), most of whom were in Germany, England and

Japan, were born with very serious malformations to mothers who had used thalidomide, a tranquilizer, during their pregnancies. Most of the infants had major limb defects, or absence of arms and/or legs and other abnormalities. (Thanks to the insistence of Dr. Frances Kelsey of the Federal Food and Drug Administration, thalidomide, which was manufactured by a West German pharmaceutical company, was not permitted to be marketed in the United States.)

The case that attracted most attention was that of Madame van de Put, who at 24, during her pregnancy with her first child, had taken 11 thalidomide pills prescribed by her family doctor Dr. Casters. Her child Corinne was born May 22, 1962, with no arms or shoulder structure and flipperlike embryos of hands protruding from the end of each shoulder. Her feet were deformed, her face was disfigured and her anal canal emptied into her vagina. Despite all her deformities, however, chances of survival seemed good. When the family and the mother saw her, they were stunned and decided that the baby must not be allowed to live. The grandmother told the doctor "Don't condemn the child to live," and the mother pleaded with her gynecologist, Dr. Weerts, and the midwife attendant, to do away with the baby. Both refused to end the infant's life; the nun replied, "It is God who gives life and God who takes life away." The grandmother then requested and obtained from Dr. Casters a prescription for enough barbiturates to kill an infant. Later, at the trail, Dr. Casters said he knew the risk, but when he thought of the future facing the baby, he said, "I found it atrocious. I gave them the prescription. . . . I do not regret it."

The mother, after asking her family to go away because she "wanted to do it alone," picked up the infant in her arms and, rocking her gently, fed her a bottle of milk and honey—and barbiturates. Dr. Weerts had become suspicious and warned the police that the baby might be killed, but it was too late. Madame van de Put was indicted on a murder charge and her husband, mother, sister, and family doctor were arraigned as aiders and abettors.

At the trial, November 5, 1962, Madame van de Put said, "I just thought you could not let a baby like that live. I thought it could never be happy in its whole life." When the president of the court asked her why she had not put the baby in a home as the gynecologist had suggested, she replied "I did not want it. Absolutely not. For me, as an egoist, I could have been rid of her. But it wouldn't have given her her arms." When the president stated that the child was mentally normal she said, "That was only worse. If she had grown up to realize the state she was in, she would never have forgiven me in her whole life for letting her live."

The family doctor testified that there would have been no possibility of fitting her with artificial limbs since there was no shoulder bone structure, only cartilage; some experts said the child had a chance of one in ten of living. The gynecologist who had refused to terminate the baby's life explained his refusal by saying, "I am a doctor. I cannot kill. I must let live. The day doctors start killing I shall change my profession."

During the six-day trial many witnesses testified in support of the accused and the family doctor who was described as "the doctor of the poor" and beloved by his patients. At the conclusion of the evidence the prosecutor demanded a verdict of guilty, although he indicated that he would support a recommendation from the jury for a royal pardon. An acquittal, he claimed, would set a terrible precedent and open the door to great abuse. He said, "You must affirm that the principle of respect for life is sacred. Thousands of thalidomide mothers who kept their children alive in spite of malformations have their eyes on your verdict."

The defense attorney broke down and sobbed "For this terribly deformed child there was no possible place of happiness on this earth." The court admitted as evidence stacks of letters supporting the defendants and a public opinion poll by Radio Luxembourg that showed popular opinion to be ten to one in their favor. *Newsweek,* describing the courtroom scene, said, "Even the lawyers, reporters, and gendarmes felt tears welling up as the story of the final hours of Corinne was told by the four others in the dock alongside Suzanne." When the foreman of the jury, which consisted of 12 men, announced the verdict, which was not guilty, wild applause burst out in the crowded courtroom.

The prominent British author and lawyer Dr. St. John-Stevas, a staunch Catholic and strong opponent of euthanasia, described the reaction:

> The verdict was greeted with frenzied joy by the thousand people who had crowded into the court for the last day of the trial. Their rejoicing was taken up by the crowds outside the court when the news became known. . . . Undoubtedly popular sympathy in Belgium and elsewhere was on the side of the mother and her family doctor. This is hardly surprising. Both had suffered intensely. They had been five months in custody, and had experienced the harrowing public ordeal of the trail. Whether misguided or not, both had acted from what they imagined to be unselfish motives, and the element of malice present in ordinary murders was totally lacking. The mother was a pathetic figure; the doctor, a revered one, regarded as a saint by the poor of Liége. No one wanted further punishment inflicted on them.

However, in his book *The Right to Life,* St. John-Stevas said that if there is a right to life, Corinne van de Put possessed it as much as anyone else. "The Liége verdict . . . is fundamentally uncivilized and dangerous; it invites imitation." He said that while Corinne was deformed, she was not a monster, and that no one had suggested that she was not a human being. "If she had been a 'monster,' that is, one in whom the full elements of a human being were not present, it would have been a different matter. . . . Corinne was never consulted."

Of course Corinne was not consulted. Newborn infants never can be consulted. Responsible parents must make decisions for them in efforts to serve their best interests. Perhaps the time has come to put less emphasis on the right of hopelessly defective infants to live and more emphasis on the rights and responsibilities of parents to spare a child from a life of extreme abnormality. In the case of Corinne, and many other seriously defective children, it would seem that her right to a peaceful death was much more important than her right to life.

Regarding the argument that a child is God-given and only God can determine when life shall end, it should be pointed out that certainly in the case of the thalidomide babies, and many other defective infants, it was not God who was responsible for the tragically deformed bodies. It was the chemists and companies that produced and marketed the thalidomide, the physicians who prescribed it, the mothers who took it, and the society that allowed it to be put on the market. This case and those of the several thousand other thalidomide babies make it clear beyond the shadow of a doubt that man, not God, was responsible for the interference with the normal development of the embryo and fetus and the tragic deformities that resulted. Does it not then seem proper for man to accept responsibility for sparing such children from the resultant suffering and subnormal existence that he had inadvertently caused?

Ten years after the Liége trial the debate over the thalidomide babies continued, and the sad plight of the defective children was brought to public attention again on television and in the newspapers. In England on January 5, 1973, the Distillers Corporation, which produced and marketed the thalidomide there under the trade name Distaval, bowed to the strong pressure of public opinion and offered its limbless thalidomide victims a total of 51 million dollars to be paid over ten years to the 404 families whose mothers had taken the drug—an average of about 126,000 dollars per child.

THE EUTHANASIA MOVEMENT IN THE UNITED STATES TODAY

The Euthanasia Society

During the Sixties there was no effort by the Euthanasia Society of America to press for legislation. This has been a great disappointment to many members, but the board adopted a policy of limiting its efforts to education rather than legislation. Its position is that further efforts toward legalization would be futile until a more favorable climate of opinion has been created. In 1967 it established the Euthanasia Educational Fund, a tax-exempt organization, the name of which was changed in 1972 to the Euthanasia Educational Council. The officers and board of directors are chiefly the same as for the Society, founded in 1938, but most activities are now conducted by the Council.

The purpose of the new organization as stated in 1972 is "to establish the right to die with dignity." Its statement of beliefs seems little different from the pronouncement of Pope Pius XII in 1957, and there is no expressed recognition of the need to enact new legislation to establish that right. The president, Mrs. Henry J. Mali, speaking at an annual meeting said, "As an organization we advocate passive euthanasia, the removal of supportive measures when there is no reasonable hope for real recovery." Two of the society's objectives are: to encourage the introduction of studies of dying, death, and euthanasia into the curricula of professional schools, and to influence hospitals to reexamine their procedures, teaching and attitudes toward dying patients.

Splendid as these objectives are, they seem to be a far cry from the courageous ones enunciated by the founders of the Society, who were forthright advocates of voluntary active euthanasia for incurable sufferers and of laws that would make it legally permissible.

Nonetheless, the new organization is performing a useful function. At its annual conferences, which are open to the public, able speakers have presented much valuable information. At the 1968 conference the moderator, Dr. Henry Pitney Van Dusen, President Emeritus of Union Theological Seminary and long-time supporter of the Euthanasia Society, stated, "There is no issue more important or urgent than the one that brings us here today . . . except possibly overpopulation." Among the other speakers were two doctors, a lawyer, a hospital chaplain, a social worker, Sir George Thomson of England, and Mrs. Lael Wertenbaker, author of *Death of a Man.*

Mrs. Wertenbaker told of the experience she and her husband had after he received "the sentence of death" from cancer. She said that by directly facing the fact that death was inevitable and imminent, they had "the most enormous reward." And finally when he realized that the time had come when he would no longer have efficient control of his functioning, he chose the moment to "drink the hemlock." Another widow told of her husband, a chemist, who had similarly faced death and decided the time had come when he should die. While she stood by, he took cyanide. She said she was proud of her husband for his courage, but not everyone can get cyanide.

The Living Will

The Euthanasia Educational Council has been responsible also for the preparation and distribution of "A Living Will." This document, which anyone of testamentary capacity may sign in the presence of two witnesses, has no legal validity at present, as pointed out by Kutner, Powers, and others, but it is a means of making known in advance one's wishes for an end to useless prolongation, and could influence the physician and family in making decisions if one should become terminally ill and *non compos mentis.* The Council reported in 1973 that it had distributed a quarter of a million copies of the Will. (For a copy, see Appendix.)

Marya Mannes in her *Last Rights: A Case for the Good Death* formulated a Living Will which authorizes "My Doctor–My Lawyer–My Closest Relative–My Dear Friend—to assure that certain measures be taken to end my life." This is a significant addition to the form of the Will distributed by the Euthanasia Educational Council, which only expresses "a request that I be allowed to die and not be kept alive by artificial means or heroic measures."

The publicity given to the Living Will has helped promote discussion of euthanasia; it has also had the positive effect of making doctors more aware of the current support for voluntary euthanasia. However, it is not an unmixed blessing. For some it tends to engender a false confidence that their wishes will be carried out if they sign it. Many doctors will not take the kind of action they request unless and until laws are passed making such action clearly legal. While some doctors may encourage patients to sign such a document, others say they would not feel bound by it and many point out that compliance with such a request might invite charges of malpractice. Many see it as an attempt to evade the real issue, namely the need for new legislation with safeguards.

The Living Will is, of course, no help at all to those who have not signed it, nor does it allow for the cessation of treatment of congenitally defective infants. And as generally written, no provision is made for taking positive action to terminate a life. The main advantage of the Will is in making known the wishes of the dying patient, and thus lifting at least part of the burden and responsibility from the involved families and doctors.

A promising new educational program was announced by the Euthanasia Educational Council in 1972. The president reported plans for seminars and workshops on death and dying to be held in six or eight sessions in each of several areas of the country. These programs are being sponsored jointly with organizations representing doctors, clergy, nurses, chaplains and others.

In 1971 the Council announced the formation of a chapter in Rochester, New York, the first chapter outside of New York City since that in Connecticut in 1950. At the organizing meeting, Dr. Roland Stevens, Associate Professor of Surgery and Senior Associate Surgeon at the University of Rochester Medical School and Strong Memorial Hospital, gave an address in which he said, "In plain truth, the effectiveness of medical technology has outstripped the quality of the professional conscience which guides it." Administrators and physicians, he said, are increasingly summoned to courts of law, so to protect themselves they feel obligated to prolong life. But he said, "Death is man's greatest blessing when it cancels a life wracked with suffering and stripped of its meaning. . . . Society has a role to play in this matter of euthanasia."

Another chapter of the Council was organized in Wilmington, Delaware in 1972.

The Good Death Fellowship

Another development in 1972—one that took place independently of the Euthanasia Society or its Educational Council—was the founding in Denver, Colorado of the *Good Death Fellowship*. This is "an organization of citizens who believe that withdrawal or denial of the right to die with dignity is a violation of an individual right which neither law, custom nor practice should be allowed to abridge or deny." The Fellowship publishes a quarterly journal, *Euthanasia News*, which reported in its second issue that the organization already had members in more than 40 states, plus Canada and Australia.

The president, the Reverend Richard Henry, a Unitarian minister, stated in *Euthanasia News* (Summer, 1972), that the Fellowship would not take part directly in efforts to get legislation enacted, "although legislative proposals may grow out of its educational activities." Until her death late in 1973, a moving spirit of the Fellowship was the

87-year-old Mrs. Elsie Garman of Denver. She pressed for "one more pill"—i.e., one that would permit the dying and aged to end life at a time of their own choosing.

In 1973 Ms. Frances A. Graves, who conducts a radio program in the state of Washington, started sending out a *Death-with-Dignity News Letter* to coordinate and disseminate information pertaining to euthanasia and help develop good legislation. She deplored policies that encourage secret action by doctors.

THE 1969 VOLUNTARY EUTHANASIA BILL IN ENGLAND AND REACTION TO IT

The Euthanasia Society in England has never wavered in its determination and efforts to get a voluntary euthanasia bill enacted. In 1962 it started drafting a new bill which after revision was introduced into the House of Lords in 1969 by Lord Raglan. Under the able leadership of its president, the Earl of Listowel, and its vice-president, Sir George Thomson, it has done much to promote the movement toward legalization.

The 1969 Voluntary Euthanasia Bill contained two major differences from the 1936 bill. First, it did away with the overly cumbersome safeguards that required that a committee of three, appointed by a central authority, to visit the dying patient to satisfy themselves that the patient's request for euthanasia was bonafide and the doctor's prognosis was accurate and justified. Secondly, it provided greater coverage in that it would make it possible for euthanasia to be administered to a person not of testamentary capacity provided he had previously signed a declaration of his wish attested to by two persons, neither of whom would stand to benefit from his decease. The declaration would come into force 30 days after being made and remain in force for three years unless revoked. Euthanasia was defined as the painless inducement of death. In order to qualify for it a patient would have to be over the age of majority and be certified by two physicians as suffering from an irremediable condition (see Appendix).

The bill provided that it would be an offense punishable by life imprisonment for anyone to willfully conceal, destroy or forge a declaration with intent to create a false impression of another person's wishes with regard to euthanasia. No doctor, nurse, or other person would be obligated to participate against his conscience in any treatment authorized by the act, and anyone acting under the act would not be guilty of any offense. The bill provided also that no insurance policy that had been in force for 12 months would be vitiated by the administration of euthanasia to the insured. The Secretary of State for Social Services was charged with the responsibility of making and carrying out regulations.

While the 1969 bill was broader in scope than the 1936 bill, it still did not apply to cases such as severely defective infants, nor to mentally incompetent persons including those who were comatose and had not made a previous declaration of their wishes. The bill attracted much public attention and stimulated further discussion but was defeated, 61 votes to 40. This 40 per cent support was substantially greater than the support in 1936. Many of those who voted against the 1969 bill said they supported it in principle but objected to some details. The Board of the Society has drafted amendments and plans to resubmit the bill at a later time.

Independently of the Society a member of the House of Commons, Laborite Hugh Gray, introduced a euthanasia bill in that body on April 7, 1970, but it was shouted down by members who yelled, "no, no" after a speech by St. John-Stevas, a Catholic member who has been a vociferous opponent of euthanasia. The matter was apparently affected by the fact that members were facing upcoming elections.

A significant achievement of the British Euthanasia Society was the publication in 1969 of the book *Euthanasia and the Right to Death,* a series of articles by prominent persons, with a foreword by the Earl of Listowel, Chairman of Committees of the House of Lords and President of the Euthanasia Society. Another major effort of the Society was an attempt to arrange for meaningful discussion with representatives of the British Medical Association's Board of Science and Education after the latter adopted a resolution in 1969 condemning euthanasia. The Society published *Doctors and Euthanasia,* a report in which it rebutted the arguments and statements of the BMA representatives.

In addition to the official opposition of the British Medical Association to the British bill, there was other concerted action in opposition to it as evidenced by formation of "Right to Life" societies and the founding in 1969 of the Human Rights Society, whose aim is "to defend in particular the right to life of all, including sick, the handicapped, and the aged" (*New York Times,* March 8, 1969). In 1971 *Your Death Warrant? The Implications of Euthanasia,* a book written by a group of Catholic doctors, lawyers, and members of Parliament was published. It attempted to warn society of the dangers of any legislation permitting euthanasia. It was edited by Jonathan Gould, a psychiatrist, and Lord Craigmyle, Secretary of the Catholic Union of Great Britain. The preface was written by John Cardinal Heenan, Archbishop of Westminister. On the colorful jacket of the book a drawing portrays the doctor as an executioner; he holds an axe as tall as himself and a patient lies dead at his feet. Inscribed on the jacket are statements such as "Let euthanasia be seen for what it is—a tragic attempt to patch up a morbid society," and "granting private control of the right to die would inevitably be the first step toward state control of the right to life."

On January 27, 1973, Cardinal Heenan conducted a conference at which euthanasia was one of the topics discussed and the official Catholic view was reiterated, according to an article in the London *Observer* by Christine Doyle entitled, "Heenan: Death Not To Be Avoided at all Costs."

In 1972 the Council of Social Services of the Department of Health and Social Security of the British government organized a conference attended by people from all over the country to discuss the problems of dying and whether or not legal voluntary euthanasia was desirable. This was the first such meeting called by the government. The need for more authoritative and unbiased information was emphasized; the extent to which dying patients suffer was one of the hotly disputed subjects.

And the Royal Society of Health held a conference on euthanasia in December 1973. The speakers were selected for their known support of or opposition to the legalization of euthanasia, so discussion rather than agreement was expected. But there was general agreement on the need to prevent medicated survival and lingering misery by extraordinary measures that prolong life in terminal cases. There was also strong support for the belief that more should be done to grant the wishes of terminally ill patients to end suffering.

Dr. Eliot Slater of the University of London said part of the medical profession is quite out of step with the informed laity, and there is no reason other than professional bigotry why negative euthanasia should not be standard medical practice, in hospital and out. He cited the fact that many eminent physicians are now advising patients to die at home, away from the "great impersonal technological machine" of a hospital. He added that the suffering many dying patients endure is a disgrace, entirely unnecessary, and completely pointless; but it can be corrected only if society gives a mandate that such things must not be.

RECENT EUTHANASIA BILLS IN THE UNITED STATES

The Sixties and early Seventies saw bills pertaining to euthanasia or the right to die with dignity introduced in at least ten states. In seven states—Florida, Washington, Wisconsin, Maryland, Massachusetts, Delaware, and California —the proposed bills dealt only with passive euthanasia; in three—Idaho, Montana, and Oregon—bills would permit voluntary active euthanasia; in Hawaii and Illinois, resolutions were introduced in the legislatures calling for hearings on euthanasia, but it appears no action has yet been taken (See Appendix for selected texts).

Passive or Negative Euthanasia Bills

FLORIDA.   Since 1967 Dr. Walter W. Sackett, a Catholic physician and member of the Florida House of Representatives, has sought legal authority in Florida for doctors to terminate treatment in some circumstances. His original proposal was for an amendment to the state constitution; he proposed adding the words "death with dignity" to "the right to life, liberty, and the pursuit of happiness" in the Bill of Rights. Later he decided that legislative action would be sufficient, and each year since he has introduced a bill. The earlier bills were based on "the right to die with dignity," but this right was not mentioned in his 1973 bill. His bills would permit a competent person 18 years of age or older to execute a document, which could be revoked at any time, directing that his life should not be prolonged beyond meaningful existence when two physicians attest to the fact that he is terminally ill.

The provision in the bill for the decision to terminate treatment to be made by the next of kin, or in the absence of next of kin by three physicians, if the patient were unable to make the request, was struck from the 1973 bill in committee, and the bill as thus amended was passed by the House on May 24, 1973, by a vote of 56 to 50. The bill was then sent to the Senate and was in Judiciary Committee upon adjournment. Dr. Sackett has announced that he will reintroduce his bill in 1974 and will also reintroduce a constitutional amendment to guarantee "the right to die with dignity."

Dr. Sackett rejects the label "euthanasia" when speaking of his proposals, but this is a matter of semantics because what he proposes is usually called passive or negative euthanasia and he advocates it not only for those who are able to request it for themselves but also for those unable to do so.

In testimony before Senator Church's Special Committee on Aging, in 1972, and in an article in *Medical Economics,* Dr. Sackett said, " I have let hundreds of people die." But because many doctors, especially young or insecure doctors, are unwilling to risk terminating life-sustaining treatment, he said it is necessary to enact law such as he has proposed. He said he has received thousands of letters praising him for his efforts and only a dozen protesting them.

Dr. Sackett cited the heavy cost of extending the meaningless existence of those unable to speak for themselves. He spoke specifically about the 1,500 severely mentally and physically retarded residents of two institutions in Florida, "some with heads as big as buckets, some small as oranges, grotesque and drawn up in contracture." Thirty to forty years ago such severely defective children usually died at an early age, but now they can be kept alive until they are 50 or 60. Dr. Sackett stated that it will cost the state of Florida

five billion dollars to care for that number of helpless defectives over the next 50 years; on the national level it will cost
roughly 100 billion dollars to care for them. He thought
that money might better be spent saving the lives of those
who could benefit from medical care rather than on those
so severely retarded they are "bedridden, diapered, tube-
fed and completely unaware."

However, he claimed that in no case would he end a
life; he said he would merely withdraw artificial support and
"let God take over." For so compassionate and courageous
a physician, it would seem that logic would have led him to
extend his bill to make provision for the legal and merciful
ending of such lives if religion and tradition had not de-
terred him.

WISCONSIN.   In 1971 a "Right to Die with Dignity" Bill
was introduced in the Wisconsin State Senate by request.
It stipulated that a person could execute a document requiring that his life not be prolonged by extraordinary
medical procedures. If the person were a minor or incapacitated adult, the request might be made by a parent,
spouse, child or nearest relative.

The Bill was first referred to the Committee on Health
and Social Services, which held a one-day public hearing;
then it was reassigned to the Judiciary Committee, which
also held a one-day public hearing. The Bill was given a
second reading but was refused a third reading by a vote
of 19 to 10. It lacked many of the safeguards found in other
euthanasia bills.

WASHINGTON.   A "Death with Dignity" Bill was introduced in the Senate of the State of Washington in February
1973 by three members at the request of the Governor's
Task Force on Aging. It provided for an individual over the
age of 18 to execute a witnessed written declaration, with
fingerprints, "authorizing the withdrawal of life-sustaining

mechanisms" when the individual is suffering from an irremediable condition as certified by two physicians. The bill provided for a waiting period of 30 days after the signing of the declaration before life support could be withdrawn.

While the Bill declared that an individual should be "allowed the right to make the crucial final decision as to the manner in which he dies," it still did not authorize active euthanasia—only the withdrawal of life-prolonging measures. And the Bill did not provide for the termination of treatment for a person who had not signed the required document—thus it did not allow nonvoluntary passive euthanasia. Safeguards similar to those in other euthanasia bills were included. One hearing in the Senate Committee on Social and Health Services produced so much controversy that further consideration was postponed.

MASSACHUSETTS AND DELAWARE.   Bills to legalize the Living Will and give doctors complying with it immunity from criminal prosecution were introduced in Massachusetts and Delaware in 1973. Both bills met with strong opposition. John Ames, of the Massachusetts House of Representatives, said that he will submit the bill again in the next session of the legislature.

MARYLAND.   A bill that would have legalized the Living Will—a passive euthanasia bill—was introduced in the Maryland Senate in February 1974. It was assigned to the Committee on Economic Affairs. Strong Catholic opposition was expressed, and the committee speedily refused any adequate consideration of the bill which had been proposed by Senator Julian Lapides.

CALIFORNIA.   The California passive euthanasia bill is the most unusual proposed to date because of its brevity. Introduced on May 16, 1974, by Assemblyman Keene as an amendment to the Civil Code relating to death, the bill consists of only one sentence: "Every person has the right to die without prolongation of life by medical means."

Active or Positive Euthanasia Bills

IDAHO. In 1969 the Health and Welfare Committee of the Idaho House of Representatives introduced a "Voluntary Euthanasia" Bill to legalize the "painless inducement of death" at the request of a patient suffering from an "irremediable condition." The patient must have made a witnessed declaration in writing that he wished the administration of euthanasia if he should suffer such a condition which would have to be certified by two physicians. This bill seems to be one of the most detailed introduced in the United States to date, stating among other things that "A person who willfully conceals, destroys, falsifies or forges a declaration under this act with intent to create a false impression of another's wishes . . . is guilty of murder in the first degree." But one might question the provision that compliance with the declaration is left to "the discretion of the physician in charge" if the patient is incapable of expressing his wishes, and there is no requirement that the physician confer with the legal guardian or family of the patient.

OREGON. Governor Tom McCall of Oregon called for discussion of "death with dignity" after he conferred with the Oregon delegates who had attended the 1971 White House Conference on Aging. In February, 1972, he announced that he would open public dialogue on the subject by arranging a symposium with members of the health and legal professions, theologians, government leaders, sociologists, philosophers, and the White House delegates. He said death with dignity was "an unclear right that somehow must be made more visible and legally available," but he stated that "death with dignity" does not mean early termination of life by administration of a medication, but rather a conscious decision to refrain from life-supporting machines and medicines to prolong the pain, suffering and degradation of the death bed. He called attention to the possibility of using the Living Will to indicate one's wishes.

This seemed to be a call to enact legislation that would permit passive euthanasia. It received much publicity, some newspapers reported him as favoring "mercy killing," and this caused the epithet "Hitler" to be hurled at him. However, of 501 letters he received within the next two months, 59.9 per cent agreed with his general position and only 32.5 per cent disagreed.

In spite of this favorable public response, the Governor later seemed to have changed his position significantly. In August, 1972, he said, "I believe it is quite possible that to carry the issue into the political arena could be an error of great magnitude. Probably we should not try to put into law what might be accomplished through the leadership of medical doctors and religious bodies. Possibly it should be a process of humane intuition based on medical fact."

In spite of this later position taken by the Governor, ten senators introduced a strong voluntary active euthanasia bill in the 1973 session of the Oregon legislature. This bill was similar to the British bill; it would provide for administration of euthanasia, which was defined as "the painless inducement of death," upon request by a patient suffering from an "irremediable condition" as certified by two physicians, or at the discretion of the physician if the patient had signed an advance declaration to be effective if he became "incapable of rational existence." Specific regulations would be made by the Department of Human Resources. It was tabled after a single hearing.

Another bill was introduced in the Oregon House in 1973 to provide "death with dignity." It authorized doctors to forego heroic measures to extend life that was beyond preserving. It too was tabled after one hearing.

MONTANA.   When Mrs. Joyce Franks was unsuccessful in getting the 1972 Montana Constitutional Convention to include the right to die in the revised Declaration of Rights (see p. 42), she took her campaign for legalized euthanasia to the State Legislature. At her request a voluntary euthanasia bill was introduced in the 1973 session of the Montana House. The bill was based on the firm conviction that any individual after he had reached majority should "be allowed the right to make the crucial, final decision as to the manner in which he dies." It seems that the bill was given inadequate study and public hearings before being voted on unfavorably 83 to 15.

The Montana bill was very much like the British and Oregon bills. It provided for "painless inducement of death" to an individual over the age of eighteen who had signed a fingerprinted and witnessed declaration for euthanasia if he were suffering from an irremediable condition as certified by two physicians. Safeguards included a waiting period of at least 15 days after the filing of the declaration before euthanasia could be administered; a spouse or person of first degree of kinship or a physician could direct the administration of euthanasia if the patient were "incapable of giving directions." Also, it provided that the county board of health should be available at all times to carry out the wishes of the patient if any physician refused to administer euthanasia to a qualified patient. Mrs. Franks has directed a revision of this bill for reintroduction in 1974 with the title "Montana Self-Determination of Death Act," based on the First Amendment of the United States Constitution.

MEDIA COVERAGE OF THE MOVEMENT

There has been a phenomenal increase in the number of radio and television programs and press reports on euthanasia and the right to die with dignity, and much evidence of support for it. Following a WOR radio program in New York in 1965 when Dr. H. Leslie Wenger, a prominent New York surgeon and strong advocate of the legalization of voluntary euthanasia, was one of the speakers, the station reported that it received about a hundred letters, favoring euthanasia by a ratio of ten to one.

And following a 1972 nationwide television progran called "The Advocates," broadcast by the Public Broadcasting Service on the subject "Should the Law Permit Voluntary Euthanasia for the Terminally Ill?" the station received 4,836 letters. Of these, 63.3 per cent indicated that they were in favor of such a law, and 36.4 per cent were opposed—a ratio of five to three.

There was sharp disagreement among some of the professional members of "The Advocates" panel regarding active euthanasia, although all were agreed that there were times when passive euthanasia was desirable. There was no disagreement, however, among several residents of Pilgrim Place, a retirement community in Claremont, California; they were united in their desire to be able to choose death when life became too burdensome. They had recently petitioned the California State Bar urging that steps be taken to protect physicians from civil suits if they fail to prolong the lives of those terminally ill who want to die.

One member of the panel who took a strong position in favor of legalization was Dr. Arval Morris, professor of law at the University of Washington. He commented that many of the arguments of the opponents were "two-faced" and that he had not heard any of the speakers give any reason why the person who is terminally ill and expected to suffer severe distress should be required to live. He chided the doctor who had implied that she thought it a good and right thing to terminate treatment in some cases but considered it a bad thing and wrong to "pull the plug" and by so doing get caught. Dr. Morris thought this could lead to a lawless society and he said,

> There is no doubt that the only way in which the law is to have respect is if the law in fact promotes freedom in human dignity, while at the same time protecting vital interests. And the way to do it, it seems to me, is to have a law that authorizes voluntary euthanasia.

On a recent television program in Washington, D.C., Canon Michael Hamilton of the Washington Cathedral also deplored the deception and conspiracy of silence that surrounds the dying. In reply to the priest on the panel who argued that we should merely terminate extraordinary treatment and allow "natural" death to occur, Canon Hamilton said he thought it would be natural to intervene sometimes in order to prevent the suffering that is "natural" in cancer patients, for instance. He expressed approval of active euthanasia. Another television program which has portrayed the problems of the terminally ill, entitled "The Right to Die," was broadcast by ABC television in January, 1974, and is now available for public showing.

Numerous other stations and networks, especially the BBC in England, have carried discussions of the subject since the late Sixties, as have many newspapers and magazines. These discussions and articles reveal a common tendency for many to evade facing the issue squarely.

A related issue is that of psychosurgery, which can destroy enough of the brain tissue to leave the patient dull, or even little better than a vegetable. According to law, there must be informed consent for this or other surgery or experimental treatment, so a competent patient can refuse it. But when there is a question as to whether or not the patient is competent to make a judgment and to give or refuse consent, serious arguments may arise regarding when relatives may step in to make decisions for the patient. When cases have been taken to court, decisions have varied. The rights of patients in such instances clearly need to be spelled out, as Jessica Mitford and others have pointed out.

RECENT MERCY DEATHS

Many fewer mercy killings were reported during this period than in either of the preceding two decades. The reason for this can only be surmised. Might it be due to an unwillingness on the part of doctors to report such cases, or to a change in what is considered newsworthy, rather than to an actual reduction in the number of such cases?

The following are among those cases that have received publicity in the American press:

Robert Waskin, 23 years old, of Chicago, Illinois, was acquitted on grounds of insanity after he killed his 52-year-old cancer-stricken mother in 1967. After the trial he said "The moral issue of euthanasia . . . was not taken up at the trial, and it should have been faced squarely. Someday it will have to be."

In June 1973 Dr. Vincent A. Montemarano of the Nassau County Medical Center in New York was indicted for murder, accused of giving Eugene Bauer, a 59-year-old patient near death from cancer of the throat, a fatal injection of potassium chloride. The verdict returned by the jury was not guilty.

Also in 1973 Lester Zygmaniak of New Jersey was charged with murder for killing his 26-year-old brother, who had been paralyzed from the neck down in a motorcycle accident and who had pleaded with Lester to kill him. In the November 1973 trial, Lester was acquitted on grounds of temporary insanity, being "crazed with love" when he shot his brother.

A case that might be regarded as a negative mercy killing (which did not result in a court case) is that of Mrs. Anna Meir of Denver, who in 1973 gave her approval to turning off the machines keeping the body of her ten-year-old son functioning when doctors told her the boy's brain was dead following an auto accident.

In a similar case of brain death following an auto accident, Lester and Madeline Wojcik of Orlando, Florida requested the doctors to remove life-sustaining apparatus from their 20-year-old son so his kidneys might give life to two other patients. This action was taken after conference with five surgeons and a priest.

In 1964 Gizela Kafri of Tel Aviv was given a one-year sentence which was reduced to nine months, for drowning her three-year-old defective daughter who was blind, deaf and retarded.

In London in 1965, Arthur Gray was put on two years probation on the doctrine of "diminished responsibility," a special provision in British law, for having killed his 12-year-old son.

In 1971, 74-year-old Jean Picquereau of Leige, Belgium was acquitted of strangling his wife whom he had nursed for three years when she was suffering "unbearable pain and mental breakdown" from cerebral sclerosis which had incapacitated her.

PUBLIC OPINION POLLS

In August, 1973, George Gallup reported that public approval of mercy killing had increased sharply in the United States since his 1950 survey when only 36 per cent approved. In reply to the same question as used in 1950, the poll indicated that 53 per cent held to the view that "When a person has a disease that cannot be cured, doctors should be allowed by law to end the patient's life by some painless means if the patient and his family request it." Thus the majority expressed support for positive euthanasia even though safeguards were not specifically mentioned in the question.

This latest survey shows that men and women hold similar views (53 per cent to 53 per cent), Protestants and Catholics are also in close accord (53 per cent to 48 per cent), and the higher the level of a person's formal education the more likely he is to support euthanasia. Six in ten among the college group think doctors should be allowed to administer positive euthanasia, and 67 per cent of young people under 30 years of age approve of it.

In 1949, 62 per cent of the Canadians could not think of any reason for mercy killing, but in 1959 the Canadian Institute of Public Opinion conducted a poll that was reported under the caption, "Belief that mercy killing for some is right spreads," and in 1968 it released a report announcing that mercy killing was gaining wider and wider acceptance. The 1968 question was, "When a person has an incurable disease that causes great suffering, do you, or do you not think that competent doctors should be allowed, by law, to end the patient's life through mercy killing, if the patient has made a formal request in writing?"

Gallup reported that Canadians were about equally divided on this difficult problem—43 per cent said that it should *not* be allowed by law, but 45 percent thought that it should be. These findings indicate that a marked change in thinking had taken place in recent years.

In 1967 *Good Housekeeping* conducted a poll of 1,000 members of its Consumer Panel. Statements by Dr. H. Leslie Wenger were quoted as the basis for this sampling of opinion. The main statements were:

> Prolonged and hopeless physical anguish degrades and dehumanizes ... Euthanasia is a proper extension of the exercise of human freedom. An incurable sufferer ... should be able to ask for euthanasia under a procedure which assures all necessary legal safeguards ... There are times when it is morally right to speed life's end.

More than half (53 per cent) of the panel members agreed in general with these statements. The comments revealed that most of the respondents had lived through the agony of slow death of a loved one, often more than once. The preponderence of those who opposed did so on religious grounds.

About 71 per cent opposed using extraordinary medical efforts when there was no hope of recovery, and 65 per cent approved of discontinuance of medication in such cases. The question pertaining to actively hastening death did not make any mention of safeguards, so the finding that 72 per cent opposed that must be regarded as inconclusive.

A 1973 Harris survey indicated that 62 per cent of Americans believe that "a patient with a terminal disease ought to be able to tell his doctor to let him die rather than to extend his life when no cure is in sight," while 28 per cent thought this would be wrong. When asked "Do you think the patient who is terminally ill, with no cure in sight, ought to have the right to tell his doctor to put him out of his misery, or do you think this is wrong?", thirty-seven per cent thought this ought to be allowed, while 53 per cent thought it wrong and 10 per cent were not sure.

It should be noted that in the questions no mention was made of legal authority for the doctor or safeguards for the patient hence the findings may be misleading.

POSITIONS OF THE CHURCHES

There is abundant evidence that the churches and many religious leaders are reexamining traditional views pertaining to life and death and demanding that society evolve more humane ways of dealing with the dying than those currently practiced. This stands out in marked contrast to the action of some churches in the early Fifties that passed resolutions denouncing euthanasia. This reappraisal in the Sixties and Seventies extends from the beginning of life to its end. Church officials and laymen of all faiths, as well as those of no religious faith, are earnestly seeking answers to such questions as: should abortion be permitted in certain circumstances, especially if it is known that the fetus is defective? Should an infant born grossly malformed or severely mentally deficient be kept alive? Should aged, dying, and incurably ill or injured persons be kept alive against their will? Should people in an irreversible coma be kept alive?

Since Pope Pius XII made his historic pronouncements in 1957, there has developed a steadily increasing protest against useless prolongation of life. There is also an increasing demand, though to a lesser degree, for positive euthanasia and laws to make it legally permissible in some cases.

The first Protestant denomination to appoint a commission to take a fresh look at the subject appears to have been the Church of England. In 1965 its National Assembly Board for Social Responsibility published a report entitled *Decisions about Life and Death: A Problem of Modern Medicine,* which showed clearly the new concern over futile prolongation of life and the need for new practices. The report stated, "We do not respect life the less for recognizing the boon of death. There comes a moment, life being what it is, that it is good to die."

In discussing comatose patients the question was asked; is this life any longer a human life? The answer was that it depends on whether the patient is still in human relationship with others. "There may come a point when it becomes inhuman for relatives and others to cling to this distorted and incomplete relationship, insofar as it is diverting them from others and from their duty of coming to terms with themselves and accepting the new situation." The report gave consideration too to the exorbitant costs involved in keeping patients alive by artificial respiration and other extraordinary means. A commission was appointed to study the matter further, but its report has been delayed, partly due to the illness and death of its chairman, the Very Reverend Dr. Ian Thomas Ramsey, one of England's leading theologians.

In the United States

In the United States the Episcopal Church at its General Convention in 1967 appointed a Joint Commission on the Church in Human Affairs and directed it to consider, with the aid of appropriate consultants, the moral issues raised by the present and prospective advances in scientific and medical technology and euthanasia. An interim report was made at the next General Convention in which the idea of any deliberate termination of life was rejected, but the withholding of treatment in some circumstances was viewed with approval. A reconstituted Joint Commission was appointed and presented a revised report on the subject at the General Convention in 1973, still rejecting positive euthanasia as "not an appreciable problem in our society at the present time," but calling passive euthanasia "a genuine and pressing moral problem in today's world." The Commission called for further study and for consultation with other religious bodies to seek "a unified and ecumenical approach to both the theological and social issues facing us all."

The American Friends Service Committee in 1966 appointed a "working party" of Quaker scholars representing medicine, law, religion, philosophy and biology to explore the ethical, moral, and religious issues pertaining to abortion and to study its effect on the quality of life. Soon the study was extended to include euthanasia. In 1970 the report was published with the title, *Who Shall Live? Man's Control over Birth and Death,* which reviewed man's increased ability to prolong life and control birth, and asked what man ought to do with this great power. Regarding the prolongation of life of the dying and congenital defectives, the authors asked, is the extra life span and degree of rehabilitation worth the discomfort, the psychological hazards, long hospital stay, the enormous cost, and the tying up of a large part of a hospital staff—especially in cases of heart transplants and dialysis programs for chronic kidney patients—when other patients are deprived of the care they need? The importance of being concerned with quality rather than quantity of life was emphasized; the effect on the family was also considered and the tremendous cost that often results in sacrificing the future development of other members of the family.

The report expressed deep concern for the lonely, depressed, confused, dependent, senile, and often unconscious men and women waiting to die in nursing homes and geriatric wards of mental hospitals, and said that society must find the right solution to the problem. Before taking a position on the subject of positive or active euthanasia, the report said there should be more study, but it expressed approval of withdrawing or withholding supportive therapy in cases such as those with irreparable brain damage and said, "We believe that human life is a gift that is meaningful only as long as the receiver is able to function as a person."

At least two other major denominations have adopted resolutions that clearly support passive euthanasia and have committees studying also the pros and cons of active euthanasia. The United Methodist Church, at its General Conference in 1972, adopted a statement of social principles, one of which read, "We assert the right of every person to die in dignity, with loving personal care and without efforts to prolong terminal illnesses merely because the technology is available to do so." And the United Church of Christ at its General Synod meeting in June 1973 adopted most of a statement on "The Right to Die" that was prepared and adopted by the Church's Council for Christian Social Action in February 1973. It called for fresh deliberations and possibly new answers and asked its members "to seek to determine, with tolerance and prayer, the Will of God in today's world."

The statement adopted says:

> When illness takes away those abilities we associate with full personhood, leaving one so impaired that what is most valuable and precious is gone, we may well feel that the mere continuance of the body by machine or drugs is a violation of the person. We believe there comes a time in the course of an irreversible, terminal illness when, in the interest of love, mercy and compassion, those who are caring for the patient should say: "Enough." We do not believe simply the continuance of mere physical existence is either morally defensible or socially desirable or is God's will.

No stand was taken on the issue of actively intervening to end a life.

The Board of Social Ministry of the Lutheran Church of America has been making a comprehensive study of death and dying, including euthanasia. The third draft of the report raises such pertinent questions as: How shall human life be defined? Should there be a legal process by which a team of persons may arrive at and implement a decision that euthanasia in certain situations and according to specific guidelines is justified? If so, who should constitute the team?

This draft concluded, "In a time of increasing consciousness of an imminent population crisis, there is need for a reevaluation of public policy on suicide and euthanasia with respect to persons of advanced age, those who are born with gross physical abnormalities or mental deficiencies, and individuals who suffer from diseases which are both incurable and fatal." However, the biennial convention of the Missouri Synod of the Lutheran Church adopted in July, 1973, a report of the Committee on Theology and Church Relations stating "Whereas, The willful taking of the life of one individual by another is contrary to the word of God (Ex. 20–13); therefore be it Resolved, That the Synod cannot condone euthanasia."

The United Presbyterian Church has not taken any official stand on the subject since its resolution in 1951 condemning euthanasia. However, its Office of Church and

Society has prepared (although not published as of early 1974) a paper on matters pertaining to the artificial prolongation of life and other biomedical problems, a section of which deals with euthanasia. The paper does not take a stand but is rather a study essay; it "speaks positively concerning 'passive euthanasia,' " according to the church office.

The Unitarian Church has not made any official study of euthanasia but does have under consideration a study of problems of death, according to the church secretary.

The National Association of Evangelicals at its 1972 annual conference adopted a resolution affirming "the right of persons to die with dignity without the use of extraordinary means to prolong biological life," but it stated that "in no case is euthanasia justified."

The Baptist Church and the Christian Science Church appear to have no plans to study the problem. The Greek Orthodox Church appears to be firmly opposed to both active and passive euthanasia, but a commission has been set up to make a report to the General Council that will deal with some matters pertaining to death and dying in the light of modern medical advances.

The Roman Catholic Church appears to have made no change in its official position since the Pontiff's encyclical in 1957. In the 1971 edition of *Ethical and Religious Directives for Catholic Health Facilities,* issued by the United States Catholic Conference to serve as the national code subject to the approval of the bishop in the diocese, directive 10 states, "The directly intended termination of any patient's life, even at his own request, is always morally wrong." Directive 28 states, "Euthanasia (mercy killing) in all forms is forbidden. The failure to supply the ordinary means of preserving life is equivalent to euthanasia. However, neither the physician nor the patient is obliged to use extraordinary means;" and Directive 29 states: "It is not euthanasia to give a dying person sedatives and analgesics for the alleviation of pain, even though they may deprive the patient of the use of reason, or shorten his life."

The orthodox Jewish position is similar to the Roman Catholic, except that it does not extol the value of suffering. It appears that no change in its official position has been made since 1950, when a special committee was appointed by the Central Conference of American Rabbis to study the matter. The committee reported: "The conclusion from the spirit of Jewish law is that while you may not do anything to hasten death, you may, under special circumstances of suffering and helplessness, allow death to come." The orthodox position (as reported by Cohon) is that active euthanasia is positively forbidden by Jewish law, but passive euthanasia seems to be sanctioned. In *Jewish Medical Ethics*, published in 1959, Rabbi Immanuel Jakobovits stated, "Any form of active euthanasia is strictly prohibited. At the same time, Jewish law sanctions, and perhaps even demands the withdrawal of any factor—whether extraneous to the patient himself or not—which may artificially delay his demise in the final phase."

In effect this asserts that while active or direct euthanasia is prohibited, passive euthanasia may be not only permissible but perhaps sometimes laudable.

Other Official Positions and Personal Views

At the first International Congress of Learned Societies in the Field of Religion, in 1972, the main theme was the need to relate religion to man's problems in **this** world. The emphasis was on man's needs during his lifetime rather than on doctrines of the past or on speculation about the future. Also at the World Council of Churches Assembly in 1968, Dr. Eugene Carson Blake, the general secretary, called upon the churches to give up doctrines that are irrelevant for our time. In 1968, the Moderator of the United Church of Canada, Dr. Robert McClure, a Fellow of the Royal College of Surgeons and a highly regarded medical missionary, publicly expressed his *personal* belief in euthanasia for congenitally deformed infants particularly when there was evidence of serious mental damage, and for hopelessly ill old people for whom death is inevitable and imminent and for those whose minds have so deteriorated that they do not even recognize their own children. And speaking at that church's annual conference, Dr. H. L. Trueman spoke of the credibility gap between man and the beliefs held by the church. He said today's people cannot be expected to accept the doctrine that we must not question God's purpose in permitting useless suffering, or the idea that all things work together for good if only we trust Him.

The British Humanist Association in 1968 passed a resolution calling for early passage of legislation to permit voluntary euthanasia. And the same year the National Secular Society and the National Council for Civil Liberties in England each passed a resolution at their annual meetings calling attention to "the natural right of individuals to seek euthanasia for themselves when their lives become intolerable, and for their doctors to be able to help them without risking a criminal prosecution." And the American Humanist Association in 1969 repeated the position they had taken in 1959 and issued a Statement of Social Policy, approved by a majority of the Board of Directors, item 28 of which read "We urge all humanists to work for changes in existing laws that prohibit an individual the right to make a rational choice concerning the termination of his own life when faced with incurable illness or irreparable damage."

The Dutch Reformed Church, Holland's biggest Protestant church, published in February of 1972 an explosive report entitled "Euthanasia, Sense and Limitation of Medical Treatment." The report, drawn up by a committee of doctors, theologians and ethicists in response to requests from doctors for guidance in ethical problems resulting from advances in medical services, was passed unanimously by the General Synod of the church for pastoral guidance. The report called for the acceptance of passive euthanasia. It took no position regarding active euthanasia, but it recognized that sometimes it is difficult to determine a borderline between active and passive euthanasia.

Other Breaks with Tradition

In 1966 *Christian Century* broke the traditional silence of Protestant church periodicals on the subject of euthanasia by publishing an article, "Coup de Grace," by Mary McDermott Shideler, in which she told how her mother had begged for months before she died to be put to death. Mrs. Shideler said that many times over the years her mother had expressed a horror of ending her life the way she finally did, with excruciating pain and physiological deterioration which eroded her mind and spirit as well as incapacitated her body. She had often said, " If that time comes, I hope you will see to it that I die before I go completely to pieces." During her final months, her mother said "This is the time"; and when Mrs. Shideler and the physician refused to give her merciful release, her mother asked her to write an article justifying their refusal.

Mrs. Shideler wrote, "I could not give her the overdose she begged for because it would have meant taking into my own hands a decision that involved society, as for example, marriage and birth also do. But there was no procedure by means of which society could participate in that decision, as it does in licensing marriage and bestowing citizenship on infants." She resolved to work for appropriate euthanasia legislation that would permit euthanasia not only for those suffering from terminal illness, but also for those in comas and infants with severe abnormalities that prevent bodily or mental development. Many letters to the editor followed Mrs. Shideler's article, most of which were favorable.

Since then many church sponsored periodicals have had articles on euthanasia. One that probably received the most attention was published in the *Episcopalian* in 1969, by Rial and Morrison entitled "What Are We Doing With Our Power Over Death?" This was reprinted in the *Observer,* the official publication of the United Church of Canada, with the title, "Privilege of Dying: Today we have the power to deny death, what are we doing with this power?" There followed a flood of letters to the editor, nearly all of which were favorable and protested useless prolongation of life.

The *Journal of Religion and Health* ran an editorial in 1971 that commented on the Living Will: "It is hard to imagine a greater and more loving gift that a person could make to one he loves than that of a peaceful death. . . . The living will asks each person involved in the choice to take the moral responsibility for the final act of love."

The Catholic journal *Linacre Quarterly* carried an article by a British physician, Dr. K. F. M. Pole, which, although it asserted that "the Christian cannot have any part" of positive euthanasia, said that the doctor might be under obligation in some terminal cases "to discontinue extraordinary treatment and thereby make the facilities free for the benefit of others." And in 1973 *Commonweal* published an article by Daniel C. Maguire, professor of theology at Marquette University, entitled "The Freedom to Die," in which positive as well as negative euthanasia in some circumstances was strongly defended.

Professor Maguire spoke of the deceit and the myths that have long marked the dying process and called upon people from all walks of life to have meetings to study the problems openly and then energetically publicize their conclusions and work creatively for new solutions. Death education, he said, is needed at all levels. He called for a lobby including the dying and gravely ill to petition politicians, national health organizations, medical and legal societies, news media, writers, and others to study "the atmosphere in which man's moral right to die with dignity can receive its needed re-evaluation" and the law be updated to make this right legally permissible. He concluded, "We can proclaim moral freedom to terminate life directly in certain cases." He said the conscious terminal patient must consider his social responsibility and beware lest he yield to societal pressures, but asserted, "direct action to bring on death . . . *in some situations* may be moral."

Professor Maguire said that to say that something is morally right or wrong in all possible circumstances is nonsense and to maintain bodily life at a vegetable level without cause is "irrational, immoral and a violation of the dignity of human life." This unusually forthright endorsement of euthanasia in a Catholic magazine would have been unthinkable a few years ago. In his 1974 book *Death by Choice,* Professor Maguire defends the right to choose death, asserting, "There are times when ending life is the best that life offers."

Another liberal Catholic thinker, John Reedy, CSC, editor of *A.D. Correspondence,* said in recent articles that the next great controversy that will clamor for our attention is euthanasia. "While we are still battling over the issue of liberalized abortion laws, the scene is being set for a new conflict—for efforts to legalize euthanasia." He said people are mistaken if they assume that there will be no public support for it. "Too many people have gone through the emotional anguish of watching someone they love linger on, either with no sign of a response or in a half-conscious endurance of pain."

Father Reedy warned that as the debate grows in scope and intensity, all the accusations of the abortion debate will be repeated. People should not make decisions or act on the basis of an emotional tidal wave but should insist that law be developed in a manner completely consistent with

the best of our legislative tradition and carefully formulated to serve the legal needs of society; society must also
be vigilant in protecting human rights of both competent
and incompetent individuals, he said.

Dr. Daniel Callahan is a Catholic philosopher who also
is courageously urging new and rational thinking on this
issue. In his numerous writings and in his position as co-
founder and director of the prestigious and influential Institute of Society, Ethics and the Life Sciences, Dr. Callahan
is giving leadership in efforts to establish a basic moral and
professional context in which to deal with problems pertaining to life and death. He seeks moral principles that are
not tied to a particular religious history or to traditional
conceptions of natural law but to human experience today.
He said that central to Catholic and Protestant theology is
the principle that God is the Lord of life and death, and
man cannot take it upon himself to act as master, but many
do not accept this concept so it cannot provide a norm
acceptable to all. He thinks, however, that everyone can
agree on the sanctity of life principle and on the belief that
there must be respect for life.

Dr. Callahan has said in his article "The Sanctity of
Life," "It is an utter abdication of human responsibility to
passively place on God's shoulders the care and protection
of human life . . . it is man who is responsible for man. . . .
Contraception, abortion, euthanasia, medical experimentation, and the prolongation of human life are all problems
which fall totally within the sphere of human rules and
human judgments."

It is interesting to note that although the Roman Catholic Church is generally regarded as the strongest force
opposing euthanasia, some of the most powerful leaders of
the Catholic faith have been the most influential in opening
the door to new thinking on the subject. The great Catholic
scholar Sir Thomas More may be regarded as the father of
the euthanasia movement, though this was disputed in

Catholic World; and it was Pope Pius XII who modified the traditional doctrine of suffering and expressed approval of what is generally called passive or negative euthanasia. Catholics have recently been influential in the development of research foundations to study problems pertaining to birth and death and in promoting discussion of how they should be dealt with.

The most significant recent departure from traditional views has come from one of the foremost Catholic moral theologians in America today, Father Richard A. McCormick, a professor at the Joseph and Rose Kennedy Institute for the Study of Human Reproduction and Bioethics at Georgetown University. Writing in *America* and *JAMA* in July, 1974, Professor McCormick suggests that deformed babies with no potential for human relationships should be allowed to die. He suggests this course not only in cases where human relationships are "simply non-existent," but also where the potential, even if it exists, would be "utterly submerged and underdeveloped in the mere struggle to survive." The duty to preserve life, he said, must be limited by consideration of other values. Rejecting an "idolatry of life" attitude, he asserts that life is a relative rather than an absolute good, and that new medical and legal guidelines are badly needed.

Some Protestant ministers who previously opposed all euthanasia have modified their position recently. The Reverend Dr. Paul Ramsey, professor of religion at Princeton, is an example. In his 1970 book *The Patient as Person* he expressed the belief that there are some circumstances in which it would be ethical to hasten deliberately the process of death. He limited these circumstances to patients "when they are irretrievably inaccessible to human care," and "when there is a kind of prolonged dying in which it is medically impossible to keep severe pain at bay."

It is not entirely clear whether Dr. Ramsey is sanctioning active or only passive euthanasia, but he appears to approve of both when the patient is no longer a person. He asked such thought provoking questions as: How much blood are we going to give a terminal patient? Should cardiac surgery be performed to save a mongoloid child? If an old man who is slowly deteriorating gets pneumonia, should antibiotics be used to save him from death? Dr. Ramsey concluded that we need to discover moral limits of efforts to save life and recognize that death is not necessarily a disaster.

Theologians of all faiths in increasing numbers have spoken out against the useless prolongation of life, and many have endorsed the idea that death should be hastened in some circumstances.

Dr. Leslie Weatherhead, past president of the Methodist Conference of England, wrote in his book *The Christian Agnostic* that if a euthanasia bill were enacted and proper safeguards strictly imposed, he "would be willing to give a patient the Holy Communion and stay with him while a doctor, whose responsibility I should thus share, allowed a patient to lay down his useless body and pass on in dignity and peace into the next phase of being." This famous theologian expressed the view that far from its being cowardly or wrong to release the patient and his loved ones from their agony, it would be reasonable, liberating and altruistic. He also thought it "absurd casuistry" to maintain that if a doctor gives an overdose of narcotic deliberately to end the patient's life, this is ethically wrong, but if he gives the same amount of narcotic having in his mind the thought that he is relieving pain, it is ethically right.

Dr. Joseph Fletcher, who has for so long championed the right of the person to choose death, and urged that euthanasia, both active and passive, be made legally permissible in accord with proper safeguards, has stated in an article in the *American Journal of Nursing* that it is harder to justify morally letting someone die a slow, ugly, dehumanized death than it is to justify helping him to escape from such misery. He claims that acts of deliberate omission (i.e., passive euthanasia) are morally not different from acts of commission. "The plain hard logic of it is that the end or purpose of both negative and positive euthanasia is exactly the same: to contrive or bring about the patient's death. ... It is naive and superficial to suppose that because we don't 'do anything positively' to hasten a patient's death we have thereby avoided complicity in his death. Not doing anything is a decision to act every bit as much as deciding for any other deed." He said that negative euthanasia is already a *fait accompli* in modern medicine, and that so-called "code 90" stickers are put on many medical record jackets, indicating "Give no intensive care or resuscitation."

In the 1970 book *Deadline for Survival: A Survey of Moral Issues in Science and Medicine,* sponsored by the Academy of Religion and Mental Health, Kenneth W. Mann asserted that it is increasingly clear that the church's main focus should be on the quality of life, not on its mere existence. He said we must make intelligent use of new knowledge instead of being its victims; we must exercise moral responsibility.

Unquestionably revolutionary changes are taking place in the thinking and attitudes of many churchmen of all faiths and an ever increasing number realize that there can be no satisfactory solution to the problem of senseless suffering until new laws with adequate safeguards are enacted.

AUSTRALIAN SOCIETY ORGANIZED

An Australian Voluntary Euthanasia Society was formed in New South Wales in October 1973 with Tom Parramore as president; Mrs. Jennie Parramore is also a leader in the movement. Another society has since been organized in Victoria, with others expected in other states. A council of representatives will coordinate their activities.

Part III

Legalization of Euthanasia:
Arguments and Proposals

Chapter 8

WHAT THE OPPONENTS SAY

The most common arguments against euthanasia and its legalization are based on ancient religious teachings, the Hippocratic Oath formulated in the fourth century B.C., and unrealistic fears.

THE ROLES OF GOD AND MAN

1. *The Sixth Commandment says "Thou shalt not kill."* That, opponents say, is sufficient reason to condemn any active euthanasia and is justification for denouncing it as a violation of God's law.

Reply: If we are going to be bound by the command, "Thou shalt not kill," we would most certainly have to condemn all war in which men are sent to kill and be killed. It is ironic that a society that permits, and even requires, the killing of healthy young men in the armed forces, and of innocent civilians as well, against their will, refuses to permit a compassionate ending of the lives of hopelessly ill or aged persons who have nothing to live for and who want to die.

Moreover, many biblical scholars say that a proper translation of the commandment is "Thou shalt not mur-

..er." Murder is defined as "the unlawful killing of a human being with malice aforethought." Surely it is absurd to regard a merciful act of acceding to a person's wish to be put out of his suffering, or to be given the means to do so, as a malicious act. But present law, except in a few non-English speaking countries, does not distinguish between the two. Clearly it is time for law to enunciate and recognize such a distinction.

When cases of mercy killing have been brought to trial, judges and juries, moved by compassion when they learned the tragic circumstances, have almost always refused to convict the person of crime. Almost always they have found some pretext for circumventing the law, even when the evidence was clear that the person did in fact kill. Surely this is an undesirable state of affairs. If the laws are so inadequate and inhumane that compassionate people will not enforce them, it is time for new laws to be enacted. The intent of the Ten Commandments was obviously to promote justice for all men and advance their welfare. Laws should do the same thing.

The greatest commandment is to love one's fellow man. Jesus said, "Do unto others as you would that they should do unto you," and "Blessed are the merciful." There are many situations in which to end hopeless suffering would be a merciful act. The Bible says "There is . . . a time to be born, and a time to die . . . a time to kill, and a time to heal." (Ecclesiastes 3:2)

2. *Only God has the right to determine when life shall end. Man must not play God.*

Reply: If so, it would be wrong to prolong life. But every day doctors prolong life, and usually this has been regarded as good. Perhaps it would be no more a trespass of God's prerogative if, in hopeless cases, doctors were given authority to shorten it. We do not leave it to God alone to meet our needs throughout life; why should we abdicate our responsibility if and when the time comes when our greatest need and most fervent wish is for death? Perhaps man has a responsibility to help meet this final need too.

Society now recognizes that men and women have responsibility for intelligent planning of birth. Has not the time come to recognize also their responsibility for intelligent planning of death? Now that the successes of medical science and technology have made it possible for doctors to keep many bodies functioning technically almost indefinitely, they are in effect, already playing God, and in a way that often results only in increased suffering. Moreover, some doctors admit that they give enough drugs to end suffering even when they know it will hasten the death of the dying patient, and Pope Pius XII expressed approval of this in certain circumstances. It is clear that the medical profession is already dedicated to playing a role in determining when life shall end. And as Leroy Augenstein has said in his book *Come, Let Us Play God,* though we must never be arrogant and cannot be God, God has given us dominion over the earth, and man's increasing knowledge now forces him to make decisions of life and death that cannot be sidestepped. And Fletcher writes in *Morals and Medicine,* "In any ethical outlook of religious faith, men are people and not puppets. It is a false humility or a subtle determinism which asks us to 'leave things in God's hands.' "

3. *Human life is sacred and must not be taken by man.*

Reply: It is the life of the *person* that is sacred. A person has rights and one of those rights is surely the right to avoid needless suffering. Does society or any individual have the right to deny him the freedom to choose death to avoid hopeless suffering, provided that by so doing he neither harms another nor deprives society of useful services? Because human life is sacred, a person should not be degraded by being required to endure prolonged, useless suffering or humiliating deterioration of mind and body while waiting for physiological death.

In this day of organ transplants, there is much pressure to develop a new definition of death; already a few states have accepted brain death, i.e., absence of spontaneous brain function, as a new criterion for pronouncing a person dead. Many believe the time has come to give more attention to cerebral death—partial brain death—and even to what some have called "social death" and "psychological death." That is to say we should differentiate between death of the body and death of the person. If one is no longer conscious or able to communicate with others as a human being, one might say he is already socially, psychologically, and spiritually dead. It is the quality of life rather than longevity that is important. It is the person and his rights as a person that are sacred. The traditional concept of the sanctity of life must be modified by concern for the quality of life.

THE ROLE OF MEDICINE

4. *The Hippocratic Oath prohibits doctors from granting a request for euthanasia; it is a doctor's duty to save life, not destroy it.*

Reply: It is commonly said that doctors are bound by the Hippocratic Oath to use all means within their power to maintain life at all costs, but such a requirement is not stated in the oath. Doctors who take it feel pledged both to preserve life and to relieve suffering, and sometimes these duties present the doctor with a dilemma. In many cases if he prolongs the patient's life he also prolongs suffering. Then the only way to relieve suffering is to either end the life or render the patient unconscious. Many doctors now believe that the duty to relieve suffering should take priority over the duty to maintain life in some instances.

The oath states among other things, "I will follow that method of treatment which, according to my ability and judgment, I consider for the benefit of my patients. . . ." and "Into whatever houses I enter I will go into them for the benefit of the sick." In the translations in common use there is nothing in the oath that prevents a doctor from deciding that the inducement of death might be the noblest and most beneficial thing he can do for the patient.

Dr. Eric Cassell has pointed out that an ethic requiring beneficence toward the ill is not the same as an ethic requiring preservation of life at all costs:

> Indeed it is the perversion of "do benefit but no harm" into "preserve life at all costs" that has gotten us into trouble—and not solely in the care of the aged. . . . Profound problems arise for society when considerations of a human being as a "person" and the utility of death for life are excluded from the operating purview of doctors. . . . The effort to save life at all costs has not only in many instances made a mockery of life, it has stolen from us the utility and meaning of death.

The clause in the oath that states, "I will give no deadly drugs" was aimed at preventing the practice of some doctors in the time of Hippocrates of entering a conspiracy with politicians who wanted the death of their opponents, according to the historian Ludwig Edelstein.

Many medical schools today do not require their students to pledge themselves to the oath, and many physicians have never done so. Moreover, the demand today for a revised oath and for new medical guidelines is increasing. If man can promulgate such an oath, then he can also revise it. Hippocrates, who lived more than 2,000 years ago, could not possibly have foreseen many of the problems physicians face today in this age of oxygen tents, dialysis machines, blood transfusions, intravenous feeding and organ transplants.

Medical schools in the past have mainly ignored the subject of death and dying and have taught that life, no matter what its quality, must be maintained at all costs. Death was viewed as an enemy that should always be fought to the very end. Today views are changing; some medical schools now realize that doctors must be trained to deal more forthrightly and humanely with dying patients. An increasing number of doctors believe that life should be ended when distress cannot be relieved or life has become meaningless with no reasonable hope of recovery, and they recognize that separate judgments must be made in each case. Such clichés as "Preserve the life of the patient" are tempting escapes from responsibility, but they ignore the individual needs of the person.

5. *There would always be the possibility of a mistaken diagnosis and judgment of incurability or remission.*

Reply: No one is omniscient, so this is a possibility. But the chance of a mistaken diagnosis in advanced terminal cases is negligible. Even if there is some doubt in certain cases, when prognosis is made by two or more doctors after such open collaboration as should ordinarily be required by a good euthanasia law, the chance of significant error is infinitesimal. Moreover, since the law would in no case be mandatory, a diagnosis of incurability would not necessitate euthanasia. The decision would still be in the hands of the patient or his family if he were not of testamentary capacity. Legal safeguards would protect his right to live if that were his wish.

6. *Future discoveries hold a promise of a cure just around the corner; a disease or condition considered incurable today may be curable tomorrow.*

Reply: This too is possible, and, in fact, likely. However, for a person who is already in the advanced stages of a terminal illness or who has had massive brain injury, it is highly unlikely that there will be a discovery capable of undoing the irreversible damage and deterioration that has already taken place. It is a cruel hoax for doctors or others to pretend otherwise. Moreover we must ask, is it fair to deny a dying patient the freedom to choose merciful death just because someone else might like to hold out a little longer in the hope of some discovery that might conceivably permit him to live a little longer?

7. *The legalization of euthanasia would destroy the patient's confidence in his doctor. A patient would view his physician as an executioner instead of a healer; he would be anxious lest he or the nurses end his life.*

Reply: This argument is often used by opponents to frighten people into opposing any euthanasia law no matter how adequate its safeguards. A good law, however, would, on the contrary, give further protection to the person's right to live. Any termination of life contrary to the patient's wish would still be murder and punishable as such. The law would provide only for merciful action taken at the request of the patient if he is conscious, or at the request of his next of kin or guardian if he is irreversibly *non compos mentis.* This argument of the opponents is as illogical as it would be to argue that surgery should not be permitted lest the doctor "do the patient in."

For many people, it would inspire confidence and relieve anxiety instead of creating fear to know that their physician could legally carry out their wishes if the time should come when they are permanently incapacitated and want to die.

8. *Many doctors oppose any euthanasia legislation.*

Reply: This is true, although recent surveys have shown that many doctors favor it. In both England and the United States, doctors have been in the forefront in pointing out the need for legislation. Many of those who argue against legalization admit that they sometimes make decisions to stop treatment, and some privately admit that they prescribe drugs in doses that are lethal. Surely this kind of secretive action should not be encouraged or sanctioned.

If the action is morally justifiable, it should be legally permissible. Doctors should abide by the law and by medical guidelines openly decided upon by the medical profession. Clandestine action is to be deplored; it is dangerous business.

Changed times and conditions require that vital decisions be made only after open consultation; but as long as the law remains unchanged, many doctors will be unwilling to risk open discussion of discontinuing treatment, much less any hastening of death. Some will risk taking secret action; others will continue to refuse their dying patient's request for either active or passive euthanasia until new legislation is enacted. Under present law, the right of the person to choose euthanasia is not recognized; as a result, whether or not a patient gets his wish granted depends on the views of a particular doctor and his willingness to risk violation of law. This ought not to be, even if some doctors do want it that way. It inevitably opens the door to abuse and unequal treatment of patients. It is well known that the medical profession is a conservative body that has usually opposed new legislation such as that pertaining to birth control, abortion, and Medicare.

FACING DEATH

9. *Very few would request euthanasia even if it were legal. Nobody wants to die.*

Reply: Various surveys have shown that this simply is not true. For example, a National Opinion Poll of 2,000 doctors in England revealed that 48.6 per cent had been asked by a dying patient for euthanasia. Countless nurses, chaplains and clergymen who attend the dying testify that many patients do indeed want death and ask for it. Moreover, the high number of suicides by the elderly is proof that many reach the stage where their preference for death is so great they take their own lives in desperation. A 1973 report of the World Health Organization which gave suicide statistics for various countries concluded that while there had been an increase in suicide in the younger age groups, most suicides continued to occur among the elderly.

Some physicians, among them Dr. Cicely Saunders, have asserted, "We never get asked for euthanasia." But unknown numbers of dying patients might ask for death had they not been taught that such a request is wrong. Some have been taught that suffering is part of the divine plan for the good of man's soul, and that it must be accepted willingly. But it is likely that once euthanasia became generally recognized as a moral and legal act, desirable in some hopeless cases, this reluctance to ask for it would diminish. And even if only a few patients wanted it, there still remains no justification for denying them the right to choose it.

10. *Patients racked with pain or suffering from a temporary mental depression might make impulsive and ill-considered requests for euthanasia.*

Reply: A good euthanasia law would prevent the granting of such a request. Safeguards would require that at least two qualified physicians certify that there was no reasonable prospect of recovery. In addition there would be a waiting period before authorization would be given for the administration of euthanasia.

11. *Most deaths are peaceful, and modern pain-relieving drugs make euthanasia unnecessary.*

Reply: It is true that there are powerful pain-killing drugs today, and it is also true that many people die peacefully. But the fact remains that there are many kinds of distress that cannot be controlled without rendering the patient unconscious, and many of the so-called peaceful deaths come only after a long period of great suffering.

For many patients there is the terror of breathlessness, uncontrollable vomiting, paralysis, incontinence, inability to swallow, and sheer weakness and helplessness. Often there is loss of sight and hearing, and anxiety over the financial burden, grief and hardship that their prolonged period of illness is causing their families. Drugs cannot alleviate many of these problems. John Hinton, in his study of dying, reported that 15 to 30 per cent of dying patients have a difficult time at the end. In human terms, this is certainly a lot of suffering to prolong.

And even if drugs are effective in dulling pain, the question must arise, what is the point of continuing in an unconscious state while medical bills mount, and the family's sadness and burden become intolerable?

THE DANGER OF ABUSE

12. *Legalization would lead to abuse of the law and foul play.* The heirs or enemies of an invalid or dying patient might pressure doctors to hasten death.

Reply: Abuses of laws are always possible, but this is no justification for not enacting and enforcing a good law designed to protect and extend the rights and welfare of all persons. The possibility of abuse by heirs and enemies exists at present and would only be reduced by a good euthanasia law designed to dispel the present trend toward secrecy of action. Any abuses that might arise from legalization would be insignificant compared with the anguish that now results from forcibly prolonging the life of patients who want to die.

13. *Legalization of voluntary euthanasia would be the opening wedge to state-imposed, compulsory euthanasia and Nazi-like elimination of all unwanted persons.*

Reply: The "wedge argument" or "slippery rope" argument is a device used to try to defeat many kinds of legislation, and if heeded, would prevent almost any kind of innovative legislation regardless of its merit. Though some may sincerely think that there is a real danger in any legislation, many opponents use the wedge argument to arouse an emotional response instead of a reasoned one. The shock and horror of the Nazi crimes are still so vivid that everyone rightly wants to avoid any possibility of such terrible action. But to argue that the enactment of good legislation would lead to police-state action is fallacious and indefensible. As C. R. Sweetingham, secretary of the Voluntary Euthanasia Society of England, has said, "Humane proposals may lead to more humane ones but not to inhumane ones." What the Nazis did was not "mercy killing" but merciless killing, done secretly and in violation of German law.

As long as we have a free society in which policies and practices are openly discussed and legislation arrived at by democratic process, there is no need to have such fears. On the contrary, the safeguards of a good law would protect the patient's right to live and prevent the kind of secret action employed by doctors in Germany in which the rights of the patient and his family were completely ignored and secret action taken without their knowledge, much less consent.

We ought not let a rightful abhorrence for what was done by the Nazis obscure the wisdom and compassion underlying present day proposals for euthanasia which would, instead of violating individual human rights, protect and extend them and do so in accordance with the best democratic principles, and with legal safeguards.

MORAL DILEMMAS

14. *The patient who had become a burden might feel pressure to sacrifice himself in consideration of others and request euthanasia.*

Reply: John Donne's reply to this first objection seems a good rebuttal: "and, in a shipwreck, may I not give my plank to another and drown?" Captain Oates of the Antartic Expedition, on becoming sick, went to voluntary death rather than endanger the lives of his comrades, Martyrs, saints, and heroes have been lauded for risking or sacrificing their lives for others, and nowhere in the Bible is suicide condemned. If a person is in an irremediable condition and has become a grievous burden to his family and friends as well as himself, is there anything wrong with his wanting his family to be spared what in some cases may be disastrous consequences of caring for him or financing his care over a long period of time? And if he is helpless and completely dependent on others and wants his death to be hastened partly because he wants the hospital facilities and medical personnel required to keep him alive to be made available to others whose lives could be saved, and perhaps wants to make the organs of his body available for transplantation purposes, should this be regarded as wrong and be denied him?

As for pressures from those who stand to gain from one's demise, it is always possible that some unscrupulous person would attempt to circumvent the law and pressure old or dying persons to request euthanasia; there is no doubt that vigilance is needed, just as it is now needed in regard to possible pressures on such persons to make changes in their wills. But an individual would be free to reject such pressure as long as he is of testamentary capacity, and a good law would give him more protection from unscrupulous, scheming relatives or doctors than he has now when secrecy of action by a single doctor is being encouraged by those who say, "Don't legalize euthanasia; just leave the matter to the doctor."

15. *"I believe in passive euthanasia but not in active euthanasia."*

Reply: Once the difficult decision has been made to terminate treatment because there is no chance of recovery, it would often be much more humane to deliberately end the person's life. Why should the patient be required to wait for "natural" death, which is often a long period of cruel suffering, after all concerned have agreed that further treatment is useless and that death would be a blessing? It seems there is no logical reason to deny the right to choose active euthanasia in such cases. Those who object do so because of their unwillingness to break with tradition, religious dogma, superstition and fear. Everyone has the right to hold such views and to refuse euthanasia of any kind, but no one should have the prerogative to deny others with different views the right to a deliberate hastening of death.

The dividing line between active and passive euthanasia is often less real than is generally supposed or admitted. Professor Louis Lasagna of the University of Rochester Medical Center claims that the difference is a nondifference—"If one is murder, the other is too." He thinks the distinction made by Pope Pius XII is "pretty darn fuzzy." According to Professor Yale Kamisar, the physician who withholds life-preserving treatment "commits criminal homicide by omission." The difference is less one of kind than of degree or speed of death's arrival. It is true that one is a negative kind of action while the other is positive, and some doctors and others assert that there is a definite psychological difference. But as Fletcher has said, it is morally evasive to suppose that we can condemn positive acts to hasten death while approving negative strategies to achieve the same purpose. And Dr. John M. Freeman of Hopkins said at the time of controversy over the mongoloid child that was left to die, "It is time that society and medicine stopped perpetuating the fiction that withholding treatment is ethically different from terminating life."

16. *"I believe in voluntary euthanasia but not in involuntary euthanasia."*

Reply: As stated earlier in this book, any compulsory euthanasia without regard for the wishes of the patient or his legal guardian, as practiced by the Nazis, and as is usually implied by "involuntary euthanasia," is to be condemned. But it is necessary to distinguish between such action and what we have called nonvoluntary euthanasia—

that is, action taken at the request of the legal guardian in cases in which the patient is not of testamentary capacity, and taken only in accord with legal safeguards designed to protect the best interests of the patient. Many who favor euthanasia only when it is at the request of the patient seem to fail to recognize man's responsibility for making decisions on behalf of those dependent on them. They are content to be guided by religious dogmas and clichés that assert or imply that human life must be stretched to the limit regardless of its quality. Under present laws the next of kin or other legal guardian accepts the responsibility for committing a dependent loved one to an institution for the rest of his or her life. Surely laws should also provide that they might accept responsibility for having a life ended when that clearly would be a merciful act.

17. *There would be borderline cases in which decisions would be difficult, and a law permitting euthanasia would result in making more problems than it would solve.* This would put too heavy a burden on doctors and families and result in feelings of guilt.

Reply: Undoubtedly difficult decisions would have to be made in borderline cases, and certainly where such doubt exists, no euthanasia should be permitted. Of course, if one can disregard an individual's suffering and his right to merciful death, it is easier to act on the simple rule of never permitting euthanasia. But as Joseph Fletcher wrote in *Morals and Medicine,* "Choice and responsibility are the very heart of ethics, and the *sine qua non* of a man's moral status. . . . The whole history of man's moral growth . . . has been the steady march upward in the scale of responsibility from predetermined to self-determined action. . . . The dimensions of our moral responsibility expand, of necessity, with the advances in medical science and medical technology." Value judgments are often not easy to make but they are the mark of intelligent, mature adults.

The burden on doctors would actually be lightened if euthanasia were legally permissible, as they would be spared the difficult experience of having to refuse a patient's request when they know that death would be a great blessing. They could have open discussions with other doctors and the family, and instead of having to make any decision alone, their responsibility in decision-making would be shared with others. This sense of shared responsibility would dispel any feelings of guilt that might otherwise arise.

Doctors would then have the peace of mind that comes from having ended useless human suffering. Similarly, members of the family might have hard decisions to make, but many would undoubtedly feel less guilt having relieved their loved one of senseless suffering, than they have now, knowing that it is really inhumane to keep him alive and to refuse him the peace of death. Much of the present fear of a sense of guilt is based on traditional teachings and present failure of law to differentiate between a compassionate and a malicious act.

18. *Legalization of euthanasia would cause a general weakening of public and social morality and a demoralization of doctors.*

Reply: Opponents of any proposed new social legislation try to frighten people into believing that dire consequences would follow. But if the law is well written and its safeguards are adequate without being too burdensome, and if its purpose is to meet a humanitarian need, there need be no fear, provided the safeguards are enforced.

Instead of causing a weakening of morality there is every reason to think that legalization would increase confidence in man's capacity and will to match noble words of compassion with noble deeds. The present tendency to encourage violation of law in order to be compassionate is indefensible. It is also morally indefensible to condemn human beings to useless suffering or a meaningless existence. We need a change in law in keeping with humanitarian instincts in today's world. Without such a change our problems will increase until they become unmanageable.

EUTHANASIA

Justifications and Specifications

GROUNDS FOR JUSTIFYING EUTHANASIA AND ITS LEGALIZATION

1. *Compassion and plain common sense for today's world must be the basis of any consideration of euthanasia.* A person should not be required to endure useless suffering or the indignity of prolonged and humiliating helplessness and deterioration of mind or body or both, when there is no reasonable possibility of meaningful recovery. If euthanasia were legally permissible, the fear many people now have of prolonged dying and dependency would be greatly reduced. It is only logical that society allow useless suffering to be ended.

2. *The right to die with dignity should be recognized as a basic human right.* Just as the right to live is a fundamental human right, to be protected from all incursions, so the right to die should also be recognized and protected.

The Declaration of Independence states that "life, liberty and the pursuit of happiness" are unalienable rights. It does not, however, state that there is any compulsion to live when the pursuit of happiness is impossible because of irremediable incapacitation of body or mind. Nor does any other legal document state that the right to live implies compulsion to live.

The preamble to the U. N. Declaration of Human Rights declares that we aspire to "A world in which human beings shall enjoy . . . freedom from fear," but today fear of prolonged suffering, helplessness and dependency are being recognized, more and more, as the greatest fear of the elderly and others. The preamble states also, "The recognition of the inherent dignity . . . of all members of the human family is the foundation of freedom." Article 5 of the Declaration states, "No one shall be subjected to torture," but countless incapacitated, aged, and dying persons have to endure torture today while waiting for death, even though, of course, no intent to torture is involved.

As long ago as 1891, the U.S. Supreme Court stated, "No right is held more sacred, or is more carefully guarded, by the common law, than the right of every individual to the possession and control of his own person, free from all restrain or interference of others, unless by clear and unquestionable authority of law" (Union Pacific v. Botsford).

Cardozo in the 1914 Schloendorff case held, "Every human being of adult years and sound mind has a right to determine what shall be done with his own body." Brandeis spoke in the Olmstead case in 1928 of "the right to be left alone," and a Kansas court in the 1960 Natanson case held, "Each man is considered to be master of his own body and he may, if he be of sound mind, expressly prohibit the performance of life-saving surgery, or other medical treatment."

And the ruling of the Supreme Court in Griswold v. Connecticut that there is a constitutionally guaranteed right to privacy should support the claim that the individual has the right to decide the extent to which his life should be prolonged.

Thus it would seem that the right of a person to choose permanent relief from suffering or a meaningless existence is a basic right; also it would seem that parents or other guardians should not only have the right but be encouraged to accept the responsibility of requesting that persons entrusted to their care be spared useless suffering or a tragic existence.

Those who oppose euthanasia on moral or religious grounds have, of course, the right to do so. But they should not be permitted to block legislation that would permit others with different beliefs to exercise their right to choose death for themselves or for persons for whom they are legally responsible. The epithets of murderer or executioner, often hurled freely by opponents of euthanasia, are patently inapplicable to the act of mercifully ending a painful and meaningless life.

It should be noted, however, that "the right to die with dignity" can be interpreted in various ways. To some it means only the right to be left alone to die without unnatural prolongation of life by modern techniques and skills. To others it means the right to choose an end to life and to have the services of a qualified doctor in bringing it about painlessly. There can be little doubt that as long as we permit the former of these interpretations, while forbidding the latter, we will find ourselves faced with increasingly inconsistent and hypocritical moral situations.

3. *Numerous highly regarded theologians, ethicists, physicians and others have expressed the conviction that euthanasia, both active and passive, is morally justified in certain circumstances.* Although this is not in itself justification for administering euthanasia, it is impressive and significant that so many responsible people now believe that it is morally indefensible to deny release from hopeless suffering or the indignity of helplessness. Indeed, they believe that society is not justified in denying release from hopeless suffering or indignity. Though some persons still believe in the redemptive value of suffering and condemn euthanasia for anyone, there is now widespread agreement that the relief of useless, hopeless suffering is morally justified and that at least passive

euthanasia should be permitted in certain circumstances. And as this book has documented, numerous religious leaders have indicated that it is their view that active euthanasia is also morally permissible in many cases, and that to deny it is morally indefensible.

While the Catholic Church and many fundamentalist and other conservative groups strongly condemn any intentional hastening of death. and such action is still a criminal act according to current law, Pope Pius XII stated that it is morally right to take action to alleviate pain and suffering even if by so doing it would hasten the death of the dying patient; few would disagree with this view, though opinions still differ regarding the ethics of intentionally ending a life. But it is evident that there is a rapidly growing number of persons of all religious faiths who approve of the right to positive as well as negative euthanasia in certain circumstances and believe that the freedom to choose death should not be denied to irremediably ill persons.

4. *What is morally right should be made legally permissible.* The Judeo-Christian ethic demands of man that he act mercifully. Yet mercy and legality—as it now stands—can pull a man in two opposite directions at once. Some kindly physicians obey the injunction, "Do unto others as you would that they should do unto you," and without legal authority prescribe or administer a lethal drug or take other action that has the effect of ending the life of a dying or hopelessly incapacitated patient. Surely it should not be necessary for a doctor to have to choose between such merciful action and violation of the law. Society has the duty to make legally permissible action that is merciful and widely recognized as morally right. It is a dangerous course to encourage secret action in violation of the law.

A sound euthanasia law would be permissive—not/ mandatory—and no doctor, nurse, or other person would be required to take any action contrary to his wishes, judgment, conscience, or religious principles and no patient would ever be required to submit to either positive or negative euthanasia against his will.

WHO SHOULD BE ELIGIBLE FOR EUTHANASIA? AND WHO SHOULD DECIDE?

To answer these questions it might be helpful to consider the following:

If it were legally permissible for a physician to follow the course requested, which course do you think you would want for yourself if suffering from a condition from which there was no reasonable hope of meaningful recovery, remission, or happiness? Would you request (a) that the physician use every possible means to prolong your life as long as possible regardless of uncontrollable suffering, economic consequences, and grief or hardship for your family, (b) that treatment be terminated and suffering be kept to the minimum until "natural" death occurs, even if that would result in increased distress or being drugged into unconsciousness, or (c) that death be induced painlessly in accordance with your wishes and legal safeguards?

And if you were in an irreversible state of unconsciousness, senility, or otherwise not of testamentary capacity, which of the above courses do you think should be followed, provided your next of kin or legal guardian requested it?

Also, if for any reason you think you would never ask for euthanasia—either passive or active—for yourself or for anyone for whom you might be legally responsible, do you think you are justified in opposing laws that would make it permissible for others?

A Special Plea on Behalf of Severely Defective Infants

With the medical developments of the Seventies has come a new concern with the problems of severely defective infants. In ancient times and in many cultures, seriously defective children were not allowed to live, and until recently, a high proportion of these infants died soon after birth. But the successes of modern medicine now provide defective infants with a greatly increased lifespan, thus adding to the extent of the problem for the children themselves, their parents, and society. And as long as society and parents adhere to the teaching that life must be prolonged as long as possible, the problem is bound to continue to grow.*

A case that has received much attention is that of a mongoloid infant born at Johns Hopkins Hospital that was left to starve to death because its parents refused to permit the surgery needed to remove an intestinal obstruction (see p. 46). A film describing the case and the doctors' dilemma entitled "Who Shall Survive?" was presented at an international symposium on human rights, mental retardtion, and biomedical research conducted by the Joseph P. Kennedy, Jr. Foundation in Washington, D.C. in 1971.

Discussants differed widely regarding how such defective infants should be dealt with, but all agreed that merely awaiting the natural death by starvation was a less than desirable method. The film graphically depicted the power to "play God" with which modern medicine has endowed man. Clearly there is now an urgent need for new guidelines for dealing with such problems.

In 1973 two pediatricians, Drs. Raymond S. Duff and A. G. M. Campbell at Yale-New Haven Hospital reported in the *New England Journal of Medicine* that 43 infants had been deliberately allowed to die with the consent of the parents between January, 1970 and July, 1972. The doctors involved said that the infants' deformities could not have been overcome to afford "meaningful humanhood." The

*For further information on defective infants, see Eckstein, Engelhardt, John Fletcher, and Sidel.

infants ranged in age from a few hours to several months; they accounted for 14 per cent of the infant deaths in the special care nursery during that two and a half-year period. The hospital's chief of staff said that to withhold treatment in such hopeless cases was nothing new but rather accepted practice in many hospitals, although people are often afraid to report it. Nothing was said in the report about taking positive steps to induce death, but the doctor involved states, "If working out these dilemmas in ways such as we suggest is in violation of law, we believe the law should be changed."

I myself became convinced that it was cruel to keep severely defective infants alive as the result of experiences in state hospitals for the mentally defective. As a college professor I arranged annually for senior students in abnormal psychology to visit the state hospital. The sight of one little boy in particular made a lasting impression that can never be erased. On our first visit the boy, a hydrocephalic, was about four years old. He was lying on his back in his crib with his monstrous head on the pillow, and his eyes, like those of a trapped animal, peered out from their sunken sockets. His tiny arms thrashed about wildly, hitting his huge head, which was badly bruised from such beating. The next year we visited him he had been provided with padded gloves to ease the blows he kept giving his head, but his head, nevertheless, had many sores both from the knocks he had given it and from the sheer weight of its rubbing on the pillow. The following year that pathetic little boy was still there. This time his arms were tied to the sides of the crib so he could no longer beat his head.

Many of the students and their teacher came away convinced that our society has a strange concept of what is right or Christian when we permit such cruelty to an innocent little child. Who can justify it? Though the fluid was drained off occasionally to reduce the inner pressure on the child's head, there was absolutely no possibility of his ever being anything but a helpless, hopeless bed patient. Is it not perfectly clear that such a defective child should be painlessly put out of his misery either at birth, or as soon thereafter as diagnosis makes it possible for physicians to predict with reasonable certainly that life can be nothing but tragic? Can anyone honestly argue that it is more moral or humane to have such a severely deformed and mentally defective child institutionalized for the rest of his life, or cared for at home at the risk of the health and happiness of his family, rather than have his life ended?

Although the various euthanasia societies have not included such cases in their bills—these have applied only to those capable of requesting euthanasia for themselves—it is significant that many of the doctors who have been the pioneers of the movement to legalize euthanasia have made a special plea on behalf of defective infants. One critic of any euthanasia, Yale Kamisar, has chided the euthanasia societies for excluding tragically defective infants from their proposed bills. He said that if compassion is the chief justification for euthanasia, surely these helpless infants should be in the forefront of consideration.

In 1901 Dr. Goddard advocated euthanasia for hopeless idiots and others incapable of improvement; in the 1930's Drs. Wolbarst, Roberts, and Kennedy urged that euthanasia be legalized for severely mentally deficient and congenitally deformed children. Dr. Roberts said he would not hesitate to violate the law to end such "human mental monstrocities," and Dr. Kennedy strongly advised that euthanasia be legalized for them. In the 1950's Dr. Walter C. Alvarez strongly supported euthanasia for severely defective children as well as for those adults requesting it.

But today, due to new medical skills and devices, more and more congenitally defective infants are being kept alive for many years. Physicians often go to great lengths, including resuscitation and surgery, to prolong the lives of these unfortunates, just as they do for the hopelessly brain-damaged, the senile, and the dying for whom there can be no happiness.

A review of the cases of mercy killing—Brownhill, Re-pouille, Greenfield, Braunsdorf and others—that have been brought to trial reveals again and again the same pattern. A parent after caring devotedly for a helpless idiot or imbecile for many years, unable to endure any longer the hopelessness of the situation, finally ended the child's life. Seldom has a person served a prison sentence for such an act, even when it was in clear violation of criminal law. Judges and juries usually feel only sympathy for such people when they learn of the tragic condition of the child and intolerable burden it created.

Public opinion has nearly always been on the side of the person who ended the hopeless suffering. In the famous case of the thalidomide baby in Belgium, Madame van de Put testified about having killed her eight-day-old infant, "I just thought you could not let a baby like that live. I thought it could never be happy in its whole life." Public opinion was such that when she was pronounced not guilty, wild applause broke out in the courtroom.

One of the many cases that demonstrate the cumulative burden on both parents and child is that of Herman H. Nagel of Arizona who, on learning that he had cancer, killed his 28-year-old daughter Betty, a life-long victim of cerebral palsy. He feared dying before her and leaving her helpless. The father said "No one knows better than I the torture she went through; she was completely helpless. I dressed her, fed her and looked after her every need. Her condition was getting worse and she was in constant pain." Nagel was acquitted on grounds of temporary insanity.

Dr. N. J. Berrill, a Canadian zoology professor, deplored the way society pushes defectives out of sight by placing them in institutions, where they live out their futile and tragic lives. The decision as to whether they should live or die is thus avoided. The issue must be faced squarely, according to Berrill, who wrote, "When the abnormality verges on the monstrous or if the brain itself is so poorly formed or so badly damaged that only an incoherent idiot can emerge, for what reason should it be kept alive as long as possible at great expense and effort? . . . If there is no possibility for the growth and flowering of the human spirit, there is no reason for existence of the human body."

Though some doctors do in fact decide not to respirate profoundly defective infants at birth, it appears that the only case in the United States in which a doctor was brought to trial for failure to save the life of a defective infant was that of Dr. H. J. Haiselden of Chicago. In 1917 he allowed a baby born hopelessly deformed and mentally defective to die by not performing an operation which would have saved the child's life. The baby's mother had approved the doctor's decision not to act, and Dr. Haiselden was exonerated, although his medical career was ended as a result of the publicity.

THE EXTENT OF THE PROBLEM.   According to the 1973 fact sheet of National Foundation—March of Dimes, every year about 250,000 American babies are born with some defect, mental or physical; this is "about seven per cent of all live births." And in the 1962 report of the President's Panel on Mental Retardation, it is estimated that one child out of every 1,000 born is so severely or profoundly retarded mentally that it will need constant care or supervision for as long as it lives; there are about 4,000 such births a year. No statistics pertaining to the number of babies born mentally defective can be entirely reliable, but an estimate commonly quoted by the U.S. Department of Health, Education and Welfare, is that 3 out of every 100 children are born mentally retarded to the extent that they can benefit little or not at all from regular school classes. According to the

1970 report of the President's Task Force on the Mentally Handicapped, the total number of residents in institutions for the mentally defective at any one time is about 215,000; many of these have severe physical as well as mental disabilities. The report stated that the cost of custodial care, special education, and other services is 2.5 billion dollars a year. It is generally estimated that the lifetime care of a severely retarded child comes to well over 100,000 dollars.

One of the most common of the birth defects is *mongolism*, more properly called Down's Syndrome. It occurs once in every 600 to 700 births, and no cure is known. The child is both mentally and physically defective, with an IQ typically of about 30, though it may range from 20 to 50.* Rarely does a mongoloid attain a mental age beyond that of a five-year old.* Parents who care for them at home often become emotionally attached to them, since they tend to be affectionate, but by adolescence the grim reality of their future becomes increasingly apparent. A few learn to read and write a little and even do routine tasks, but many can do none of these things and will always be dependent on others to care for them as long as they live. (see p. 251)

Many mongoloids are born with obstructed intestines, heart disease, and susceptibility to pneumonia and other diseases that in the past caused them to die at an early age. But with new surgical skills and the use of antibiotics, the survival rate has greatly increased.

It is now known, due to a scientific breakthrough in 1959, that the Down's syndrome is caused by the presence of an extra chromosome—there are 47 instead of 46—but it is still not known what causes the extra chromosome, although it is attributed to some drug or other environmental factor affecting prenatal growth, rather than to a hereditary factor. It is now possible to detect this defect before birth, and an increasing number of expectant mothers decide on an abortion if this defect is discovered. If the defect is not discovered before birth, it is possible for the diagnosis to be made with certainty at almost any large hospital at the time of birth.

Only two of the other kinds of severe birth defects will be mentioned here. Spina bifida (open spine), often with meningomyelocele, is a malformation of the central nervous system in which the spine fails to develop properly and usually protrudes from the surface of the body; it results in varying degrees of irreversible paralysis especially of legs, bladder, and bowels, and often results in destruction of brain tissue and an abnormally large head.** Until about ten years ago, 80 per cent died at birth or soon after, but today many of these children have numerous operations and now about 75 per cent survive. (see p. 251)

Tay-Sachs disease is an inherited genetic disorder that causes destruction of the nervous system. It affects fewer children than mongolism but is a more serious defect. The infant may appear normal for about six months, but after that point there is a fairly rapid deterioration, and death is certain at an early age, usually by the fourth year. The suffering of the parents is great as they helplessly watch the deterioration of their child while waiting for death. The financial burden is also great. One such child was paralyzed, blind, and mentally retarded. She was cared for at home until the parents could no longer care for her or endure her suffering, and then put in a hospital where she died at four and a half. The hospital bill was nearly 60,000 dollars.

PREVENTING BIRTH DEFECTS   According to the March of Dimes, it is now believed that about 20 per cent of birth defects are hereditary, 20 per cent caused by circumstances at or before birth, and 60 per cent a combination of both. These defects are permanent, and although many children can be helped to overcome their disability to some extent, no amount of loving care or training can make them normal or near normal. Therefore, while every effort must continue to assist such unfortunate children, it is necessary to focus special attention on the prevention of such abnormalities. This point is emphasized in a 1974 report by the World Council of Churches, "Genetics and the Quality of Life," which describes the importance of genetic counseling and says it is important for the churches to help men and women understand and discharge their responsibilities in this regard.

Recent research has added greatly to knowledge of the causes of these congenital defects, so it should be possible to reduce the number, but new causes keep arising at a disturbing rate. There is a very real possibility that at the current rate of population growth, the total number of infants born with congenital defects may increase rather than decrease. Gerald Leach, in his book *The Biocrats: Implications of Medical Progress,* writes of the "surging rise in the number of physically and mentally crippled children," and attributes it, at least in part, to the population explosion. Readers are referred to Hamilton's *The New Genetics and the Future of Man,* and the Institute of Society, Ethics and the Life Sciences for in-depth coverage of these questions.

In many ways our own technology is backfiring, creating new agents that may cause damage to the embryo or developing fetus. These include new forms of radiation and industrial chemicals, gene-damaging X-rays, atomic radiation, new viral diseases, some pesticides, food additives, tranquilizers, and various untested drugs. Rubella (German Measles) contracted by the mother during pregnancy and incompatability of the Rh factor are two other major causes of brain damage that are fortunately now preventable. The spread of Rubella vaccination will have a dramatic impact on the number of mentally and physically defective children born.

Another recent development is the discovery of the technique known an amniocentesis. The test involves inserting a needle into the womb and withdrawing some of the mother's amniotic fluid; analysis of the fluid enables doctors to detect many kinds of defective fetuses. As yet, however, the method is not feasible until about the sixteenth week of pregnancy, when abortion is not as simple and safe as it would be earlier.

It is predicted that within a couple of years a new instrument known as a "fetoscope" will allow doctors to look directly at a baby in its mother's womb and get a clear view of any physical defects. Some scientists look to the day when by genetic engineering or by surgery in utero, doctors will be able to prevent or correct birth defects, but it will be years before these techniques are developed and perfected.

Many newspaper reporters have recently been calling attention to the pathetic individuals hidden away in institutions across the land. Leon Dash in the *Washington Post,* for example, brought to public attention the tragic lives of 200 severely mentally defective individuals. Their ages ranged from 8 to 60, but all had mental ages of two to three. They lived in a Washington, D.C. institution called Forest Haven, where they required complete nursing care. Many had been there from early childhood and would remain there indefinitely. An editorial on the subject that the *Post* ran later said, "The heart cries out for something, anything, that could be done to alleviate this misery."

Another article in the *Post,* "Repackaging the Inquisition," by Nicholas von Hoffman, described the condition of the 2,600 residents at the Rosewood State Hospital, Maryland. About 1,000 of these were profoundly mentally retarded, with IQ's below 20; most of them had multiple physical handicaps; 800 were helpless, bedridden patients who had to be fed by hand. Would not painless death in infancy be more humane and therefore more moral than requiring this kind of existence year after year?

On the basis of an excellent follow-up study of 524 infants at the University of Sheffield Hospital suffering from myclomeningocele who were given intensive treatment, which included major operations for most of them, the British pediatrician Dr. John Lorber found that most were living pitiful, fruitless lives. He concluded, "Therapeutic efforts should be concentrated only on those who have the potential to benefit from treatment." He claims that accurate prognosis in such cases is possible from the day the child is born and thinks the pendulum has now swung too far in efforts to save such children.

At the June 11, 1974 hearings of the Senate subcommittee on Health, under the chairmanship of Senator Edward Kennedy, Warren Reich of the Bioethics Center at Georgetown University, an opponent of euthanasia, argued that a baby's life must always be saved if possible, no matter how severe the defects and how great the costs to the family and/or society. However, Dr. Raymond S. Duff, Associate Professor of Pediatrics at Yale University, predicted that if modern technology is used to force the survival of large numbers of the severely handicapped, a backlash could result because of the devastating financial and emotional effects on families, and the drain on taxpayers. He said this might lead to the chilling prospect of "socially mandated" death. Such a prospect is surely a more frightening possibility than the rather unlikely risk of a mistaken diagnosis. When Senator Kennedy asked Dr. Duff to estimate how many severely handicapped babies are left to die nationally, he replied, "I'm sure several thousand a year." (Reports of these hearings appeared in the *Washington Star* and the *New York Times*, June 12, 1974.)

It is encouraging to learn that according to a 1973 survey of nearly 2,000 adults conducted by sociologists of the National Opinion Research Center in Chicago for the *National Catholic Reporter,* a majority of Catholics, Protestants and Jews now favor abortion to prevent birth of a defective child. 83 per cent of the Protestants polled, 77 per cent of the Catholics, and 100 per cent of the Jews favored such abortions.

It would be a good idea if prospective parents were to face ahead of time the possibility of having a seriously defective child and decide what their wish would be if a child such as one of the following were born to them: a child born with a grotesque head, the brain partially missing and a mass of tumors at the base of the spine—it could never develop normally though it might survive for three or four years; a child born with a cancerous growth that was eating away at the optic nerves leaving him blind and causing him to shriek with pain almost constantly, and threatening him with a slow and painful death in a year or so, or a child such as the thalidomide baby Corrine.

The Plight of the Elderly

A discussion of euthanasia would be incomplete without mention of the conditions under which many elderly and aged persons live out their days. According to the 1970 Census Bureau report of the U.S. Department of Commerce, about 800,000 persons 65 and over live in institutions and other group quarters, and of this number about one-third require nursing care. More recent figures put the total at over one million in nursing homes and other institutions, not including general hospitals. Recent studies of nursing homes and other institutions for the aged have revealed shocking conditions under which many are "waiting their time." Fortunately many people and agencies are now concentrating on improving those conditions.

The report in 1961 by J. H. Sheldon to the Birmingham Regional Hospital Board in England on its geriatric services did much to alert the public to the shocking conditions in which many old people and others die. The report stated that while many of those dying at home received devoted care by their relatives, some had frighteningly inadequate and impersonal care and experienced great hardship. In addition, the burden on other members of the family was often intolerable. Of those dying in hospitals, homes for the aged, nursing homes and institutions for the chronically ill, some were given excellent and devoted care, but many died in what Sheldon described as "human warehouses" and "storage space for patients."

Congressman David Pryor of Arkansas pointed out in 1971 after his investigation of nursing homes in the United States that nine out of ten of them exist for profit and that during the 1960's nursing homes became a glamor stock on the stock exchanges. In 1971, according to the *Washington Post,* about a million Americans of all ages were housed in approximately 20,000 nursing homes. The number has greatly increased since that time, and nearly one-third of the homes are not licensed. And as Haynes Johnson of the *Post* has stated, "Countless horror stories of deplorable conditions, callous treatment, heartless overcharging, and indifference have been documented by congressional and other investigators." Ralph Nader's *Old Age: The Last Segregation* is another exposé of such practices. And Nelson H. Cruikshank, president of the National Council of Senior Citizens, which has about three million members, has been among those effective in alerting the public to the plight of the elderly.

A 1968 report by the National Institute for Mental Health states, "A large and tragic group of patients in state mental hospitals are old people. Mental hospitals have long been used as a place to send the aging and senile whose families cannot or do not want to care for them. Many do not actually need psychiatric treatment and might not be in hospitals at all if other care were available. Yet state hospitals for many years have provided minimal custodial geriatric care to more than one-fourth of their entire resident population." Government statistics for 1974 indicate that there are about 100,000 persons aged 65 or over in state mental hospitals in the United States.

But the physical surroundings and conditions, though often distressing, do not approach the tragedy of the mental anguish that is often all too evident. One can only wonder how many, if any, of the residents of these "homes" willingly continue their existence.

The health and financial conditions of the aged add to their problems. John B. Martin, former commissioner of the Administration on Aging, has reported that four-fifths of those over 65 years of age have one or more chronic conditions, and of those over 75, only one in eight is free from some chronic health problem. Compounding the problem is financial stress; statistics for 1971 indicate that nearly five million, or one out of every four people in the United States aged 65 or over, live on or below the poverty level, often in extreme poverty. *Time,* in a 1970 article entitled "The Old in the Country of the Young," pointed out that for too many of the 20 million elderly in the United States, "the golden years" are a time of neglect, isolation, and despair.

Surely the time has come to face up to the sad possibilities with which many elderly persons are confronted. While every effort must be made to improve the conditions under which they live, there must also be consideration of their wishes to live or to die. Can any thoughtful person really think that it is more humane or moral to commit an elderly person to an institution for the rest of his life against his will rather than to permit him merciful termination of a hopeless existence if that is what he wishes?

Our society must become more sensitive to the needs and problems of the aging. Both their physical and psychological needs must be provided for, and their potential for valuable contributions to society more fully recognized. But attempts to prolong the lives of the aged and dying, beyond the point at which they themselves desire to die, seem cruel and unwarranted. It is essential that we develop without further delay a philosophy of life that provides for the acceptance of death when meaningful life has ended. For some, as Socrates said, "Death may be the greatest of human blessings."

It is to be hoped that the newly organized International Federation on Aging, based in Washington, D.C., will put the subject of euthanasia high on its list of priorities, and that efforts will be made at all levels—international, national, state, and local—to find a satisfactory solution.

Recently a new National Institute on Aging was established within the National Institutes of Health, by the 1974 Research on Aging Act. Hopefully it, too, will give serious consideration to ways of dealing with the suffering of the elderly who want to die, and of those in irreversible comas. This new agency for research on aging was a major recommendation of the 1971 White House Conference on Aging.

WHAT WOULD YOUR CHOICE BE?

It would be helpful if every adult would ask himself or herself which he thinks he or she would choose—prolongation of life as long as possible, or the release of death—if circumstances arose when there was no reasonable chance of a remission or recovery, as was the case in each of the following instances:

An 85-year-old patient described by Dr. Walter Sackett in Testimony before the 1971 White House Conference on Aging who had a terminal blood condition received three blood transfusions daily, to a total of 65, and the emergency resuscitation team was called six times before the man was allowed to die.

An 89-year-old woman whose physician described her as "a poor old soul who is totally deaf, totally blind, cannot speak and is totally paralyzed." She was being kept alive by intravenous feeding which the physician told the hospital superintendent she would like to order stopped. Permission was refused.

A veteran of World War II with no sight or hearing, no arms or legs, just a torso lying helplessly on a bed.

Many readers will doubtless recall some friend or member of their family who had a long period of senseless suffering before death finally came. Cases range from profoundly defective infants to chronic senility or helplessness and dependency at the other end of life. Prognosis may be certain and death near, or there may be some slight possibility of a temporary remission, and death still some distance away. What cannot be called into question is the extent of human suffering in all these cases.

Undoubtedly if a good euthanasia law were enacted, many difficult decisions would have to be made. Such difficult decisions are far preferable, however to the moral side-stepping of current law. Each individual case would be decided upon only after adequate consideration of all factors, and the concurrence of at least two physicians would be required to ensure well-reasoned and humane action.

---

* It is exceptional for the I.Q. to exceed 70 or the mental age to exceed eight or nine but with good care and training, a few reach higher mental levels and become self-supporting.

** The destruction of brain tissue and the large head are not generally thought to be *caused* by the spina bifida but by the hydrocephalus which accompanies it in about 4 out of 5 cases. In many, perhaps most, cases this may be controlled by a surgical shunting procedure.

Chapter 10

CURRENT EUTHANASIA
LEGISLATION AND
PROPOSALS FOR CHANGE

PRESENT LAWS REGARDING EUTHANASIA

Legislative Provisions for Euthanasia

Laws and court decisions regarding euthanasia vary from country to country. While no country has yet legalized euthanasia, in recent years in some non-English speaking countries—Belgium, France, Germany, Holland, and Italy, for instance—compassionate motive has been recognized in laws as an extenuating circumstance in mercy killings and cases of assisted suicide. Especially when the action was taken at the request of the patient, penalties for such killings are very lenient. Switzerland's revised Criminal Code of 1942 provided that punishment could be as little as three days' imprisonment or even merely a fine. In Uruguay and Peru a person who aids or abets a suicide from an altruistic motive is exempt from penalty; and article 37 of the penal Code of Uruguay provides that though mercy killing is regarded as a crime, "The judges are authorized to forego punishment of a person whose previous life has been honorable where he commits a homicide motivated by

compassion, induced by repeated requests of the victim."
The code of Czechoslavakia seems to leave punishment in
cases of merciful homicide to the determination of the
judge.

The presiding justice of the High Court of Nogoya,
Toichi Kobayashi, formulated in 1963 guiding principles to
distinguish legal euthanasia from culpable homicide. The
case involved Komei Yamanouchi, who had given poison to
his incurably ill father upon his urgent request for death.
The court published an opinion stating that euthanasia
would be legal provided six conditions were satisfied:

1. The victim must be suffering from an illness not curable
   by modern medicine.
2. The victim must be suffering unbearable pain, obvious to
   any observer.
3. The purpose of the doctor must be the relief of pain.
4. The victim's consciousness must be clear and he or she
   must have seriously requested or approved the mercy
   killing.
5. Wherever possible the means of inducing death must be
   administered by a physician.
6. The method of inducing death must be morally acceptable.

A sentence of "homicide upon request" was delivered
against Yamanouchi because he failed to meet the last two
conditions. His sentence, however, was reduced from three
years to one and then suspended with a three-year period
of probation. The case was considered a very significant
step toward the legalization of euthanasia in Japan.

One case in Sweden in 1964 provoked discussion of
passive euthanasia throughout medical and legal circles.
The Medicolegal Committee of the Swedish National
Board of Health approved the action of a physician who
stopped the intravenous support of an elderly comatose
patient. The Committee, according to *Medical World News,*

considered such life-shortening action "perfectly responsible and legitimate."

But motive has not been recognized as an important legal factor by criminal law in the United States or in any other English-speaking country. Present American laws designate any intentional shortening of another person's life as murder, regardless of motive. Humanitarian aims, consent of the victim, and the victim's hopeless condition are all irrelevant in the eyes of the law. Any omission in the efforts of a physician to prolong the functioning of a patient's body leaves him open to a charge of negligence or nonfeasance. But the law on the books and the law applied in courts are clearly not the same. The fact that they are not illustrates that the law on the books is out of step with current concepts of mercy and justice. This discrepancy is at the heart of the current demand for new legislation.

As noted earlier, courts have seldom convicted a person in a case of mercy killing, and even in cases of conviction, judges have been very lenient in sentencing. As J. Sanders has shown, the record is mostly one of failure to indict, acquittals on grounds of insanity, suspended sentences, and reprieves. It has been said by some authorities that rulings in this field are a conglomerate of common law, theological pronouncements, and ethical and moral considerations, and that juries have taken on the job of correcting the inequities of law and have in effect rewritten criminal law to sanction compassionately motivated killing. Harry Kalven says motive has become *de facto* mitigation. But still laws have not yet been altered to conform to new needs and demands. The present state of affairs in law and in practice is, as Dr. Eliot Slater has said, "a patent absurdity."

Cases of Prosecution of Doctors

In my research I have found only seven cases in which doctors were prosecuted for mercy killings. Only in Holland—in two instances—have these cases resulted in convictions.

In 1917, Dr. Haisdelden of Chicago was cleared of having failed to save the life of a hopelessly deformed and defective newborn infant.

Dr. Hermann Sander of New Hampshire was acquitted of a murder charge in 1950 on the defense that the patient was virtually dead before he injected air into her veins after the patient's request for death.

In England in 1957, Dr. John Bodkin Adams was acquitted of murder after having administered narcotics which apparently caused the death of his patient. The judge held that a doctor who administers narcotics to relieve pain is not guilty of murder merely because the measures he takes incidentally shorten life.

A Swedish court in 1964 refused to indict a doctor who had stopped the intravenous feeding of an aged patient.

And in February, 1974, Dr. Vincent A. Montemarano of New York was held not guilty of the death of a terminal cancer patient to whom he was accused of giving an injection of potassium chloride.

It appears that only in the Netherlands has a court convicted a physician in a similar instance. In a 1950 case there, a 50-year-old doctor received a one-year suspended sentence for giving sleeping pills and painkillers to hasten the death of his brother, who was suffering from an incurable disease, and who had asked that his life be ended. And in 1971 Dr. Gertruida Postma-von Boven was charged with mercy killing when she reported that she had ended the life of her hopelessly ill mother who had repeatedly begged that her life be ended. Under Dutch law this is a lesser charge than murder and carries a penalty of only up to 12 years. At the 1973 trial Dr. Postma said her mother's "mental suffering became unbearable . . . [That] was most important to me. Now, after all these months, I am convinced I should have done it much earlier." Because of her admission, the court decided that it could do nothing but find her guilty, but gave her only a one-week suspended sentence and a year's probation. Her supporters considered even this minimal sentence a defeat. Dr. Postma said, "I don't think my action based solely on the grounds of humanity deserves any punishment however light." She said she would consider appealing the case. Eighteen doctors from her community said they had practiced euthanasia at one time or another, and 45 other doctors signed a letter in support of her.

Other Cases of Mercy-Killing Prosecutions

In the cases of mercy killing in which a parent, spouse, or other member of the family ended the life of a loved one in order to end hopeless suffering, judges and juries have shown great sympathy and an unwillingness to punish, even when the evidence showed clearly that the person had indeed violated criminal law. The public response to an acquittal in such cases has usually been overwhelmingly favorable, giving further evidence that the law is not in accord with what is commonly believed to be humane and justifiable action.

In only two widely reported cases, Roberts in Michigan, 1920, and Noxon in Massachusetts, 1943, has the defendant been convicted of murder, and even in them the leniency of the sentences indicated that the court in effect recognized a distinction between murder and euthanasia. But this distinction has not been clearly claimed and established.

Court decisions have varied on the legality of terminating treatment and the patient's right to refuse treatment. United States courts have in many cases upheld the right of a competent adult patient to refuse medical treatment (See Martinez, Raasch and Osborne cases). In one of the most recent cases (Yetter, 1973), Judge Alfred T. Williams, Jr. said:

> In our opinion the constitutional right of privacy includes the right of a mature competent adult to refuse to accept medical recommendations that may prolong one's life and which, to a third person at least, appear to be in his best interests; in short, that the right of privacy includes a right to die with which the State should not interfere where there are no minor or unborn children and no clear and present danger to public health, welfare or morals.

But courts have ordered treatment of adults in cases in which the competence of the patient is questioned (Bettman and Heston cases), to prevent minors from becoming wards of the state (if rejection of treatment would probably result in the parent's death), and in cases in which patients voluntarily sought treatment but later either changed their minds or became incompetent. There are also cases of court-ordered treatment of children over parental objections, based on the right of the state to protect neglected or dependent children.

But questions regarding the legal rights of parents to make decisions regarding their severely defective newborn infants have probably been greatly compounded by the decision of Maine Superior Court Judge David G. Roberts in the case of "Baby Boy Houle." A child born February 9 to Mr. and Mrs. Houle had several severe malformations including some nonfused vertebrae and a tracheal esophageal fistula that prevented normal feeding and respiration. When the parents refused to authorize corrective surgery, the attending physician and the Maine Medical Center appealed for a court order to give intravenous feeding and to repair the fistula. On February 11, the Judge ordered the feeding. Meanwhile the child's condition had deteriorated to the extent that the physician reported "virtual certainty of some brain damage resulting from anoxia," and he now favored "the opinion that all life-supporting measures should be withdrawn." In spite of this, Judge Roberts held, "The most basic right enjoyed by every human being is the right to life itself . . . the doctor's qualitative evaluation of the value of the life to be preserved is not legally within the scope of his expertise. In the court's opinion the issue before the court is not the prospective quality of the life to be preserved, but the medical feasibility of the proposed treatment." Thereupon the Judge ordered surgery, which was performed on February 15. The baby died on February 24, 1974, fifteen days after birth.

However, courts have also held that the performance of medical procedures without the consent of the patient or his guardian constitutes assault and battery. It is for this reason that doctors and hospitals have sometimes applied

Table 2:   U.S. COURT DECISIONS IN SOME WIDELY

First Degree Murder	Lesser Homicide	Acquitted
Roberts Michigan 1920 fixed poison for wife life imprisonment	*Repouille* New York 1939 chloroformed 13-yr.-old mongoloid son susp. 5–10 yr. sentence	*Greenfield* New York 1939 chloroformed 17 yr. old imbecile son
Noxon Massachusetts 1943 electrocuted 6 mo. old mongoloid son life imprisonment then life sentence then life parole	*Mohr* Pennsylvania 1950 killed blind & cancer- stricken brother 3–6 yr. sentence & $500 fine	*Haug* Pennsylvania 1947 indicted for drugging invalid mother *Werner* Illinois 1958 indicted for suffocating bedridden wife *Zygmaniak* New Jersey 1973 indicted for shooting paralyzed brother

to the courts for the appointment of a guardian in cases of patients whom they claim to be incompetent.

One writer has said, "the distinction between refusal of compulsory lifesaving treatment and euthanasia is all but illusory," and many agree with Glanville Williams, who has said, "There is no moral chasm between what may be called shortening life and accelerating death." It may be that Arthur Levisohn is right in saying that part of the problem pertaining to euthanasia is an inadequate public awareness of the need for legal clarification of the situation. Tables 2 and 3 give an overview of court decisions regarding euthanasia that points up just how ambiguous and inconsistent the courts have been in determining its legal status.

PUBLICIZED "MERCY-KILLINGS" BY OTHERS THAN DOCTORS

ACQUITTED ON GROUNDS OF TEMPORARY INSANITY		REFUSED TO INDICT
Kirby New York 1832 drowned 2 children	*Braunsdorf* Michigan 1950 shot 29 yr. old invalid daughter	*Johnson* New York 1938 accused of suffocating cancer-stricken wife
Reichert New York 1942 shot 26 yr. old mental patient brother	*Nagel* Arizona 1953 shot 28 yr. old invalid daughter	*Reinecke* Illinois 1967 accused of strangling 74-yr.-old cancer-stricken wife
Paight Connecticut 1949 shot cancer-stricken father	*Waskin* Illinois 1969 shot cancer-stricken mother	

Table 3

WIDELY PUBLICIZED "MERCY-KILLING" COURT CASES AGAINST DOCTORS

LESSER HOMICIDE	ACQUITTED	ACQUITTED AS AIDER & ABETTOR	REFUSED TO INDICT
Dutch doctor, 1950 (name not reported) drugged invalid brother 1 yr. susp. sentence	*Haiselden* Illinois 1915 & 1917 indicted for allowing defective babies to die	*Casters* Belgium 1962 in Van de Put case	*Swedish doctor, 1964* (name withheld) stopped intravenous feeding of aged patient
Postma Holland 1971 drugged 79 yr. old invalid mother 1 week susp. sentence & 1 yr. probation	*Sander* New Hampshire 1950 indicted for injecting air in vein of dying cancer patient		
	Adams England 1957 drugged patient		
	Montemarano New York 1973 accused of drugging dying cancer patient		

COURSES OPEN TO US

Negative Positions

OPPOSE ANYTHING CALLED EUTHANASIA AND ITS LEGALIZATION
FOR ANYONE UNDER ANY CIRCUMSTANCE.   One may adhere
to the traditional doctrines of various religions, and specifically the teachings of the Roman Catholic Church, and
condemn anything called euthanasia as an immoral en-
croachment on God's dominion over life. In the foreword
to Sullivan's 1950 book on Catholic teaching on the morality of euthanasia, the Reverend Francis J. Connell, of Catholic University of America, stated that the Catholic Church
vigorously opposes any acceleration of death: "The teaching of the Church has always been the same as it is today,
and it will remain the same until the end of time. For the
Church proposes her doctrine on the subject of mercy killing as the law of God, and God's law does not change with
changes of human customs or the advance of science."
     In 1957, however, as has already been noted, Pope
Pius XII took a less rigid attitude toward suffering than that
held by the Church traditionally. And Father Gerald Kelly,
in his book setting forth directives for Catholics, and especially for physicians, stated that while moral principles do
not change and the Church makes no claim to the power
of changing them, "our understanding of these principles
and their implications can grow. . . . Certainly the applications of the principles can change from time to time, and
even from case to case, according to the changing factors
upon which the applications depend."
     Both Directive 21 and the Pontiff stated that "eu-
thanasia in all forms is forbidden," but they also made it
clear that the alleviation of suffering is permissible, even
when such action shortens the patient's life. Both the Directive and the Pontiff have also specified that extraordinary
measures need not be taken to prolong the life of the dying.

Such inaction, however, is commonly referred to as passive or negative euthanasia, so the problem is partly one of semantics. Nevertheless, the Catholic Church and fundamentalist religions still strongly condemn active euthanasia, and many other churches do too, though many, as indicated in Chapter 8, are calling for a re-examination of their stand on euthanasia.

LEAVE IT TO THE DOCTORS.   Many doctors say the matter should be left with them and some people who prefer to shirk their decision-making responsibilities are happy with the status quo. Any broadening of participation in such crucial matters is regarded by some doctors as interference with their traditional prerogatives even though they recognize that many of the dilemmas they face require decisions that are ethical, moral, and social judgments rather than medical ones.

This view ignores the right of the individual to choose euthanasia when life has become too great a burden and recovery is not possible. The action taken or not taken might depend more on the personal philosophy or religious views of the physician than on the wishes of the patient or his legal guardian. Moreover, few doctors are willing to risk the possible charge of murder by administering or prescribing a lethal dose, or even by terminating treatment.

Is it not selfish for people who have a personal physician they think they can count on to grant their wish for euthanasia covertly, if and when the time comes they want it, to be unconcerned about the countless others who can have no such assurance until it becomes legally permissible for a physician to grant such a request?

The changed and changing role of the doctor in our society is also an important point to take into consideration. The old image of the kindly physician sitting by the bedside of the critically ill patient, as immortalized in the picture "The Country Doctor," is fast becoming a thing of the past. Relatively few patients have such personal attention; hospital care today involves large numbers of specialists who cannot give the personal and concerned care that might be desirable.

In the book *The Crisis in American Medicine,* published in 1961, John Fischer stated that millions of Americans are bitterly dissatisfied with the medical care they are receiving. A few of the problems cited were the critical shortage of doctors, soaring charges, scandal in the marketing and pricing of drugs, rising costs of medical care for old people, and the depersonalization of medicine.

Reluctantly one must recognize that doctors are neither infallible nor incorruptible, as has been documented in *The Doctors* by Martin L. Gross, and in other books and articles. Many of the incidents reported come as a shock to laymen: useless surgery; the new speed-up technology with computerized assembly-line, dehumanizing methods of dealing with patients that provide almost no opportunity for exchange between the doctor and the patient; the many errors and faulty lab reports; the fact that so many doctors have virtually eliminated the "house call;" the restriction of practice to wealthy patients by some doctors and the increasing tendency to place the interest of research over day-to-day care and the welfare of the seriously ill patient.

These disturbing facts should not cause anyone to lose confidence in the thousands of dedicated and competent doctors whose ethical and professional conduct is above reproach. But they do point to the need to recognize that doctors should not be exempted from practicing within the law, nor should they be encouraged to act secretively. Decisions that in effect determine who shall live and who shall die and when should be made only after appropriate consultations and consensus, in accordance with safeguards prescribed by law and new medical guidelines formulated by the medical profession. It should be remembered that it was secrecy of action by several hundred doctors in Nazi Germany that made possible the extermination of "unwanted persons" without their consent or that of their family, and also the most cruel and revolting experiments on human subjects, done in the name of science.

RELY ON THE LIVING WILL.   Some people assert that the Living Will (see p. 181) is sufficient to take care of the problem of useless prolongation, but this document has no legal status under present law and as generally written it does not provide for an executor with legal power to enforce the dying person's wishes. Persons who sign such a will may be enjoying a false sense of security, for they have no legal guarantee that their stated wishes will be acted upon. And one must ask, is it fair to a doctor to make such a request until legal authority has been clearly established for him to carry out the request without fear of a charge of malpractice or assisted suicide? In a few states, unsuccessful attempts have been made to make such a will legal; but although some think that such a will might serve as effective defense if a doctor were sued, it has yet to be made legally valid.

The "Advance Declaration" provided for in the 1969 British Bill and in several of the bills proposed in the United States is similar in intent and content to the Living Will, but differs from it in that the Declaration would be incorporated in a law providing authority and safeguards and would apply to positive as well as negative euthanasia.

Partial Solutions of Significant but Limited Value

AMEND THE UNITED STATES CONSTITUTION AND SIMILAR DOCUMENTS IN OTHER COUNTRIES.   An amendment to the U. S. Constitution might be adopted which would recognize that the right of an individual to life, liberty and happiness includes the right to death as well. However, the passage of such an amendment would probably be long and difficult, and there would still have to be legislation to establish appropriate safeguards.

Two decades ago an attempt was made at the international level to establish this right; a petition signed by more than two thousand distinguished people was sent to the United Nations requesting that the U. N. Declaration of Human Rights be amended to include specifically the right of incurable sufferers to euthanasia when meaningful life has ended. Such an amendment, however, may not be feasible until after this right has been established in several countries (See Appendix).

AMEND THE SUICIDE LAWS.   In the United States, England, and France, it is no longer a criminal offense to commit suicide, although, ironically, an unsuccessful attempt to commit suicide is a felony in some states. To assist or abet suicide, however, remains a crime in most states and in most countries, so a physician who provides a person with the means to commit suicide is liable to a criminal charge.

If laws were amended to make assisted suicide legal in certain circumstances and in accord with legal safeguards, a physician could provide his patient with a lethal pill or other means of ending his life in a socially acceptable manner.

It should be recognized, however, that such an amendment to the suicide laws could not benefit persons who were already unconscious, paralyzed, or otherwise too helpless to take a lethal drug even if it were available, and of course it could not apply to defective infants or minors. Its value would be significant but limited.

In England some prominent members of the Euthanasia Society, when fearful that the 1969 euthanasia bill might be defeated, proposed that the Society, as a compromise first step, work for an amendment to the 1961 Suicide Act that would make it no longer a crime for a doctor to provide the dying patient who requested it with the means to end his life. In Texas in 1902 and again in 1906 a judge ruled that since it was no longer a crime to commit suicide, it was not a crime to assist one to do so, but it seems that this interpretation has not been made elsewhere in the U.S., and was reversed by Texas Statute in 1974.

AMEND THE CRIMINAL CODE SO AS TO DISTINGUISH EUTHANASIA FROM MURDER.   This might be done by legislative action or by litigation. Since the kind of euthanasia being discussed would clearly not be a "malicious" act, it should be possible to exclude it from the definition of murder. This would probably require also court reversal of the long standing legal interpretation that "malice" means merely *intent* to kill or cause bodily harm, and not necessarily with ill will or evil intent. In the first reported case involving euthanasia, *People v. Kirby* (1823), in which a father drowned his daughter and stepson, the defense said, "There was no evidence of malice against the children, but on the contrary, it appeared he was very much attached to them," but the court ruled, "Every willful and intentional taking of the life of a human being, without a justifiable cause, is murder, if done with deliberation and not in the heat of passion, and legal malice is always implied in such cases." But in spite of this, Kirby was acquitted on grounds of insanity at the time of the drownings.

As late as 1966 this interpretation was reinforced by *People v. Conley* in which the court said, "One who commits euthanasia bears no ill will toward his victim and believes his act is morally justified, but he nonetheless acts with malice if he is able to comprehend that society prohibits his act regardless of personal belief." Such a differentiation has already been made in the criminal codes of some European and other countries, as has been reported. In a few countries, as Silving points out, motive *a priori* determines the classification of an act and affects the punishment accordingly; positive euthanasia is still regarded as a criminal act, but the punishment is generally negligible, especially if it is clearly established that the act was a compassionate one. The Swiss Code stated that the mark of the murderer is the depraved mind or the dangerousness of the actor.

John C. Hirschfeld, writing in *Notre Dame Lawyer,* proposed that there should be a "special niche" in American criminal law that would classify voluntary euthanasia as a lesser crime than other forms of premeditated homicide. His proposal, however, and the codes of the above-mentioned countries, would still leave the person who committed the compassionate act a criminal in the eyes of the law, though his punishment would be less than for murder. A doctor might still have to risk the hardship of a criminal trial for performing a humane act; furthermore, such an amendment would not establish a person's right to choose euthanasia or the doctor's legal right to administer it.

In 1953 the British Royal Commission on Capital Punishment considered a special status in the law for euthanasia but took no action on the matter.

BRING ABOUT REFORM BY LITIGATION.   There are two directions such litigation could take. One course would be to challenge in court the criminal nature of euthanasia. This would involve a defendent in a mercy-killing case basing his defense on the grounds that his act should not be regarded as murder, and should not be a prosecutable offense.

It appears that to date no doctor or other defendant has attempted to present such a defense, preferring instead to argue their cases on grounds such as mercy or temporary insanity. A defense based instead on the distinction between euthanasia and murder would make a valuable contribution by establishing a legal precedent for acceptance of euthanasia, but it would pose certain risks for the practicing physician who undertook it. If successful, such a test case might lead to a change in the criminal code that would differentiate between a malicious act of murder and a compassionate act of euthanasia.

Another possible legal course to take would be to challenge the right of the state to deny a person the right to choose death. Such a challenge would posit that every individual, when faced with hopeless suffering or prolonged unconsciousness, has the constitutional right to die with the assistance of a qualified doctor.

Under the equal protection clause of the fifth and fourteenth amendments to the U. S. Constitution, a person might claim that it is his prerogative to have his life ended if competent doctors have certified that his condition is incurable and is such that there was no reasonable possibility of his being of service or of ever finding further happiness or satisfaction in living. It appears that no such claim has been made in a court case to this time, but competent attorneys might be able to get such an issue before the Supreme Court.

The fact that the Supreme Court, in its recent ruling on abortion, has given to women greater power to determine what course their own bodies will take leads one to hope that it might rule similarly on the right to euthanasia if a suitable case were appealed to it.

The right to refuse treatment, and in effect to choose death, has been upheld in some court cases and denied in others. In the 1971 Martinez case, the judge held, "A person has the right not to suffer pain. A person has the right to live or die in dignity." On the other hand in the Heston case, Chief Justice Joseph Weintraub said, "It seems correct to say there is no constitutional right to choose to die."

In 1972 the framers of a revised Montana State Constitution refused the plea of Mrs. Joyce Franks to include in the Bill of Rights a guarantee of the right of every citizen to "choose the manner in which he dies," yet in Milwaukee, the right of Mrs. Raasch to refuse surgery was upheld on the grounds that "It is not the prerogative of this court to make decisions for adult, competent citizens, even decisions relating to life or death." And in the District of Columbia, the judge refused the plea of a hospital to order a blood transfusion for Charles Osborne, holding that the patient had knowingly "chosen this course for his life," and concluded that there was no "compelling state interest which justifies overriding" his decision.

It is evident the rights of patients are not uniformly recognized and clarification is needed. Glanville Williams has said, "The main issue is one of personal liberty . . . there is a sphere of conduct in which men are, or ought to be, free to act according to their consciences." Recently the American Hospital Association evidenced its recognition of the right to refuse treatment and the need for new guidelines when it adopted in 1973 a "Bill of Rights for Patients."

We must ask, does society have the right to deny euthanasia to patients for whom life is clearly an intolerable and hopeless burden?

MAKE BRAIN DEATH A LEGAL CRITERION OF DEATH.   As previously stated, this would help reduce some useless prolongation and would be helpful when organs are wanted for transplant purposes, but it would solve only a very minor part of the total problem.

ENACT A EUTHANASIA LAW PERTAINING ONLY TO NEGATIVE (PASSIVE) EUTHANASIA.   In order to clarify the rights and responsibilities of doctors in regard to termination of treatment, and also to clarify the rights of patients and their guardians if the patient is not of testamentary capacity, bills pertaining to passive euthanasia have been proposed.

Since there is at present no legal immunity for a doctor who causes death by failure to prolong life as long as possible, many physicians continue treatment long after it is obviously useless to do so rather than risk a charge of malpractice or nonfeasance, or censure by their profession. So, while it has been ruled in several court cases that a competent adult does have the right to refuse treatment, it is often found that if a patient does so he is likely to be dismissed from the hospital. This may present great hardship for him and his family, so he may agree to the proposed treatment that may be expensive, painful, and useless.

Also, to date there have been few court cases, if any, in which the next of kin, or guardian of a minor or of a person ruled incompetent, has been given the authority to demand that treatment be stopped or not started. New guidelines are clearly needed. At present the doctor often feels compelled to do what his conscience and experience tell him is a mere prolongation of agony for both the patient and his family and often at great expense to society.

Dr. Sackett's Florida bills have been attempts to meet this need for authority and legal immunity for a doctor who desists from or terminates treatment for those irremediably ill patients who request it themselves, or whose next of kin or guardian requests it. In his 1973 bill Dr. Sackett provided for better safeguards than those of earlier editions of the bill by requiring certification by two doctors that the patient was terminally ill. Regrettably, however, he put less emphasis on the patient's right to request termination of prolongation than in his earlier "Right to Die with Dignity" bill. The later bill was passed by the Florida House in 1973, but only after the portion dealing with incompetents had been deleted; it still had not been passed by the Senate in early 1974.

A bill introduced into the State Senate of Washington, to be known as the "Death with Dignity Act of 1973," expressed the conviction that a person who has reached the age of majority should be "allowed the right to make the crucial, final decision as to the manner in which he dies," provided he had made a witnessed, notarized declaration of his wishes, and is suffering from an "irremediable condition." The bill would authorize the withdrawal of life-sustaining mechanisms ("artificial means"), and provide that in cases in which distress could not otherwise be relieved, the patient would be "entitled to drugs rendering him continuously unconscious" if he has declared in advance that that is his wish. This would, in effect, give legal status to the currently popular Living Will, and provide safeguards for physicians who act on it.

The safeguards of this Washington bill are stringent, even though only those who have previously signed a declaration of wishes regarding euthanasia are eligible. Its scope, therefore, is more limited than the original 1973 Florida bill which would give authority to surrogates to speak for those not of testamentary capacity even when they have not signed a declaration of their wishes.

The best elements of these bills combined would seem to provide the basis for a good model bill pertaining to passive euthanasia—both voluntary and nonvoluntary. This would not permit action to hasten death intentionally, however, no matter how hopeless the condition. One may well ask what is the justification of limiting a bill to withdrawal of life-sustaining measures when perhaps the only means of relieving distress is to keep the patient continuously unconscious. What is to be gained by keeping a patient permanently unconscious instead of taking positive steps to induce death if withdrawal of treatment does not cause death? Moreover, many dying patients never had any treatment that would be described as artificial or "extraordinary," so a passive euthanasia bill would not apply to them. Such patients would still have to endure hopeless suffering for months or years, unless there is legislation permitting active euthanasia.

ENACT A VOLUNTARY, POSITIVE (ACTIVE) EUTHANASIA LAW SIMILAR TO THE 1969 BRITISH VOLUNTARY EUTHANASIA BILL AND THE IDAHO, MONTANA, AND OREGON BILLS.   These four bills all recognize the right of the patient to choose death with the assistance of a qualified physician, or person he designates, acting in accordance with the bill's provisions and safeguards. They apply only to persons who have made a witnessed, written declaration of their wish for euthanasia. They do not provide for nonvoluntary euthanasia. However, the advance declaration would, in the event the person became *non compos mentis,* permit the next of kin or guardian to request the termination of life thus providing, in effect, nonvoluntary euthanasia. Anyone who had not previously signed the document, however, would not be eligible for euthanasia, thus excluding defective infants.

Judge Michael T. Sullivan has said, "The law's failure to recognize the dying person's rights, the dichotomy and confusion of case law regarding persons who have religious convictions about medical treatment, the officious assumption of authority over people's death style by professionals, all point to a pressing need for state legislation. . . . The polestar of any legislation must be the dying person's right to make the decisions concerning all his interrelationships."

A Recommended Solution

A comprehensive euthanasia law combining the best features of those bills proposed to date, with additional provisions as well, is the only solution that is not in some way merely a preliminary step. A bill more comprehensive than any put forward to date is desirable: one that would provide for both active and passive, voluntary and nonvoluntary euthanasia (not involuntary); one that would meet a broad spectrum of needs and provide adequate safeguards for every case.

Many will protest that to get such a radical measure enacted would be impossible and that it is wiser to take one step at a time on the theory that "half a loaf is better than none." This may well be true. But it is also true that when the British Voluntary Euthanasia Bill was being widely debated, one of the criticisms by both advocates and opponents was that it would not permit euthanasia for persons who could not speak for themselves, such as defective infants. Perhaps it is better to have a comprehensive, radically definitive bill that one can defend wholeheartedly and in good conscience, than a compromise that would solve too small a part of the problem.

It is not my intention to draft a proposed bill. Members of the legal profession have the special skills necessary to create and promulgate just and workable laws. Able and highly respected lawyers have repeatedly deplored the disrespect for present laws on questions of euthanasia; now is the time for them to take the action necessary to end this disrespect for law. Yale Kamisar has said, "When a mercy killing occurs the Law in Action is as malleable as the Law on the Books is uncompromising," and Arthur Levisohn agreed: "There is a steadily expanding galaxy of examples of apparent disrespect for the written law in euthanasia cases."

Legal experts, with the collaboration of physicians, nurses, hospital chaplains, social workers, religious leaders, legislators, and others, can certainly draft a good, comprehensive bill if they have the will and determination to do so. Efforts should continue in individual states to draft and enact euthanasia legislation, but in order to have a uniform law throughout the United States, it seems urgent for some group such as the National Conference of Commissioners on Uniform State Laws to prepare a model bill pertaining to euthanasia. The model bill prepared by this group on anatomical gifts in 1968 led to its quick passage by all the states. The American Law Institute could also be helpful, as it was in drafting a model statute pertaining to abortion, which has been adopted by several states and is in the legislatures of several others.

Other groups such as the American Civil Liberties Union, foundations such as Russell Sage, Ford, and Rockefeller, and the Institute of Society, Ethics and Life Sciences, the Thanatology Foundation, the American Association of Retired Persons, and many church and civic groups concerned with these problems of life and death could no doubt be counted on to assist or give active leadership in the formulation and enactment of appropriate legislation.

To initiate action it might be helpful if an appropriate national commission such as the one on Health Science and Society proposed by Senator Mondale would direct a study of the matter with a view to drafting a model bill that could then be presented to the individual states for their consideration and action. In 1973, Congressman Tim Lee Carter introduced in the House of Representatives "A Bill to Establish a Commission on Medical Technology and the Dignity of Dying"; such a commission could be very helpful.

Also, the United Nations Commission on Human Rights might establish a committee to study the matter and encourage all countries to do likewise with a view to establishing the right to choose euthanasia in accordance with safeguards to be established by law.

SUGGESTIONS FOR A COMPREHENSIVE EUTHANASIA BILL. It is proposed that the bill be known as "A Euthanasia Bill" and that it be divided into three parts as follows:

Part I would provide for negative (passive) euthanasia, voluntary and nonvoluntary, as in the 1973 Florida bill before it was amended.

Part II would provide for positive (active) euthanasia at the request of the patient, similar to the 1969 British Voluntary Euthanasia Bill and the Idaho, Montana and Oregon bills, all of which make provision also for a person to make an advance declaration of his wishes in the event he is suffering from an irremediable condition as specified in his witnessed statement.

Part III would provide for positive (active) euthanasia at the request of the next of kin or legal guardian, for those individuals who are unable to speak for themselves and have not made a prior declaration of their wishes.

Such a provision appears not to have been made in any bill publicly proposed to date. It would make it legally permissible for a physician who observed all safeguards to terminate at the request of parents the life of a severely defective infant. It would also allow them to administer euthanasia to those not of testamentary capacity when it is requested by their legal guardian. This provision would include irreversibly comatose or totally paralyzed patients, or those who are chronically senile or insane.

Since no personal liberty is absolute—as Justice Holmes said, freedom of speech does not embrace the right to falsely cry "fire" in a crowded theatre—the freedom to choose euthanasia must be subject to some restrictions in order to protect the physician, the patient, and society from foul play or tragic human errors in diagnosis.

It would seem that the following provisions and safeguards should be among those included in a good euthanasia law:

1. Legislation would be permissive only, not mandatory or compulsory.

2. No secrecy of action for either negative or positive euthanasia would be permitted, and action taken would be officially recorded.

3. A written, witnessed and notarized request for euthanasia would be made by the patient, or if he is not of testamentary capacity, by his guardian. Such a declaration of wishes could be made in advance, while in good health, and would specify that euthanasia was to be administered in accordance with safeguards prescribed by law, if the signer was incapacitated and unable to make his wishes known. The documents should designate a surrogate and contingency surrogate to take action on the patient's behalf in such event. Such a request could be revoked at any time and would have to be reaffirmed if the patient were capable of doing so before euthanasia could be administered.

4. Two or more physicians who would not stand to gain by the decease of the patient would certify that in their judgment the patient's condition is such that there is no

reasonable chance of significant recovery, usefulness or happiness, and that the request for euthanasia is bonafide, executed without pressure from relatives or others.

5. The application for euthanasia would be made only after consultation and agreement among the patient or his legal guardian if he is incompetent, the attending physician, and at least one other physician who has certified that it is his judgment that the patient "qualifies" for euthanasia. In most cases, before an application would be made, there would be consultation also with other people such as a clergyman, hospital chaplain, nurse, psychologist or social worker, and in practically all cases with at least some members of the family.

This idea of a team approach is now being used in some hospitals to help physicians determine which patients will get the use of lifesaving machines, blood for transfusions, or organs for transplantation which are in short supply. An advisory panel or committee such as that recommended by the California Medical Association might be established in each hospital and be available for consultation if desired, especially when there are no relatives, but such a committee would not be empowered to make decisions regarding euthanasia, unless possibly in such extreme circumstances as might be stipulated in the law.

6. The formal request for euthanasia accompanied by the "qualifying" statements by two doctors would be filed with the appropriate officer in the County Court House or other legally constituted authority whose duty it would be to deal with the application. If the official had any reason to suspect that the documents were not authentic or not properly completed, or if he suspected that there might have been coercion or foul play, he would immediately, in cooperation with the Board of Health or other appropriate officials, direct an investigation and withhold the granting of a permit for euthanasia until such time as they were satisfied that the documents were legal and proper. A per-

mit would then be issued for the kind of euthanasia requested—negative or positive—in accordance with the
waiting period provided for in the law and in accordance
with the physician's recommendation.

Negative euthanasia might be made more readily available than positive in most cases. Perhaps permission for it
in hospital cases might be authorized without application to
a central official. Possibly at the request of the patient or his
guardian for termination of treatment, a physician might
describe the facts of the case to a hospital advisory committee including at least two doctors which would be authorized, not to make the decision to terminate treatment, but
to provide in writing its judgment regarding the advisabil-
ity of further treatment. If the report stated that the committee concurred in the decision that no further treatment
was advisable, the physician might then terminate the treatment at the request of the patient and/or the family, or
both, depending on the circumstances.

7. A waiting period would be required in most cases
to assure that a request for euthanasia by either the patient
or his or her guardian had not been made in a moment of
emotional distress. This period might vary depending on
the severity of the suffering, the certainty of irremediability,
and the nearness to death. The British bill stipulated a
30-day waiting period; the Montana bill a 15-day period;
possibly, to prevent unnecessary hardship in some terminal
cases, special provision might be made that would permit
the request to be granted within as short a period as 24
hours.

This authorization of a permit would be comparable to
the issuance of a marriage license in that it would grant
permission by the state for an authorized person to carry
out the request of the applicant.

8. The administration of euthanasia—either positive
or negative—would be the responsibility of the patient's
physician, or of a qualified nurse or other medical or

paramedical personnel specially designated to carry out the physician's instructions and the patient's wishes. If the patient so desired, the permit would allow the physician to provide the patient with means to end his own life.

9. The death certificate would indicate the kind of action taken.

10. No physician, nurse or other person would ever be required to administer euthanasia contrary to his conscience, judgment, religious beliefs, or will.

11. It would be a criminal offense to willfully falsify, forge, conceal, destroy or otherwise tamper with a declaration or request for euthanasia with intent to create a false impression of the wishes of the patient or his surrogate. An appropriate penalty would be provided.

12. A physician, nurse or other specialist who performs an authorized act of euthanasia would not be guilty of any offense.

13. No policy of insurance in force would be vitiated by the administration of negative euthanasia; no policy that has been in force for a specified period would be vitiated by the administration of positive euthanasia.

14. Any person knowing or suspicious of coercion or any malpractice or any pressure brought to bear on either the patient or his physician or physicians should immediately notify the license officer who should immediately stay any action until an investigation and decision by his office would be made. This would apply especially to physicians who for reasons other than religion or conscience refuse to sign a qualifying statement either because of uncertainty regarding prognosis or judgment, or suspicion of foul play by anyone concerned.

15. As a protection against the stress of the moment in the event a seriously defective infant is born, prospective parents should discuss in advance with their physician and obstetrician what their wishes would be in the event their

newborn baby should be seriously defective. A calmly thought-out and signed declaration of their desire could be of great assistance in making a decision at the crucial moment, or could even provide that the doctor, with the written concurrence of at least one other physician, be permitted the authority to administer euthanasia in accordance with the parents' wishes. Or, in cases in which the severity of the defect or mental abnormality could not be determined with certainty until some weeks or months later, or the parents should change their minds, the request would not be acted upon until such time as diagnosis and prognosis were established and the parents reaffirmed their request for euthanasia.

16. Some special provision might be made for exceptional circumstances. There must be no relaxation of safeguards, but unnecessary hardship should be avoided by making provision for some special situations. For instance, if a person were critically and terminally ill, especially if he were aged and living in a rural community far from even one doctor, it would be impracticable or impossible unless the family were very wealthy to obtain a second doctor's diagnosis and prognosis. In such a situation it would seem wise to provide for a substitute for the second physician's certification: a statement signed by a clergyman, probate judge, or other highly regarded citizen in the community who would not stand to benefit by the estate of the patient might be an acceptable substitute for the second doctor. And as Medical Data Centers and "tele-diagnosis" centers become established on a nationwide basis—i.e., centers which would permit a patient's physician to consult with a distant doctor and/or with computer medical centers— these means of communication might provide a substitute for personal examination by a second doctor in some special cases. Perhaps the law should make provision also for emergency situations in which a physician has to make a

life-or-death decision without any possibility of consultation. In such instances, the physician might be exempt from prosecution unless it was proven that he acted irresponsibly.

17. It is suggested that each person who has reached the age of maturity be encouraged to lodge with the appropriate office his or her desires pertaining to euthanasia as well as his wishes pertaining to anatomical gifts and disposal of his body, and the whereabouts of his next of kin or surrogate. He would then be issued a notarized and legally executed card (or bracelet) which he would carry with him, indicating these wishes and authorizing action by appropriate persons, just as it is now possible to determine whether one's organs are to be transplanted or one's body donated to a medical school after death.

Consideration should be given to the enactment of the euthanasia bill on a trial basis. This is a sound legislative procedure, though not often used. Such a suggestion was made by Dean Claude L. Sowle in 1968 while he was Professor of Law at the University of Cincinnati. He proposed that whatever bill is passed should remain in effect only until a specified later session of the legislature, at which time it would have to be considered again after there had been careful research and appraisal of its effects.

In England, in a letter to *The Lancet* in 1962, T. H. Gillison also proposed that there be a "sort of pilot scheme" in which a few cities would be empowered to permit voluntary euthanasia for a trial run for, say, three years. During that period the advantages and shortcomings of the bill would be assessed. He thought such a scheme would tell more of the practicability of euthanasia than scores of debates. The proposal has merit and might well be considered by individual States. However, some regulation would have to be made to prevent an influx of persons from outside the area requesting euthanasia.

THE CHALLENGE

In an age when man has succeeded in transplanting human hearts and exploring outer space and now seems on the verge of even being able to create human beings with characteristics of his own choosing, we can certainly, if we wish, devise a good euthanasia bill that would help to resolve many of the problems of senseless, cruel suffering of persons at each end of life, and in between.

Professor Harry Kalven of the University of Chicago Law School has said if there were already a good law permitting euthanasia, there would be no strong case that could be made for changing it. But we do not now have such a law. One is urgently needed. Chief Justice Burger has said "The law always lags behind the most advanced thinking in every area. It must wait until the theologians and the moral leaders and events have created some common ground, some consensus."

It would seem that such common ground and consensus is fast developing regarding euthanasia. The right to choose death with dignity is an idea whose time has come. There is a rapidly growing demand that the dying and the hopelessly incapacitated be treated more humanely and that the right to death not be denied them when life has no further beauty or value.

Clearly new legislation is needed: legislation based on compassion, justice, common sense, and enlightened public opinion. To get such legislation, efforts must be energetic and persistent. Opposition is to be expected. It is not easy to break with custom and the inflexible stupidities of the past. Sir William Osler, addressing the Royal College of Physicians in London in 1906 on "The Growth of Truth," described the long years of labor required and the opposition to be overcome, among both physicians and the general public, in order to obtain knowledge of the anatomy and functioning of the human body and the causes of disease. He said that opposition came chiefly from men who could not, not who would not, see the truth. But ultimately the fetters of dogma and authority are severed, and acceptance of new knowledge, new beliefs and new laws finally comes; sometimes suddenly. Illustrating resistance to change he quoted these lines that reputedly came to Henry Sidgwick in his sleep:

> We think so because all other people think so;
> Or because—or because after all, we do think so;
> Or because we were told so, and think we must think so;
> Or because we once thought so, and think we still think so;
> Or because, having thought so, we think we will think so.

This kind of thinking explains much of the opposition to euthanasia and the search to find acceptable ways of avoiding useless suffering or a meaningless existence. It explains why 60 years ago Margaret Sanger was jailed for championing the right to birth control. Great changes have taken place since then in the beliefs and practices of most people in regard to their rights and responsibilities in control of birth.

Practices pertaining to the creation and termination of life are matters of conscience to be decided chiefly by the individuals concerned, or by their next of kin or guardians in cases of individuals who are not of testamentary capacity. As long as the exercise of the right to choose death does no harm to anyone else or to society, it would seem that society has no right to deny it.

This book has presented strong evidence of the need for new legislation now. And as we look toward the future it seems certain that the magnitude of the problem will continue to accelerate unless intelligent action is taken. Due chiefly to ever-increasing medical skills and pharmaceutical and technological advances, the proportion of persons reaching old age and senility is much greater than formerly, when acute diseases and epidemics resulted in premature death. Statistics indicate that the population over 75 years of age is increasing at about two and one-half times the rate of the general population, and some scientists have predicted that the average lifespan will be increased by at least 15 years within the next couple of decades. Such facts compounded with the high survival rate of severely and permanently defective infants make it clear that there is a gradually growing number of helpless, dependent individuals, many of whom are no longer real persons able to communicate, but patients requiring medical, nursing and hospital services that are already in short supply and very expensive.

Reverence for life and freedom of choice must be the basis for any action regarding euthanasia. Society must recognize also that undesirable pressures arise when freedom and justice are denied and also when citizens are required to bear useless, unreasonable expenditures and suffering. To avoid such undesirable pressures, society must act now to permit an easy and dignified exit from life when life is no longer something to be desired. We must treat death as an inevitable part of existence to be faced realistically, not evasively; it is often man's friend.

It seems certain that it is only a matter of time until laws will be passed that will permit the administration of painless death when the only alternative is an agonizing or meaningless existence. It is a challenge to every citizen to hasten that day.

APPENDIX

# ATH OF HIPPOCRATES

I swear by Apollo, the Physician, and Aesculapius and health and all-heal and all the Gods and Goddesses that, according to my ability and judgment, I will keep this oath and stipulation:

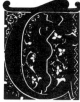o reckon him who taught me this art equally dear to me as my parents, to share my substance with him and relieve his necessities if required: to regard his offspring as on the same footing with my own brothers, and to teach them this art if they should wish to learn it, without fee or stipulation, and that by precept, lecture and every other mode of instruction, I will impart a knowledge of the art to my own sons and to those of my teachers, and to disciples bound by a stipulation and oath, according to the law of medicine, but to none others.

I will follow that method of treatment which, according to my ability and judgment, I consider for the benefit of my patients, and abstain from whatever is deleterious and mischievous. I will give no deadly medicine to anyone if asked, nor suggest any such counsel; furthermore, I will not give to a woman an instrument to produce abortion.

With Purity and with Holiness I will pass my life and practice my art. I will not cut a person who is suffering with a stone, but will leave this to be done by practitioners of this work. Into whatever houses I enter I will go into them for the benefit of the sick and will abstain from every voluntary act of mischief and corruption; and further from the seduction of females or males, bond or free.

Whatever, in connection with my professional practice, or not in connection with it, I may see or hear in the lives of men which ought not to be spoken abroad I will not divulge, as reckoning that all such should be kept secret.

While I continue to keep this oath unviolated may it be granted to me to enjoy life and the practice of the art, respected by all men at all times but should I trespass and violate this oath, may the reverse be my lot.

285

PETITIONS

Petition to the Legislature of the State of New York (1949)

We, the undersigned Ministers of Religion, taking note of the fact that a distinguished company of a thousand physicians of New York State have courageously advocated the legalization of voluntary euthanasia, desire to affirm our conviction also that the ending of the physical existence of an individual at his request, when afflicted with an incurable disease which causes extreme suffering is, under proper safeguards, not only medically indicated, but also in accord with the most civilized and humane ethics and the highest concepts and practices of religion.

Our profession takes us constantly into the presence of sickness and death. Every one of us has seen suffering which has passed beyond any possibility of an ennobling effect upon character and has become protracted torture, when the only merciful prayer would be that the end might come speedily. We have seen the degradation and disintegration of personality through the prolonging of existence by the administration of deadening drugs.

Since humanity was endowed by its Creator with powers that entail the responsibility to determine human destiny, powers which are increasingly exercised in the light of growing knowledge, we believe we must not shirk the responsibilities of mercy.

We believe in the sacredness of the human personality, but not in the worth of mere existence or "length of days." We no longer believe that God wills the prolongation of physical torture for the benefit of the soul of the sufferer. For one enduring continual and severe pain from an incurable disease, who is a burden to himself and his family, surely life has no value.

We believe that such a sufferer has the right to die, and that society should grant this right, showing the same mercy to human beings as to the sub-human animal kingdom. "Blessed are the merciful."

Resolved, therefore, that we, the undersigned ministers of religion in New York State, hereby petition the Legislature of the State of New York to amend the law to permit voluntary euthanasia for incurable sufferers, when authorized by a Court of Record, upon receipt of a signed and attested petition from the sufferer, and after investigation of the case by a medical committee designated by the Court.

Signed by:

387 PROTESTANT AND JEWISH
MINISTERS IN NEW YORK STATE*

Petition to the United Nations (1950)**

For Amendment of the Declaration of Human Rights to include the Right of Incurable Sufferers to Voluntary Euthanasia

If the rights proclaimed in the Declaration of Human Rights as approved by the United Nations' General Assembly are to be fully realized and enjoyed by mankind, it is essential that a further right be recognized and observed—the right of incurable sufferers to euthanasia or merciful death.

In Article 5, the Declaration states, "No one shall be subjected to torture." This freedom cannot be fully assured unless sufferers from the torture of prolonged and painful incurable disease, for which no lasting relief is known, may legally secure release by death.

According to the preamble of the Declaration, we aspire to "a world in which human beings shall enjoy . . . freedom from fear . . ." Then let us relieve them from fear of a slow, painful death, by granting them the right to prompt release from incurable suffering, should they ever be subjected to it.

The preamble further declares that "the recognition of the inherent dignity . . . of all members of the human family is the foundation of freedom . . ." But the dignity of the human being is degraded, his personality is disintegrated, by suffering that breaks down his self-control, or by the repeated administration of deadening drugs for the temporary relief of such suffering.

In Articles 3 and 18 the Declaration States, "Everyone has the right to life, liberty and the security of person . . . to freedom of . . . conscience and religion." But the *right* to life does not mean the obligation to live: —a humane society will not condemn its members to live when life is

---

*While the printed copy of this petition gives the number of signers as 387, the final number was actually 379.

**Signed by 2,513 prominent persons in England and the U.S.

nothing but prolonged suffering. By granting incurables the right to merciful release, society would confer no power upon the state to deprive anyone of life, liberty or security of person. Whether the individual sufferer would avail himself of the right would depend entirely upon his own volition; he would have complete freedom to act in accordance with the dictates of his own conscience or religion.

Inasmuch as this right is, then, not only consonant with the rights and freedoms set forth in the Declaration of Human Rights but essential to their realization, we hereby petition the United Nations to proclaim the right of incurable sufferers to euthanasia.

Petition Sent to the New Jersey State Legislature (1957)*

WHEREAS, large numbers of our population, notwithstanding the advance of medical science, suffer from painful disease for which neither prevention, cure, nor lasting relief has been found, and

WHEREAS, the proportion of the aged in our population who are subject to the painful, chronic, degenerative diseases, is rapidly increasing and the death rate from cancer has reached a new high, and

WHEREAS, many incurable sufferers, facing months of agony, attempt crude, violent methods of suicide; while in other cases distraught relatives of hopeless incurables who plead for merciful release, secretly put them out of their misery and thereby render themselves liable to prosecution as murderers, and

WHEREAS, to permit the termination of useless, hopeless suffering at the request of the sufferer is in accord with the humane spirit of this age, therefore be it

RESOLVED that voluntary euthanasia (merciful release petitioned for by an incurable sufferer) should be permitted by law, brought out into the open and safeguarded against abuse rather than, as at present, practiced illegally, surreptitiously and without supervision or regulation; and be it further

RESOLVED that we, the undersigned, 174 physicians of New Jersey, hereby petition the legislature of the State of New Jersey to amend the law to permit voluntary euthanasia for incurable suffers, when authorized by a Court of Record, upon receipt of a signed and attested petition from the sufferer and after investigation of the case by a medical committee designated by the Court.

*Circulated by the Euthanasia Society, this petition was signed by 174 New Jersey physicians.

LEGISLATIVE PROPOSALS

Connecticut Assembly Bill No. 2527 (1959)

AN ACT TO LEGALIZE EUTHANASIA

Section 1. As used in this act, "euthanasia" means the termination of human life by painless means for the purpose of ending severe physical suffering; "patient" means the Person desiring to receive euthanasia; "physician" means any person licensed to practice medicine in this state.

Sec. 2. Any person of sound mind over twenty-one years of age who is suffering from severe physical pain caused by a disease for which no remedy affording lasting relief or recovery is at the time known to medical science may have euthanasia administered. The desire to anticipate death by euthanisia under these conditions shall not be deemed to indicate mental impairment.

Sec. 3. Any judge of the superior court sitting in the county in which the patient resides or may be, to whom a petition for euthanasia is presented, shall have jurisdiction of and shall grant euthanasia upon the conditions and in conformity with the provisions of this act.

Sec. 4. A petition for euthanasia shall be in writing signed by the patient in the presence of two witnesses who must add their signatures and the post-office addresses of their domicile. Such petition must be made in substantially the following form: To the Superior Court of . . . . County

I . . . .   residing   at . . . .
hereby declare as follows:

I am . . . . years of age and am suffering severe physical pain caused, as I am advised by my physician, by a disease for which no remedy affording lasting relief or recovery is at this time known to medical science.

I am desirous of anticipating death by euthanasia and hereby petition for permission to receive euthanasia.

The names and addresses of the following persons are as follows or, if unknown to me, I so state:

Father . . . .
Mother . . . .
Spouse . . . .
Children . . . .
Uncles . . . .
Aunts . . . .
      Signed . . . .

In the presence of

.... residing at ....

.... residing at ....

Date ....

Such petition must be accompanied by a certificate signed by the patient's attending physician in substantially the following form:

To the Superior Court of .... County

I .... of .... do hereby certify as follows:

I have attended the patient, ... since ....
...

It is my opinion and belief that the patient is suffering severe physical pain caused by a disease for which no remedy affording lasting relief or recovery is at the present time known to medical science.

The disease from which the patient is suffering is known as ....

I am satisfied that the patient understands the nature and purpose of the petition in support of which this certificate is issued and that such disease comes within the provisions of section 2 of this act.

Signature ....

Date .... Medical Qualifications ....

If, for any reason, the patient is unable to write, he may execute the petition by making his mark which shall be authenticated in the manner provided by law.

Sec. 5. The judge to whom a petition for euthanasia has been presented shall appoint a committee of three competent persons, who are not opposed to euthanasia as herein provided, of whom at least two must be physicians and members of a county or district medical society, who shall forthwith examine the patient and such other persons as they deem advisable or as the court may direct and, within five days after their appointment, shall report to the court whether or not the patient understands the nature and purpose of the petition and comes within the provisions of section 2 of this act. The court must either grant or deny the petition within three days of its receipt. The said committee shall serve without compensation. If the said committee shall report in the affirmative the court shall grant the petition unless there is reason to believe that the report is erroneous or untrue, in which case the court shall state in writing the reason for denying the petition. If the petition shall be denied an appeal may be taken to the supreme court of errors, in the manner prescribed by law.

Sec. 6. When the petition has been granted as herein provided, euthanasia shall be administered in the presence of the committee, or any two members thereof, appointed according to section 5 of this act, by a person chosen by the patient or by said committee, or any two members thereof, with the patient's consent; but no person shall be obliged to administer or to receive euthanasia against his will.

Sec. 7. A person to whom euthanasia has been administered under the conditions of this act shall not be deemed to have died a violent or unnatural death nor shall any physician or person who has administered or assisted in the administration thereof be deemed to have committed any offense criminal or civil, or be liable to any person whatever for damages or otherwise.

Sec. 8. Death resulting from euthanasia administered pursuant to and in accordance with the provisions of this act shall not constitute a crime or be punishable under any provisions of chapter 939 of the general statutes.

Sec. 9. This act shall take effect from its passage.

STATEMENT OF PURPOSE: To legalize euthanasia to allow those afflicted with severe physical suffering to have their lives terminated by painless means under the sanction of law.

British Voluntary Euthanasia Bill (1969)

An Act to provide in certain circumstances for the administration of euthanasia to persons who request it and who are suffering from an irremediable condition, and to enable persons to request in advance the administration of euthanasia in the event of their suffering from such a condition at a future date.

1.—(1) Subject to the provisions of this Act, it shall be lawful for a physician to administer euthanasia to a qualified patient who has made a declaration that is for the time being in force.

(2) For the purposes of this Act:

"physician" means a registered medical practitioner:

"euthanasia" means the painless inducement of death:

"qualified patient" means a patient over the age of majority in respect of whom two physicians (one being of consultant status) have certified in writing that the patient appears to them to be suffering from an irremediable condition;

"irremediable condition" means a serious physical illness or impairment reasonably thought in the patient's case to be incurable and expected to cause him severe distress or render him incapable of rational existence:

"declaration" means a witnessed declaration in writing made substantially in the form set out in the schedule to this Act.

2.—(1) Subject to the provisions of this section, a declaration shall come into force 30 days after being made and shall remain in force (unless revoked) for three years.

(2) A declaration re-executed within the 12 months preceding its expiry date shall remain in force (unless revoked) during the lifetime of the declarant.

3. A declaration may be revoked at any time by destruction or by notice of cancellation shown on its face, effected (in either case) by the declarant or to his order.

4.—(1) Before causing euthanasia to be administered to a mentally responsible patient the physician in charge shall ascertain to his reasonable satisfaction that the declaration and all steps proposed to be taken under it accord with the patient's wishes.

(2) Euthanasia shall be deemed to be administered by a physician if treatment prescribed by a physician is given to the patient by a state registered or state enrolled nurse.

(3) No person shall be under any duty, whether by contract or by any statutory or other legal requirement, to participate in any treatment authorised by this Act to which he has a conscientious objection.

5.—(1) A physician or nurse who, acting in good faith, causes euthanasia to be administered to a qualified patient in accordance with what the person so acting believes to be the patient's declaration and wishes shall not be guilty of any offence.

(2) Physicians and nurses who have taken part in the administration of euthanasia shall be deemed not to be in breach of any professional oath or affirmation.

6.—(1) It shall be an offence punishable on indictment by a sentence of life imprisonment wilfully to conceal, destroy, falsify or forge a declaration with intent to create a false impression of another person's wishes with regard to euthanasia.

(2) A person signing a declaration by way of attestation who wilfully puts his signature to a statement he knows to be false shall be deemed to have committed an offence under section 2 of the Perjury Act 1911.

7. No policy of insurance that has been in force for 12 months shall be vitiated by the administration of euthanasia to the insured.

8. For the removal of doubt it is declared that a patient suffering from an irremediable condition reasonably thought in his case to be terminal shall be entitled to the administration of whatever quantity of drugs may be required to keep him free from pain, and such a patient in whose case severe distress cannot be otherwise relieved shall, if he so requests, be entitled to drugs rendering him continuously unconscious.

9.—(1) The Secretary of State for Social Services shall make regulations under this Act by statutory instrument for determining classes of persons who may or may not sign a declaration by way of attestation, for regulating the custody of declarations, for appointing (with their consent) hospital physicians having responsibility in relation to patients who have made or wish to make a declaration, and for the prescribing of any matters he may think fit to prescribe for the purposes of this Act.

(2) Any statutory instrument made under this Act shall be subject to annulment in pursuance of a resolution of either House of Parliament.

10.—(1) This Act may be cited as the Voluntary Euthanasia Act 1969.

(2) This Act does not extend to Northern Ireland.

FORM OF DECLARATION UNDER THE VOLUNTARY
EUTHANASIA ACT 1969
Declaration made   19   [and re-executed
                                    19   ]

by
of
I DECLARE that I subscribe to the code set out under the following articles:—

A. If I should at any time suffer from a serious physical illness or impairment reasonably thought in my case to be incurable and expected to cause me severe distress or render me incapable of rational existence, I request the administration of euthanasia at a time or in circumstances to be indicated or specified by me or, if it is apparent that I have become incapable of giving directions, at the decretion of the physician in charge of my case.

B. In the event of my suffering from any of the conditions specified above, I request that no active steps should be taken, and in particular that no resuscitatory techniques should be used, to prolong my life or restore me to consciousness.

C. This declaration is to remain in force unless I revoke it, which I may do at any time, and any request I may make concerning action to be taken or withheld in connection with this declaration will be made without further formalities.

I WISH it to be understood that I have confidence in the good faith of my relatives and physicians, and fear degeneration and indignity far more than I fear premature death. I ask and authorise the physician in charge of my case to bear these statements in mind when considering what my wishes would be in any uncertain situation.

SIGNED
[SIGNED ON RE-EXECUTION]

WE TESTIFY that the above-named declarant [signed] [was unable to write but assented to] this declaration in our presence, and appeared to appreciate its significance. We do not know of any pressure being brought on him to make a declaration, and we believe it is made by his own wish. So far as we are aware, we are entitled to attest this declaration and do not stand to benefit by the death of the declarant.

Signed by	Signed by
of	of
[Signed by .	[Signed by
of	of
on re-execution]	on re-execution]

Florida House Bill No. 407—Introduced by Dr. Walter W. Sackett (1973)*

A bill to be entitled An act relating to medical treatment; providing for termination of sustaining treatment of a terminally ill or injured patient in certain circumstances; providing immunity for physicians; exempting persons complying with this act from the provisions of § 782.08, Florida Statutes; providing for revocation of a document authorizing the termination of sustaining medical treatment; providing an effective date.

Be It Enacted by the Legislature of the State of Florida:

Section 1. As used in this act, "terminal illness" or "injury" means any illness or injury that would result in natural expiration of life regardless of the use or discontinuance of medical treatment to sustain the life processes. Any person eighteen (18) years of age or older and competent may at any time execute a document directing that medical treatment designed solely to sustain the life processes be discontinued. However, said document shall not take effect until said person has been declared terminally ill or injured by two (2) licensed physicians and attested to by written statement.

Section 2. In the event any terminally ill or injured person has failed to comply with section 1 because he is unable to make such a decision due to mental or physical incapacity, as determined by two (2) licensed physicians, a spouse or person of the first degree of kinship shall be allowed to make such a decision, provided written consent is obtained from a majority of all persons of the first degree of kinship.

*Passed by the House on May 24, 1973 by a vote of 56 to 50 after the deletion of Sections 2 and 3 and the last four words of section 6.

Section 3. In the event the terminally ill or injured person is incompetent and the procedure authorized by section 2 cannot be complied with because no person of the first degree of kinship can be located within thirty (30) days, then the decision to terminate medical procedures solely to sustain the life processes may be ordered by three (3) licensed physicians and attested to by a written statement.

Section 4. A physician who relies on a document authorized by section 1, 2 or 3 to refuse medical treatment or who makes a determination of terminal illness or injury shall be presumed to be acting in good faith and, unless negligent, shall be immune from civil or criminal liability that otherwise might be incurred.

Section 5. No person participating in good faith in the execution of a statement or document required by the provisions of this act shall be deemed to be in violation of § 782.08, Florida Statutes.

Section 6. A person who has executed a document to refuse medical treatment shall have the power to revoke said document at any time by oral or written statement; provided, however, that such revocation must be witnessed by two (2) persons.

Section 7. This act shall take effect upon becoming a law.

Hawaii House Resolution No. 44 (1972)

REQUESTING THE HOUSE COMMITTEE ON PUBLIC HEALTH, YOUTH, AND GENERAL WELFARE TO HOLD HEARINGS IN THE AREA OF EUTHANASIA.

WHEREAS, among the rights of every human being is included the right to die with dignity; and

WHEREAS, because of the advances in medicine and treatment of illnesses, the process of dying is changing and man can now begin to determine if life is really being served by prolonging the act of dying; and

WHEREAS, in certain cases, prolonging the act of dying often means deterioration, dependence, hopeless pain, and above all, indignity for the patient, not to mention the suffering and anguish on the part of the family; and

WHEREAS, for many persons, the idea of euthanasia is shrouded in the confused atmosphere of "mercy killing" when in fact, the word "euthanasia" is of Greek origin meaning "happy or good death" which does not necessarily include the voluntary inducement of death; and

WHEREAS, with the liberalization of abortion laws throughout the country the idea of euthanasia is beginning to emerge from its stigma as man assumes a much greater role in the determination over his own life or death; and

WHEREAS, physicians often find themselves in a dilemma when a patient requests that all medical services be withdrawn and that medical efforts be reduced to making him comfortable, since a physician carrying out this humane wish stands in danger of legal action by a disgruntled or greedy survivor; and

WHEREAS, the law should recognize the validity of instructions given by a patient to his physician in such a personal and individual matter as the choice of dying; now, therefore,

BE IT RESOLVED by the House of Representatives of the Sixth Legislature of the State of Hawaii, Regular Session of 1972, that the House Committee on Public Health, Youth, and General Welfare be, and is hereby requested, to conduct hearings in the area of euthanasia, exploring all its facets including the social, judicial, and public health and welfare implications of such a practice; and

BE IT FURTHER RESOLVED that the House Committee on Public Health, Youth, and General Welfare report its findings to the Legislature prior to the ending of the 1972 session; and

BE IT FURTHER RESOLVED that certified copies of this Resolution be transmitted to the Chairman of the House Committee on Public Health, Youth, and General Welfare.

THE LIVING WILL*

TO MY FAMILY, PHYSICIAN, MY CLERGYMAN, MY LAWYER—
If the time comes when I can no longer take part in decisions for my own future, let this statement stand as the testment of my wishes:
If there is no reasonable expectation of my recovery from physical or mental disability, I, _____ request that I be allowed to die and not be kept alive by artificial means or heroic measures. Death is as much a reality as birth, growth, maturity and old age —it is the one certainty. I do not fear death as much as I fear the indignity of deterioration, dependence and hopeless pain. I ask that drugs be mercifully administered to me for terminal suffering even if they hasten the moment of death.

This request is made after careful consideration. Although this document is not legally binding, you who care for me will, I hope, feel morally bound to follow its mandate. I recognize that it places a heavy burden

*As distributed by the Euthanasia Educational Council, 1972.

of responsibility upon you, and it is with the intention of sharing that responsibility and of mitigating any feelings of guilt that this statement is made.

Signed _____

Date _____

Witnessed by:

_____

_____

DEFINITIONS OF DEATH

Criteria of the Ad Hoc Committee of the Harvard Medical School (1968)*

1. *Unreceptivity and Unresponsivity.*—There is a total unawareness to externally applied stimuli and inner need and complete unresponsiveness—our definition of irreversible coma. Even the most intensely painful stimuli evoke no vocal or other response, not even a groan, withdrawal of a limb, or quickening of respiration.

2. *No Movements or Breathing.*—Observations covering a period of at least one hour by physicians is adequate to satisfy the criteria of no spontaneous muscular movements or spontaneous respiration or response to stimuli such as pain, touch, sound, or light. After the patient is on a mechanical respirator, the total absence of spontaneous breathing may be established by turning off the respirator for three minutes and observing whether there is any effort on the part of the subject to breathe spontaneously. (The respirator may be turned off for this time provided that at the start of the trial period the patient's carbon dioxide tension is within the normal range, and provided also that the patient had been breathing room air for at least 10 minutes prior to the trial.)

3. *No Reflexes.*—Irreversible coma with abolition of central nervous system activity is evidenced in part by the absence of elicitable reflexes.

*Reprinted by permission.

The pupil will be fixed and dilated and will not respond to a direct source of bright light. Since the establishment of a fixed, dilated pupil is clear-cut in clinical practice, there should be no uncertainty as to its presence. Ocular movement (to head turning and to irrigation of the ears with ice water) and blinking are absent. There is no evidence of postural activity (decerebrate or other). Swallowing, yawning, vocalization are in abeyance. Corneal and pharyngeal reflexes are absent.

As a rule the stretch of tendon reflexes cannot be elicited; ie, tapping the tendons of the biceps, triceps, and pronator muscles, quadriceps and gastrocnemius muscles with the reflex hammer elicits no contraction of the respective muscles. Plantar or noxious stimulation gives no response.

4. *Flat Electroencephalogram.*—Of great confirmatory value is the flat or isoelectric EEG. We must assume that the electrodes have been properly applied, that the apparatus is functioning normally, and that the personnel in charge is competent. We consider it prudent to have one channel of the apparatus used for an electrocardiogram. This channel will monitor the ECG so that, if it appears in the electroencephalographic leads because of high resistance, it can be readily identified. It also establishes the presence of the active heart in the absence of the EEG. We recommend that another channel be used for a noncephalic lead. This will pick up space-borne or vibration-borne artifacts and identify them. The simplest form of such a monitoring noncephalic electrode has two leads over the dorsum of the hand, preferably the right hand, so the ECG will be minimal or absent. Since one of the requirements of this state is that there be no muscle activity, these two dorsal hand electrodes will not be bothered by muscle artifact. The apparatus should be run at standard gains $10\mu v/mm$, $50\mu v/5mm$. Also it should be isoelectric at double this standard gain which is $5\mu v/mm$ or $25\mu v/5mm$. At least ten full minutes of recording are desirable, but twice that would be better.

It is also suggested that the gains at some point be opened to their full amplitude for a brief period (5 to 100 seconds) to see what is going on. Usually in an intensive care unit artifacts will dominate the picture, but these are readily identifiable. There shall be no electroencephalographic response to noise or to pinch.

All of the above tests shall be repeated at least 24 hours later with no change.

The validity of such data as indications of irreversible cerebral damage depends on the exclusion of two conditions: hypothermia (temperature below 90 F [32.2 C])

Proposal of Alexander M. Capron and Leon R. Kass (1972)*

A person will be considered dead if in the announced opinion of a physician based on ordinary standards of medical practice, he has experienced an irreversible cessation of spontaneous respiratory and circulatory functions. In the event that artificial means of support preclude a determination that these functions have ceased, a person will be considered dead if in the announced opinion of a physician, based on ordinary standards of medical practice, he has experienced an irreversible cessation of spontaneous brain functions. Death will have occurred at the time when the relevant functions ceased.

Virginia Statute (1973)

Be it enacted by the General Assembly of Virginia:
1. That the Code of Virginia be amended by adding a section numbered 32–364.3:1 as follows:

§ 32–364.3:1 A person shall be medically and legally dead if, (a) in the opinion of a physician duly authorized to practice medicine in this State, based on the ordinary standards of medical practice, there is the absence of spontaneous respiratory and spontaneous cardiac functions and, because of the disease or condition which directly or indirectly caused these functions to cease, or because of the passage of time since these functions ceased, attempts at resuscitation would not, in the opinion of such physician, be successful in restoring spontaneous life-sustaining functions, and, in such event, death shall be deemed to have occurred at the time these functions ceased; or (b) in the opinion of a consulting physician, who shall be duly licensed and a specialist in the field of neurology, neurosurgery, or electroencephlography, when based on the ordinary standards of medical practice, there is the absence of spontaneous brain functions and spontaneous respiratory functions and, in the opinion of the attending physician and such consulting physician, based on the ordinary standards of medical practice and considering the absence of the aforesaid spontaneous brain functions and spontaneous respiratory functions and the patient's medical record, further attempts at resuscitation or continued supportive maintenance would not be successful in restoring such spontaneous functions, and, in such event, death shall be deemed to have occurred at the time when

*Reprinted by permission from the *University of Pennsylvania Law Review,* Nov. 1972, 121:87–118.

these conditions first coincide. Death as defined in subsection (b) hereof, shall be pronounced by the attending physician and recorded in the patient's medical record and attested by the aforesaid consulting physician.

Notwithstanding any statutory or common law to the contrary, either of these alternative definitions of death may be utilized for all purposes in the Commonwealth, including the trial of civil and criminal cases.

SOURCES

The sources listed below were either mentioned or quoted in the text. Books and signed articles are listed by name of author; editorials, unidentified articles, news items, and symposia are under the name of the periodical listing them; official reports are listed under the organization or committee responsible for them. Bills and the individual cases mentioned are listed separately on pages 329–335.

Books marked with an asterisk are recommended for the general reader. References used in the supplement have not been added to this list.

The Advocates. Should the law permit voluntary euthanasia for the terminally ill? Transcript of a Public Broadcasting Service Program, May 2, 1972.

Aldrich, C. K. The dying patient's grief. *JAMA,* May 4, 1963, 184, **5:** 329–331.

Alexander, L. Medical science under dictatorship. *New England J. Medicine,* Jul. 14, 1949, 241, **2:** 39–47.

Altman, L. K. Doctor and patient: Bill of Rights a break with old paternalism. *N.Y. Times,* Jan. 9, 1973: 1; Jan. 10, 1973: 24.

Alvarez, W. C. Ethics in medicine. *G. P.* (Journal of Am. Acad. of General Practice), Sept. 1950, 2, **3:** 81–83.

Alvarez, W. C. Care of the dying. *JAMA,* Sept. 13, 1952, 150: 86–91.

American Broadcasting Company. See: *The right to die.*

*American Friends Service Committee. *Who shall live? Man's control over birth and death.* N.Y.: Hill & Wang, 1970.

American Hospital Association. *Bill of Rights of patients.* See: Altman, L. K. Also *Newsweek,* Jan. 22, 1973, p. 77.

Apgar, V. & Stickle, G. Birth defects: their significance as a public health problem. *JAMA,* April 29, 1968, 204, **5:** 79–82.

Appel, J. Z. Ethical and legal questions posed by recent advances in medicine. *JAMA,* Aug. 12, 1968, 205, **7:** 101–104.

Auerbach, S. AMA aide sees place for euthanasia. *Washington Post,* June 29, 1973: A 14.

Augenstein, L. *Come let us play God.* N.Y.: Harper & Row, 1969.

Aurelius, Marcus. See: Saffron, M. H.; Moore, C.; Haines, C. R. (p. 321.)

Avorn, J. Beyond dying: experiments using psychedelic drugs to ease the transition from life. *Harper's,* Mar. 1973, 246, **1474:** 56–64.

Ayd, F. J., Jr. The hopeless case: medical and moral considerations. *JAMA,* Sept. 29, 1962, 181, **13:** 1099–1102.

Ayd, F. J., Jr. Voluntary euthanasia. *Medical-Moral Newsletter,* Jan.–Feb. 1970, VI, **5–6.**

Ayd, F. J., Jr. Voluntary euthanasia: the right to be killed. *Medical Counterpoint,* June, 1970, 2, **6:** 12.

Ayd, F. J., Jr. When is a person dead? *Medical Sci.* Ap. 1967, 18, **4:** 33–38.

Bard, B. & Fletcher, J. The right to die. *Atlantic Monthly,* Ap. 1968, 221, **4:** 59–64.

Baughman, W. H., Bruha, J. C., & Gould, F. J. Euthanasia: criminal, tort, constitutional and legislative considerations. *Notre Dame Lawyer,* June 1973, 48, **5:** 1202–1260.

Beavan, J. The patient's right to live and die. *N.Y. Times,* Aug. 9, 1959, VI: 14; Aug. 23, 1959, VI: 4.

Becker, A. As quoted in *Time,* Nov. 25, 1935, 26: 39.

Beckman, M. A. Humanizing the management of death: a psychiatric social worker's viewpoint. *Euthanasia Education Council Report,* 1968: 18–19.

Beecher, H. K. Ethical problems created by the hopelessly unconscious patient. *New England J. Medicine,* June 27, 1968, 278, **26:** 1425–1430.

Berrill, N. J. Abnormal babies should not be encouraged to live. *Saturday Night* (Toronto), Dec. 6, 1958, 73, **25:** 12–13.

Berrill, N. J. The crime of keeping worn-out bodies alive. *Maclean's* (Toronto), Feb. 11, 1961, 74, **3:** 18; 29–30.

Bonnell, J. S. Sanctity of human life. *Theology Today,* May–Jul. 1951, 8: 194–201.

Brill, A. A. Is mercy killing justified? *Vital Speeches of the Day*, Dec. 16, 1935, 2, **6**: 165–167.

Brill, A. A. Reflections on euthanasia. *J. Nervous and Mental Diseases*, Jul. 1936, 84, **1**: 1–2.

*Brim, O. G., Jr. (Ed.) *The dying patient*. N.Y.: Russell Sage Foundation, 1970.

British Medical Association. The problem of euthanasia: report of a special panel of the Board of Science and Education of the BMA, January 1971. *British Medical J.*, Jan. 23, 1971: 187.

British Medical J. Distress in dying. Aug. 17, 1963, 2: 400–401.

British Medical J. Killing of patients (editorial). Ap. 5, 1969, 2: 4–5.

British Medical J. Reports on the founding of the Voluntary Euthanasia Society and proposed bill: Nov. 2, 1935, 2: 856; Nov. 30, 1935, 2: 1052; Dec. 14, 1935, 2: 1168.

Brody, J. E. New medical specialty urged to help one die with dignity. *N.Y. Times*, Jan. 16, 1972: 46.

Brown, N. K., *et al.* How do nurses feel about euthanasia and abortion? *Am. J. Nursing*, Jul. 1971, 71, **7**: 1413–1416.

Brown, N. K. The preservation of life. *JAMA*, Jan. 5., 1970, 211, **1**: 76–82.

Burger, W. E. The law and medical advances. *Annals of Internal Medicine*, Sept. 1967, 67, **3**: 15–18.

Butler, E. P. Euthanasia: M.D.'s asked for study. *Boston Herald American*, June 29, 1973: 1.

Butler, R. N. & Lewis, M. I. *Aging and mental health: positive psychosocial approaches*. St. Louis, Mo.: C. V. Mosby Co., 1973.

CA (Bulletin of Cancer Progress). Let me go quietly (editorial). May–June 1959, 9, **3**: 72.

CA. Thanatopsis. Jan.–Feb. 1960, 10, **1**.

California Medical Association. Euthanasia—an overview for our time—a report by the CMA Committee for Continuing Study of Evolving Trends in Society Affecting Life. *Calif. Medicine*, Mar. 1973, 118, **3**: 55–58.

Callahan, D. Ethics, law and genetic counseling. *Science*, Ap. 14, 1972, 176: 197–200.

Callahan, D. New Questions on life and death. *Event*, Dec. 1972: 3–5.

Callahan, D. The sanctity of life. In D. R. Cutler (Ed.), *Updating life and death*. Boston: Beacon Press, 1969, pp. 181–223.

Canadian Medical Assn. *Code of Ethics*. Ottawa, Canada: Canadian Medical Assn. 1970.

Canadian Medical Assn. J. The ethical basis of medical practice. Ap. 3, 1965, 92: 782–783.

Canadian Medical Assn. J. Matters of life and death (editorial). Sept. 25, 1965, 93: 718–719.

Cappon, D. Attitudes of and toward the dying. *Canadian Medical Assn. J.*, Sept. 29, 1962, 87: 693–700.

Cappon, D. Attitudes toward death. *Postgraduate Medicine,* Feb. 1970, 47: 257.

Cappon, D. The dying. *Psychiat. Q.,* Jul. 1959, 33: 466–489.

Cappon, D. The psychology of dying. *Pastoral Psychol.,* Feb. 1961, 12: 35–44.

Capron, A. M. Determining death: do we need a statute? *Hastings Center Rep.,* Feb. 1973, 3, 1: 6–7.

Capron, A. M. & Kass, L. R. A statutatory definition of the standards for determining human death: an appraisal and a proposal. *U. of Penn. Law Rev.,* Nov. 1972, 121, 1: 87–118.

Cassell, E. J. Permission to die. *BioScience,* Aug. 1973, 23, **8:** 475–478.

Cassell, E. J. Learning to die. *Bull. N.Y. Acad. Medicine,* Dec. 1973, 49, **12:** 1110–1118. (Quoted on p. 221).

Catholic World. Thomas More, the mercy killer. Ap. 1949, 169: 3.

Church Assembly Board for Social Responsibility. *Decisions about life and death: a problem in modern medicine.* London: Church Information Office, 1965. (See *Crucible,* July 1970).

Ciba Foundation Symposium. See: Wolstenholme, G. & O'Connor, M.

Cohon, B. D. Euthanasia: theory and practice in Judaism. *Nat. Jewish Monthly,* Mar. 1969, 83: 24.

Colebrook, L. *A plan for voluntary euthanasia.* London: Voluntary Euthanasia Society, 1962. Appeared also in *Lancet,* Dec. 8, 1962, 2: 1205.

Commonweal. A bill in the New York Legislature (editorial). Feb. 10, 1939, 29, **16:** 422–423.

Commonweal. Ite ad Joseph (editorial). Jan. 21, 1949, 49, **15:** 363.

Commonweal. Quality of mercy (editorial). Jan. 13, 1950, 51, **14:** 380–381.

Connecticut State Medical Society. Definition of Death. Adopted by the House of Delegates of the Society, April, 1967. As reported in J. A. Fabro, *New England J. Medicine,* Mar. 9, 1972, 286, **10:** 549.

Connecticut State Medical Society. Dignity in life and death. Adopted by the House of Delegates of the Society, Ap. 24, 1973. As reported in *N.Y. Times,* Ap. 26, 1973: 40.

*Curtin, S. *Nobody ever died of old age.* Boston: Little, Brown & Co., 1972.

Cutler, D. R. (Ed.) *Updating life and death: essays in ethics and medicine.* Boston: Beacon Press, 1969.

Dash, L. Forest Haven: 200 retarded wait mindlessly for death. *Washington Post,* May 26, 1971: 1.

Davidson, H. A. Should we legalize mercy killing? *Medical Economics,* May 1950, 27, **8:** 64–66.

Davis, B. The nurse's dilemma. *Euthanasia Educational Council Report,* 1971: 14–18. Also 1970 Report p. 24.

Davis, E. Should we prolong suffering? *Nebraska State Medical J.,* Oct. 1950, 35, **10:** 310–312.

Dawson, Lord. See: *Parliamentary Debates.*

Dempsey, D. Learning how to die. *N.Y. Times,* Nov. 14, 1971, VI: 58.

Dept. of Health and Social Security. Care of the dying (a symposium). *British Medical J.,* Jan. 6, 1973, 31, **2.**

Deutsch, F. Euthanasia: a clinical study. *Psychoanal. Q.,* Jul. 1936, 5: 347–368.

*Downing, A. B. (Ed.) *Euthanasia and the right to death: the case for voluntary euthanasia.* London: Peter Owen, 1969; N.Y.: Humanities Press, 1970.

Doyle, C. Heenan: death not to be avoided at all costs. *Observer* (London), Jan. 28, 1973: 2.

Duff, R. S. & Campbell, A. G. M. Moral and ethical dilemmas in the special-care nursery. *New England J. Medicine,* Oct. 25, 1973, 289, **17:** 890–894. See also: *Time,* The hardest choice. Mar. 25, 1974: 84; *Washington Post,* Deformed infants are allowed to die. Oct. 28, 1973: B5.

Earengey, W. G. Voluntary euthanasia. *Medico-Legal and Criminal Rev.* (Cambridge), 1940, 8: 91–110.

Eckstein, H. B., Hatcher, G., & Slater, E. New Horizons in medical ethics: severely malformed children. *British Medical J.,* May 5, 1973, 2: 284–288.

Edelstein, L. *The Hippocratic Oath: text, translation and interpretation.* Baltimore: The Johns Hopkins U. Press, 1943.

*Eissler, K. R. *The psychiatrist and the dying patient.* N.Y.: International Universities Press, 1955. (p. 118 is quoted on p. 125).

Episcopal Council of the Protestant Episcopal Church. *Report of the Commission.* New York, 1973.

Euthanasia Educational Council. Reports of annual conferences are available from the Council's office in New York City. Titles are as follows: *The right to die with dignity,* 1968. *Today's student takes a new look at life and death,* 1969. *Attitudes toward euthanasia in ancient times and today,* 1970. *Dilemmas of euthanasia,* 1971. *Euthanasia—rights and realities,* 1972. *Euthanasia: an examination of current attitudes,* 1973.

Euthanasia Society of America. Organization as reported in *N.Y. Times,* Jan. 17, 1938: 21; *Time,* Jan. 31, 1938, 31, **5:** 24. Questionnaire to N.Y. doctors as reported in *N.Y. Times,* May 23, 1941: 23. N.Y. Bill as reported in S. James, *Survey Graphic,* May, 1948; H. Davidson, *Medical Economics,* May 1950; *N.Y. Times,* Dec. 15, **1947:** 30.

Exton-Smith, A. N. Terminal illness in the aged. *Lancet,* Aug. 5, 1961, 2:305–308.

Feifel, H., *et al.* Physicians consider death. *Proceedings, Amer. Psychol. Assn. Convention,* 1967, pp. 201–202.

Ferriar, J. *Medical histories and reflections.* Vol. 3. London: Cadell & Davies, 1798.

Filbey, E. E. Some overtones of euthanasia. *Hospital Topics* (Chicago), Sept. 1965, 43:55–61.

Fischer, J. The easy chair. Letter from Leete's Island: a case of termination. *Harper's,* Feb. 1973, 246, **1473:** 25–27.

Five times I have taken a life. *N.Y. Times,* Nov. 8, 1935: 1. See also: *Literary Digest;* and *Time,* Nov. 18 & 25, 1935.

Fletcher, G. P. Prolonging Life. *Washington Law Rev.,* June 1967, 42. **4:** 999–1016.

Fletcher, G. P. Legal aspects of the decision not to prolong life. *JAMA,* Jan. 1, 1968, 203: 65–68.

Fletcher, John. Attitudes toward defective newborns. *Hastings Center Studies,* Jan. 1974, 2, **1:** 21–32.

Fletcher, John. Parents in genetic counseling: the moral shape of decision-making. In B. Hilton, *et al.* (Eds.), *Ethical issues in human genetics.* N.Y. Plenum Press, 1973.

Fletcher, Joseph. Dysthanasia: the problems of prolonging death. *Tufts Folia Medica,* Jan.–Mar. 1962, 8, **1.**

Fletcher, Joseph. Elective death. In E. F. Torrey (Ed.), *Ethical issues in medicine.* Boston: Little, Brown & Co., 1968.

Fletcher, Joseph. Ethics and euthanasia. *Am. J. Nursing,* Ap. 1973, 73, **4:** 670–675.

Fletcher, Joseph. Indicators of humanhood: a tentative profile of man. *Hastings Cr. Rep.,* Nov. 1972, 2, **5:** 1–4.

Fletcher, Joseph. *Moral responsibility: situation ethics at work.* Phil.: Westminster Press, 1967.

*Fletcher, Joseph. *Morals and medicine.* Boston: Beacon Press, 1960.

Fletcher, Joseph. The patient's right to die. *Harper's,* Oct. 1960, 221: 139–143.

Fletcher, Joseph. Voluntary euthanasia: the new shape of death. *Medical Counterpoint,* June 1970, 2, **6:** 13.

Fortune. Survey and table on mercy killing. July 1937, 16: 106.

Foye, L. W., Jr. See: U.S. Senate Special Committee on Aging Hearings.

Franklin, R. K. The question of transplants. *New Republic,* Mar. 16, 1968, 158: 7–8.

Franks, J. As reported in C. S. Johnson, *Sunday Missoulian*, Joyce Franks wages a lonely crusade for legalized euthanasia. Dec. 17, 1972: 33; C. S. Johnson, *Miami Herald*, Housewife pleads for right-to-die law. Feb. 5, 1972.

Freeman, J. M. Is there a right to die quickly? *J. Pediatrics*, May 1972, 80, **5**: 904–908.

French Academy of Medicine. See: Gould, D.; Franklin, R. K.

Gale, Z. Charlotte Perkins Gilman. *Nation*, Sept. 25, 1935, 141: 350.

Gale, Z. The right to die. *Forum*, Feb. 1936, 95: 110–112.

Gallup, G. H. *The Gallup Poll: public opinion 1935–1971.* N.Y.: Random House, 1972. Polls cited include those of Jan. 17, 1937; Ap. 24, 1939; June 21, 1947; Feb. 6, 1950.

Gallup, G. H. Poll by the British Inst. of Public Opinion. As reported in *N.Y. Times*, Ap. 23, 1939, III: 4.

Gallup, G. H. Poll released Aug. 2, 1973. As reported in *N.Y. Times*, Aug. 2, 1973: 41.

Garman, E. M. Euthanasia—after four years. *Rocky Mountain Medical J.*, May 1971, 68, **5**: 3.

Gaylin, W. M. Sharing the hardest decision. *Hospital Physician*, Jul. 1972: 33–48.

Gillison, T. H. Letter to the editor. *Lancet*, Dec. 22, 1962, 2: 1327.

Gilman, C. P. The right to die. *Forum*, Nov. 1935, 94:297–300. Also, as reported in *Forum*, Dec. 1935, 94: 323: *Literary Digest*, Nov. 23, 1935, 120: 17; *Survey*, Sept. 1935, 71: 274.

Glaser, B. G. & Strauss, A. L. *Awareness of dying.* Chicago: Aldine, 1965.

Glaser, B. G. & Strauss, A. L. *Time for dying.* Chicago: Aldine, 1968.

Glaser, R. J. Innovations and heroic acts in prolonging life. In O. Brim, *op. cit.*, pp. 102–108.

Glass, B. Human heredity and ethical problems. *Perspectives in Biology and Medicine*, Winter 1972, 15: 237–253.

Glass, B. Science: endless horizons or Golden Age. *Science*, Jan. 8, 1971, 171, **3966**: 23–29.

Goddard, C. E. Suggestions in favour of terminating absolutely hopeless cases of injury and disease. *Medical Times and Hospital Gazette* (London), Oct. 19, 1901, 29: 657–659.

Good Housekeeping. Should mercy killing be permitted: Dr. Leslie Wenger says yes. Ap. 1967, 164: 82.

Gould, D. When is death? *New Statesman.* June 10, 1966, 71: 841.

Gould, J. (Ed.) *Your death warrant? Implications of euthanasia.* London: Geoffrey Chapman, 1971.

Graham, E. A good death: increasing support for euthanasia spurs heated medical debate. *Wall Street Journal*, Jan. 31, 1972: 1.

Gray, H. Bill in House of Commons reported, Euthanasia in England: a Growing Storm. *America,* May 2, 1970: 122: 463.

Green, P. *The problem of right conduct.* London & N.Y.: Longmans, Green & Co., 1931.

Gross, M. L. *The doctors.* N.Y.: Random House, 1966.

Hall, A. As reported in *N.Y. Times,* Jan. 24, 1906: 2; Jan. 25, 1906: 8.

Hamilton, M. P. (E.) *The new genetics and the future of man.* Grand Rapids, Mich.: William B. Eerdmans Publishing Co., 1972.

Hamlin, H. Life or death by EEG. *JAMA,* Oct. 12, 1964, 190: 112–114.

Hansard. See: Parliamentary debates.

Harden-Hickey, J. A. *Euthanasia: the aesthetics of suicide.* N.Y.: The Truth Seeker Co., 1894.

Harding, R. The legalization of voluntary euthanasia. *Nineteenth Century.* Aug., 1938, 124: 238–248.

Harvard Medical School Ad Hoc Committee to Examine the Definition of Brain Death. A definition of irreversible coma. *JAMA,* Aug. 5, 1968, 205, 6: 85–88; 337–340. See also: *British Medical J.,* 1970, 1: 750–751.

*Hendin, D. *Death as a fact of life.* N.Y.: Norton, 1973

Hinton, J. M. Distress in the dying. In J. N. Agate (Ed.), *Medicine in old age.* London: Pitman, 1966, pp. 180–187.

Hinton, J. M. *Dying.* Baltimore: Penguin, 1967.

Hinton, J. M. Facing death. *J. Psychosomatic Research,* Jul. 1966, 10: 22–28.

Hinton, J. M. The physical and mental distress of the dying. *Quarterly J. Medicine* (London), Jan. 1963, 32, 125: 1–21.

Hippocratic Oath. See: Edelstein, and Appendix.

Hirschfeld, J. C. Recent Decisions. *Notre Dame Lawyer,* May, 1959, 34: 460–464.

Horder, Lord. See: Parliamentary Debates.

Hume, D. Essays on suicide. *Essays and Treatises,* 1777.

Hurst, A. Euthanasia. *Quarterly Rev.,* Ap. 1940, 274, 544: 319–324.

Independent. Euthanasia once more, (editorial) Feb. 1, 1906, 60: 291–292.

Inge, W. R. *Science and ultimate truth.* London: Longmans, Green & Co., 1930.

Institute of Society, Ethics and the Life Sciences. *The institute: Goals and history.* Hastings-on-Hudson, N. Y. See also: C. Pepper, Should Science Have a Conscience? *R F Illustrated,* Oct. 1972, 1, 1.

Institute of Society, Ethics and the Life Sciences. Facing Death. Hastings Center Studies, May 1974, 2: 2.

Institute of Society, Ethics and the Life Sciences, Task Force on Death and Dying. Refinements in criteria for the determination of death: an appraisal. *JAMA,* Jul. 3, 1972, 221:1, 48–53.

Ivy, A. C. Nazi crimes of a medical nature: some conclusions. *JAMA* Jan. 15, 1949, 139, 3: 131–135.

Jackson, E. N. Is Euthanasia Christian? *Christian Century,* 67: 300–301, Mar. 8, 1950.

Jacoby, G. W. *Physician, pastor and patient.* N. Y.: Hoeber Inc., 1936.

Jakobovits, I. The dying and their treatment in Jewish law. *Hebrew Medical J.* 1961, 2: 242–251.

Jakobovits, I. *Jewish medical ethics: a comparative and historical study of the Jewish religious attitudes to medicine and its practice.* N.Y. Philosophical Library, 1959.

James, S. Euthanasia—right or wrong? *Survey Graphic,* May 1948, 37: 241–243.

Johnson, H. Nursing homes: the end of the line. *Washington Post,* Ap. 4, 1971: 1.

Josephs, D. The right to die with dignity. *N. Y. Times,* Sept. 25, 1971: 31.

J. Religion and Health. See: Meserve, H. C. regarding the Living Will. July 1971, 10:3.

Kamisar, Y. Some non-religious views against proposed 'mercy killing' Legislation. *Minnesota Law Review,* May 1958, 42, 6: 969–1042.

Karnofsky, D. A. Why prolong the life of a patient with advanced cancer. *CA,* Jan.–Feb. 1960, 10, 1: 9–11.

Kass, L. R. Death as an event; a commentary on Robert Morison, *Science,* Aug. 20, 1971, 173: 694–702.

Kass, L. R. Man's right to die. *The Pharos* Ap. 1972: 73–77.

Kass, L. R. The new biology: what price relieving man's estate? *Science,* Nov. 19, 1971, 174, 4011: 779–788.

Katz, S. Are they better off dead? *Maclean's* (Toronto), Nov. 1, 1947, 60, 21: 78: 69–73.

Kaunitz, J. An address reported in *Euthanasia Society Bulletin,* 1957.

Kelly, G. *Medico-moral problems.* St. Louis: Catholic Hospital Assn., 1958.

Kelly, G. Euthanasia. *Hospital Progress,* Mar. 1950, 31, 3: 91–92; April 1950, 31, 4: 118–119; Mar. 1955, 36, 3: 58.

Kennedy, F. Euthanasia: to be or not to be? *Collier's,* May 20, 1939, 103: 15–16; Ap. 22, 1950, 125: 13. See also: *N. Y. Times,* Feb. 14, 1939: 2.

Kubler-Ross, E. *On death and dying.* N.Y. Macmillan, 1969.

Kutner, L. Due process of euthanasia: the living Will. A proposal. *Indiana Law J.,* Summer 1969, 44, 4: 539–554.

Lancet. Against Euthanasia. Jan. 30, 1971: 320.

Lancet. Euthanasia (editorial) Aug. 12, 1961, 2: 351–352.

Lancet. The prolongation of dying (editorial). Dec. 8, 1962, 2: 1205.

Lancet. The right to die (letter to the editor by Sir Geo. P. Thomson). Nov. 14, 1970, 2: 1037.

Lasagna, L. *Life, death and the doctor.* N.Y.: Knopf, 1968.

Lasagana, L. Physicians' behavior toward the dying patient. In O. Brim, *op. cit.,* pp. 83–101.

Lawrence, R. Death for mercy's sake is gaining support in Toronto. *Toronto- Daily Telegram,* Jul. 3, 1963.

Laws, E. H., Bulger, R. J., Boyce, T. R., Thompson, D. J., & Brown, N. K. Views on euthanasia. *J. Medical Education,* June, 1971, 46: 540.

Leach, G. *The biocrats: implications of medical progress.* N.Y.: McGraw-Hill 1970.

Levine, S. & Scotch, N. S. Dying as an emerging social problem. In O. Brim, *op. cit.,* pp. 211–224.

Levisohn, A. A. Voluntary mercy deaths, social-legal aspects of euthanasia. *J. Forensic Medicine,* Ap.–June 1961, 8, 2: 57–79.

Life. Reader response: what do you think of your medical care? Aug. 11, 1972, 73, 6: 38–39.

Linacre Q. Murder by another name (editorial). Feb. 1950, 17, 1: 1.

Literary Digest. Five times I have taken a life. Nov. 23, 1935, 120: 17.

Long, P. H. On the quantity and quality of life. *Medical Times,* May 1960, 88, 5: 613–619.

Lorber, J. Results of treatment of myelomeningocele. *Developmental Medicine and Child Neurology,* June 1971, 13: 279–303.

MacPherson, J. As quoted in *Euthanasia Educational Council Report, 1971, op. cit.,* p. 32; *Euthanasia Educational Council Report, 1972, op. cit.,* pp. 44–48.

*Maguire, D. C. *Death by choice.* N.Y.: Doubleday, 1974.

Maguire, D. C. The freedom to die. *Commonweal,* Aug. 11, 1972, 96, 18: 423–427.

Mahoney, W. J. As quoted in *N.Y. Times,* Jan. 7, 1949: 15.

Mann, K. W. *Deadline for survival: a survey of moral issues in science and medicine.* N.Y.: Seabury Press, 1970.

*Mannes, M. *Last rights: a case for the good death.* N.Y.: William Morrow & Co., 1974.

Martin, T. O. Euthanasia and modern morality. *The Jurist,* Oct. 1950, 10, 4: 437–464.

Maryland State Medical J. Symposium on euthanasia. Mar. 1953, 2, 3: 120–140.

Matthews, W. E. *Voluntary euthanasia, the ethical aspect.* London: The Voluntary Euthanasia Society, 1950.

McCall, T. Death with dignity: unsolicited responses to a gubernatorial statement. Salem, Oregon: Office of the governor, undated.

McCall, T. Publicity releases from the Office of the Governor of Oregon, Feb. 28, 1972; Aug. 2, 1972.

McCormick, R. A. To save or let die. *JAMA,* Jul. 8, 1974, 229, 2: 172–176.

Mead, M. Answers: are you in favor of mercy deaths? *Redbook,* Jul. 1973, 141: 33–34.

Medical J. of Australia. Euthanasia legislation. May 10, 1969, 1: 987–988.

Medical J. of Australia. A time to die. Oct. 8, 1966, II: 710; Jan. 18, 1969, I: 127–128.

Medical Record. The euthanasia problem (editorial). Mar. 4, 1936, 143, 5:177.

Medical Society of the State of New York. News release, Jan. 11, 1973. Also, as reported in *N.Y. Times,* Physicians back the right to die. Jan. 13, 1973: 35.

Medical World News. The right to die with dignity. Feb. 21, 1969, 10, 8. (The 1968 Florida bill).

Meserve, H. C. Editorial, *J. Religion and Health,* Jul. 1971, 10, 3.

Middleton, J. S. As quoted in *N.Y. Times,* Jan. 10, 1949: 23.

Millard, C. K. Case for euthanasia. *Fortnightly Rev.,* Dec. 1, 1931, 136: 701–718.

Millard, C. K. A plea for the legalization of euthanasia. *Public Health,* Nov., 1931, 45: 39–47.

Millard, M. As reported in *N.Y. Times,* May 6, 1959: 49; and in *Newsweek,* The old lady slept, May 18, 1959: 44.

Mitchison, N. The right to die. *Medical World* (London), Aug. 1956, 85, 2: 159–163.

Mitford, J. Experiments behind bars: doctors, drug companies and prisoners. *Atlantic Monthly,* Jan. 1973, 231, 1: 64–73.

Mondale, W. F. The issues before us. *Hastings Center Report,* June 1971, 1, 1.

Moore, C. *A full inquiry into suicide.* London: 1790.

Morgan, A. E. Statement before the U.S. Senate Special Committee on Aging, Aug. 7, 1972.

Morgan, L. G. On drinking the hemlock (with introduction by A. E. Morgan). *Hastings Center Report,* Dec. 1971, 1, 3: 4–5.

Morison, R. S. Death: process or event? *Science,* Aug. 20, 1971, 173: 694–702. See also: Kass, L. R.; Robertson, M. G.

Morris, A. A. Voluntary euthanasia. *Washington Law Rev.* Ap. 1970, 45: 239–270.

Mosher, L. When there is no hope—why prolong life? *National Observer,* Mar. 4, 1972: 1.

Mountford, W. *Euthansy: or, happy talk towards the end of life.* N.Y.: D. Appleton & Co., 1848.

Muller, H. J. See: Wolstenholme, G. E. W. & O'Connor, M.

Munk, W. A. *Euthanasia: or medical treatment in aid of an easy death.* London: Longmans, Green & Co., 1887.

Nader, R. Thalidomide children. *New Republic,* Feb. 10, 1973, 168, 6: 10–11.

The National Foundation—March of Dimes. *Facts '73.* N.Y.:1973.

National Opinion Polls, Ltd. Report of two polls conducted in Jan. 1964 and Jan. 1965. Unpublished, available from the organization's office in London.

National Opinion Research Cr., U. of Chicago. National survey of attitudes toward abortion. As reported in *Washington Post,* Nov. 14, 1973: C4.

Neasden Hospital. As reported in *N.Y. Times,* London doctors get live or die decision. Sept. 23, 1967: 1; Sept. 24, 1967: 21; M. Jones, Euthanasia. *Observer Rev.* (London), Sept. 24, 1967; *Observer Rev.,* Right to die, Oct. 1, 1967: 21.

Nelson, H. AMA adopts report on 'dignified death.' *Washington Post,* Dec. 6, 1973: A1.

New England J. Medicine. Life in death (editorial). Ap. 18, 1957, 256, 16: 760–761.

New Medica Materia. A survey of how physicians feel about euthanasia. Oct. 1962, 4, 10; 31.

N.Y. Times. Death with dignity (editorial). Dec. 29, 1972: 24.

N.Y. Times. Mercy death bill filed in Nebraska. Feb. 3, 1937: 7; Feb. 14, 1937: 17.

N.Y. Times. Mercy death law ready for Albany. Feb. 14, 1939: 2.

N.Y. Times. Position of Pope Paul. Oct. 13, 1970: 2; June 4, 1972: 13.

N.Y. Times. The right to die (editorial). Jul. 3, 1973: 22.

N.Y.U. Law Rev. Morals, medicine and law—a symposium. Nov. 1956, 31: 1157–1245. Includes articles by T. A. Cowan, I. P. Frohman, J. D. Hassett, H. M. Kallen, H. Kalven, Jr., M. Ploscowe, E. Rackman, & P. Ramsey.

Norton, C. E. As reported in *N.Y. Times* (editorial). Jan. 6, 1906: 8.

Osler, W. The growth of Truth. In *Selected writings.* London: Oxford U. Press, 1951.

Osler, W. *Science and immortality.* Boston: Houghton, 1904.

Outlook. Shall we legalize homicide? Feb. 3, 1906, 82: 252.

Parliamentary Debates. Dec. 1, 1936, 103, 11: 466–506. See also *Law Times,* Nov. 28, 1936, 182: 412–413; *Lancet,* Dec. 5, 1936, 2: 1369; *British*

Medical J., Dec. 12, 1936, 1: 1232–1234; *N.Y. Times*, Nov. 5, 1936: 29; *N.Y. Times*, Nov. 11, 1936: 22; *N.Y. Times*, 1936: 29, Dec. 2, 1936: 29.

Parliamentary Debates. 1951, 169: 552–598.

Parliamentary Debates. March 25, 1969, 300, 50: 1143–1254. See also: *British Medical J.*, Ap. 5, 1969, 2: 4–5.

Peck, R. L. When should the patient be allowed to die? *Hospital Physician*, Jul. 1972, 8: 29–33.

Pestalozzi-Henggeler, A. Euthanasia under the Swiss penal code. *Southwestern Law J.*, 1961, 15, 3: 393–398.

Philbrick, I. C. As reported in *N.Y. Times*, Feb. 3, 1937: 7.

Peterson, O. L. Control of medical conduct. In O. Brim, *op. cit.*, pp. 225–252.

Platt, R. As quoted in *British Medical J.* Killing of patients (editorial). Ap. 5, 1969, II: 4–5.

Pole, K. F. M. Euthanasia or a peaceful death. *Linacre Q.*, Feb. 1971, 38: 45–49.

Pope Pius XII. As quoted by *Acta Apostolicae Sedis*, 1957, 49: 1027–1033; *Catholic Medical Q.*, Oct. 1956, 10: 6–13; *New York Times*, Feb. 25, 1957: 1; Nov. 25, 1957: 20. *The Pope Speaks*, Medical law and morality. Winter 1956–1957, 3, 3: 216–270; *The Pope Speaks*, Anesthesia: three moral questions. Summer 1957, 4, 1: 33–49; *The Pope Speaks*, Prolongation of life. Spring 1958, 4, 4: 393–398.

Postgraduate Medicine. When should patients be allowed to die. Some questions of ethics (symposium). Ap. 1968, 43, 4: 197–200; May 1968: 222–225.

Potter, C. F. Should Mercy Killing be legalized? The case for voluntary euthanasia. *Reader's Scope*, May 1947, 4, 12: 111–114.

Pryor, D. H. Where we put the aged. *New Republic*, Ap. 25, 1970, 162, 17: 15–17.

Quint, J. C. The dying patient: a difficult nursing problem. *Nursing Clinics of North Am.*, Dec. 1967, 2: 763–773.

Quint, J. C. *The nurse and the dying patient.* N.Y.: Macmillan, 1967.

Quint, J. E. The threat of death: some consequences for patients and nurses. *Nursing Forum.* 1969, 8, 3: 286–298.

Ramsey, P. *Fabricated man: the ethics of genetic control.* New Haven: Yale U. Press, 1970.

Ramsey, P. On updating death. In D. R. Cutler, *op. cit.*

*Ramsey, P. *The patient as person: explorations in medical ethics.* New Haven: Yale U. Press, 1970.

Rattray, R. F. The right to painless death. *Quarterly Rev.* (London). Jan. 1940, 274, 543: 39–49.

Reader's Digest. Shall we legalize mercy killing? Nov. 1938, 33: 94–98.

Reedy, J. Coming up: campaign for euthanasia. *A.D. Correspondence: Personal Reflections on Catholic Life.* June 1971, 2, 13.

Reedy, J. Thoughts on the next controversy: cooperating with death. *A.D. Correspondence: Personal Reflections on Catholic Life.* March 18, 1972, 4, 6.

Reese, T. V. Doctor isn't accepting new patients. *Medical Economics,* Aug. 7, 1967, 44:72–77.

Reeves, R. B., Jr. *Recognizing the death of the individual: a clergyman's viewpoint.* N.Y.: Euthanasia Educational Fund, 1968, no. 23, pp. 11–14.

Reid, F. W. Prolongation of life or prolonging the act of dying. *JAMA,* Oct. 9, 1967, 202, 2:162.

Restak, R. Death. *Washington Post,* Dec. 17, 1972:B1.

Rial, W. Y. & Morrison, M. What are we doing with our power over death? *The Episcopalian,* Dec. 1969, 134, 12.

Riddle, O. As quoted in *N.Y. Times,* Mercy death law ready for Albany. Feb. 14, 1939: 2.

The right to die. American Broadcasting Company Television documentary, Broadcast Jan. 5, 1974.

Riley, C. G. Doctor's moral obligation to his patients. *New Zealand Medical J.,* Oct. 1967, 66: 686–688.

Roberts, H. *Euthanasia and other aspects of life and death.* Ann Arbor, Mich.: Finch Press, 1973.

Roberts, H. May doctors kill? *Living Age,* Oct. 1934, 347: 159–162.

Robertson, M. G. Criteria of death. *Science,* Feb. 11, 1972, 175: 581.

Roosevelt, P. P. I love a Roosevelt. As excerpted in *Good Housekeeping,* Eleanor Roosevelt: a great lady's last brave days. June 1967, 164: 80–83.

Royal Soc. of Health. Report of Dec. 1973 conference. *The Voluntary Euthanasia Soc. Newsletter* (London), Ap. 1974.

Royal Soc. of Medicine. The cost of life (symposium). *Proceedings of the Royal Society of Medicine* (London), Nov. 1967, 60, 11, Part 2.

Royal Soc. of Medicine. Euthanasia (conference of the Royal Soc. of Medicine, Oct. 13, 1969). As reported in *British Medical J.,* Oct. 1969, 4, 229; *Proceedings of the Royal Soc. of Medicine,* Jul. 1970, 63, 7: 659–670.

Rusk, H. A. Science in the Nazi era. *N.Y. Times,* May 31, 1959: 62.

Russell, O. R. The right to choose death. *N.Y. Times,* Feb. 14, 1972: 29.

Rynearson, E. H. You are standing at the bedside of a patient dying of untreatable cancer. *CA,* May–June 1959, 9: 85–87.

Sackett, W. W. I've let hundreds of patients die. Shouldn't you? *Medical Economics,* Ap. 2, 1973, 50: 92–114.

Saffron. M. H. Euthanasia in the Greek Tradition, *Euthanasia Educational Council Conference Report,* 1970, pp. 3–7.

Sanders, J. Euthanasia: none dare call it murder. *J. Criminal Law, Criminology, and Police Science,* Sept. 1969, 60, 3: 351–359.

Sanders, M. K. (Ed.) *The crisis in American medicine* (with foreward by J. Fischer). N.Y.: Harper & Brothers, 1961.

Saunders, C. *Care of the dying.* London: Macmillan Co, 1959.

Saunders, C. The treatment of intractable pain in terminal cancer. *Proceedings of the Royal Soc. of Medicine,* 1963, 56: 195–197.

Schiff, A. F. Euthanasia? Yes, but what kind?, *Medical Economics,* May 25, 1970, 47: 259–273.

Schiff, A. F. The final specialty. *Medical Opinion and Rev.* Nov. 1969, 5, 11: 16d–25.

Schwab, R. S. Today's student takes a new look at life and death. *Euthanasia Educational Council Conference Report,* 1969, 7–9.

Seneca, L. A. Epistulae Morales (R. M. Gummere, Trans.). N.Y.: G.P. Putnam's Sons, 1917, op. cit., pp. 181–192. Epistles LXX: 11–14. See also Moore, C.

Sheldon, J. H. *Report to the Birmingham Regional Hospital Board on its Geriatric Services.* Birmingham, England; Birmingham Regional Hospital Board, 1961.

Shideler, M. M. Coup de grace. *Christian Century,* Dec. 7, 1966, 83: 1499–1502; Jan. 4, 1967, 20 & 18: 82–83.

Shirer, W. L. Mercy deaths in Germany, *Reader's Digest,* June 1941, 38: 55–58.

Silving, H. Euthanasia: a study in comparative criminal law. *U. of Penn. Law Rev.* 1954, 103: 350–389.

Simpson, C. K. *Forensic Medicine.* (6th. ed.). London: Edward Arnold, 1969.

Slater, E. The case for voluntary euthanasia. *Contemporary Rev.* (London), Aug. 1971, 219, **1267**: 84–88.

Slater, E. The fear of death. *British Medical J.* Ap. 12, 1958, 1: 885.

Slater, E. Give man the right to die, British MD says. *JAMA,* Oct. 27, 1969, 210, **4**: 657.

Smith, H. An appeal to doctors. *Lancet,* Dec. 20, 1969: 1353. Also Nov. 21, 1970: 1088.

Smith, H. Suicide and euthanasia. *British Medical J.,* June 5, 1971, 2: 591.

St. John-Stevas, N. *The right to life.* N.Y.: Holt, Rinehart & Winston, 1964.

Stevens, R. Euthanasia: a doctor speaks. Address to the Rochester, N.Y. chapter of the Euthanasia Educational Council, Feb. 4, 1971. Leaflet.

Straight, M. Germany executed her 'unfit'. *New Republic,* May 5, 1941, 104: 627–628.

Strauss, A. L. & Glaser, B. G. Patterns of dying. In O. Brim, *op. cit.,* pp. 129–155.

Sudnow, D. Dying in a public hospital. In O. Brim, *op. cit.,* pp. 191–208.

Sudnow, D. *Passing on: the social organization of dying.* Englewood Cliffs, N.J.: Prentice-Hall, 1967. (cited on p. 172).

Sullivan, J. V. *Catholic teaching on the morality of euthanasia.* Washington, D.C.: Catholic U. Press, 1949. Also published in 1950 by Newman Press, Westminister, Md., under title *The morality of mercy killing.*

Sullivan, M. T. The dying person—his plight and his right. *New England Law Rev.,* Spring 1973, 8: 197–216.

Sweetingham, C. R. Euthanasia—a human right. *Freethinker: The Humanist World Weekly,* Jan. 26, 1968, 88, 4: 29.

Swenson, W. M. Attitudes toward death among the aged. *Minn. Medicine,* Ap. 1959, 42, 4: 399–402.

Swenson, W. M. Attitudes toward death in older persons: a symposium. *J. Gerontology,* Jan. 1961, 16, 1: 49–53.

Time. The old in the country of the young. Aug. 3, 1970, 96: 49–54.

Todd, M. As quoted by S. Auerbach, *op. cit.,* E. P. Bulter, *op. cit.*

Tollemache, L. A. The cure for incurables. *Fortnightly Rev.,* 1873, 19: 218.

Tollemache, L. A. *Stones of Stumbling.* London: C. F. Hodgson & Sons, 1884 (4th edition in 1895).

Townsend, C. *Old age: the last segregation.* N.Y.: Grossman Publ., 1971.

Trowbridge, C. Today's student takes a new look at life and death. *Euthanasia Educational Council Conference Report* 1969, p. 14.

*Trubo, R. *An act of mercy: euthanasia today.* Los Angeles: Nash Publishing Co., 1973.

Turano, A. M. Murder by request. *American Mercury,* Dec. 1935, 36: 423–429.

United Church of Christ. *The Right to Die* (Statement adopted by General Synod), Washington D.C.: United Church of Christ, 1973.

United Methodist Church. Statement of Board of Global Ministry. N.Y.: United Methodist Church, 1972.

U.S. Catholic Conference Dept. of Health Affairs. *Ethical and religious directives for Catholic health facilities* (Approved by the Committee on Doctrine of the National Conference of Catholic Bishops, Washington, D.C.: Oct. 30, 1971.)

U.S. Dept. of Commerce, Social and Economic Statistics Admin. *Persons in institutions and other group quarters.* U.S. Gov. Printing Office, Washington, D.C. 1970.

U.S. Dept. of Health, Education, and Welfare. *Report of the President's Panel on Mental Retardation,* Oct. 1962. U.S. Government Printing Office, Washington, D. C.: 1962.

U.S. Senate Special Committee on Aging. *Death with dignity: an inquiry into related public issues.* Hearings Aug. 7–9, 1972. U.S. Gov. Printing Office, Washington, D.C.: 1972.

*Vaux, K. (Editor.) *Who shall live?* Phil.: Fortress Press, 1970.

Vickery, K. O. A. Euthanasia at 80? *Newsweek,* May 12, 1969, 73, **77**.

Vickery, K. O. A. The right to die. *Sunday Star Magazine* (Washington, D.C.), Aug. 17, 1969: 4–5.

Voluntary Euthanasia Soc. *The case for voluntary euthanasia.* London: Voluntary Euthanasia Soc. 1961, and 1962.

Voluntary Euthanasia Soc. *Doctors and euthanasia: a rejoinder to the British Medical Assn. 's report.* London: Voluntary Euthanasia Soc. 1971.

Von Hoffman, N. Repackaging the inquisition. *Washington Post,* Mar. 6, 1970: B1.

Walsh, J. J. Life is sacred. *Forum,* Dec. 1935, 94: 330–334.

Washington Post. Deformed infants are allowed to die. Oct. 28, 1973: B5.

Washington Post. Infant deaths. Nov. 16, 1973: D19.

Washington Post. Permitted to die. Aug. 31, 1973: A10. (Wojcik case).

Watson, J. D. Moving toward clonal man: is this what we want? *Atlantic Monthly,* May 1971, 227: 50–53.

Weatherhead, L. *The Christian agnostic.* London: Hodder & Stoughton, Ltd., 1965. (p. 267 quoted on p. 45 & 213).

Weisman, A. D. *On dying and denying: a psychiatric study of terminality.* N.Y.: Behavioral Publ., 1972.

Wells, S. R. Is euthanasia ever justifiable? *Transactions of the Medico-Legal Society* (London), 1906–1907.

*Wertenbaker, L. *Death of a man.* N.Y.: Random House, 1957. (1974 paperback by Beacon Press).

White House Conference on Aging. Toward a national policy on aging. Washington, D.C.: U.S. Govt. Printing Office, 1971.

Williams, G. Euthanasia. *Proceedings, Royal Soc. of Medicine,* Jul. 1970, 63: 663–670.

Williams, G. Mercy-killing legislation—a rejoinder. *Minn. Law Rev.,* 1958–1958, 43: 1–12.

*Williams, G. *The Sanctity of life and the criminal law.* N.Y.: Knopf, 1957.

*Williams, R. H. The end of life in the elderly. *Postgraduate Medicine,* Dec. 1973, 54, **6**: 55–59. Also appears as a chapter in R. H. Williams (Ed.), *To live and to die: when why and how.* N.Y. Springer-Verlag, 1973.

Williams, R. H. Our role in the generation, modification and termination of life. *Arch. Internal Medicine* (Chicago), Aug. 1969, 124, **2**: 215–237; and *JAMA*, Oct. 11, 1971, 218, 2: 249.

Williams, S. D. *Euthanasia.* London: Williams & Norgate, 1872.

Williamson, W. P. Life or death—whose decision? *JAMA*, Sept. 5, 1966, 197, **10**: 793–795.

Williamson, W. P. Should that patient be kept alive? *Medical Econcomics*, Jan. 9, 1967, 44, 1: 60–63.

Williamson, W. P. & Reid, F. W., Jr. Prolongation of life or prolonging the act of dying? *JAMA*, Oct. 9, 1967, 202, 2: 162–163.

Wilson, J. R. The freedom to die. *Spectator*, Feb. 7, 1969, 222: 169.

Wolbarst, A. L. The doctor looks at euthanasia. *Medical Record*, May 17, 1939, 149: **10**, 354–356.

Wolbarst, A. L. Legalize euthanasia. *Forum*, Dec. 1935, 94: 330–334.

Wolstenholme, G. E. W. & O'Connor, M. (Eds.) *Ethics in medical progress with special reference to transplanatation.* Boston: Little, Brown & Co., 1966.

World Council of Churches. *Genetics and the quality of life.* Geneva, Switz.: June, 1973.

World Medical Assn., 1950 meeting. As reported in *N.Y. Times*, Oct. 18, 1950: 22; *JAMA*, June 10, 1950, 143, **6**:: 561.

World Medical Assn. Declaration of Sydney. *Medical News*, Aug. 16, 1968: 9; *N.Y. Times*, Aug. 10, 1968: 25.

Ziemer, G. How Hitler builds his 'Super Race'. *Maclean's* Toronto, Oct. 15, 1941, 54, **2**: 43–45.

BIBLIOGRAPHY

The books and articles listed below, while not mentioned directly in the text, provide useful background information. Though they are listed by subject, many items belong under several headings.

Birth Defects

Bundey, S. Mongolism, the most common autosomal abnormality. *Modern Medicine*, Sept. 3, 1973, 41, **18**:32.

Engelhardt, H. T., Jr. Euthanasia and children: the injury of continued existence. *J. Pediatrics*, July 1973, 83:170–171.

Etzioni, A. *Genetic Fix.* N.Y.: Macmillan, 1973.

Etzioni, A. A testing time for fetal flaws. *Washington Post,* Dec. 9, 1973: Bl.

Gustafson, J. M. Mongolism, parental desires, and the right to life. *Perspectives in Biology and Medicine,* Summer 1973, 16:529–557.

Nelson, H. Life or Death for Brain-damaged Infant? *Los Angeles Times,* Mar. 17, 1972.

Reedy, J. The mentally retarded: the forgotten minority, A.D. *Correspondence,* Aug. 5, 1972, 3:105–107.

Shaw, A. Dilemmas of "informed consent" in children. *New England J. Medicine,* Oct. 25, 1973, 289,17:885–890.

Shaw, A. Doctor, do we have a choice? *N.Y. Times,* Jan. 30, 1972, VI:44

Definitions of Death

Beecher, H. K. Definitions of life and death for medical science and practice. *Annals of the N.Y. Acad. of Sciences,* Jan. 21, 1970, 169:471–474.

British Medical J., Moment of Death, 2:533. Aug. 27, 1966.

Cohn, R. Updating the definition of death. *Medical World News,* Ap. 28, 1967: 47.

Corday, E. Definition of Death—a double standard. *Hospital Tribune.* May 4, 1970:8.

Curran, W. J. Legal and medical death: Kansas takes the first step. *New England J. of Medicine,* Feb. 4, 1971, 284,5:260–261.

Curran, W. The legal meaning of death. *Am. J. of Public Health,* 1968, 58, 10:1965–1966;1968.

Dusinberre, R.K.Y. Statutory definition of death. *New England J. Medicine,* March 9, 1972, 286,10:549.

Fletcher, Joseph. New definitions of death. *Prism,* Jan. 1974:13.

Halley, M. & Harvey, W. F. Medical v. legal definitions of death. *JAMA,* May 6, 1968, 204,6:423–425.

Hannah, J. E. The signs of death: historical review. *N.C. Medical J.,* 1967, 28,11:457.

Hillman, H. & Aldridge, T. M. Towards a legal definition of death. *Solicitor's J.,* Ap. 28, 1972, 116:323.

Inst. for Judaism and Medicine. *Medical survey of the problems surrounding the criteria and definitions of death.* Jerusalem: July 1968.

Kennedy, I. M. The Kansas Statute on death—an appraisal. *New England J. Medicine,* Oct. 21, 1971, 285,17:946–949.

Mills, D. H. The Kansas Death Statute: bold and innovative. *New England J. Medicine,* Oct. 21, 1971, 285,17:968–969.

Taylor, L. F. A statutory definition of death in Kansas. *JAMA,* Jan. 11, 1971, 215,**2**:296.

Veatch, R. M. Brain death: welcome definition or dangerous judgment? *Hastings C. Report,* Nov. 1972, 2,**5**:10–13. *World Medical J.* The Moment of Death. 1967, 14:133–134.

The Elderly

Garvin, R. M. & Burger, R. E. *Where they go to die: the tragedy of America's aged.* N.Y.: Delacorte Press, 1968.

Mendelson, M. A. *Tender loving greed: How the incredibly lucrative nursing home industry is exploiting America's old people and defrauding us all.* N.Y.: Knopf, 1974.

Miller, M. B. Decision-making in the death process of the ill aged. *Geriatrics,* May 1971, 26,**5**:105–1116.

National Council on the Aging. *The golden years—a tarnished myth.* Washington, D.C.: U.S. Govt. Printing Office, 1970.

N.Y. Times. Mental hospitals: last refuge of the aged. Dec. 1, 1968, IV:4.

Paulson, G. W. Who should live? *Geriatrics,* Mar. 1973, 28,**3**:132–136.

Roberts, J. L. Kimsey, L. R. & Logan, D. L. How aged in nursing homes view dying and death. *Geriatrics,* Ap. 1970, 25:115–119.

Free choice and the right to death with dignity

Alsop, S. The right to die with dignity. *Good Housekeeping,* Aug. 1974:69; 130; 132.

Bavin, C. The right to die. *Spectator,* Ap. 7, 1950, 184,**6354**:466.

Briggs, W. L. Suicide may be one's right when life lacks hope, dignity. *National Observer,* Jan. 27, 1973:20.

Bryant, H. Death with dignity: is your life your own? Pros and cons of the right to die. *Seattle Post-Intelligencer,* Mar. 19–23, 1973.

Choron, J. *Suicide.* N.Y.: Scribner's Sons, 1972.

Cleland, J. T. (Ed.) The right to live and the right to die. *Medical Times,* 1967, 95:1171–1196.

Cooke, R. E. Is there a right to die—quickly? *J. Pediatrics,* 80,**5**:904–908.

Euthanasia Society of America, Inc. *The Euthanasia Soc. Bull.* was published quarterly until 1968, when the Euthanasia Educational Fund was established and the Society's *Bulletin* was discontinued. Since its foundation in 1971 the Fund, which later changed its name to the Euthanasia Educational Council, has published its *Bulletin* periodically.

Farrell, J. J. The right of a patient to die. *J. South Carolina Medical Assn.,* Jul. 1958, 55,**7**:231–233.

Gould, D. The right to die. *New Statesman,* Mar. 21, 1969, 77:402.

Gould, D. A better way to die. *New Statesman,* Ap. 4, 1969, 77:474.

Haines, C. R. *The communings with himself of Marcus Aurelius.* N.Y.: G. P. Putnam's Sons, 1961.

Hollobon, J. The power of life and death: now it's in your hands. *Homemakers's Magazine* (Canada), Jan.–Feb. 1973, 8,1:9–20.

The Humanist. A plea for beneficent euthanasia. Jul.–Aug. 1974, 34,4: 4–27.

Kelly, G. Survey on euthanasia. *Linacre Q.* Nov. 1950, 17,4:3–17.

Krant, M. J. *Dying and dignity: the meaning and control of a personal death.* Springfield, Ill.: Charles C Thomas, 1974.

Leeman, J. S. Euthanasia: man's right to die. *J. Religion and Health,* Oct. 1968, 7:342–349.

Lisker, J. Euthanasia: murder or mercy? *Boston Sunday Globe,* Jul. 15, 1973:Al.

Lister, J. Voluntary euthanasia. *New England J. Medicine,* May 29, 1969, 280, **22**:1225–1227.

Medical Times. The right to live and the right to die: symposium. 95,**11**: 1171–1196.

Miller, R. C. Humility and compassion—why hast thou forsaken us? *G. P.,* Oct. 1964, 30,4:213–215.

Moore, P. Let the dying die. *Saturday Evening Post,* Sept. 10, 1966: 12–14.

The Observer (London), Death: consumer's choice (editorial). Mar. 30, 1969.

Powers, C. T. Decisions for death with dignity. *Washington Post,* Aug. 5, 1973:K2.

Reeves, R. B., Jr. When is it time to die? Prolegomenon to voluntary euthanasia. *New England Law Rev.,* Spring 1973, 8:183–196.

Robitscher, J. B. The right to die. *Hastings Cr. Report,* Sept. 1972, 2,4: 11–14.

Sackett, W. W. Death with dignity. *Medical Opinion and Rec,* June 1969: 25–31.

Sackett, W. W. Death with dignity. *Southern Medical J.,* Mar. 1971:330–332.

Small, P. Euthanasia—the individual's right to freedom of choice. *Suffolk U. Law Rev.,* Fall 1970, 5:190–212.

Stallworthy, J. The right to live. *J. of the Royal College of General Practitioners,* Ap. 1970, 19:93.

Szasz, T. The ethics of suicide. *Antioch Rev.,* Spring 1971, 31:7–17.

The Times (London). Voluntary euthanasia (editorial). Mar. 24, 1969.

Tribe, D. The right to die. *Freethinker,* Jan. 26, 1968, 88, **4**:1;27.

Veatch, R. M. Choosing not to prolong dying. *Medical Dimensions,* Dec. 1972, 1,5:8–10.

The Voluntary Euthanasia Soc. (London). In addition to special reports, it publishes a *Newsletter* periodically.

Weber, L. J. Ethics and euthanasia: another view. *Am. J. Nursing,* Jul. 1973, 73,**7**:1228.

Wilkes, P. When do we have the right to die? *Life,* Jan. 14, 1972, 72:48–52.

Williams, P. N. The nature and dignity of man—AAAS Symposium. *Science,* Nov. 7, 1969, 166,**3906**:778.

Legislation, the Law and Euthanasia

Brill, H. W. Death with dignity: a recommendation for statutory change. *Univ. of Florida Law Rev.,* Winter 1970, 12, **3**:368–383.

Cannon, W. P. Euthanasia: the right to die. *Houston Law Rev.,* May 1970, 7,**5**:654–670.

Cantor, N. L. A patient's decision to decline life-saving medical treatment: Bodily integrity v. the preservation of life. *Rutgers Law Rev.,* Winter 1973, 26:228–264.

Colebrook, L. The Liége trial and the problem of voluntary euthanasia. *The Lancet,* Dec. 8, 1962:1225.

Friedman, G. A. Suicide, Euthanasia and the law. *Medical Times,* June 1957, 85,**6**:681–689.

Gallahue, J. Tragedy at Liege. *Look,* Mar. 12, 1963, 27, **72–74**.

Gurney, E. J. Is there a right to die? A study of the law of euthanasia. *Cumberland Samford Law Rev.,* Summer 1972, 3, **2**:235–261.

J. of the Medical Assn. of the State of Ala. Now would be a good time to foster a euthanasia bill (editorial). Feb. 1964, 38,**8**:764.

Kelly, W. A. The physician, the patient, and the consent. *U. of Kansas Law Rev.,* 1960, 8: 405–434.

Koessler, M. Euthanasia in the Hadamar Sanatorium and international law. *J. Criminal Law, Criminology, and Police Science,* Mar.–Ap. 1953, 43,**6**:735–755.

Louisell, D. W. Euthanasia and biathanasia: on dying and killing. *Catholic U. Law Rev.,* Summer 1973, 22,**723**:45.

Meyers, D. W. *The human body and the law: a medico-legal study.* Chicago: Aldine Pub., 1970.

Meyers, D. W. The legal aspects of medical euthanasia. *Bioscience,* Aug. 1973, 23,**8**:467–470.

Moore, M. M. The case for voluntary euthanasia. *UMKC law Rev.,* Spring 1974, 42,**3**:327–340.

Orth, C. E. Legal aspects relating to euthanasia. *Maryland Medical J.,* 1953, 2:120.

Platt, Lord R. *Private and controversial.* London: Cassell & Co., 1972.
Prevezer, S. The English Homicide Act: a new attempt to revise the law of murder. *Columbia Law Rev.,* 1957, 57: 624–629.
Scher, E. M. Legal aspects of euthanasia. *Albany Law Rev.,* 1972, 36,4 :674–697.
Sharpe, D. J. & Hargest, R. F. Lifesaving treatment for unwilling patients. *Fordham Law Rev.,* 1967–68, 36: 695–706.
St. John-Stevas, N. *Life, death and the law.* Cleveland: World Publishing Co., 1964.
Stevens, R. E. Do patients ever have rights in the timing of their own deaths. *New England Law Rev.,* Spring 1973, 8: 181–182.
Szasz, T. Medicine and the state: the first Amendment violated. *The Humanist,* Mar.–Ap. 1973:4–9.

Medical ethics and decision-making

Abelson, P. H. Who shall live. *Medical Sci.,* Nov. 1967, 18,11:38–44.
Aitken, P. W. The right to live and the right to die. *Medical Times,* Nov. 1967, 95,1184.
Banks, A. L. Euthanasia. *Practitioner,* 1948, 161:101–107.
Campbell, A. V. *Moral dilemmas in medicine: a coursebook in ethics for doctors and nurses.* Baltimore: Williams & Wilkins, 1972.
Cant, G. Deciding when death is better than life. *Time,* Jul. 16, 1973, 102:36–37.
Carlova, J. New supports for doctor-aided deaths. *Medical Economics,* May 25, 1970, 47:254–258.
Carr, J. L. The coroner and the common law: death and its medical implications. *Calif. Medical J.,* 1960, 93:32–34.
Clouser, K. D. The sanctity of life: an analysis of a concept. *Annals of Internal Medicine,* Jan. 1973, 78:119–125.
Collins, V. J. Limits of medical responsibility in the prolongation of life: a guide to decision—a dying score. *JAMA,* Oct. 7, 1968, 206,2: 389–392.
Dedek, J. F. *Human life: some moral issues.* N.Y.: Sheed & Ward, 1972.
Dickinson, G. T. Matters of life and death. *Canadian Medical Assn. J.,* Sept. 25, 1965, 93:718.
Downing, A. B. Euthanasia: the modern context. *St. Thomas' Hospital Gazette,* Winter 1967–1968, 65:4.
Edmonds, A. We don't want the job of God: should doctors hasten death? *Canadian Magazine,* Feb. 3, 1973:4–8.
Etzioni, M. B. The Physician's creed. Springfield, Ill.: Charles C Thomas, 1973.

Fletcher, Joseph. Medicine and the nature of man. *Science, Medicine and Man: An International J.*, Dec. 1973, 1,**2**:93–102.

Frazier, C. A. (Ed.) Should doctors play God? Nashville, Tenn.: Broadman Press, 1971.

Freeman, E. The God committee. *N.Y. Times,* May 21, 1972, VI: 84.

Gastonguay, P. R. Euthanasia: the next medical dilemma. *America,* Mar. 2, 1974: 130:152–153.

Goodfield, J. Reflections on the Hippocratic Oath. *Hastings C. Studies,* 1973, 1, 2: 79–92.

Gumpert, M. Euthanasia—pro and con: a false mercy. *Nation,* Jan. 28, 1950, 170, 179.

Haynes, W. S. Preservation of the unfit. *Medical J. Australia,* Mar. 20, 1971, 1,**12**:650–651.

Hofling, C. K. Terminal decisions. *Medical Opinion and Rev.,* 1966, 2,1: 40–49.

Ingelfinger, F. J. Bedside ethics for the hopeless case. *New England J. Medicine,* Oct. 25, 1973, 289,**17**:914–915.

Levine, M. The Hippocratic Oath in modern dress. *Cincinnati J. of Medicine,* 1948, 29:257–262.

Macdougall, A. K. Euthanasia: murder or mercy? *Humanist,* 1958, 1:38.

Mansson, H. H. Justifying the final solution. *Omega,* May 1972, 3:79–89.

McCormick, R. A. To save or let die. *JAMA,* Jul. 8, 1974, 229, 2:172–176.

McIntyre, R. V. Voluntary euthanasia: the ultimate perversion. *Medical Counterpoint,* June 1970, 2,**6**:26.

Medical World News. Doctors reply to survey on four key ethical sticklers. Sept. 15, 1972; 25–30.

Miller, B. Euthanasia and the ethics of self-fulfillment. *Ethical Platform,* May 1959.

Morse, J. Euthanasia: are mercy killings ever justified? *Boston Sunday Herald Advertiser,* Jul. 8, 1973:23.

O'Donnell, T. J. *Morals in medicine.* Westminister, Md.: Newman Press, 1960.

Rabinowitch, I. M. Euthanasia. *McGill Medical J.,* Oct. 1950, 19,**3**:160–176.

Rhoads, P. S. Medical ethics and morals in a new age. *JAMA,* Aug. 12, 1968, 205,**7**:517–522.

Ritchie-Calder, Lord. The doctor's dilemma. *Center Magazine,* Sept.–Oct. 1971, 4,**5**.

Romanell, P. A philosophic preface to morals in medicine. *Bull. N.Y. Acad. Medicine,* Jan. 1974, 50:3–27.

Saunders, C. Euthanasia. *Lancet,* 1961, 2:548.

Sidel, V. (Ed.) Resuscitation: who makes the decision. *New Physician,* Oct. 1972, 21,**1**:588.

Silverlight, J. The rights and wrongs of euthanasia. *London Observer,* Jan. 14, 1973:9.

Sperry, W. L. *The ethical basis of medical practice.* N.Y.: Harper & Bros., 1956.

Taylor, T. R. Annotations on the Oath of Hippocrates and the Geneva Version of the Oath. *Linacre Q.,* May 1956, 23:34–37.

Torrey, E. F. Euthanasia: a problem in medical ethics. *McGill Medical J.,* Oct. 1961:127–133.

Torrey, E. F. (Ed.) *Ethical issues in medicine.* Boston: Little, Brown & Co., 1968.

Trowell, H. *The unfinished debate on euthanasia.* London: SCM Press, 1973.

*Vaux, K. *Biomedical ethics: morality for the new medicine.* N.Y.: Harper & Row, 1974.

Verwoerdt, A. Euthanasia: a growing concern for physicians. *Geriatrics,* Aug. 1967, 22:44–60.

Washington Post. Doctors discuss ethics: justice, utility and emotion. Sept. 9, 1973:C3.

White, K. L. Life and death and medicine. *Scientific American,* Sept. 1973, 229,**3**:22–33.

Williams, G. Euthanasia. *Medico-Legal J.,* 1973, 41:14–34.

Modern Technology and Medical Care

Ehrenreich, B. & Ehrenreich, J. *The American health empire: an analysis of power, profits and politics in American medicine.* N.Y.: Vantage Books, 1971.

Ehrlich, P. *The population bomb.* N.Y.: Ballantine Books, 1968.

Fletcher, J. *The ethics of genetic control: ending reproductive roulette.* N.Y.: Doubleday Anchor, 1974.

Fuller, W. (Ed.) *The biological revolution: social good or social evil?* N.Y. Doubleday Anchor, 1972.

Gaylin, W. We have the awful knowledge to make exact copies of human beings. *N.Y. Times Magazine,* Mar. 6, 1972:10.

*Glasser, R. J. *Ward 402.* N.Y.: George Braziller, 1973.

Greenberg, S. *The quality of mercy: a report on the critical condition of hospital and medical care in America.* N.Y.: Atheneum, 1971.

Hanzlik, H. Population crisis. *Science,* Mar. 13, 1970, 167:1438.

Harmer, R. M. *The high cost of dying.* N.Y.: Crowell-Collier, 1963.

Jonas, H. *Philosophical essays: from ancient creed to technological man.* Englewood Cliffs, N.J.: Prentice-Hall, 1974.

Knowles, J. H. The hospital. *Scientific American,* Sept. 1973, 229,**3**:128.

*Kohl, M. *The morality of killing: euthanasia, abortion and transplants.* N.Y.: Humanities Press, 1974.

Kramer, J. R. Medical care: as costs soar, support grows for major reform. *Science,* Nov. 28, 1969, 166, **3909:**1126–1129.

Lewis, H. P. Machine medicine and its relation to the fatally ill. *JAMA,* Oct. 7, 1968, 206,**2:**387–388.

Martin, H. Inside the insane asylum. *Saturday Evening Post,* Ap. 8, 1968, 241:32–36.

Mendelsohn, E., *et al. Human aspects of biomedical innovation.* Cambridge, Mass.: Harvard U. Press, 1971.

Ramsey, P. Genetic engineering. *Bull. of the Atomic Scientist,* Dec. 1972:14–17.

Sinsheimer, R. L. Prospects for future scientific developments: ambush or opportunity? *Hastings Cr. Report,* Sept. 1972, 2, 4:4–7.

Spitzer, S. & Folta, J. Death in the hospital: a problem for study. *Nursing Forum,* 1964, 3, **4:**85–92.

Time. Man into superman. The promise and peril of the new genetics. Ap. 19, 1971:33–52.

Veatch, R. M. Life and death arbiters with a vested interest. *N.Y. Times,* June 15, 1972:40.

Villanova Law Rev. The medical, moral and legal implications of recent medical advances—a symposium. Summer 1968, 13:732–792.

The psychology of death; treating the fatally ill

Becker, E. *The denial of death.* N.Y.: Free Press, 1973.

Blaker, C. W. Thanatopsis. *Christian Century,* Dec. 7, 1966, 83:1503–1506.

Bok, S. Euthanasia and the care of the dying. *Bioscience,* Aug. 1973, 23, 8:461–466.

Colen, B. D. A time to die. *Washington Post,* March 10–12, 1974: A1.

Eisenberg, L. The human nature of human nature. *Science,* Ap. 14, 1972, 176:123–128.

Farrar, C. B. Euthansia. *Am. J. Psychiat.,* May 1963, 119, **2:** 1104.

Feifel, H. Perception of death. *Annals of N.Y. Acad. of Science,* Dec. 19, 1969, 164: 669–677.

Feifel, H. (Ed.) *The meaning of death.* N.Y. McGraw-Hill, 1959.

Foundation of Thanatology. Dealing with death: thanatology looks at the doctor and the dying patient. *Medical World News,* May 21, 1971, 12, **20:**30.

Freireich, E. J. The best medical care for the "hopeless patient." *Medical Opinion,* Feb. 1972:51–55.

Freud, S. Thoughts for the times on war and death. *Standard Edition,* London: Hogarth Press, 1957, pp. 273–300.

Kalish, R. A. Some variables in death attitudes. *J. Social Psychol.*, Feb. 1963, 59:137–145.

Kalish, R. A. The aged and the dying process. *J. Social Issues*, 1965, 21, 4:87–96.

Kalish, R. A. Life and death: dividing the indivisible. *Social Science and Medicine*, 1968, 2:249–259.

Kastenbaum, R. The mental life of dying geriatric patients. *The Gerontologist*, June 1967, 7:97–100.

Kastenbaum, R. & Aisenberg, R. *The psychology of death.* N.Y.: Springer, 1972.

Kelly, G. The duty to preserve life. *Theological Studies*, Dec. 1951, 12: 550–556.

Krant, M. J. The organized care of the dying patient. *Hospital Practice,* Jan. 1972, 7, 1:101–108.

Kübler-Ross, E. What is it like to be dying? *Am J. Nursing*, Jan. 1971, 71: 54–60.

Kübler-Ross, E. On death and dying. *JAMA*, Jul. 10, 1972, 221, 2:174–179.

Kübler-Ross, E. The art of dying: let's only talk about the present. *N.Y. Times*, Jan. 15, 1973:29.

Kutscher, A. H. (Ed.) *Death and bereavement.* Springfield, Ill.: Charles C Thomas, 1969.

Lamerton, R. *Care of the dying.* London: Priory Press, 1973.

Medical Tribune. Heroic treatment (editorial), Ap. 10, 1961, 2, 15:15.

Morison, R. S. Dying. *Scientific American*, Sept. 1973, 229, 3:54–62.

Neale, R. E. *The art of dying.* N.Y.: Harper & Row, 1973.

Ogilvie, H. Journey's end. *Practitioner* (London), Nov. 1957, 179:584–591.

Pastoral Psychology. Death and education. Nov. 1971, 22.

Pearson, L. (Ed.) *Death and dying: current issues in the treatment of the dying person.* Cleveland: Case Western Reserve U. Press, 1969.

Peretz, D., *et al.* Survey of physicians' attitudes toward death and bereavement: comparison of psychiatrist and nonpsychiatrist. *J. Thanatology*, Mar. 1971, 1, **91**.

Poe, W. D. Maranthology, a needed specialty. *New England J. Medicine*, Jan. 13, 1972, 286, 2:102.

Randal, J. New approach to the dying needed. *Evening Star* (Washington, D.C.), Feb. 10, 1972:A12.

Rees, W. D. The distress of dying. *British Medical J.*, Jul. 8, 1972, 3:105–107.

Ross, N. L. Death and the young. *Washington Post*, Feb. 11, 1973: G6.

Saunders, C. The last stages of life. *Am. J. Nursing*, Mar. 1965, 65:70–75.

Shneidman, E. S. (Ed.) *Death and the college student.* N.Y.: Behavioral Publ., 1972.

Shneidman, E. S. *Deaths of man.* N.Y.: Quadrangle, 1973.

Shneidman, E. S. *On the nature of suicide.* San Francisco: Jossey-Bass, 1969.

Still, J. W. Three levels of human life and death. *Medical Annals* (Washington, D.C.), June 1968, 37:316.

Toynbee, A., *et al. Man's concern with death.* N.Y.: McGraw-Hill, 1968.

Weisman, A. D. & Kastenbaum, R. *The psychological autopsy.* N.Y.: Behavioral Publ., 1968.

White, D. Death control. *New Society,* Nov. 30, 1972, 22:502–505.

Williams, R. H. Number, types and duration of human lives. *Northwest Medicine,* Jul. 1970, 69:493–496.

Winter, A. (Ed.) *The moment of death.* Springfield, Ill.: Charles C Thomas, 1969.

Religion, Death and Euthanasia

Bustanoby, A. The right to die. *Christianity Today,* May 24, 1963, 7:39.

Cooper, R. M. Euthanasia and the notion of death with dignity. *The Christian Century,* Feb. 21, 1973, 90, **8:** 225–227.

Kelly, C. The duty to preserve life. *Theological Studies,* Dec. 1951, 12:550–556.

Kron, S. D. Euthanasia: a physician's view. *J. Religion and Health,* Oct. 1968, 7:333–341.

Rosner, F. Jewish attitudes toward euthanasia. *N.Y. State J. Medicine,* Sept. 15, 1967, 67:2499–2506.

Societal attitudes toward death

Choron, J. *Death and Western Thought.* N.Y.: Collier Books, 1973.

Crane, D. *Social Aspects of the Prolongation of Life.* N.Y.: Russell Sage Foundation, 1969.

Crane, D. Physicians' attitudes toward the treatment of critically ill patients, *BioScience,* Aug. 1973, 23,8:471–474.

Forbes, C. A. Death: no more taboos. *Christianity Today,* May 26, 1972, 16:41.

Geriatrics. On death and attitudes toward death: a symposium. Aug. 1972, 27,8:52–60.

Lester, D. Attitudes toward death today and thirty-five years ago. *Omega.* Aug. 1971, 2,3:168.

Psychology Today, You and death. Aug. 1970, 4,**3**:67–72. June 1971, 5,**1**: 43–45.

Ross, U. L. Mercy-killing issues still causing debate. *Washington Post,* Jan. 13, 1974: B4.

Rudikoff, S. The problem of euthanasia. *Commentary,* Feb. 1974, 57,**2**: 62–68.

Williams, M. Changing attitudes to death. *Human Relations,* Nov. 1966, 19,**4**:405–423.

Woodward, K. L. How America lives with death. *Newsweek,* April 6, 1970:81–88.

CASES

Index and References

The following cases were mentioned in the text.

Court cases involving allegations of mercy killing

Haiselden, Dr. H. J., p. 63, 241, 255, 260.
  Illinois, 1917.
  N.Y. Times, Jul. 25, 1917:11; Jul. 26, 1917:10; Nov. 16, 1917:4; Jan. 8, 1950, IV:2.

Haug, Ella, p. 102, 258.
  Pennsylvania, 1947.
  N.Y. Times, Jul. 23, 1947:30.

Johnson, Harry C., p. 84, 259.
  New York, 1938.
  N.Y. Times, Oct. 2, 1938:1; Oct. 12, 1939:30; Oct. 19, 1938:46.

Kafri, Gizela, p. 198.
  Israel, 1964.
  N.Y. Times, Nov. 2, 1964:2.

Kirby, William, p. 259, 266.
  New York, 1823.
  2 Parker Crim. Rep. (N.Y.) 28 (1823).

Long, G. R., p. 101.
  England, 1946.
  N.Y. Times, Nov. 23, 1946:7; Nov. 29, 1946:7. *Time*, Dec. 2, 1946, 48:32.

Mohr, Harold, p. 136, 258.
  Pennsylvania, 1950.
  N.Y. Times, Mar. 12, 1950:41; Ap. 4, 1950:60; Ap. 8, 1950:26; Ap. 11, 1950:20.

Montemarano, Dr. Vincent A., p. 46, 197, p. 255, 260.
  New York, 1973.
  N.Y. Times, June 28, 1973:1; June 29, 1973:42; Jul. 1, 1973:E3; Nov. 2, 1973:86; Feb. 6, 1974:1. *Newsweek*, Jan. 28, 1974, 83:45.

Nagel, Herman H., p. 240, 259.
  Arizona, 1953.
  N.Y. Times, Sept. 7, 1953:31; Dec. 24, 1953:20.

Noxon, J. F., p. 99, 101, 256, 258.
  Massachusetts, 1943.
  N.Y. Times Sept. 28, 1943:27; Sept. 29, 1943:23 Oct. 29, 1943:27; Aug. 8, 1946:42; Jan. 4, 1949:16; Jan. 15, 1949:30.

Paight, Carol, p. 102, 259.
  Connecticut, 1949.
  N.Y. Times, Jan. 24, 1950:23; Jan. 28, 1950:30; Feb. 1, 1950:54; Feb. 2, 1950:22; Feb. 3, 1950:11; Feb. 8, 1950:1. *Time*, Feb. 6, 1950:15.

Piquereau, Jean, p. 198.
    Belgium, 1971.
    N.Y. Times, Jan. 16, 1972:8.
Postma-von Boven, Dr. Gertruida, p. 255, 260.
    The Netherlands, 1971.
    Time, Implications of Mercy Mar. 5, 1973, 101:70.
Price, James
    England, 1971.
    N.Y. Times, Dec. 26, 1971:47.
Ramsberg case, p. 97.
    Canada, 1947.
    Sidney Katz, *Maclean's,* Nov. 1, 1947, 60, 21:7–8; 69–73.
Reichert, Mrs. G., p. 259.
    New York, 1942.
    N.Y. Times, June 27, 1942:15; Jul. 2, 1942:23; Jul. 3, 1942:19.
Reinecke, William, p. 259.
    Illinois, 1967.
    Chicago Daily News, Aug. 10, 1967:5.
Repouille, Louis, p. 84, 99, 118, 240, 258.
    New York, 1939.
    N.Y. Times, Oct. 13, 1939:25; Dec. 6, 1941:17; Dec. 10, 1941:27; Dec. 25, 1941:44.
Roberts, p. 256, 258.
    Michigan, 1920.
    People v. Roberts: 211 Mich. 187, 178 N.W. 690 (1920).
Sander, Dr. Hermann, p. 102, 104–109, 111, 127, 137, 255, 260.
    New Hampshire, 1949.
    N.Y. Times, Dec. 30, 1949:1; Jan. 2, 1950:25; Feb. 24, 1950:1; Mar. 2, 1950:5; Mar. 3, 1950:1; Mar. 7, 1950:1; Mar. 8, 1950:1; Mar. 10, 1950:1. *Time,* Jan. 16, 1950:20; Mar. 6, 1950:20. *Mich. Law Rev.,* 1950, 48:1197.
Swedish Doctor (name withheld), p. 253, 255, 260.
    Sweden, 1964.
    Medical World News, Nov. 20, 1964:56; Ap. 2, 1965:49.
van de Put, Suzanna, p. 175, 240.
    Belgium, 1962.
    Colebrook, *Lancet.* Dec. 8, 1962:1225. *Newsweek,* Nov. 19, 1962, 60:62. Gallahue, *Look.* Mar. 12, 1963:72.
Waskin, Robert, p. 197, 259.
    Illinois, 1967.

N.Y. Times, Aug. 9, 1967:77. Kutner, *Indiana Law J.,* Summer 1969: 539–554. Small, P., *Suffolk U. Law Rev.,* Fall 1970: 190–212.

Werner, Otto, p. 117, 258.
Illinois, 1958.
Hirschfeld, *Notre Dame Lawyer,* May 1959:460–464. Williams, G., *U. Colorado Law Rev.,* Winter 1966, 38:178–201.

Yamanouchi, K., p. 253.
Japan, 1963.
Miyano, A. Historic decision—euthanasia legal in Japan. *Euthanasia Soc. Bull.* (N.Y.), Spring 1963, XVI, 1.

Zygmaniak, Lester, p. 46, 197, 258.
New Jersey, 1973.
N.Y. Times, June 23, 1973:65; June 26, 1973:94; Jul. 14, 1973:59; Oct. 30, 1973:90; Oct. 31, 1973:93. Cant, G., *Time.* Jul. 16, 1973: 36–37. *Washington Post,* Nov. 6, 1973:A5.

Court cases involving the rights of patients

Bentley, Patricia, p. 41.
Washington, D.C., 1974.
Washington Post, Ap. 26, 1974:B1; Ap. 27, 1974:A15.
Superior Court of the District of Columbia, Civil Division, Misc. No. 65–74.

Bettman, Clarence A., p. 39, 257.
New York, 1972.
N.Y. Times, Jan. 28, 1972:42.

Heston, Delores, p. 40, 257, 268.
New Jersey, 1971.
N.Y. Times, Jul. 14, 1971:16.
Hoover, J. F. *Notre Dame Lawyer,* Feb. 1972, 47:571.
58 N.J. 576, 279 A 2d 670 (1971).

Houle, Baby, p. 257.
Maine, 1974.
Auerbach, S. Court ruled surgery fails to save baby. *Washington Post,* Feb. 25, 1974: A1.
State of Maine, Superior Court, Civil Action, Docket No. 74–145.

Martinez, Carmen, p. 38, 256, 268.
Florida, 1971.
N.Y. Times, Jul. 3, 1971:21; Jul. 4, 1971:22. *Time,* Jul. 19, 1971: 98:44. Palm Springs Gen. Hospital V. Martinez, case no. 71–12678, Cir. Ct. of Dade Cy., Fla., Jul. 2, 1971.

Osborne, Charles, p. 256, 268.
  Washington, D.C., 1972.
  294 A. 2d 372 (D.C. App. 1972)

Raasch, Gertrude, p. 39, 256, 268.
  Wisconsin, 1972.
  Guardianship of Gertrude Raasch, Cy. Court for Milwaukee Cy.,
  Probate Div., no. 445–996, Jan. 25, 1972.

Yetter, Maida, p. 256.
  Pennsylvania, 1973.
  N.Y. Times, June 8, 1973:84. Opinion of Judge Alfred T. Williams,
  Jr., Third Judicial District,. Commonwealth of Pennsylvania, June 6,
  1973, *Washington Post.* June 8, 1973:C8.

Court cases involving the definition of death

Lyons, Andrew D., p. 31.
  California, 1973.
  Washington Post, Sept. 14, 1973:A3; May 15, 1973:A3.
  San Francisco Chronicle. Editorial, May 22, 1974. *N.Y. Times,* May 20,
  1974:23; May 24, 1974:20.

Tucker, Bruce, p. 31.
  Virginia, 1968.
  N.Y. Times, May 25, 1968; May 24, 1968:6; May 27, 1968:15; June
  4, 1972, IV:7. *Washington Post,* May 24, 1972: B3; May 26, 1972:A1;
  May 29, 1972:A3. Robert M. Veatch, *Hastings Cr. Report.* 1972, vol.
  2, 5:10–13.

Court opinions cited

Union Pacific v. Botsford: 141 U.S. 250, 251 (1891), p. 233.

People v. Conley: 49 Cal. Rptr. 815, 822, 411 P. 2d 911, 918 (1966),
p. 266.

Griswold v. Conn.: 381 US 479 (1965), p. 233.

Natanson v. Kline: 186 Kan. 393, 406–407, 350 P. 2d. 1093, 1104 (1960),
p. 233.

Olmstead v. U.S.: 277 U.S. 438 (1928), p. 233.

Schloendorff v. Society of N.Y. Hospital: 211 N.Y. 125, 129–130, 105 N.E. 92,
93 (1914), p. 233.

Grace v. State: 44 Tex. Crim. 193: 69 S.W. 529 (1902), p. 265.

Cases not taken to Court

Harwis, Sara, p. 63.
    Independent, Dec. 12, 1912, 73:1385–1387; *Literary Digest,* Should we
    kill when we cannot cure? Oct. 11, 1913, 47:627.

"Hopkins case," p. 46, 237.
    Baltimore, 1971.
    Gaylin, W. M. Sharing the hardest decision. *Hospital Physician,* Jul.
    1972: 33–38. Peck, R. L. When should the patient be allowed to die?
    Hospital Physician, Jul. 1972: 29–33. *N.Y. Times,* Oct. 15, 1971:31;
    Oct. 17, 1971:33.

Meir case, p. 197.
    Colorado, 1973.
    N.Y. Times, May 9, 1973:53.

Wojcik case, p. 198.
    Florida, 1973.
    N.Y. Times Aug. 31, 1973:14.

EUTHANASIA BILLS AND RESOLUTIONS

1906.   Ohio, p. 60–61, 63, 68, 72.
    Outlook. Shall We legalize Homicide? Feb. 3, 1906, 82: 252.
    N.Y. Times, Jan. 24, 1906: 2; Jan. 25, 1906: 8; Jan. 29, 1906:8.
    Independent, Euthanasia Once More (editorial). Feb. 1, 1906,
    60:291–292.

1937.   Nebraska, p. 71.
    Bill no. 135, 52d Session (sponsored by Dr. Inez C. Philbrick)
    N.Y. Times, Feb. 3, 1937: 7; Jan. 14, 1937: 17.

1951.   Connecticut, p. 133.
    Euthanasia Soc. Bull., Summer 1950, III, 3.

1959.   Connecticut, p. 134, 291.
    Bill no. 2527.

1968–1974.   Florida, p. 22, 188, 270, 274, 298.

    House joint Resolution 91, Dec. 9, 1968.
    House Bill 68, 1970.
    House Bill 2914, 1971.
    House Bill 2614, 1972.
    House Hill 407, 1973.

1969.   Idaho, p. 188, 192, 271, 274.
        House Bill 143.
1971.   Wisconsin, p. 188, 190.
        Senate Bill 670 & 715.
1973.   Delaware, p. 188, 191.
        House Bill 251.
        Montana, p. 22, 188, 194, 271, 274, 277.
        House Bill 137.
        Oregon, p. 22, 188, 192, 193, 271, 274.
        House Bill 2997 and Senate Bill 179.
        Washington, p. 22, 188, 190, 270.
        Senate Bill 2449.

1974.   California, p. 188, 191.
        Assembly Bill no. 4444
        Maryland, p. 188, 191.
        Senate Bill 700.
        Massachusetts, p. 188, 191.
        House Bill 3641.

Resolutions:

1971.   Walter F. Mondale, p. 15, 274.
        U.S. Senate Joint Resolution 75, Congressional Record 117,
        March 24, 1971.
1972.   Hawaii House Resolution 44, p. 25, 188, 300.
1973.   Tim Lee Carter, p. 274.
        U.S. House Resolution 2655, Jan. 23, 1973.
1973.   Illinois House Resolution 45, p. 25, 188.

Bills proposed but apparently never introduced:

1939.   New York, p. 74
1946–1949.   New York, p. 94–97, 133.
1952.   New York, p. 132.
1957.   New Jersey, p. 133.

Euthanasia Bills in England:

House of Lords: 1936, p. 68–71, 89, 127, 184.
                  1950 (debate), p. 70, 111.
                  1969, p. 22, 70, 111, 127, 151, 184, 264, 271, 274,
                  277, 295.
House of Commons: 1970, p. 185.

SUPPLEMENT TO THE FIRST EDITION: DEVELOPMENTS FROM EARLY 1974 TO LATE 1976

THE "LIVING WILL" AND PATIENTS' BILLS OF RIGHTS 382

INCREASED EFFORTS TO HELP THE AGED AND DYING 385

PUBLIC OPINION POLLS 387

MORE CASES THAT DEMONSTRATE THE NEED FOR LEGISLATIVE ACTION 388

CONCLUSION 395

SUPPLEMENT TO THE FIRST
EDITION: DEVELOPMENTS FROM
EARLY 1974 TO LATE 1976

Since this book *Freedom To Die: Moral and Legal Aspects of Euthanasia* went to press in early 1974, there have been many significant developments in the march toward recognition of a right to die and the legalization of voluntary euthanasia. There has been an avalanche of literature on the subject and numerous radio and television programs study the aspects of death and dying, death with dignity, the right to die, and euthanasia. An ever-increasing number of seminars, symposia, courses, and study groups for the public and students at colleges, professional schools, and even secondary schools focus on this hitherto taboo topic.

Also the daily press, professional journals, and popular magazines, in reporting the case of Karen Quinlan, the suicide of Dr. and Mrs. Van Dusen, and the indictment of Dr. Haemmerli of Zurich and numerous other cases of "mercy deaths" or attempted suicide, have brought to public attention the fact that law today is not in step with the needs of this age of greatly increased ability of doctors to prolong the life of dying patients—when we have what has been called "mechanized dying."

The advocates of a change of law were greatly encouraged when on September 30, 1976, Governor Edmund G. Brown of California signed into law a bill that will permit passive euthanasia. Under this law physicians may refrain from prolonging the dying process at the request of the patient. This is the first such law enacted in the United States. However, no state or country to date has made it legally permissible ever to hasten or directly bring about death, which would be active euthanasia. Many believe that a law providing for such a choice is urgently needed and in several states such legislation has been introduced and debated.

Another important development was the first international conference on euthanasia held in Tokyo in August 1976. Here the signing of the Tokyo Declaration recognized "a right to die with dignity."

CASES THAT ATTRACTED WORLDWIDE ATTENTION

The Quinlan Case

The case of Karen Ann Quinlan has stimulated worldwide controversy over the problems of death and dying. Since the case has been so widely reported, mainly the legal aspects will be discussed here.

Karen, aged 21, fell into a coma on the night of April 15, 1975, apparently as a result of a mixture of drugs and alcohol. From that time on she has been in what expert physicians have called a "chronic persistent vegetative state." Until very recently her body was kept functioning by artificial means but there was "no longer any cognitive function." At first it was the opinion of the experts that she could not survive without the assistance of the respirator. It was agreed that no form of treatment which could cure or improve her condition was known or available. Karen's weight dropped to half of her normal weight. Her grossly deformed body, drawn in a fetal position, was described in this condition: ". . . her arms and legs have pulled in toward her body and have calsified in that position to the extent that she now resembles a praying mantis." Karen's physicians have fought a running battle against infections with massive doses of antibiotics and she has been fed high-caloric liquid through a tube inserted in her nose.

In the fall of 1975 her father, Joseph Quinlan, went to court seeking appointment as her guardian with the express power to authorize that all extraordinary medical procedures allegedly sustaining her vital processes and hence her life be discontinued, since these measures presented no hope of her eventual recovery. He said he wanted his daughter to be allowed to die "with grace and dignity." Mr. Quinlan also sought "to enjoin the prosecutor from prosecuting for homicide when the authorization sought is effected." His appeal was opposed by the doctors, the hospital, the Morris County Prosecutor, the State of New Jersey, and a court-appointed guardian.

The decision of Judge Robert Muir, Jr. was handed down on November 10, 1975 (137 N.J. Super. 227, 1975). This decision will probably stand as a most thorough exploration of the possibility of handling the problems involved in this tragic case by judicial means and the conclusion that the courts are not the proper source of the decisions required. While Judge Muir repeated the statement that Justice Weintraub had made in the Heston case (N.J. 1971) that there is "no constitutional right to die," he still seemed to acknowledge that this did not adequately meet the needs of the Quinlan case.

In a footnote to another point in his opinion, Judge Muir said,

> Certainly the question must be asked, did the Common Law contemplate the continued existence of a human being,

where that human being, although medically and legally
alive, has been given all the diagnostic and therapeutic treatment available and should not the natural functions of that
human being be permitted to progress in a normal way
without the law against homicide being a deterrent?

Yet because "testimony of other doctors reflects an
inclination that the use of the respirator is an ordinary
medical practice," Judge Muir said the termination of the
respirator "would be homicide and an act of euthanasia. . . .
The authorization . . . would be to permit Karen Quinlan
to die." He seemed to decline such authorization because
of the possibility of setting a precedent. "In this age of
advanced medical science, the prolongation of life, and
organ transplants," he stated, "it is not my intent, nor can
it be, to resolve the extensive civil and criminal legal dilemmas engendered. . . . The precedential effect on future litigation, particularly in light of the raging issue of
euthanasia, would be legally detrimental."

Still Judge Muir seemed to think there should be some
way to end the hopeless condition of Karen and the suffering of her family. He discussed her condition at length and
said, "All agree she is in a persistent vegetative state. She
is described as having irreversible brain damage . . .
chances for useful sapient life or return of discriminative
functioning are remote." While there was testimony that
Karen had said she would not want to live in such a condition, the Judge said her comments were "theoretical" but
"this is not the situation of a Living Will which is based
upon a concept of informed consent." This seems to imply
that if a Living Will had been signed by the patient, a
different solution to the problem might have been possible.

Judge Muir did not at all deal with the possibility of
solving the dilemma by the enactment of statutory law, so
it was not surprising when he passed the problem back to
the medical profession. He concluded, "The nature, ex-

tent, and duration of care by societal standards is the responsibility of a physician. . . . What justification is there to remove it from the control of the medical profession and place it in the hands of the courts? . . . It is a medical decision, not a judicial one."

Judge Muir then appointed a guardian for Karen, rejecting her father's appeal for this role. *Time* said Judge Muir had sentenced Karen "to life." Early in 1976 Karen's father appealed the court's decision to the Supreme Court of New Jersey.

On March 31, 1976 Chief Justice Richard J. Hughes of the Supreme Court of New Jersey handed down the unanimous decision of the Court (Sup. C. of N.J. A-116, Sept. Term 1975). He reviewed the facts of Karen's condition and said, "No form of treatment which can cure or improve that condition is known or available." He noted that "developments in medical technology have obfuscated the use of the traditional definition of death," and went on to admit the testimony of Bishop Lawrence B. Casey of the New Jersey Catholic Conference.

Bishop Casey stated that "the decision of Joseph Quinlan to request the discontinuance of this treatment is, according to the teachings of the Catholic Church, a morally correct decision," based on the November 24, 1957 allocution of Pope Pius XII. The Justice said he admitted such testimony "only in the aspect of its impact upon the conscience, motivation, and purpose of the intending guardian, Joseph Quinlan, and not as a precedent in terms of civil law."

Justice Hughes pointed out:

> that many physicians have refused to inflict an undesired prolongation of the process of dying on a patient in irreversible condition when it is clear that such 'therapy' offers neither human nor humane benefit. We think these attitudes represent a balanced implementation of a profoundly realis-

tic perspective on the meaning of life and death and that they respect the whole Judeo-Christian tradition of regard for human life. No less would they seem consistent with the moral matrix of medicine, 'to heal,' very much in the sense of the endless mission of the law, 'to do justice.' Yet this balance, we feel, is particularly difficult to perceive and apply in the context of the development by advanced technology of sophisticated and artificial life-sustaining devices. . . . one would have to think that the use of the same respirator or like support could be considered 'ordinary' in the context of the possibly curable patient but 'extraordinary' in the context of the forced sustaining by cardio-respiratory processes of an irreversibly doomed patient. And this dilemma is sharpened in the face of the malpractice and criminal action threat which we have mentioned.

Discussing "the constitutional right of privacy," Justice Hughes said:

Ultimately there comes a point at which the individual's rights overcome the State interest. . . . We have concluded that Karen's right of privacy may be asserted on her behalf by her guardian under the peculiar circumstances here present. If a putative decision by Karen to permit this noncognitive, vegetative existence to terminate by natural forces is regarded as a valuable incident of her right of privacy, as we believe it to be, then it should not be discarded solely on the basis that her condition prevents her conscious exercise of the choice. . . . It is for this reason that we determine that Karen's right of privacy may be asserted in her behalf, in this respect, by her guardian and family under the particular circumstances presented by this record. . . . Determination as to these (underlying human values and rights) must, in the ultimate, be responsive not only to the concepts of medicine but also to the common moral judgment of the community at large.

The evidence in this case convinces us that the focal point of decision should be the prognosis as to the reasonable possibility of return to cognitive and sapient life, as distinguished from the forced continuance of that biological vegetative existence to which Karen seems to be doomed. . . . We conclude that there would be no criminal homicide in the circumstances of this case. We believe, first, that the ensuing death would not be homicide but rather expiration from existing natural causes. Secondly, even if it were to be regarded as homicide, it would not be unlawful. These conclusions rest upon definitional and constitutional bases. The termination of treatment pursuant to the right of privacy is, within the limitations of this case, *ipso facto* lawful. . . . There is a real, and in this case, determinative distinction between the unlawful taking of the life of another and the ending of artificial life-support systems as a matter of self-determination.

Justice Hughes then commented favorably on the proposal of Dr. Karen Teel, a pediatrician from Austin, Texas (*Baylor Law Review*, Winter 1975). Dr. Teel suggested that an Ethics Committee of physicians, social workers, attorneys and theologians be organized to give advice in difficult cases. The work of such a committee would diffuse professional responsibility for difficult decisions much as a multijudge court resolves difficult questions of law. But Justice Hughes added, "We consider that a practice of applying to a court to confirm such decisions would generally be inappropriate." He then appointed Joseph Quinlan "as guardian of the person of Karen Quinlan with full power to make decisions with regard to the identity of her treating physician."

Justice Hughes further declared that if the hospital Ethics Committee or like-body of the institution in which Karen is then hospitalized "agrees that there is no reasonable possibility of Karen's ever emerging from her present comatose condition to a cognitive, sapient state, the present life-support system may be withdrawn and said action shall be without any civil or criminal liability therefor on the part of any participant, whether guardian, physician, hospital, or others."

This decision was both widely praised and severely criticized. The Reverend Richard A. McCormick, S.J., of Georgetown University's Kennedy Institute, called the decision "just great. The responsibility is primarily the patient's or the family's, with the advice and counsel of the physician. Judge Muir had it just backwards." But Dr. McCarthy DeMere, a former chairman of the American Bar Association's committee on law and medicine said, "I am sad about it. I think it is unfortunate because I think the few of us left who respect life think it will be a far-reaching and devastating decision." He continued that in his opinion, by using the word "sapient," the Court paved the way for physicians to end the life of any patient who is not "wise," such as a retarded child whom doctors feel might come out of a coma but would never be mentally normal.

In May, Karen was removed from the respirator but oxygen was used as she needed it. However, St. Clare's Hospital, where Karen had been for over 13 months, refused to set up the Ethics Committee as recommended by Justice Hughes. So on June 9 she was moved to Morris View Nursing Home in Morris Plains, N.J. The feeding and treatment with antibiotics were continued but a respirator was not used. There an Ethics Committee was established as recommended, composed of two clergymen, a social worker, the chairman of the welfare board, and a physician. This committee will make recommendations for future action and treatment.

The idea of having an Ethics Committee recommend the fate of a patient is being discussed in medical and legal circles throughout the world. Such committees have been set up at hospitals including the Massachusetts General Hospital, the University of Virginia Hospital, Childrens' Hospital in Pittsburgh, and The Johns Hopkins Hospital.

Since the publication of her *Baylor Law Review* article, Dr. Teel says she has "had a very uneasy feeling" about how these Ethics Committees will work. Dr. DeMere has said, ". . . these ethical committees include non-doctors who are reviewing the medical decisions of a doctor. This is a very nebulous and gray area."

In the *Journal of Legal Medicine* (May 1976), Francis I. Kittredge said, "In many or most situations, the realities of clinical practice will preclude the opportunity to have an ethics committee decide whether life-support systems should be administered or continued."

As of late-October 1976, Karen Quinlan was still "alive."

The Suicide of Dr. and Mrs. Van Dusen

As noted earlier in this book, Dr. Henry P. Van Dusen, President Emeritus of Union Theological Seminary, an organizer and leader of the World Council of Churches, and long-time supporter of the Euthanasia Society, opened the 1968 Euthanasia Conference of the Society. Dr. Van Dusen declared, "There is no issue more important or urgent than the one that brings us here today—except possibly over-population."

Then in January 1975, after Dr. Van Dusen had suffered for five years from a severely crippling stroke and Mrs. Van Dusen was seriously incapacitated by arthritis, they left a letter addressed "to all friends and relations." The letter said:

> We have both had very full and satisfying lives. . . . Nowadays it is difficult to die. We feel that this way we are taking will become more usual and acceptable as the years pass. . . . We are both increasingly weak and unwell and who would want to die in a nursing home. . . . O Lamb of God that taketh away the sins of the world, have mercy upon us. O Lamb of God that taketh away the sins of the world, grant us thy peace."

Then by taking overdoses of sleep pills, they carried out a suicide pact. Mrs. Van Dusen died immediately but Dr. Van Dusen had to endure another 15 days before the relief of death came.

Disclosure of their suicide stirred widespread comment. Dr. John C. Bennett, who followed Dr. Van Dusen as president of Union Theological Seminary, said he had no doubt that the Van Dusens "sincerely believed that in this act they were doing the will of God for them. . . . There may be degrees of mental as well as physical suffering and degrees of life's denial of everything that one has been, which can be read as indications that suicide is in accordance with God's will. . . . (The Van Dusens) had come to reject the church's absolutistic attitude toward suicide as a form of euthanasia and their own long reflection on the theological issues involved supported their intuition that they were acting in accordance with God's will."

The Case of Dr. Haemmerli

On January 15, 1975, Dr. Urs Peter Haemmerli of Zurich, an internationally known specialist in liver disorders and chief of medicine at the 700 bed Triemli Hospital, was arrested. The charge was murder, "without a corpse known." A member of the city council had filed a complaint against the doctor, charging that he refused to force-feed terminally-ill patients. Although he was soon released, Dr. Haemmerli was suspended from his medical practice for 10 weeks. On July 9, 1976 he was cleared of all charges that had been filed against him.

An exhaustive review of five years of records of 1500 deaths showed that Dr. Haemmerli had been involved in withholding food from 10 comatose permanently-ill patients during that period. Commenting on his practice, Dr. Haemmerli said:

I have never done anything or ordered anything to be done to my patients that I would not have done for my own mother or father if they were in the same position. If I myself were in such a condition, then I would want my doctor to treat me in the same way. . . . Most of our patients are elderly, chronically-ill patients and I have been concerned for a long time about how to care properly for such people. . . . This is the backside of medicine . . . for many people, tube-feeding, even when they are comatose, is an extremely unpleasant thing that causes them to gag and retch and vomit. I and the members of my staff would see these poor people suffering, and we asked ourselves, 'Isn't our real duty to make their last hours as comfortable as possible rather than make them suffer even more?' So what we did in some of these cases was to stop the force-feeding and give them only water and saline solution. . . . It was always a collective decision in which all the members of my staff had to concur. . . . We took as our rule what seemed to be best for the comfort and peace of the patient in his last hours. . . . It's not correct to characterize such a procedure as euthanasia or mercy-killing. . . . What we used were passive measures to ease a patient's last moments. . . . All I ever tried to do was make some decisions striking a balance between humanity, reason, and sound medical practice—and that's what a doctor is supposed to do.

In response to his position, Dr. Haemmerli received thousands of letters, many from old people who said they hoped their doctors would have the same attitude.

In late 1975 Dr. Haemmerli addressed the Committee on Social and Health Questions of the Council of Europe and assisted in the drafting of a resolution on patients' rights, asserting "a right not to suffer." In an address to the Eighth Annual conference of the Euthanasia Educational Council on December 6, 1975, in New York, Dr. Haemmerli asked:

Are there times when a physician has a duty to do nothing? If you have a living corpse, it is because of advances in medicine which have forced people to consider as never before the issue of dying naturally. If my case stimulates discussion about a doctor's responsibility to the dying and makes clear how patients themselves want to be treated, it could be of incalculable help to doctors everywhere.

As a result of the Haemmerli case, the Swiss Parliament has created a Commission on Euthanasia to provide guidelines on proper hospital handling of terminally-ill patients. A poll in Switzerland showed that 60 per cent of the people questioned were in favor of active euthanasia, while only 23 per cent were opposed to it. In France a similar poll of 1200 people who were aged 18 and over was taken from the electoral roll. The French poll revealed that 60 per cent thought that a doctor ought to end the life of an invalid who is incurably ill and when with this knowledge the patient then asks the doctor to do so.

Confessions of a Surgeon

Dr. George B. Mair, retired Scottish physician, stirred up widespread discussion of euthanasia and the physician's role with his book *The Confessions of a Surgeon* (London: Luscomb, 1974). He told how over the years he had carried out mercy-killings on incurable patients, but always with three criteria: (1) the initiative by the patient; (2) the patient being incurably-ill; and (3) the agreement of two doctors on the diagnosis. As a young doctor he saw his seniors carrying out euthanasia from time to time and he assumed it was legal since those of impeccable character did it. Dr. Mair said he used the word "kill" deliberately when he referred to euthanasia because he did not like euphemisms. "Surely people should be allowed to terminate their lives with dignity," he said. ". . . This is not unhealthy thinking. It is compassionate and humane."

There were calls for indictment of Dr. Mair but in Parliament the Lord Advocate said, "Crown Counsel, on my behalf, have studied the book with care and I have read relevant passages myself. Although on page one the author has made vague and unspecified claims to have coped with one or two cases of euthanasia in England, he does not claim to have done the same in Scotland and I am satisfied there is no *prima facie* evidence of euthanasia in Scotland."

A British Medical Association official said, "We do not comment on individual cases but our official policy is to condemn euthanasia."

Although Charles Sweetingham of the British Euthanasia Society said he admired Dr. Mair's courage and humanity, he added, "I think it does reveal the desirability of having the position made lawful."

Lord Platt, past president of the Royal College of Physicians, supported Dr. Mair, saying, "A large number of colleagues will admit privately that they have hastened patients' deaths. Few doctors could say that they have never done it. . . . It is mischievous to keep patients alive if they have no chance of recovery to meaningful life. Almost everyone in the profession agrees that it is merciful to withhold antibiotics from someone who is dying from cancer." Lord Platt refused to say what his practice had been but he said he was prepared to die by euthanasia. He concluded, "I don't want my family to spend years nursing me when I ought to be a corpse."

The Appeal of Stewart Alsop

The tragic experience of well-known writer Stewart Alsop before he died of cancer also received wide attention. During a brief mysterious remission of the disease, Alsop wrote of his suffering and the agony of others in the ward in spite of medication and the most sophisticated medical care. In a *Newsweek* article (March 11, 1974), he said, "It seems to me that a patient suffering beyond endurance should be given the option of ending his own life, and the means to do so should be supplied on request."

DEVELOPMENTS IN LEGISLATION

In the United States

The long struggle in the United States for legislative action on the problem of useless prolongation of life had its first success in California. A bill popularly called the "Right To Die" bill was signed into law by Governor Edmund G. Brown, Jr., on September 30, 1976, to become effective on January 1, 1977. Officially named the "Natural Death Act," the new law provides for cessation of medical care in a case of "an incurable injury, disease, or illness certified to be a terminal condition by two physicians." It is stated:

> The Legislature finds that adult persons have the fundamental right to control the decisions relating to the rendering of their own medical care, including the decision to have life-sustaining procedures withheld or withdrawn in instances of a terminal condition. The Legislature further finds that modern medical technology has made possible the artificial prolongation of human life beyond natural limits. . . . The Legislature hereby declares that the laws of the State of California shall recognize the right of an adult person to make a written directive instructing his physician to withhold or withdraw life-sustaining procedures in the event of a terminal condition. (1975–76 Assembly Bill 3060).

There shall be a waiting period of 14 days after a person has been declared to be in a terminal condition before he can execute in the presence of two witnesses a directive which may be revoked at any time. This directive would be legally recognized as a form of "Living Will." A physician not wishing to comply with the directive shall direct the patient to another physician. A physician complying with the directive is relieved from any civil or criminal liability for withholding or withdrawing life-sustaining procedures. Such action would not constitute suicide or invalidate insurance.

The charge that this law would authorize active euthanasia was answered by this provision:

> Nothing in this chapter shall be construed to condone, authorize, or approve mercy killing, or to permit any affirmative or deliberate act or commission to end life other than to permit the natural process of dying as provided in this chapter.

This California bill was sponsored by Assemblyman Barry Keene and was supported by groups of elderly persons, the California Medical Association, and the American Civil Liberties Union. A bill stating simply, "Every person has the right to die without prolongation of life by extraordinary means," had been sponsored unsuccessfully by Assemblyman Keene in the 1973–74 session of the legislature. This new law which has been called a passive euthanasia law is hailed as a means of ending the useless attempt to extend the life of a patient in a terminal condition: some, however, refuse to use this term to describe it.

But such cessation can only follow the request of the patient. It offers no relief to patients such as Karen Quinlan, to seriously defective infants, or to comatose or senile persons and others unable to make the request. In these cases where action to end the terminal condition is prohibited, there may still be a long period, as in the Quinlan case, in which the suffering of the patient and the family may continue until "the natural process of dying" brings relief to all concerned. So while this new law dealing with "the right to die" is welcomed, it is limited.

In other states the effort to enact legislation against useless prolongation of life has been going on since the unsuccessful effort in Ohio in 1906. Since that time such bills have been presented in at least 27 states. In 1976 there were bills introduced in at least 17 states,* for the first time in 10 of those states.

One of the longest efforts for legislation has been made by Walter Sackett, M.D., a member of the Florida House of Representatives, who has introduced "death with dignity" bills for 10 years. In 1973 his bill was passed by the House but died on the Senate calendar. Since then Dr. Sackett has returned to his original idea of a constitutional amendment listing "a right to die with dignity" in the Bill of Rights.

LEGISLATIVE MANUAL   In 1975 a "Death With Dignity Legislative Manual" was published by the Society For the Right To Die, Inc. successor to the Euthanasia Society, (250 West 57 St., New York 10019), with a 1976 revised edition. The manual includes very helpful suggestions for effective legislation on this subject, the texts of 10 bills that have been introduced, and a model bill for passive euthanasia.

In Great Britain

Baroness Wooton introduced a bill on the rights of incurable patients in the House of Lords on December 4, 1975. The bill provided:

---

*Alabama, Alaska, Arizona, California, Delaware, Florida, Georgia, Hawaii, Kentucky, Massachusetts, Missouri, New Jersey, New York, Ohio, Pennsylvania, Tennessee, Virginia

> An incurable patient shall with his consent, and notwithstanding any refusal on his part to receive intensive care or other life-sustaining treatment, be entitled to receive whatever quantity of drugs may be required to give him full relief from pain and physical distress, and to be rendered unconscious if no other treatment is effective to give such relief. . . . An incurable patient who causes his own death by overdosing or other intentional action shall be deemed to have died by misadventure.

The bill provided that a person might make a written statement attested by two witnesses that he should not receive treatment in the event he became incapable of making his will known. During the debate on this bill the Lord Bishop of Durham said, "This debate will do good if it is widely reported and makes the medical profession more aware now of the deep disquiet felt by many ordinary people about some cases."

In discussing the problem Lord Raglan said:

> There is, I suppose, a difference between cutting off a means of life and inducing a means of death, but I do not find it very clear for both mean killing. If one accepts that good medical practice sometimes entails removing life-sustaining equipment, one inevitably accepts that good medical practice sometimes entails killing. I think we should not shy away from facing that fact in these terms. . . . Something is very wrong with regard to our care for the dying.

Baroness Gaitskell said:

> My Lords, it is not the prospect of death or pain or incurability that fills me personally with terror. What fills me with terror is the thought of senility and brain damage and the results of these two. On this I am in the greatest sympathy with the purpose of this bill.

Nevertheless, on February 12, 1976 the Lords failed to pass the bill on second reading.

Writing in the *British Medical Journal* (January 31, 1976), J. F. Searle said:

> I doubt if legislation is the right way in which to protect their rights . . . are there not other ways of correcting this situation such as the proper education of doctors in the management of severe pain, rather than resorting to statute? The fact that Lady Wooton has brought in this bill ought to compel the profession to pay very much more attention to the dying and to incurable patients than is perhaps usual and to ensure that they die in comfort and with dignity.

In Europe

Action that may eventually lead to legislation was taken by the Parliamentary Assembly of the Council of Europe on January 29, 1976. A lengthy recommendation was passed calling on the Committee of Ministers to invite the governments of the 18 member states to establish national commissions of enquiry, composed of representatives from the medical, legal, theological, psychological and other professions "to establish ethical rules for the treatment of persons approaching the end of life."

The Assembly pointed out that "the rapid and continuing progress of medical science creates problems, and may even pose certain threats with respect to the fundamental human rights and the integrity of sick people. . . . The prolongation of life should not in itself constitute the exclusive aim of medical practice, which must be concerned equally with the relief of suffering" (*Nordisk Medicin,* 1976, Vol. 91, 3, p. 67).

In several European countries there have been movements to develop attitudes favorable toward the legalization of euthanasia.

Euthanasia Societies

The Euthanasia Society in the United States

The Euthanasia Society of America founded by the Reverend Charles Francis Potter in 1938 has been relatively inactive in recent years. A companion organization, the Euthanasia Educational Fund, was established in 1967 and changed to the Euthanasia Educational Council in 1972. In early 1975 the Society was reorganized as the Society For The Right To Die with Dr. Joseph Fletcher as president. He was succeeded in 1976 by lawyer Sidney Rosoff.

In choosing the new name the Board felt that including the word "euthanasia" would be a detriment to legislative work. The Board explained, "Experience has shown that legislators and lawyers have expressed gratitude for receiving material on 'death with dignity' but object to receiving it from an organization with the word 'euthanasia' in its title. Secondly, it was felt that 'The Right To Die' more closely approximates what the Society stands for."

The new society promptly promoted legislative work by publishing a *Legislative Manual* which included the drafts of bills that had been introduced in 10 states, a model bill, and suggestions for judging the merits of such bills. There is a 1976 revision of the manual.

Meanwhile the other arm of the organization, the Euthanasia Educational Council, published the first issue of *Euthanasia News* in February 1975. It was announced that the Good Death Fellowship organized in Denver in 1972 had merged with the EEC in organization and publishing.

The Euthanasia Educational Council holds a prestigious annual conference in New York City and also sponsors numerous seminars and regional conferences. In

Seattle in May 1976 a conference on "The Dying Patient" was cosponsored by the new Northwest Institute of Ethics and the Life Sciences, organized in 1975 for the study of bioethical issues. The Student Medical Society of the University of Washington was also a sponsor for this conference.

Dr. Daniel Maguire, professor of theology at Marquette University and author of *Death By Choice,* was the principal speaker. Dr. Maguire declared, "Life is a good thing and the precondition of all good things but there are times when the ending of life is the best that life offers. . . . We make no legal provision for motive. When the law forbids it but morality dictates it, we play games." To make his point he quoted Saint Thomas Aquinas as saying, "Human actions are right or wrong depending on the circumstances."

In October 1976, a regional conference in Nashville on "The Right To Die" was cosponsored by the Vanderbilt University Schools of Medicine, Law and Divinity, and the Scarritt College Center of Continuing Education.

The first international conference on euthanasia was held in Tokyo in 1976. Mr. and Mrs. Sidney Rosoff, Mr. and Mrs. C. Dickerman Williams, Dr. and Mrs. Milton D. Heifetz, and Mrs. Francis F. Randolph represented the Educational Council and the Society For The Right To Die.

The Voluntary Euthanasia Society of Great Britain

The Voluntary Euthanasia Society of Great Britain prepared and published a reply to the report of the Anglican Church on euthanasia. This is discussed further elsewhere in this Supplement.

In February 1975 the Reverend A. B. Downing resigned as chairman of the Society when he was appointed to a church far from London. He had served as chairman for 10 years and among other things had edited the very successful book *Euthanasia and The Right To Die.* The new chairman is Miss Mary Rose Barrington, M.A., Solicitor to the Supreme Court. Miss Barrington has been very active in the Society for some years. She contributed an essay to the book edited by Dr. Downing, presented a paper on euthanasia to the Royal Society of Health Conference in December 1974, and has often spoken publicly on the subject of euthanasia.

The British Society has called attention to the fact that the opposition to euthanasia has shifted arguments. Instead of the old objection that the elderly and handicapped would be done away with by scheming relatives, the current argument is that because modern medicine now ensures a gentle death, euthanasia is irrelevant.

Mr. Charles R. Sweetingham, executive secretary, and Mr. Michael J. Berridge, a director, represented the Society at the August 1976 international conference on euthanasia in Tokyo.

The Australian Voluntary Euthanasia Society

The Australian Voluntary Euthanasia Society, which was formed in October 1973, started publishing an *A.V.E.S. Newsletter* in March 1974. Since then, the organizers, principally Jenny and Tom Parramore, have worked vigorously in many parts of Australia holding discussion meetings and organizing societies. Their stated aim is:

> To create a public opinion favorable to the view that an adult person, suffering, through illness or disability, severe pain or distress for which no relief is available, should be entitled by law to the mercy of a painless death if, and only if, that is his expressed wish; and to promote legislation to this effect.

In October 1974 the Society drew up a formal proposal for the creation of a Euthanasia Commissioner. The Commissioner and five assistants would operate as ombudsmen to receive applications from patients for euthanasia. These persons would be drawn from the professions of law, medicine, and social work. They would investigate each application to determine that it met the requirements of the law and that there had been no pressure on the patient to apply. If requirements had been complied with, they would give approval and arrange for carrying out the euthanasia.

In March 1975 the Society drew up a detailed statement regarding the need for legislation to permit voluntary euthanasia for the relief of suffering. The statement was submitted to the Royal Commission on Human Relations.

The Society also proposed that the law relating to suicide be revised to remove any legal taint. They held:

> If, after a suitable period of counselling, the person in distress still shows a firm wish for an end to life, we believe that assistance should be available. Assisted suicide could be the answer for those suffering from an irremediable disease which results in physical or mental distress; the answer also for the aged person who at the end of a long and happy life fears the indignity of existence in a nursing home in a senile state. The availability of assisted suicide would, we believe, reduce the need for voluntary euthanasia. However, there will still be a need for this when the patient is completely paralysed or unconscious.

To take care of the latter situation, they proposed the signing of a declaration of wishes ahead of time.

In March 1976 the Society composed a similar statement on suicide and the need for revising the law regarding it. This was distributed to members of Parliament, State and Federal Law Reform Commissions, law societies, bar associations, libraries, and law schools. Materials for use on radio and television, as well as letters to the press, have been prepared.

Tom Parramore says, "So long as a person can hold a glass and swallow a pill, I do not think he should ask more of his doctor than to be supplied with the right sort of pill. When he is no longer capable of helping himself to that degree, then he needs voluntary euthanasia."

Mr. and Mrs. Parramore represented the Australian Society at the international conference on euthanasia in Tokyo in August 1976.

The Netherlands Euthanasia Society

Following the trial of Dr. Gertruida Postma-von Boven the Netherlands Euthanasia Society was formed in 1973. Dr. Postma-von Boven was tried for having ended the life of her seriously-ill mother who had repeatedly begged that her life be ended. She received a one-week suspended sentence and a year's probation. At her trial the court listed conditions that would automatically exclude a Dutch doctor from being charged under Article 293 of the Dutch penal code prohibiting euthanasia. The conditions were as follows:

(1) that the patient is incurably ill;
(2) that his suffering, physical or mental, is inhuman;
(3) that he has expressed the will to end his life or to be assisted in ending his suffering;
(4) that the patient is dying or is very near death.

A 1976 committee of eminent lawyers and physicians is preparing plans to have Parliament extend the rights of patients. The Society is also making efforts to interest a university in conducting scientific research on the medical aspects of euthanasia. They are seeking government support for this project as well.

Miss Nelly Folpmers, secretary of the Society, represented it at the Tokyo Conference in August 1976.

The South African Euthanasia Society

The South African Voluntary Euthanasia Society, formed in 1974, now has seven branches in various parts of the country. It is holding well-attended public meetings discussing euthanasia and is enjoying excellent publicity in the press. The Natal Council of Churches conducted a symposium on euthanasia in late 1976 with Dr. Urs Peter Haemmerli of Zurich as a principal speaker.

Mrs. Sylvia Kean of Natal, secretary, and Professor H. Grant-Whyte, president, represented the Society at the international conference on euthanasia in Tokyo in August, 1976.

Action In Japan

Under the leadership of Dr. Tenrei Ota, the Japan Euthanasia Society was formed January 20, 1976. Dr. Ota is a noted obstetrician and gynecologist and a former member of the Japanese Diet, who has written many books on medical subjects, including euthanasia. Working with Dr. Ota as officers and associates are 25 prominent professionals from the fields of medicine, law, architecture, publishing, and economics. Among them are one member of Parliament and three former members.

Increasing approval of euthanasia in Japan was indicated in an October 12, 1976 report from Tokyo to a meeting of the Japan Gerontological Society. The report stemmed from a survey which questioned 145 nurses at 70

TOKYO DECLARATION OF AUGUST, 1976.

東京宣言 1 9 7 6 年 8 月

In recent years, we have become aware of the increasing concern of the individual over his right to die with dignity, or euthanasia. We believe in the rights and freedom of all men. This brings us to affirm this right to die with dignity, which means in peace and without suffering.

Death is unavoidable. But we believe that the manner of dying should be left to the decision of the individual, assuming such demands do not result in harm to society other than the sadness associated with death.

The Declaration of a person's wishes, or the "Living Will", should be respected by all concerned as an expression of intrinsic human rights. Therefore, at least for the present, we request that this Declaration, or the "Living Will", be made legally effective, and pursuant to this, efforts toward its legalization should be made.

Through the Tokyo International Conference on Euthanasia, or Death with Dignity, the national movements of each country can achieve international cooperation, as well as solidarity. Let us promise ourselves to strive to achieve the above objectives, through the establishment of a liaison center whose purpose will be an exchange of information, as well as the convening of periodically held international conferences.

TOKYO INTERNATIONAL CONFERENCE ON EUTHANASIA

近年、いわゆる安楽死について、個々の関心が高まってきた。われわれは人間の権利と自由を確信し、品位ある死の権利を保有する。

死は避けられない必然である。人がいかなる死を選ぶかは、自らの決定にゆだねられるものであって、それは死の別れに伴う悲しみの他には、周囲の人々に害を及ぼすものであってはならない。

この意味で、個人の願いの表明または「生者の意志」は人間個有の権利として尊重されるべきである。したがって、われわれは、この種の書類が法的に効力を持つことを要求し、当面、この線にそって立法化の努力をすすめる。

今回東京の国際安楽死会議を通じて、各国の運動が国際協力と連帯を持つに至った。今後さらに情報交換のため連絡センターの設置、国際会議の定期開催などによって目的の達成にまい進する。

1 9 7 6 年 8 月 2 4 日

東京国際安楽死会議

******

Australia   Voluntary Euthanasia Society

by ___Thomas I. Parramore___
Thomas I. Parramore

Japan   Euthanasia Society

by ___Tenrei Ota___
Tenrei Ota

Netherlands   Voluntary Euthanasia Society

by ___Nelly Folpmers___
Nelly Folpmers

United Kingdom   Voluntary Euthanasia Society

by ___Charles R. Sweetingham___
Charles R. Sweetingham

United States   Society for the Right to Die

by ___Sidney D. Rosoff___
Sidney D. Rosoff

Euthanasia Educational Council

by ___C. Dickerman Williams___
C. Dickerman Williams

(1976.8.24.)

hospitals. It stated that 21 nurses had told investigators that they had carried out mercy-killings of terminally-ill patients without consulting doctors but always at the request of the patients, or their relatives. Another 76 nurses said they had received such requests.

Furthermore *Newsweek* (February 16, 1976) reported that thousands of elderly Japanese are making pilgrimages to pray to a god known as Pokkuri-sama. This worship began 250 years ago when an old man asked for and received a painless quick end to his life. The word "pokkuri" means at a snap or instantly. Although the first shrine was in a distant part of the island of Shikoku, there are now several temples dedicated to the pokkuri faith. There is also an organization called Jiiren or The League to Decline Medicare which campaigns for the right to die.

The Japan Euthanasia Society, along with the Mainichi newspaper, called and conducted a first International Conference For Euthanasia in Tokyo in August, 1976. This was attended by representatives of euthanasia societies in Great Britain, the United States, Netherlands, South Africa, and Australia as well as representatives of Family and Population Planning organizations of Malaysia and the Philippines.

The conference deliberations resulted in the formation and signing of the declaration on the preceding page.

POLICIES OF ORGANIZATIONS AND VIEWS OF PROFESSIONAL LEADERS

Action by Legal Organizations and Discussion in Legal Journals

There is much evidence that members of bar associations are seriously struggling with the problems pertaining to life and death. At the August 1976 meeting of the American Bar Association Professor Oliver C. Schroeder, Jr., director of the Law-Medical Center at Case Western Reserve University, declared the state of "life and death law" to be "oscillating between confusing and chaotic."

A panel agreed that confusion results from the fact that some old concepts are being "unhinged" as theology, law, and medicine are being forced to reconsider and redefine life and death. Speakers asserted that it will be difficult to achieve agreement while many people feel threatened rather than helped by the technology that can prolong life. Professor Schroeder cited the statement of the Nairobi assembly of the World Council of Churches earlier in the year deploring the spiritual state of mankind. He said, "We are not going to get any law that is worth a tinker's damn while human society is in spiritual confusion."

In February 1975, The House of Delegates of the American Bar Association approved this statement: "For all legal purposes, a human body with irreversible cessation of total brain function, according to usual and customary standards of medical practice, shall be considered dead." Hence it was said that the $750,000 wrongful-death suit being brought against St. Louis University Hospital for the death of a patient whose life-support machine was detached after he had recorded no brain waves for 48 hours would probably be a most significant case.

In Canada a definition of brain death has been embodied in the Manitoba Vital Statistics Act. In contrast, the Ontario Human Tissues Act makes death official when two or more doctors decide that a death has taken place. A step toward recognizing the right to die was taken by the criminal law section of the Canadian Bar Association when they approved the right of a mortally-ill person to refuse treatment.

Legal Journals

There is a rapidly growing volume of discussions of euthanasia and its legal ramifications in legal journals. Principal attention seems to focus on the unsatisfactory state of present statutory law regarding the rights of persons in view of "mechanically prolonged death." The result is that it is becoming increasingly difficult to die. It is being emphasized that we are becoming "trapped in life" by the proficiency of modern science making this one of the most complex and perplexing problems today.

The argument that a person should have a right to choose death is based on the general constitutional right of privacy as expounded in *Roe v. Wade* (410 U.S. 113, 1973) and *Doe v. Bolton* (410 U.S. 179, 1973). It is argued that this is a fundamental right that can be limited by the state only to the extent of seeing that surviving dependents are not left destitute and a burden on the state.

A person's right to die is claimed because there are no criminal sanctions against suicide and present case law recognizes a person's right to refuse medical treatment and, by so doing, risk or choose death. Thus any issue does not depend upon whether the patient's decision agrees with the sensibilities of others, but only whether he has freely and knowingly made the choice to die.

The argument that legalized euthanasia might be abused ignores the fact that it is now practiced despite its present illegal status. It is because of this disparity between the law on the books and the law in practice that the jury has become "the conscience of society," thus being the intermediary between the two.

The unsatisfactory status of present statutory law has led to several proposed drafts for new law. One such proposal is by Sheila Schiff Cole and Marta Sachey Shea, entitled "Voluntary Euthanasia: A Proposed Remedy." (*Albany Law Review*, 1975, 39:4). They define their proposal as "an Act to provide terminally injured persons the means to effect their death through the assistance of a physician." The person would voluntarily petition the New York Supreme Court for authorization of an assisted termination of life, with an affidavit by a physician indicating that he believes the petitioner to be a qualified person under the law. The Court would then conduct an investigation, including a report by a court-appointed physician. Afterward the Court would make a determination, within one week if possible, and then issue an order effective for seven days authorizing the assisted termination of life. This would mean provision to the petitioner by a physician "of an instrumentality designed to induce a painless death, to be administered to the person by the physician in the presence of a witness, or by the person in the presence of the physician and a witness."

According to this proposal, the physician would be immune from criminal and civil liability and the death of the person would be deemed a natural death. The authors conclude, "There is a great need for the relief a Voluntary Euthanasia Act would provide. We call upon the members of the New York State Legislature to consider the Proposed Euthanasia Bill and enact it or a similar bill into law." Still one questions whether quite such stringent requirements as Miss Cole and Miss Shea propose are necessary.

Another draft entitled "Self-Death—A Defense to Murder" has been proposed by Walter W. Steele, Jr., and Bill B. Hill, Jr., in "A Legislative Proposal for a Legal Right to Die." (*Criminal Law Bulletin,* March–April 1976, 12:2). The same draft is published in *Oklahoma Law Review* (Spring 1976, 29:2) under the title, "A Plea for a Legal Right to Die." The latter article concludes with a note on the Karen Quinlan case. This draft is open to several criticisms, partly because of the terminology. Comments and rebuttals to appear in later issues of the first journal have been invited by the editor. It is encouraging to have lawyers working on such drafts but further effort is needed. Other drafts had been proposed by Margaret J. Orbon (Loyola

Univ. of Chicago Law Journal, Summer 1976), and by Ronald P. Kaplan (American Journal of Law and Medicine, Summer 1976).

Study by the ACLU

The due process committee of the American Civil Liberties Union has prepared a tentative proposed policy statement pertaining to euthanasia, living wills, suicide, and the definition of death. Study of the draft is continuing and it is scheduled to be considered at a meeting of the Board of ACLU in December 1976.

Opinions and Actions of Physicians, Nurses, and Medical Organizations

At the 1971 annual health conference of the New York Academy of Medicine, Lord Ritchie-Calder said, "Medical science has produced an ethical crisis which transcends our conventional ideas of Good and Evil." In response to the admonition of that statement the Academy studied the problems involved and approved this statement:

> When, in the opinion of the attending physician, measures to prolong life, which have no realistic hope of effecting significant improvement, will cause further pain and suffering to the patient and the family, we support conservative, passive medical care in place of heroic measures in the management of a patient afflicted with a terminal illness.

Following the 1974 resolution of the Canadian Medical Association that it is ethical for a doctor to write "no resuscitation" on a dying patient's chart, *Modern Medicine of Canada,* (July 1974, Vol. 29:7) conducted a survey of over 1700 physicians to determine their views on euthanasia. Of this number, 95 per cent said dying patients should have the right to reject life-prolonging treatment. However, 61 per cent said the decision to terminate treatment should be made by a committee of physicians, and whoever makes the decision should be legally protected. There were 89 per cent who said they had faced situations in which euthanasia could have been involved. And 79 per cent thought the legal position on euthanasia should be re-examined. One doctor commented, "Obviously we need to discuss euthanasia. At the moment we are so conscious of avoiding abuse of euthanasia that we allow many patients and their relatives to suffer needlessly."

At the 1975 meeting of the CMA, delegates defeated a move to rescind the resolution passed at the 1974 meeting which had given its approval to "no resuscitation." In arguing to rescind the resolution it was said that the Criminal Code had not yet been amended to protect physicians. But in response there was another call for the Code to be amended to protect doctors who practice passive euthanasia and it was decided to obtain further legal advice about "no resuscitation."

These questions were discussed again at the 1976 meeting. Dr. John S. Bennett, director of professional affairs of the CMA, indicated the increased public interest in "the right to die" (whether or not expressed in those terms), the living will, automatic resuscitation, or euthanasia. The Committee on Ethics reported agreement that "the major factor in making decisions must continue to be the clinical judgment of the physician," and that there should be further consideration of the "Living Will." The concern of CMA members with these problems is indicated by the growing number of articles in the *CMA Journal* with such titles as "Pulling the Plug: Who Decides?," "Palliative Care. It's the Quality of Life Remaining That Matters," "The Problem of Caring for the Dying in a General Hospital," and "Terminal Care: Toward an Ideal."

Medical Opinion (May 1974) reported a survey of 3000 physicians in the United States, selected at random, from whom 933 replies were received. The report was entitled "Doctors and Dying: Is Euthanasia Now Becoming Accepted?" There were 79 per cent who agreed on the right to make one's wishes known regarding treatment before serious illness strikes. And 82 per cent would practice a form of passive euthanasia on a member of his family and 86 per cent would practice it on themselves. And 10 per cent would actively bring on death. Commenting on the survey the *New York Times* said, "The medical mandate for euthanasia is far stronger than was previously known." (*New York Times*, June 16, 1974, IV, p. 7).

A study of opinions regarding euthanasia of 151 physicians in 10 medical specialities reported by *Omega* (1975, 6:4, p. 291–302) concluded that most doctors felt that patients should be told the facts of their condition. There was strong opposition to the use of heroic measures in hopeless cases, and older physicians were the most negative in their responses.

In another study reported in *International Journal of Psychiatry* (1974, Vol. 5:1), all 3,223 physicians in the state of Iowa were questioned regarding the care of terminally-ill patients. Nearly half of the 1,602 who responded revealed that they frequently omitted life-prolonging procedures. But the vast majority opposed a change in social attitudes which would permit physicians to hasten death. Those doctors with greater exposure to terminal patients more readily discussed a patient's prognosis with him, received more requests for interrupting treatment, and more frequently omitted life-prolonging measures. Physicians in their 20's and 70's claimed they much less frequently omitted life-prolonging measures than did physicians in their 40's and 50's.

The report concluded

It is interesting to note that physicians in their 60's and 70's view their terminal patients as less aware they are dying and, accordingly, appear to discuss the prognosis with them less frequently. This may suggest that the closer a physician comes to his own death, the more he avoids reminders of that eventuality, including the awareness of death in his patients. In support of his own denial he may avoid communication regarding death.

One may suppose that it might also be that the older physicians tend to be more bound by tradition and past medical training.

At its 1975 meeting, the Maryland State Medical Society urged all hospitals and nursing homes to set up permanent committees to give advice on when to stop the use of heroic measures. To this end, the Society adopted a statement drafted by Dr. Leslie Miles, head of the Society's committee on medicine and religion. Among other things, the statement read: "It is reiterated that all normal medical procedures must be followed and that extraordinary treatment should be avoided if it is recognized as hopeless and detrimental to the patient and the patient's family."

Nurses have also been increasingly rebelling against useless prolongation of life. A survey of the opinions of the nation's 1,500,000 nurses was reported in *Nursing 75* (August and September 1975). Of the more than 15,000 nurses who answered the survey, almost half said they favor, or slightly favor, euthanasia for dying patients who request it. Also, 96 per cent said they favor, or slightly favor, withdrawing all life-sustaining treatment from dying patients who do not want such treatment. There were 79 per cent who said they never "knowingly helped to hasten the death of a terminally-ill patient." Over 60 per cent said they are very uncomfortable or unable to cope with their feelings when a young child is dying, while fewer than 5 per cent said they were uncomfortable when the patient is elderly. An overwhelming majority favored deliberately allowing newborns with gross abnormalities to die when there is no possibility of any meaningful life, while only 8 per cent were firmly opposed to such action, and 11 per cent were slightly against it.

Medical Times (May 26, 1976) reported a poll of physicians showing that 77 per cent of them said they would "consider" passive euthanasia in cases of terminal patients "whose suffering seems unbearable." But there were 61 per cent who said they opposed active euthanasia, 17 per cent who favored it, and 22 per cent who made no comment. And 48 per cent indicated that they wished physicians had greater freedom to shorten the suffering of terminal patients, and 57 per cent said they had had a terminal patient ask to have his suffering cut short.

The doctors of the Massachusetts General Hospital and Beth Israel Hospital of Boston made an important contribution to considering human dignity and welfare when they conceded the fact that in some cases maximum therapeutic efforts may only prolong the dying process rather than extend meaningful life, (*The New England Journal of Medicine,* August 12, 1976). But they spoke only of "consultation with and concurrence of the family" and "shared responsibility for patient and family" which seems to leave too much authority to the attending physician rather than to the patient, or to his family if he is incompetent. Although the Beth Israel report discussed "the patient's right to elect and decline the benefits of medical technology," both reports spoke only of discontinuing therapy. Yet once the machines have been turned off, the relief that only death can give may still be a long way off, as is the case of Karen Quinlan.

In 1975 Dr. George Annas, Director of Boston University's Center for Law and the Health Sciences, and author of *The Rights of Hospital Patients,* made an address to the annual conference of the Euthanasia Educational Council. There Dr. Annas stated that if the patient is competent, he should make the decision to live or die. He said it is wrong to take it for granted that the physician alone should be the one to decide whether treatment should be terminated.

H. T. Engelhardt faced this aspect of the problem in his article, "On the Bounds of Freedom," (*Connecticut Medicine,* January 1976), saying, ". . . a person-oriented medicine must come to terms with human freedom." Referring to assisted suicide, he said, ". . . allowing such practice can be part of protecting rather than violating basic human freedoms . . ."

Positions and Views of Religious Leaders and Churches

The Reverend Michael P. Hamilton of the Washington Cathedral made this comment on the Karen Quinlan case in *The Christian Century* (October 22, 1975):

> ". . . despite hesitation and delay, our society is changing its mind about the process of dying and if wise and humane judgments of lawyers, doctors, ethicists, and citizens prevail, we may expect fewer cases like that of Karen Quinlan in the future."

Canon Hamilton said that the churches are ahead of other social institutions on this issue and cited the landmark pronouncement of Pope Pius XII in 1957. But this writer is not aware that the churches have made any courageous resolutions in support of a right to euthanasia since those reported earlier in this book in support of passive euthanasia. An exception is the resolution made by the Canadian Unitarian Council at its annual meeting in May 1976. By a vote of 60 to 3, the Council overwhelmingly approved the following resolution:

"That the fifteenth annual meeting of the Canadian Unitarian Council urges the Law Reform Commission of Canada to propose a modification of the criminal code, subject to proper safeguards and sanctions, expedient to the situation when the withdrawal of life-support treatment would be considered an act of compassion."

Earlier a parish poll indicated that of 634 members who replied to a questionnaire asking how they would vote on this resolution, 93% approved, 2% disapproved, and 4% abstained.

In November 1975 the District of Columbia Baptist Convention approved the right of a person of sound mind "to covenant with his family that extraordinary medical means not be used to prolong his life where no reasonable hope of recovery shall exist." The statement asserted that "the denial of this right to death imposes severe economic hardships and mental anguish upon a surviving family, as well as liability for criminal prosecution of them and their physician."

What is widely regarded as a backward step was taken by the Church of England in its 1975 report entitled, "On Dying Well." This, as well as a rebuttal it received will be discussed in the next section of this supplement. The Catholic Church has also stepped up its opposition to any deliberate hastening of death. Cardinal Cooke made this statement in St. Patrick's Cathedral in New York: "Deliberate abortion at one end of the life spectrum and deliberate euthanasia at the other end are fundamental moral evils to be opposed in every instance." (*New York Times,* January 14, 1974, 31:7). And in his Bicentennial message to the Catholic hierarchy in the United States Pope Paul VI warned that euthanasia and abortion are "special dangers" in American society, saying, "We are with you in facing the special dangers to your country and society from abortion and euthanasia." (*New York Times,* June 25, 1976, 2:4).

But some Catholics have taken significant stands differing from the official Catholic position. One such Catholic is Dr. Daniel Maguire, theologian of Marquette University and author of *Death By Choice,* who says the Church is changing its stand but not at the level of the hierarchy. Maguire believes that mercy-killing should be a matter of choice. "I believe we have the First Amendment right to give or seek assistance. I don't anticipate that any time in the future the hierarchy will recognize it and adopt it but the official view is a minority view."

In contrast, the Catholic League for Religious and Civil Rights has recently attacked what it called "the growing euthanasia movement in the United States." The League warned that ". . . each day these forces remain unchecked they grow stronger and for many the chances of dying a natural death grow more remote."

Since the World Council of Churches and other international organizations have helped focus world attention on violations of human rights, it is to be hoped that they will consider the needless suffering caused by the present laws and customs pertaining to death and dying.

Church of England Report on Euthanasia and Rebuttal by the Voluntary Euthanasia Society

The Board for Social Responsibility of the Church of England published a 67-page report in May 1975 entitled, "On Dying Well: An Anglican Contribution to the Debate on Euthanasia." It was prepared by a Working Party that had been appointed in 1970 to study the matter. Its chairman reported that "its subsequent course had not been smooth" and the death of some of its members had caused delay. When it was finally issued the report was a great disappointment to many. Considering the courageous stand that the church had taken in its 1965 report, the advocates of legalizing euthanasia viewed the present report as a definite step backward.

The Report stated that it does not commit the Church of England or its members to any one view regarding euthanasia. It also acknowledged that sometimes new situations arise that render old moral rules obsolete and that "further principles" are sometimes necessary. While it agreed that "there comes a time in the course of fatal illness when the doctor's duty to the patient is no longer to use all efforts to preserve life . . . ," it concluded that euthanasia or any hastening of death was wrong and ought not to be made legally permissible.

It said that even though there might be a very few extreme cases in which it would be moral to end life, it was important to adhere to the sanctity of life principle that it is always wrong to kill innocent life. The Working Party concluded, "In matters so fundamental to our well-being as those of life and death, we interfere at our peril with deeply felt attitudes and convictions."

The Working Party also minimized the number of persons who would want euthanasia. According to Dr. Cicely Saunders, Medical Director of St. Christopher's Hospice in London, an influential member of the group, there were many cases of dying patients who were comfortable and happy in her hospice. Dr. Saunders did not speak of the numerous persons who cannot go to such a hospice even though they might want to or have the means to do so since there simply are not enough such hospices. The increasing number of old people makes it unreasonable to think that there will ever be enough hospices. Moreover, many question how happy some of the patients in St. Christopher's really are.

The Voluntary Euthanasia Society of England published a rebuttal to the Anglican report the following year. It is entitled "Death with Dignity—A Reply to 'On Dying Well.'" It was prepared by Dr. Eliot Slater, Prof. Anthony

G. M. Flew, and Reverend A. B. Downing. One of its criticisms of the Anglican report is that it is based on theological teaching which many find unacceptable today. For instance, the idea that we must all live until such time as it shall please God to call us is questioned. The Society claimed that if this were true, instead of us being free men with rights and duties, we would be like slaves who are only responsible to their master.

The Anglican authors had said, ". . . we wish to express our strong dissent from the use of the expression 'right to die' in the discussion of euthanasia." The Society replied that a person should have the right to determine whether or not he shall live or die, either by suicide or euthanasia, if he no longer has duties to society. The Society claimed that sometimes in caring for a dying patient, Christians and others may actually have a duty to end the patient's life if that is the patient's wish.

The Anglican group rejected any legalization of euthanasia in the belief that it "would place some terminal and even some non-terminal patients under pressure to allow themselves to be put away. . . ." In response to this the Society asked, "But why is it wrong in death, as it is not, surely, wrong in life, to feel some obligation not to be a burden on others?" It must be remembered that the Society and others make it clear that they do not advocate any compulsory euthanasia, and on the contrary strongly condemn it. In the legislation proposed by the Society careful safeguards are incorporated to ensure that the patient makes the choice of his own free will, without any pressure whatsoever.

In commenting on the hospice cases described by Dr. Cicely Saunders the Society pointed out that if the helplessly-dying patients in the hospice should request death, they would not be taken seriously. Furthermore, they would be reminded that what they suggest is sinful.

The Plea by the American Humanist Association

The American Humanist Association issued "A Plea For Beneficent Euthanasia" in its July/August 1974 issue, signed by such distinguished persons as three Nobel Prize Laureates, physicians, religious leaders, philosophers, lawyers, businessmen, and academics. Almost the entire issue was devoted to articles on the subject of euthanasia or dying. The plea and conclusion read as follows:

> We, the undersigned, declare our support on ethical grounds for beneficent euthanasia. We believe that reflective ethical consciousness has developed to a point that makes it possible for societies to work out a humane policy toward death and dying. We deplore moral insensitivity and legal restrictions which impede and oppose the ethical case for euthanasia. We appeal to an enlightened public opinion to transcend traditional taboos and to move in the direction of a compassionate view toward needless suffering in dying.
>
> We reject theories that imply that human suffering is inevitable or that little can be done to improve the human condition. We hold that the tolerance, acceptance, or enforcement of the unnecessary suffering of others is immoral.
>
> We believe in the value and dignity of the individual person. This requires respectful treatment, which entails the right to reasonable self-determination. No rational morality can categorically forbid the termination of life if it has been blighted by some horrible malady for which all known remedial measures are unavailing.
>
> *Conclusion:*
>
> We believe that the practice of voluntary beneficent euthanasia will enhance the general welfare of human beings and once proper legal safeguards are established, that such actions will encourage men to act courageously, out of kindness and justice. We believe that society has no genuine interest or need to preserve the terminally ill against their will and that the right to beneficent euthanasia, with proper procedural safeguards, can be protected against abuse.

Later that year the Association established a National Commission for Beneficent Euthanasia which held its first meeting in St. Louis in May 1974. Its purpose is to study the problem of euthanasia, to enlighten public opinion to transcend traditional taboos, and to help make it possible for society to work out a humane policy toward death and dying. The Commission endorses both active and passive euthanasia.

Research and Education

At least four prestigious organizations are doing very significant research and education bearing in one way or another on this problem of death and dying. The Institute of Society, Ethics and the Life Sciences, often referred to as the Hastings Institute as it is located in Hastings-on-Hudson, continues to expand its research in the whole field of bioethics since it was founded in 1969. Its bimonthly *Hastings Center Report* is filled with challenging articles and reports of research by scientists in many fields, including lawyers, theologians, and others. It carries excellent brief reviews of current literature related to bioethics that is most valuable for students in this field.

A companion group was organized in Seattle in 1975 called "The Northwest Institute of Ethics and the Life Sciences." It is publishing a quarterly called *Bioethics Northwest* featuring research and comment by clergy, lawyers, educators, philosophers and others doing work in the broad field of bioethics. The first issue of their quarterly was mostly devoted to discussion of euthanasia. And there is the Kennedy Institute, at Georgetown University in Washington, D.C., which is conducting research and numerous educational programs and seminars on bioethics for both scholars and the public. The Foundation of

Thanatology, with its major emphasis on death and grief, is also engaged in research and educational programs.

THE LIVING WILL AND PATIENTS' BILLS OF RIGHTS

Much publicity has been given recently to the "Living Will." The Euthanasia Educational Council reported in 1975 that it had distributed 750,000 copies of their draft, which is essentially the same as the form given on pages 296–97 in this book. Many individuals write their own draft which may vary from the E.E.C. form. It should be remembered that at the present time these wills are not legal documents except in California as specified in the Natural Death Act. However many doctors and lawyers and others are encouraging patients and clients to sign them. And in 1973 the Judicial Council of the American Medical Association stated that there was consensus that "patients should not be discouraged from indicating in writing their wishes regarding refusal of medical treatment during terminal illness, and these wishes should be respected insofar as possible. . . ." In spite of the widespread popularity the Living Will has enjoyed in recent years, many disapprove of its use until it becomes legally permissible for the patient's wishes to be carried out and satisfactory safeguards for patients and physicians are incorporated in it.

Some Catholics have been stepping up their opposition to the use of the Living Will. Others believe that signing it is inviting a doctor to do covertly what he would not risk doing openly under present law. In an article entitled "Conscience and the Law" in *Catholic Lawyer* (Summer 1975), the Reverend Joseph E. Hogan, C. M., Professor of Philosophy at St. John's University, spoke of the anguish Catholics suffered over the Living Will, as well as abortion. He accused the Euthanasia Educational Council of using the will "as a form of propaganda to form the public according to their point of view." He said that if one were to read the will uncritically, it would appear to be compatible with Catholic teaching on natural dying and death.

> However: a more reflective reading, from the perspective of Catholic moral teaching on this subject, . . . reveals the absence in this form of presumptions which are implicit in our Catholic position, namely, the patient is expected to be prepared both spiritually and temporally for death; the determination not to use extraordinary means is made at a particular time and under specific circumstances, and not the long-range decision implicit in the living will.

The Reverend Hogan regards the will as a wedge to the legalization of "voluntary euthanasia and ultimately involuntary euthanasia." He says that it is contrary to the moral convictions and directives of Catholic hospitals and he views it with alarm.

Efforts of Catholics and others to block distribution of the Living Will have met with some success, at least temporarily, in some places. For instance, according to *Euthanasia News,* August 1976, the Committee on Medical Practice of the Massachusetts Medical Society had recommended unanimously that the document be made available and distribution of the forms had begun. But this was halted, due largely to the efforts of Dr. George Smithy, president of the medical staff at St. Elizabeth's Hospital in Brighton, and a decision was made to reconsider the matter at a later meeting.

Writing in the *New York State Journal of Medicine* (April 1976), Dr. Alfred Jaretzki opposed any legalization of the will, saying, "As soon as attempts are made to try to make it a legally binding document the specter of active euthanasia comes to the forefront." But he continued, "When it has been accurately determined that the patient is indeed dying and reasonable hope no longer exists and the patient and family accept this evaluation, the physician has the obligation to let death come as comfortably as possible and in as natural a setting as possible."

In England, Malcolm Muggeridge signed the legal form prepared by the Human Rights Society which was formed in 1969 to oppose euthanasia. While Muggeridge said he was opposed to euthanasia he would want to be allowed to die in peace.

One must conclude that more and more living wills are being given to physicians in spite of the fact that patients and physicians are not given the safeguards that law should provide. Also more and more doctors may resort to covert action not only to administer passive euthanasia but active as well, which is a dangerous course to take.

The state of California is to be commended, in this writer's view, for enacting law that may be regarded as a first step toward solving this difficult problem.

Patients' Bills of Rights

In January 1973 The American Hospital Association made public its Bill of Rights for patients which it distributed to 7000 member hospitals. In May 1975 the AHA indicated that while 85 per cent of the nation's hospitals have accepted the Bill in principle, only 35 per cent have used it in any form.

The Catholic Hospital Association published in 1974 a "Christian Affirmation of Life" for use by persons wishing to express their desires regarding treatment during a terminal illness. It requests that consultation be permitted if possible on medical procedures and that "no extraordinary means be used" to prolong life when there is no reasonable expectation of recovery. Catholics claim that it is not a substitute for the living will but an affirmation of beliefs in Catholic doctrines. Although there is a request that undue pain be alleviated there is never any intention of shortening life.

In July 1976 the Orthodox Jewish organization, Agudath Israel of America, published a Bill of Rights for Jewish patients. Among other rights it specifies the right to consult with spiritual advisers before deciding whether to undergo medical procedures that might pose religious questions.

INCREASED EFFORTS TO HELP THE AGED AND THE DYING

There are more indications of consideration being given to the problems and care of the aged. Dr. Walter Sackett of Florida has said that when he went into medical practice 30 years ago, the elderly were afraid to go to the hospital because it was a place to die. Now they are afraid to go because it is a place where they will not be allowed to die.

In May 1974 Congress passed a law authorizing the establishment of a National Institute on Aging as part of the National Institutes of Health. The purpose of the Institute is to conduct biomedical, social, and behavioral research related to the aging process and the needs of the aged. In May 1976 Dr. Robert Butler, winner of the 1976 Pulitzer Prize for nonfiction for his book *Why Survive? Being Old in America,* was named director of the new institute.

Dr. Butler has pointed out that there is not one chair in geriatric medicine in the United States. To care for the 1.2 million people in the nation's 23,000 nursing homes there are only 30,000 registered nurses. For a variety of reasons that have not been studied, 25% of all suicides committed in the United States are accomplished by people over 65 years of age. Obviously there are some problems to be explored.

Nursing homes continue to be subject to closer scrutiny. *Time's* June 2, 1975 cover story was on "The New Outlook For The Aged." And in a lead editorial in April 1, 1975, *The Washington Post* discussed and deplored nursing homes as "Human Warehouses." In a September 1975 report the Senate Subcommittee on Aging stated that because of fire hazards nursing homes "rank number one on the list of unsafe places to live."

There is also increasing discussion of hospices for the care of the dying. While these hospices do not seem to recognize the right of a person to choose to die, they do face the fact that it is not desirable in hopeless cases to try to postpone death and they try to make dying as easy as possible. Modeled on the program in St. Christopher's in England, Dr. Sylvia Lack is directing a new hospice in New Haven, Connecticut. A similar unit has been established in Montreal, Canada, as part of Royal Victoria Hospital, a large teaching hospital. Although it is not a separate institution, it has its own special staff of physicians and nurses assisted by a corps of volunteers. Director Dr. Balfour Mount said it was established because a study of dying patients showed that their psychological, spiritual, and even medical needs were not being met. He said, "Poor care for the dying arises out of a death-denying culture in which even doctors are ambivalent, equating good medical care with aggressive investigation and treatment."

The aim of these hospices is not to prolong life but to improve the quality of remaining life to the greatest degree possible, to keep the patient free of pain, in comfortable surroundings, and prepared to meet death in a calm state of mind.

Numerous medical schools, theological, and nursing schools have initiated courses on death and dying. The Foundation of Thantology is sponsoring research, symposia, and publications on death and the care of the dying. Its new *Thanatology Library* is a publication listing books and audio-visual materials on death, bereavement, loss, and grief, along with useful reviews of the listings.

Bicentennial Charter For Older Americans

The Federal Council on the Aging published the Bicentennial Charter for Older Americans in 1976. It is a revision of the Senior Citizens Charter of Rights and Obligations that was developed by the 1961 White House Conference on Aging.

The Charter lists nine basic rights, of which the last two are as follows:

> VIII The Right to Appropriate Institutional Care When Required. Care should provide full restorative services in a safe environment. This care should also promote and protect the dignity and rights of the individual along with family and community ties.
>
> IX The Right to a Life and Death With Dignity. Regardless of age, society must assure individual citizens of the protection of their constitutional rights and opportunities for self respect, respect and acceptance from others, a sense of enrichment and contribution, and freedom from dependency. Dignity in dying includes the right of the individual to permit or deny the use of extraordinary life support systems.

Public Opinion Polls

Much publicity has been given to four recent public opinion polls which have covered the aspects of euthanasia. Mervin Field's poll of 504 Californians in April 1975 showed that 87 per cent agreed that incurably-ill patients should have a right to refuse medication, and 63 per cent agreed that the terminally ill should have a right to ask for and receive medication to end life. Interestingly, 41 per cent of this last group were over the age of 70.

In November 1975 the William Hamilton Organization made a nationwide survey of 982 persons. The Organization posed this question: "Suppose a person is in the hospital and according to all medical evidence is dying and cannot be cured or saved. Do you feel that it would be right to simply let that person die or should every effort be made to keep them alive?" In response 59 per cent said to let the person die, while 39 per cent said to make every effort to prolong life. When asked, "Who do you feel has the right to make that decision—the patient's relatives or the patient's doctor or the relatives and doctor?", 27 per cent said the patient's relatives, 7 per cent named the doctor, and 26 per cent replied that the relatives and the doctor should assume that responsibility. Unfortunately this question did not include the patient himself.

In August 1975 Gallup reported a nation-wide poll regarding suicide following the Van Dusen case. The poll asked, "Do you think a person has a moral right to end his or her life under these circumstances: when this person has a disease that is incurable?" There were 40 per cent who said yes, 53 per cent who said no, and 7 per cent who had no opinion. When asked this same question, under the circumstance "—when this person is suffering great pain and has no hope of improvement?", 41 per cent said yes, 51 per cent said no, and 8 per cent had no opinion. To the added circumstance, "—when this person is an extremely heavy burden on his or her family?", the answers were 20 per cent yes, 72 per cent no, and 8 per cent no opinion.

Gallup said the survey revealed wide differences in attitude depending on the background characteristics of those polled. He said:

> More liberally-oriented population groups, such as young adults and persons with a college background, are more likely to favor death by choice than are older adults and persons with less formal education. For example, 54 per cent of the college-trained segment believe a person has the moral right to end his or her life while suffering great pain with no hope of improvement or when a person has a disease that is incurable. Also, 29 per cent of the college group say

a person has this right upon becoming an intolerable family burden—a higher percentage than found in any other population group.

Gallup also reported that he found little difference between the views of men and women, and also only slight differences in terms of religious affiliation.

The Ladies Home Journal reported a 16-city survey of American women in March 1976 showing that 60 per cent thought the life-sustaining machines should be turned off for Karen Quinlan, 69 per cent approved of having them turned off if the patient were a loved one, and 81 per cent would want them turned off if they were the patient; 77 per cent agreed that there should be no prosecution of a person who turned off the machine of a terminally-ill person, and 80 per cent thought a Living Will should be honored.

Dr. John W. Riley, Jr., reported a 1973 nationwide survey of attitudes and feelings about death for the Office of Social Research of Equitable Life Assurance Society. It showed that 95 per cent of those questioned agreed that each person has the right to die with dignity; 86 per cent agreed that only the manner of dying and not death itself is to be feared; 67 per cent said that if a patient is dying a doctor ought to tell him; and only 26 per cent said that "doctors should use any means for keeping a patient alive, even after the patient is no longer himself."

MORE CASES THAT DEMONSTRATE THE NEED FOR LEGISLATIVE ACTION

There is an increasing number of doctors who admit that they have either terminated treatment or ended a life of a hopelessly ill patient. In 1974 Dr. David Maclay, aged 66, of Birmingham, England, said that 40 years ago he had given a fatal dose of morphine to a newborn with spina bifida. He urged the legalization of euthanasia, saying:

I have never regretted my decision. I do not think my views conflict with the Hippocratic Oath. The baby's life, however long it lasted, would have been a burden to itself and its parents. I do not know whether you would call that killing. I would prefer to call it freeing someone from a living death. When I see people, whether children, the old, or accident victims who have been kept alive by today's wonderful advanced surgery, it sometimes distresses me. Quite often these people are being kept alive cruelly. They are never again going to be of any use to themselves or society.

There was no indictment of Dr. Maclay.

A similar case is that of Dr. Bjoern Ibsen, aged 51, of Copenhagen, Denmark. In 1974 Dr. Ibsen said on radio that he speeds up the process of dying when he considers a patient's case hopeless and that continued treatment would meaninglessly prolong pain and suffering. Also in 1974 a doctor of Stockholm, Sweden, whose name was not given, said he had stopped the respirators of 12 persons whose brains had stopped functioning. He justified this by saying, ". . . an ill person is incurably dead when his brain has ceased to function." And in 1975 Dr. Alby Hartman, aged 50, of Capetown, South Africa, was given a one-year suspended sentence on conviction of murder for having killed his 87-year-old father who was dying of cancer.

In 1974 two convictions for mercy-killings were widely reported. In Scotland, there was the trial and conviction of Jessie McTavish, a nurse at Glasgow's Ruchill Hospital. She was accused of giving elderly patients injections to ease their dying, which she claimed were to prevent choking. She was sentenced to life imprisonment, which she has appealed. Lord Platt in the House of Lords commented, "Of course the judgment was correct, the charge of murder proved, the sentence according to law. But I hope that if I live to be senile, demented, incontinent, and a nuisance and expense to those who care for me, that if Sister McTavish is by then released, they will have the good sense to let me spend my last days on her ward." But Richard Lamerton, chairman of the Human Rights Society which was founded in 1969 to oppose euthanasia, had a very different opinion. "I fear that the involuntary euthanasia which Lord Platt commends would create more social problems than it would solve. With good care, senile people can be dignified, contented, and a pleasure to serve."

The second mercy-killing conviction was that of Mrs. Elizabeth Wise, of Newbury, England, second cousin of the Queen, for having given a deadly drug to her 10-month old daughter who was born blind and deaf. She had been charged with murder but that was reduced to a charge of manslaughter for "reasons of diminished responsibility." She was put on probation for 12 months. Mrs. Wise's attorney said she had cared for the child for 10 months but when the doctors said that there was no hope that the child's condition would ever improve, she ended the life of her daughter.

In Pontiac, Michigan, Robert C. Waters, 65, a former high school principal, was convicted of manslaughter in January 1975. He was fined $3,750 and put on 30 months probation for what his attorney called "a crime of love." Mr. Waters helped his ailing wife of 40 years, also 65, to commit suicide by starting the engine of his car, helping her to the car, and leaving her inside the closed garage where she died. He explained, "The reason I didn't stop her was if she did not die here, she was going into another mental and psychiatric hospital for care which she neither wanted nor would approve to find herself in in all probability." Since 1971 he had tried to dissuade her from killing herself. "And rather than die the way she feared, a cripple maybe and mentally affected, I would rather let her make her own choice and die—if I may say—with dignity, than to go thru with what she might have faced. It had to be her decision, not mine."

There were at least three notable cases in which there

was no indictment and no prosecution. In Oakland, California, in July 1975, Lois Phillips, aged 68, was not prosecuted although she had been charged with aiding and abetting a suicide. Mrs. Phillips shot her husband of 32 years who had begged repeatedly to be killed because he had been an invalid for 12 years with a painful spinal deterioration. After shooting him, she had unsuccessfully tried to shoot herself.

No charge was made against William Plachta, 64, also of California, who watched his wife take an overdose of sleeping pills. She had suffered for 2 years with nervous disorders and multiple sclerosis. He said, "I could not let her go on like this."

And in Mineola, New York, there was no charge made in the death of Maryjane Dahl, 16 years old, when her respirator was mysteriously unplugged. Miss Dahl, who was critically ill, was described to be in a "terminal state." The District Attorney said there was insufficient evidence to put before a grand jury.

There have been several appeals for action in hopeless cases, with the appeal granted in some and not in others. In November 1975, Judith Ann Debro, 35, died while her life-support machines were still attached. She had been comatose following an auto accident. Her husband had appealed to the court for authority to have her removed from the machines which kept her heart beating "while no other part of her body is in fact alive." A St. Louis County judge ruled that his court did not have authority to order the respirator to be unhooked.

In Elyria, Ohio, Randal Carmen, 17, whose brain was dead following a football injury, lived for 22 days on machines. The hospital refused to shut off the machines despite the request of his parents. The hospital administrator said it was their policy "to do everything in our power to maintain life-saving procedures regardless of the condition of the patient."

However, in Seattle, Washington, Superior Court Judge D. J. Cunningham ruled that surgery need not be performed on "Baby Shane," aged three months, who had been born with serious abnormalities of the brain, spine, heart, kidneys, and eyes. County health officials had gone to court to force radical, high-risk surgery. Dr. David Shurtleff, director of the Birth Defects Center of the University of Washington, said, "This will become a question of balancing humaneness against needlessly perpetuating life."

In August 1976, the Massachusetts Supreme Court ruled unanimously that Hampshire County Probate Judge Harry Jekanowski had had authority to decide that chemotherapy should not be ordered for a mentally retarded patient at one of the state's schools for the retarded. The patient Joseph Saikewicz had spent 53 of his 67 years at such schools when a routine blood test revealed that he was suffering from a fatal virulent form of blood cancer which could be treated with chemotherapy. Dr. William A. Jones, director of the school, sought court authority to order the treatment because there was a 30 to 50% chance that a 2 to 13 month remission of the disease would be achieved. However, the treatment would cause great pain and suffering for the patient and be difficult to administer because the patient would not understand and be able to cooperate. It was argued that the state had an obligation to protect life and to treat Saikewicz. But Judge Jekanowski ruled that the treatment should not be given. He said, "I think I'd want to die. If I couldn't be cured, I wouldn't want to live." Dr. Jones had said, "There is a quality of life below which we might not value life." The Supreme Court, upholding Judge Jekanowski, held in a split opinion that the lower court had ruled correctly in ordering treatment withheld.

In early 1975 in Maryland, the parents of Samantha Lara Jean Teague, a severely defective infant, allowed her to die rather than have her life extended a short time by surgery. In December 1974 she was born with a hole in the base of her spine, water on the brain, a malfunctioning bladder, club feet, and deformed legs. Her parents made their decision since surgery would not have given their daughter a chance for "a meaningful life." Dr. Thomas Herrick Milhorat, of the Children's Hospital National Medical Center, said, "Personal experience, as well as that documented in medical literature, indicates that such patients never become normally functioning individuals." But the administrator of the Maryland Mental Retardation Administration instituted legal proceedings to have the baby made a ward of the state so that surgery might be performed. The child died before court action could deal with the case.

When there was a report that a seriously deformed infant in a Norfolk, Virginia, hospital had been fed to be kept alive contrary to the decision of the parents that she not be allowed to live, a Maryland couple gave a reporter their experience of having unsuccessfully tried to save their child with similar deformities. The Maryland parents said they had lived through 10 tearfilled months, had accumulated medical bills totaling $12,000 and had endured mental burdens that could be lifted only by visits to a psychiatrist. The mother said, "From the conception forward he was a planned, wanted child. But it was all a waste of energy and money. That money could have been used to help someone." They had agreed to surgery and expensive medical care on the advice of their physician who said there was hope. But the mother said, "Being Jewish, we believe very strongly in the sanctity of life. But the rabbi said, 'the life of whom?' You have another child, a husband, parents." The couple said that if they had been told the true situation from the day the child was born, they never would have authorized the original operation and their ordeal likely would have ended much sooner. They finished, "These life groups come along and say 'You've got no right to do this.' They don't know what they're dealing with."

More interest is being taken in the difficulties of making decisions regarding treatment of severely defective newborn babies. Following the Karen Quinlan decision, several doctors in the Washington, D.C. area were questioned about their practice. Dr. Anne Fletcher, of Childrens Hospital said, "I feel there are times when one has to stop therapy, and I do not feel it is passive euthanasia or playing God. . . . Life to me is far more than a heartbeat or breathing. . . . In our newborn nursery we see one or two cases a month, sometimes none in a month but sometimes three or four in which a child has been kept alive to no purpose for as long as two months and treatment then should be withdrawn."

Dr. David Abramson, chief newborn specialist at Georgetown University Hospital, was reported to have said that he and his colleagues allowed at least 50 infants a year to die when they feel the best medical outcome is death.

There is also the case of 37-year-old Chuck McCracken who chose passive euthanasia when he disconnected a kidney machine which he said caused "sheer agony." When he died about two months later, Father Daniel A. O'Callaghan, chaplain of the Catholic hospital where he died, commented, "It was his choice and I see nothing wrong with it." McCracken made his decision saying, "I look forward to a pleasant death, not painful, not traumatic. I'll go peacefully and quietly. I don't believe a person should commit suicide but to be kept alive by doctors is not quite humane. A person has a right to choose between life and death." He had said earlier that once he had made his choice to die "the world lifted from my shoulders. I have felt extreme inner peace since."

CONCLUSION

It is now widely recognized that in prolonging life, the achievements of modern medicine have produced serious problems as well as blessings. When such prolongation brings about senseless suffering, something must be done to stop it. It is the contention of many that laws must be enacted that will recognize the right of a person to choose death when there is no further chance for a meaningful life. It is also contended that the right to make such a decision should be the prerogative of the parent or guardian of a person unable to make a decision for himself. Certainly the decision of Chief Justice Hughes in the Karen Quinlan case and the newly enacted Natural Death Act in California are important first steps. These decisions are in accord with the pronouncement of Pope Pius XII in 1957 and with the views of a great number of people today.

But law has not yet been enacted in any state or country that would legalize assisted suicide or any deliberate ending of life no matter how great the suffering or how earnestly the patient pleads for death. It is time to ask why society should deny merciful death when the patient can no longer be of service to anyone, including himself, and wants nothing so much as to die. It cannot be overemphasized that we are talking only of euthanasia at the request of the patient, or, if he is incompetent, of his next of kin or guardian. It would never be compulsory—that is, never contrary to the patient's wishes.

It seems certain that it is only a matter of time until the stranglehold of tradition and religions dogma will be broken and humane laws will be enacted to ensure one's right to choose peaceful death instead of being required to endure prolonged and difficult dying. It is a challenge to every citizen to hasten that day.

INDEX

Items in the Supplement have not been indexed

Kafri, Gizela, case of, 198, 330
Kallen, Horace M., 118
Kalven, Harry J., 119, 254, 281
Kamisar, Yale, 101, 116, 229, 239, 273
Karnovsky, David A., 122
Kass, Leon R., 33, 299
Katz, Sidney, 97
Kaunitz, Julius, 112
Kelly, Garald A., 109, 132, 261
Kelsey, Frances, 176
Kempster, Walter, 61
Kennedy, Edward, 246
Kennedy, Foster, 73, 74, 113, 239
Kennedy, Joseph P., Jr., Foundation, 237
Kippon, Duncan, 162
Kirby, William, case of, 259, 266, 330
Kirchway, Freda, 73
Kobayashi, Toichi, principles on euthanasia, 253
Kubler-Ross, Elizabeth, 25, 173-175
Lancet, editorial, 149-150
Lander, Karen, 167
Langdon-Brown, Sir Walter, 71
Lasagna, Louis, 229
Last Rights: A Case for the Good Death, 182
Law
  on euthanasia, need for, 8, 9, 10, 17, 21-22, 36, 48, 107-108, 143, 156
  and right to death with dignity, 17
Law journals
  and articles on euthanasia, 115-119
  discussions on euthanasia, in 1960s, 139
Lawrence, Ron, 170
Laws, current, on euthanasia, 252-260
Laws, E. Harold, 155
Leach, Gerald, 244
Learned Societies in the Field of Religion, International Congress of, 206
"Legalize Euthanasia" (debate), 78
Legislation, on euthanasia
  bibliography, 322-323

bills and resolutions (listed), 334-335
efforts in United States in 1950s, 132-135
proposals of, 25
texts of, 289-296
United States, 188-194
Levine, Sol, 27
Levisohn, Arthur A., 48, 140, 142-144, 259, 273
License, for euthanasia, 68, 276-277
Life
  beginning of, changed beliefs and practices on, 13
  "idolatry" of, 212
  prolongation of, 7, 9, 15-16, 21-22, 23, 37, 49, 121-122, 124, 141, 143, 146, 149, 150, 151-152, 187, 191, 192, 193, 201, 202, 210, 212-213, 250-251
  attitudes toward, 170
  and defective infants, 237, 239-240
  and fear of malpractice charges, 269
  and Hippocratic Oath, 65, 220-221
  and Living Will, 181
  problems created by, 27, 32
  protests against, 29
  viewed as man playing God, 218-219
  withholding of, 18, 20
  quality of
    as focus of church, 214
    vs. quantity, 203, 220
  sanctity of, as argument against euthanasia, 219-220
"Life is Sacred" (debate), 78
"Life or Death—Whose Decision?" 144
Lineacre Quarterly, 209
Listowel, Earl of, 70, 73, 184, 184
Litigation, as means of reform, 267-269
Living death, 15
Living Will, 159, 181, 191, 193, 209, 264, 270
  text of, 296-297
  See also Advance declaration
Loneliness, of the dying, 172
Long, G. R., case of, 101-102, 330

Long, Perrin H., 140-142
Longevity, increasing, 282-283
Lopez, Rolando, 38
Lorber, John, 246
LSD, used with the dying, 169
Luther, Martin, 124
Lutheran Church of America, and euthanasia, 204
Lyons, Andrew D., case of, 31, 333

McCall, Governor Tom, 25, 102
McClure, Robert, 206
McCormick, Monsignor R. E., 95, 212
McDougall, William, 73
McMath, William, 160
MacPherson, Jennifer, 166
Maguire, Daniel, 209
Mahoney, Sen. Walter J., 96
Mali, Mrs. Henry J., 180
Malice, in interpretation of murder, 266
Malpractice charges, fear of, and physicians' attitude on euthanasia, 182, 183, 269
Mann, Kenneth W., 214
Mannes, Marya, 182
Manslaughter, negative euthanasia as, 20
Marcus Aurelius, and right to choose death, 54
Martin, John B., 249
Martin, Thomas Owen, 115
Martinez, Carmen, case of, 38-39, 256, 268, 332
Maryland, euthanasia legislation, 191
Massachusetts
  Death Education Research Group, 29
  euthanasia legislation, 191
Massachusetts Medical Society, opposition to euthanasia, 109
Mass media, and euthanasia movement, 194-196
Matthews, William R., 45, 67
Maugham, W. Somerset, 73
Medical associations, stand on euthanasia, 109, 156-160
Medical Data Centers, and consultation on euthanasia, 279

"Medical" euthanasia, 19
Medical Histories and Reflections, "On the Treatment of Dying," 56-57
Medical journals
  articles on euthanasia in 1950s, 119-123
  discussions on euthanasia in 1960s, 139
Medical organizations and groups
  American Academy of General Practice, 109
  American Medical Association, 24, 29, 33, 46, 80, 122, 159, 160
  American Physicians Association, 96, 153
  British Medical Association, 155, 156, 186
  British Royal Society of Health, 161, 187
  California Medical Association, 158, 276
  Canadian Medical Association, 157, 162
  Connecticut State Medical Association, 33, 134, 159
  French Academy of Medicine, 30
  Massachusetts Medical Society, 109
  New Jersey Medical Society, 133
  New York Medical Society, 109, 157
  World Medical Association, 30, 93, 109, 156
Medical profession
  awareness of need for ethical and social judgments, 24
  conservatism of, 224
  German, 93-94
  opposition to birth control, 13
  opposition to euthanasia, 9
Medical Record, editorial, 79-80
Medical schools
  attitude to death and dying, 222
  and Hippocratic Oath, 221-222
  research on death and dying, 28
Medical science, and prolonging of life, 7, 9, 15-16, 21-22
"Medical Science Under Dictatorship," 92
Medical skills, and defective infants, 239-240, 242, 244

406

407

117, 123
and perversion of term eutha-
nasia, 18
Neasden Hospital controversy,
160-161
Nebraska Bill, 71-72
Nebraska State Medical Association, 72
Necessity, doctrine of, 125-126
Netherlands, convictions of physicians in mercy deaths,
255-256
Newark Methodist Conference
Committee, opposition to
euthanasia, 109
*The New Genetics and the Future
of Man*, 244
New Jersey, efforts for legislation
in the 1950s, 133
New Jersey State Legislature,
petition to (text), 288
Newman, Horatio H., 73
New York State
efforts to legalize euthanasia, 74
in 1950s, 132-133
proposed bill of 1946, 94-97
New York State Legislature, peti-
tion to (text), 286
New York State Medical Society
1973 statement on euthanasia,
157-158
opposition to euthanasia, 109
New York State Naturopathic
Association, and euthanasia
bill, 96
New York Times, editorials on
euthanasia, 26
1906, 60, 61, 62
Nicolson, Sir Harold, 67
Nighswonger, Carl, 174
1984 (Orwell), 15
Nixdorff, Charles E., 74
Nobody Ever Died of Old Age,
166
Nonvoluntary euthanasia, 21. *See
also* Euthanasia
Norton, Charles Eliot, 60
Norwood, F. W., 67
Noxon, John F., Jr., case of, 99,
101, 256, 258, 330
Nuremburg trials, 92. *See also*
Nazi war crimes
Nurses, opinions on euthanasia,
165-167

Nursing homes, conditions in,
247-248

Observer (United Church of
Canada), 209
Ohio, proposed bill on euthanasia,
60-61
Old Age: The Last Segregation,
248
Olmstead v. U.S., 233, 333
Omission, acts of, and negative
euthanasia, 20
On Death and Dying, 173, 175
On Dying and Denying, 172
"On Drinking the Hemlock," 43
"On the Quality and Quantity of
Life," 140
Opponents of euthanasia, argu-
ments of, 217-231
Opposition to euthanasia, in
1950s, 109-110, 123
Oregon, euthanasia legislation,
192-193
Oregon, University of, 29
Orwell, George, 15
Osborne, Charles, case of, 256,
268, 333
Osler, Sir William, 157, 168, 281

Paight, Carol, case of, 102, 259,
330
Pain prevention, moral implica-
tions of, 128-129
Paramedical training for eutha-
nasia, 22
Passive euthanasia. *See* Eutha-
nasia, negative
Patient, rights of, 124, 127, 145,
146, 147-148, 150-151,
157, 158, 161, 224, 227,
256, 268-269
The Patient as Person, 212
"The Patient's Right to Live and
Die," 115
People v. Conley, 266, 333
People v. Kirby, 266
Perilman, Nathan A., 111
Periodicals, church-sponsored,
and euthanasia, 209
Permit. *See* License
Personality, human, vs. biologi-
cal organism, 45
Peru, law on assisted suicide, 252

Peterson, Osler L., 27
Petitions on euthanasia, 286-288
Philbrick, Inez C., 72
Physician, Pastor and Patient, 76
Physician-patient relationship, changing, 263
Physician(s)
  changing attitudes on euthanasia, 46-48
  changing role of, 262-263
  and confidence of patient, as argument against euthanasia, 223
  and decision on euthanasia, 88-89, 121, 127, 130, 152, 157, 161, 189, 223-224, 231, 262-264
  bibliography, 323-325
  dilemma about suffering (mercy vs. law), 220, 235
  laws on declaration of death, 32-33
  legal protection for, 270. *See also* Safeguards
  mercy killing cases (table), 260
  as opponents of euthanasia, 223-224
  pacts between, 38
  and polls on euthanasia, 153-156
  and positive euthanasia, 19-20, 23
  practice of euthanasia, 80, 98, 108, 136, 144, 154, 155-156
  prosecutions for mercy killings, 254-256
  questionnaire on euthanasia, 89-90
  role in euthanasia, 22, 23
  and stigma of euthanasia, 79
  views on euthanasia, 140-152
Picquereau, Jean, case of, 198, 331
Pilot scheme, for euthanasia laws, 280
Plato, and euthanasia, 53
"A Plea for the Legalization of Euthanasia," 65
Ploscowe, Morris, 119
Pole, K. F. M., 209
Polls and/or studies
  in Canada
    by Cappon, 170

    by Gallup (1949), 137, 199; (1959), 137, 199; (1968), 199
  in Great Britain
    by Exton Smith (1961), 171
    by Gallup (1939), 85
    by Hinton (1962), 171, 226
    by Lorber, 246
    by National Opinion (1946 and 1965), 35, 155, 224
    by Osler (1906), 168
  in United States
    by *CA Bulletin of Cancer Progress*, 122
    by Euthanasia Society (1941), 89
    by *Fortune Magazine* (1937), 84, 103
    by Gallup (1937), 85, 103; (1939), 85, 103; (1947), 102; (1950), 134, 198; (1973), 198
    by *Good Housekeeping*, 199
    by Harris (1973), 200
    by Levisohn, 144
    by National Opinion Research Center (1973), 170, 246
    by *New Medica Materia*, 153
    by Swenson, 169
    by Williams, 153
    of Colorado Nurses Association, 166
    of Connecticut physicians, 134
    of nurses, by Brown, 167
    of Seattle doctors, by Brown, 153
    of Seattle medical students, by Laws, 155
Polls, public opinion
  on abortion to prevent birth defects, 246
  on attitudes toward death, 170
  on euthanasia, 84-86, 102
  on mercy death, 178, 198-200, 240
  in 1950s, 137-138
  of physicians, 153-156, 224
Ponsonby, Lord, 68
Pope Pius XII, 44, 104, 121, 128-132, 144, 180, 201, 212, 219, 235, 261
Popper, Judge David, 39

Safeguards in euthanasia legislation, 68, 70, 76, 90, 93, 113, 130, 146, 184, 194, 200, 222, 223, 225, 227, 228, 230, 231, 251, 270, 275-280
Saffron, Morris H., 53
St. John-Stevas, 178, 185
"The Sanctity of Life," 120, 211
The Sanctity of Life and the Criminal Law, 116, 125
Sander, Hermann, case of, 102, 104-109, 127, 137, 255, 260, 331
and public interest in euthanasia, 111
Sanders, Joseph, 254
Sanger, Margaret, 13, 73, 111, 282
Saunders, Cicely, 169, 225
Schiff, Arthur F., 48, 148
Schloendorff v. Society of N.Y. Hospital, 233, 333
Scotch, Norman A., 27
Schwab, Robert S., 32
Seneca, on choice of death, 54
Separation, fear of, and dying, 170, 175
"Shall We Legalize Homicide," 61
"Shall We Legalize Mercy Killing?" 82
Shaw, G. Bernard, 67
Sheldon, J. H., 247
Shepherd, Canon, H. R. L., 67
Sherwood, Robert E., 73
Shideler, Mary McDermott, 208
Shirer, William L., 91
"Should Doctors Play God?" 148
Sidgwick, Henry, 282
Silving, Helen, 118, 226
Simpson, Keith, 30
Sixth Commandment, 54, 109, 154, 217-218
Slater, Eliot, 35, 151, 187, 254
"Slippery rope" argument, 226-227
Smith, Henerson, 156
Snay, Albert, 107
Social concerns, and attitudes to euthanasia, 140
"Social death," 220
Social Science and Medicine, First International Conference on, 24
Social workers, opinions on euthanasia, 163, 167-168

Society, Ethics and the Life Sciences, Institution of, 26
Task Force on Death and Dying, 33
Society of Friends. *See* Quakers
Socrates, and euthanasia, 53, 250
"Some Non-Religious Views Against Proposed 'Mercy Killing' Legislation," 117
Soul, human, effect of euthanasia, 113
Sowle, Claude R., 280
Spann, W., 34
Sperm banks, 14
Spina bifida, 243
Stanford University, 29
State mental hospitals, and elderly patients, 248
States, euthanasia bills, 188-194
Stevens, Roland, 183
Stones of Stumbling, 57
Straight, Michael, 91
Strauss, Anselm L., 167, 172
Strauss, Eileen, 165
Strickland, Mark B., 106
Studnow, David, 172
Sturgess, Wesley A., 111
Suffering
Catholic defense of, 125
fear of, 233
physical, in dying, 168-169
spiritual value of, 129, 225
"Suggestions in Favor of Terminating Absolutely Hopeless Cases of Injury and Disease," 59
Suicide, 20, 54, 55, 56, 58, 65, 66, 78, 88, 112, 147, 150, 171, 181, 204, 229, 252, 265
assisted, 265
laws on, 252
of Charlotte Perkins Gilman, 77
condemnation of, and attitudes to euthanasia, 65-66
considered by terminally ill, 171
by the elderly, 224-225
euthanasia regarded as, 54, 78
of George Eastman, 77
and the law, 55
moral aspects of, 228
positive euthanasia as, 20
St. Augustine's views of, 54

Uruguay, penal code of, and
mercy killing, 252
Utopia, 55

Value judgment, and definition of
death, 34
van de Put, Suzanne, trial of, 175-
179, 240, 260, 331
Van Dusen, Henry Pitney, 181
Vaux, Kenneth, 156
Veatch, Robert M., 33
Verulam, Lord, 58
Vickery, Kenneth O. A., 161
Virginia Statute of 1973, text of,
299-300
Voluntary Euthanasia (Legaliza-
tion) Bill, 68-71
Voluntary Euthanasia Legaliza-
tion Society, founding of,
67-68
Voluntary Euthanasia Bill of 1969
(England), 151, 184-188
Voltaire, 56
Von Hoffman, Nicholas, 245

Waiting period, and euthanasia
request, 277
See also Safeguards
Wall Street Journal article on
euthanasia, 26
Walsh, James J., 77, 78
War crimes, Nazi, 18, 87, 90-94,
104, 115, 117, 123
Washington Post
editorial on mentally retarded,
245
and nursing homes, 248
Washington (State), euthanasia
legislation, 190-191
Waskin, Robert, case of, 197, 259,
331
Watson, James D., 15
Wayne State University, Center
for Psychological Studies of
Dying, Death, and Lethal
Behavior, 28
Weatherhead, Leslie, 45, 108, 213
Wedge argument, 92-93, 115, 117,
125, 128, 226-227
Weintraub, Justice Joseph, 40, 268
Weisman, Avery, 25, 172
Wells, H. G., 67, 73
Wells, S. Russell, 62

Wenger, H. Leslie, 47, 195, 199
Werner, Otto, case of, 117, 258,
332
Wertenbaker, Lael, 181
"What Are We Doing With Our
Power Over Death?" 209
White House Conference on
Aging (1971), 24, 25, 192,
250
Who Shall Live? 156
*Who Shall Live? Man's Control
Over Birth and Death*, 202
"Who Shall Survive?" (film), 237
Wicks, Hon. Arthur H., 132
Williams, Glanville, 112, 116, 125-
127, 259, 269
Williams, Judge Alfred, 256
Williams, Rhondda, 67
Williams, Robert H., 147, 153,
172
Williams, S. D., 57
Williamson, William P., 144
Wilson, John Rowen, 47, 151
Wisconsin, euthanasia legislation,
190
Wojcik, Lester and Madeline, case
of, 198, 334
Wolbarst, Abraham L., 75, 77,
78, 79, 95, 239
Wolfe, Heinrich F., 112
World Council of Churches
Assembly, 206
report on genetics, 244
World Medical Association
Declaration of Sydney (1968),
30
opposition to euthanasia,
109-110
reactions to Nazi experiments,
93-94
resolution on euthanasia, 94,
156
World War II, effect on euthanasia
movement, 87

Yamanouchi, Komei, case of,
253, 332
Yetter, Maida, case of, 256, 333
*Your Death Warrant? The Impli-
cations of Euthanasia*, 186

Zeimer, Gregor, 92
Zygmaniak, Lester, case of, 46,
197, 258, 332